Sacred Biography in the Buddhist Traditions of South and Southeast Asia

Sacred Biography
in the
Buddhist Traditions
of
South
and
Southeast Asia

Edited by

JULIANE SCHOBER

MOTILAL BANARSIDASS PUBLISHERS
PRIVATE LIMITED • DELHI

First Indian Edition: Delhi, 2002
First Edition: USA, 1997

ISBN: 81-208-1812-1

Also available at:

MOTILAL BANARSIDASS
41 U.A. Bungalow Road, Jawahar Nagar, Delhi 110 007
236, 9th Main III Block, Jayanagar, Bangalore 560 011
8 Mahalaxmi Chamber, Warden Road, Mumbai 400 026
120 Royapettah High Road, Mylapore, Chennai 600 004
Sanas Plaza, 1302 Baji Rao Road, Pune 411 002
8 Camac Street, Kolkata 700 017
Ashok Rajpath, Patna 800 004
Chowk, Varanasi 221 001

[redacted]

Printed in India
BY JAINENDRA PRAKASH JAIN AT SHRI JAINENDRA PRESS,
A-45 NARAINA, PHASE-I, NEW DELHI 110 028
AND PUBLISHED BY NARENDRA PRAKASH JAIN FOR
MOTILAL BANARSIDASS PUBLISHERS PRIVATE LIMITED,
BUNGALOW ROAD, DELHI 110 007

Contents

Part 2

Extensions of the Buddha Biography in Texts

Part 3

The Jātakas *and Biographies of Kings*

Part 4

The Biographical Genre in Local Buddhist Cults and Practice

Preface

This volume presents previously unpublished essays on sacred biography in the Buddhist traditions of South and Southeast Asia. It introduces into the cross-disciplinary discourse methodologies and perspectives in anthropology, art history, and history of religions that center on the theme of biography in Buddhism. Each contribution examines sacred biography in one or more modalities in the texts, art, history, literature, myths, rituals, and cultures of the Buddhist tradition. Their common goal is to elucidate the ways in which these biographies function as frames of reference or, in Stanley Tambiah's words, as indexical symbols that allow for shifts in interpretation, meaning, and intentionality by alluding at once to multiple levels of discourse and contexts in the past and in the present. In Buddhism, biographies are the tools for mapping diverse realities onto one another: local cosmologies are integrated into universal ones; pristine Buddhist ideals and modes of practice are recreated in the present and in the lives of others; the present is explained in terms of causes in past lives; iconic veneration of an absent Buddha allows the community to participate in his continuing biography; and so on. Many more examples of "mapping" or shifting between contexts and interpretations can be encompassed by a frame of reference such as Buddhist biography. The narrative intention and focus of each biographical episode is manipulated through a set of relations, both internal and external to the biographical frame itself. This makes biography in Buddhism an effective device for didactic communication. It also allows for communicating at once a great variety of things, abstract and pragmatic, past and present. Although biography also plays a significant role in other "great religions," including Christianity, Judaism, Islam, and

Hinduism, its universality and multivocality in Buddhism are rooted in an epistemology that presumes an open-ended soteriology that entertains two mutually reinforcing conceptions: anyone can potentially become a Buddha; and time is cyclical—that is to say, the same kind of event can happen again and again under different circumstances and in diverse contexts.

At the same time that the volume seeks to fill a lacuna in the study of sacred biography in Buddhism, it also seeks to encourage further multidisciplinary explorations of a common theme among audiences in the humanities and social sciences who share these methodological interests in the relationships between textual, artistic, and cultural modes of religion.

Our impetus to explore Buddhist sacred biography came from two separate, though overlapping, symposia. The first one, "Interpretations of *Jātaka* Tales in Southeast Asia," focused on the stories of the Buddha's previous lives across Theravāda and Mahāyāna traditions of mainland and insular Southeast Asia and was held at Arizona State University in the spring of 1990. The essays by Robert Brown, Thomas Hudak, Frank Reynolds, and Mark Woodward were first presented in that forum. This led to a second, more broadly defined symposium: "Buddhist 'Life Stories': Sacred Biography in South and Southeast Asia," held a few months later at the University of Chicago, where Reginald Ray, John Strong, and Jonathan Walters first presented their essays. Contributions by Gustaaf Houtman, Paul Johnson, Forrest McGill, James Taylor, and my own essay were then gathered to complement approaches and case studies discussed in the two symposia.

This book would not have come about without the collegial advice and constructive comments of many scholars and the substantive support of institutions and foundations. I am indebted to Frank Reynolds, who first suggested the publication of a collection of essays on this subject. He offered his generous advice at several junctures in its conceptual and editorial development. Mark Woodward has been a steady critic who offered concrete suggestions for improvement. On several occasions in the course of the conferences and the editorial process, I have relied on Carol Withers' logistical and secretarial expertise. Steve Toth has assisted me with his expertise in editorial conventions and the conversion of some obscure software formats into readable form.

The conferences that provided the impetus for this project were supported by the Program for Southeast Asian Studies and the College for Liberal Arts and Sciences at Arizona State University; by the National Endowment for the Humanities; and by the Buddhist Studies Forum at the University of Chicago. The Department of Religious Studies at Arizona State University has generously granted me the time to bring the project to completion. Grants in support of this publication have been generously provided by John Adams Thierry, the Bucyrus-Erie Foundation, and the Program for Southeast Asian Studies at Arizona State University. My appreciation also goes to Sally Serafim and Sharon Yamamoto, editors for the press whose expertise greatly enhanced the final outcome. Finally, I am indebted to the authors in this volume for their patience with the process of bringing this collection to a wider audience and the collegiality with which they received editorial comments.

Note on Diacritical Conventions

The contributions to this volume draw on primary sources in Pāli, Sanskrit, Tibetan, Thai, and Burmese and follow the accepted conventions for transcription and diacritical marks in these respective languages. Each author chose to employ the standards appropriate to his or her respective field of study.

Sacred Biography in the Buddhist Traditions of South and Southeast Asia

Trajectories in Buddhist Sacred Biography

Juliane Schober

Sacred biographies inspire imagination, belief, and practice in many religious traditions. The popular penchant for the life stories of religious figures persists without concern for the historicity accorded to the times, places, and facts of individual lives they recount. Stories about the lives of saints and founders of religious traditions cast into relief precisely those acts and episodes that evoke salient themes throughout the broader religious tradition. They provide a narrative explication of abstract religious concepts and, at the same time, become the fabric for speculations about pervasive religious concerns. In diverse ways, this accounts for the continuity of biographic themes over time and throughout religious traditions. This book explores recurrent though distinctive variations in biographies and related narratives articulated in the arts, texts, rituals, myths, and religious practices in Buddhist traditions of South and Southeast Asia.

A pervasive theme in Buddhism, sacred biography invites comparative exploration along multiple trajectories. A religious tradition of great historic depth, Buddhism encompasses many diverse cultures throughout Asia. Through time, models of Buddhist practice—exemplified in the biographies of Buddha and of saints—became articulated and contextualized in a variety of culturally salient modes. Concerning an epistemology of text-building in Javanese shadow plays, A. L. Becker has shown how the interpretation of simultaneous voices of the past and of the present is constrained by relations within the text itself, to its literary context, and audiences.[1] Biographical episodes in Buddhist texts thus speak not only of the past, but speak simultaneously of a variety of presents in multiple cultural and linguistic contexts.

In his contribution to a comparative volume on the biographical process in the history and psychology of religions, Frank Reynolds[2] argues that stories about the Buddha's lives helped define the framework for the development of Buddhist texts and practice because they depict fundamental religious and cultural modes that are paradigmatic for the tradition as a whole and inform the construction of religious practice, texts, and cultures. The structure of sacred biographies, the process of their compilation, and their proliferation throughout the Buddhist tradition convey more than merely moral tales for religious instruction. Reynolds has shown that sacred biographies resonate among religious audiences because the Buddha biography has fundamentally shaped religious conceptions and interpretations in various religious modes throughout that tradition.

The mythic and symbolic qualities of sacred biographies often make for "good stories to tell," but these stories also have didactic value because they illustrate exemplary moral practice. However, members of religious communities accept sacred biographies "on faith" and their salience transcends concerns of morality and religious instruction. Biographical tales become meaningful only in reference to concepts central to the religious tradition. Highly evocative and polysemous, sacred biographies depict and contextualize the lives of those who emulate these ideals in religious texts and practice. In their totality, the biographies of the Buddha encompass a variety of models of and for religious practice. The tradition views these potentially limitless models of path practice as applicable to all sentient beings and particularly to those who—as *arhats* (saints) and future Buddhas—have realized in exemplary fashion a version of the path in their own lives.[3]

Religious biographies mediate between the ideal and the real, the conceptual and the pragmatic. To the extent to which individual life stories express salient and abstract religious principles, they become, in Clifford Geert's terms, "models of" exemplary religious practice.[4] They are simultaneously "models for" religious practice for they inspire others to imitate in their own lives idealized expressions of religiosity.

It is not uncommon, therefore, to discover in various Buddhist contexts that sacred biographies—as inspirational exemplars—are integral to contextualizing and legitimating the formation of local cults. Stanley Tambiah employs Burks' notion of indexical symbols to explain the multifaceted aspects of a modern Thai cult surrounding a monastic saint[5] and his nationally acclaimed biography authored by one of his chief disciples. Tambiah[6] argues that the indexical symbols of this biography provide an analytical entrée into "the study of text and context, semantics and pragmatics, meaning that refers back to classical constructs and forward to uses in the present."[7] This, it seems, allows us to conceive of the exploration of sacred biography from an encompassing perspective.

Early Buddhist scholars such as H. Oldenberg and T. W. and C. A. F. Rhys-Davids sought to reconstruct a historically accurate account of the life of the Buddha on the basis of textual evidence. They considered mythic elements of biographical texts to be irrational and detracting from the "original" message of "pure" Buddhism. These attempts to trace the life history of the Buddha as an exemplary human being mirrored in many ways the prevailing epistemological parameters in Western canons of chronological history.

More recent scholarship departs from the confines of rationalist, positivist reconstruction of chronological history, recognizing the interpretive value of mythic, artistic, and cultural themes as expressions of principal tenets underlying the tradition. While they acknowledge the historical core of later biographical developments, Reynolds and Charles Hallisey[8] note the lack of concern for chronological and narrative continuity in the biographical fragments of early texts. In their view, "the tradition of recounting biographical episodes is an integral part of early Buddhism. Episodic fragments, preserved in the Pāli and Chinese versions of the early Buddhist literature, are embedded in sermons attributed to the Buddha himself and illustrate points of practice of doctrine. Such episodes are also used as narrative frames to provide a context indicating when and where a particular discourse was taught."[9]

In commenting on the evolution of studies on the biographical genre in Buddhism, Reynolds and Hallisey mention Erich Frauwallner's[10] presupposition of a comprehensive, though no longer extant "ur-biography." Frauwallner saw this "ur-biography" as an explanation and model for later biographical fragments in the extant Vinaya literature. More recent works by Alfred Foucher,[11] Etienne Lamotte,[12] and Andre Bareau[13] proceed antithetically to Frauwallner's theory of a lost "ur-text" and favor "a gradual development of biographical cycles, with only a later synthesis of this material into a series of more complete biographies."[14] Over time, new and autonomous biographies depicting the Buddha's lives were eventually composed in diverse Buddhist schools. They reflect characteristics and orientations that are specific to the contexts of their composition and indicate reinterpretations of the Buddha's biography to justify prevailing contexts or to exemplify certain attributes and qualities of the Buddha.[15] Reynolds and Hallisey note the fluidity in the structure of the Buddhist biographical genre and the use of biographical episodes as narrative frames to contextualize and authenticate the Buddha's teachings.[16]

Among the most seminal developments in the biographical genre of the Theravāda traditions of South and Southeast Asia is the fifth-century Pāli commentary *Jātakatthakathā*, which recounts 547 of the Buddha's previous lives.[17] This Sinhalese commentary and slightly variant Southeast Asian texts describe exemplary modes of practicing the path and the ultimate nibbanic attainment of a karmically constituted "individual."[18] These stories of the Buddha's former lives are prefaced by the Sinhalese commentator's introduction, *Nidānakathā*,[19] which recounts the Buddha's biography from the time of his vow to embark on the Buddha path to his achievement of enlightenment. The *jātaka* narratives describe the Buddha's path and, to some extent, also the path of his family and disciples who follow him through several lives. Yet, as a whole, the *Jātakas* appear to have been arranged according to properties of the text (e.g., length) rather than narrative sequence of successive rebirths. They do not present a chronically ordered depiction of the Buddha's path to enlightenment.

In their essays in this volume, Frank Reynolds and Thomas John Hudak both note the consistent format followed in the classical Pāli biographical stories: they begin with "the story of the present," which provides the context and occasion for the Buddha's recollection of one of his former lives and thus "frames" the second part, "the story of the past," which is the *jātaka* or story of the former life; the rebirth identities of major characters conclude the story by linking the narrative past and present. The shift in focus, intent, and context characterizes the narrative structure of birth stories in their classical Pāli renditions. The essays in this volume show that shifts in narrative foci, intent, and contexts are formal properties of biographic depiction not only in textual modes, but also in the cultural, cultic, and artistic articulations of Buddhist sacred biography.

The biographical genre in the Buddhist world also engendered other, independent biographical traditions in vernacular languages and local mythologies.[20] In the Theravādin branch, some versions of these are recounted in historical chronicles (*vaṃsa*) which serve to legitimate local claims or contexts. A separate, though complementary, genre of Buddha biographies recounting his visits to local sites is encountered in numerous oral mythologies.[21] Finally, there is a prevailing tendency throughout local traditions of Theravāda Buddhism for disciples to compose biographies upon the death of their monastic teachers. Several recent studies of Theravāda Buddhism examine biographies of religious figures recounted in local traditions (Ruth-Inge Heinze,[22] Grant A. Olson,[23] Gustaaf Houtman,[24] and Bonnie Brereton[25]), portray biographical themes as emblematic of broader contexts (Tambiah,[26] Charles Keyes,[27] and Michael Carrithers[28]), or explore relationships between biographers, their subjects, and audiences (James L. Taylor[29]).

Other recent studies employ comparative approaches in the analysis of Buddhist biography. Reginald Ray's *Buddhist Saints in India* looks at the lives of saints in the early Buddhist tradition through a variety of textual sources.[30] In *The Legend and Cult of Upagupta*, John Strong examines Sanskrit Hīnayāna Buddhist tales about this saint and their extensions in the Theravāda rituals of Southeast Asia.[31] *Monks and Magicians*,[32] edited by Phyliss Granoff and Koichi Shinohara, presents case studies of Jain and Buddhist figures in India, Tibet, and China. Another collection, entitled *Maitreya, The Future Buddha* and edited by Alan Sponberg and Helen Hardacre,[33] features essays on the development and interpretation of the Maitreya tradition. Its primary focus is the Mahāyāna traditions of South and East Asia.

In his introduction and again in the epilogue Sponberg points to characteristics of the Maitreya biography that are directly relevant to the larger scope of Buddhist biography explored here. Sponberg contrasts the universality of core themes with the culturally specific, local elaborations of the tradition of the future Buddha Maitreya. He notes the adaptability of core themes in the Maitreya mythology, such as "continuity and legitimacy, regeneration and renewal, messianism and millennialism, the tension between liberation in this world and salvation somewhere beyond, and the tension between worldly and spiritual power and authority."[34] These implicitly stated core themes and explicit narrative motifs form "the building blocks employed to construct the distinctive variations we find in the later, more culturally specific variations."[35] Sponberg emphasizes the process of seemingly open-ended variations in local Maitreya traditions. He sees this variation as a characteristic feature in the dialectical encounter of Buddhism and the diverse cultures of Buddhist Asia.

The present collection and the Maitreya volume developed independently of one another. In spite of this, they generate comparable perspectives on the relations between continuous, universal themes in Buddhist biography and their local, culturally specific variations. Such metalevel similarities underscore the value of multidisciplinary, thematically oriented inquiry in the study of religious traditions. The present book introduces into this discourse previously unpublished essays that aim to expand upon the thematic scope and geographical orientation of previous studies on sacred biography in Buddhism. The essays seek to define encompassing frameworks, pervasive themes, and specific variations of the Buddhist biographical genre as a whole and to elucidate these in discussions of examples taken from the Buddhist traditions of South and Southeast Asia, which, until now, have not been the subject of comparative exploration.

Common Themes Explored

This book fills a thematic lacuna in the study of Buddhist sacred biography and its expressions in text, art, myth, and ritual. The essays gathered here illuminate narratives of the Buddha's life stories and other sacred biographies in terms of their salience, universality, scope, structure, and relation to other aspects of the Buddhist traditions of South and Southeast Asia. They examine local variations on Buddhist biographical themes in historical, contemporary, ritual, and cultural contexts and investigate ways in which pervasive biographical themes inform local, culturally specific articulations of Buddhist sacred biography. In doing so, they document the continuing construction of Buddhist sacred biographies in diverse modes—textual, artistic, historical, and performative—and diverse contexts—cultural and historical—in order to identify transformative processes in the larger Buddhist tradition.

This book presents a comprehensive view of a hitherto-neglected topic in the study of Buddhism from the multidisciplinary perspectives of textual scholarship, history of religions, art history, and anthropology. The essays that make up this collection share related methodological concerns underlying the multidisciplinary study of religion in the humanities and social sciences. They apply interpretive and critical methodologies to the analysis of a common religious theme in order to delineate its paradigmatic significance within the tradition. They also identify ways in which local biographical vicissitudes express salient religious themes in the texts, arts, history, and cultural performance of the larger tradition. In pursuing these approaches, the authors move toward deconstructing boundaries of disciplinary scrutiny and advance cross-disciplinary inquiry into issues of broader relevance.

The essays are grouped into four parts that offer complementary perspectives on central themes in Buddhist biography. Part 1 explores the role of sacred biography in South and Southeast Asian Buddhist traditions in terms of conceptual frameworks in the textual tradition and iconography of the Buddha biography. Part 2 examines the textual biographies of Buddhist saints and communities in light of the Buddha's biography. Part 3 presents depictions of the lives of Theravāda kings in the tradition of the *jātakas*. The essays in Part 4 interpret the Buddhist biographical genre in local cults and practice.

In Part 1, the essays by Frank Reynolds, Mark Woodward, and Robert Brown charter frameworks in Buddhist sacred biography and explore their respective parameters in its textual and artistic extensions. Emphasizing the mythological element in the biographical accounts of the Buddha, Reynolds concentrates on the Buddha's lineages as recounted in several *jātaka* traditions and leading up to the last life of Buddha Gotama (approximately sixth to fourth century B.C.E.). He argues—here and elsewhere[36]—for the systematic role of mythology in the construction of the Buddha biography and its pervasive influence on the development and structure of the Theravāda tradition. In Reynolds' view, the justification for the biographical tradition derives from the Buddha's ability to remember all his past lives during the meditational stages that lead to his enlightenment. This vision was developed in several branches of the tradition to encompass a series of intersecting lineages: the lineage of the Buddha's successive rebirths that link him to his karmic past; the lineage of Buddhas that preceded him and those who will follow him in the future; and the lineage of kings from whom he descended in his last life. Reynolds shows how biographical lineages have been used to establish the continued presence of the Buddha and ultimately serve to legitimize religious and civil institutions and practices throughout Buddhist history.[37]

Woodward's essay identifies relationships between the Buddha's biography and doctrinal formulations of the path to enlightenment. He argues for a neccessary link between biographical narrative and philosophical discourse in the Theravāda textual tradition. At a less abstract level of textual discourse, the biographical imperative is depicted in the narratives of former lives of Buddhas and their disciples. These intertwined biographies encompass numerous life spans and form a persistent rebirth pattern of "karmic cohorts." He documents how the biographical narrative is used to justify philosophical conclusions of authoritative texts like the *Vissudhimagga*, Buddhaghosa's commentary on the Theravāda Abhidhamma.

Brown's essay challenges prevailing assumptions about the didactic function of *jātaka* reliefs in ancient Indian and Southeast Asian architecture. His inquiry into the relationship between depictions of the Buddha's past lives through verbal text and relief images centers on the iconic properties of *jātaka* reliefs within the architectural space of these monuments. While he concedes that *jātaka* reliefs as icons make symbolic references to a longer, verbal text, he points out that an exclusive reliance on theories concerning their didactic use and function fails to account for the fact that many of these visual representations were partially or completely obscured from view. Their condensed, highly symbolic styles of depiction and the seeming disregard for narrative sequence in their placement within the architectural space lead him to conclude that these *jātaka* reliefs were not intended as visual illustrations that prompt, in the mind of the viewer, the mental recitation of a prior known, verbal narrative. Instead, he argues that their significance lies in their iconic function within the sacred space of these religious monuments. Brown suggests that these reliefs were the focus of worship and reverence and that the diverse visual depictions of the Buddha's former lives served to create the presence of an all-too-absent Buddha.

The essays in part 2 focus on biographical themes in Buddhist texts explaining how the Buddha's biography was extended to encompass and inform the accounts of the lives of saints and the pristine Buddhist community. John Strong critiques the Western bias for individualism and historicism, which presumes that the single life span of an individual is the meaningful and significant unit in the study of Buddhist biography. He shows that, in Buddhism, latitudinal and longitudinal extensions of karmic collectivities are affected by the development of certain biographical events. In his analysis of the Bodhisattva's Great Departure in the *Sanghabhedavastu* of the Sanskrit *Mūlasarvāstivāda Vinaya*, he finds that the Buddha's quest for enlightenment was not merely that of a solitary seeker, but also caused parallel quests for path attainment for his wife, Yaśodharā, and his son, Rāhula. Strong concludes that the Buddha's renunciation provides the mythic model for monastic ordination and nibbanic path action and that his family's parallel quest illustrates the karmic path of householders.

Reginald Ray looks at longevity as a characteristic trait in the biographies of Buddhist saints. He argues that the conception of longevity rests on a central causality between path accomplishment, meditation, and saintly longevity, and individual expressions of saintly longevity are specific to each tradition. In exploring the mythically long lives of enlightened beings in Sanskrit, Tibetan, and Pāli sources, Ray identifies parallels in the hagiographic models of saints (*arhat*), future Buddhas, and fully enlightened Buddhas. His comparison of the long lives attributed to saints, Bodhisattvas, and the Buddha according to the Madhyamaka and Theravāda schools and to Nāgārjuna shows that these hagiographies share three definitive characteristics: the lives of these extraordinary beings may extend beyond ordinary human life spans; they are compelled to live such long lives out of altruistic compassion; and their longevity is realized only through the desire of others. Ray demonstrates that longevity is a significant attribute of Buddhist hagiography in the earliest extant texts, such as the early passages in the *Mahāparinibbāna Sutta,* and concludes that the focus on sacred biography remained significant from the beginning of the tradition and throughout many of its later, divergent developments. Ray views that the biographical focus is central in Buddhism and finds multiple expressions in both its elite, monastic domain and the popular, lay domain.

Jonathan Walters interprets universalist Buddhist society in the early post-Aśokan period as described in such Pāli sources as the *Cariyāpiṭaka, Buddhavaṃsa,* and *Apadāna.* His focus there is on the ritual celebration of the Buddha's biography through *stūpa* and relic cults during the expansion and formation of the early post-Aśokan period. Walters argues that these texts depict a coherent and fully developed biographical mode of the Buddha. He also proposes that an analysis of these texts in conjunction with epigraphic and archaeological evidence allows for a historical construction of developments in the biographical tradition and its influence on subsequent conceptions.

The third group of essays considers biographies of Buddhist kings in Thai classical literature, paintings, and history. Each contribution appraises multiple voices, contexts, and narrative intentions in these biographies. The essays highlight the ambiguity and complexity in textual depictions of Theravāda kings, who are described as protectors of Buddhist fields of merit or as future Buddhas. The first of these models is informed by the Aśokan paradigm of Buddhist kingship,[38] in which a just king (*dhammarāja*) protects religion to guarantee the spiritual and material welfare of the polity, while the latter conception is informed by the Buddha's penultimate human life as King Vessantara, which led to his perfection of generosity.

In "Painting the 'Great Life,'" Forrest McGill examines nineteenth-century central Thai paintings and their accompanying inscriptions of the last of the Ten Great Pāli *jātakas*, which recounts the Buddha's penultimate life as King Vessantara. In addition to analyzing stylistic representations in these paintings from an art historical vantage, McGill turns his attention to ritual, social, and historical contexts of their use, production, and meaning. Paintings of this kind were mass-produced for purchase by lay sponsors of Buddhists rituals such as temple festivals or monastic ordinations. Lay donors also supported ritualized recitations of the *Vessantara Jātaka* that were performed as an integral part of merit-making rituals. McGill explores the ritual uses of the Vessantara story for the aspirations of lay donors as "owners" of these fields of merit and related issues of power, status, and wealth. While the sponsorship of this *jātaka* in its diverse modes was believed to bring about meritorious results in the religious lives of its sponsors, McGill, like Hudak, notes also the value of *jātaka* stories as entertainment. McGill's demonstration of the ways in which biographical modes of the *Vessantara Jātaka* are extended to encompass past, present, and future lives of those who karmically encounter the story recalls for the reader similar conclusions in contributions by Woodward, Strong, and Walters.

Thomas John Hudak's essay analyzes narrative transformations in the *Samutthākhoot kham chan*, a Thai poem about one of the Buddha's former lives. This poem borrows from established forms of the Pāli *jātakas*, but a version of the narrative does not exist in that tradition. Rather, it is part of the apocryphal *Paññāsa Jātaka* tales that developed in northern Thailand between the thirteenth and seventeenth centuries. Hudak shows how this biographical tale became a simultaneous venue for sacralizing the biography of the future Buddha and of the Thai King Narai (r.1652–1688). Through a process of multiple authors, narrative purposes, styles, and contexts, this story came to be retold as a parable for the royal biography of a wheel-turning king, Narai, glorifying his power and the artful refinement of his court. The changes in the narrative's structure and content reflect the historical contexts and intentionality of authors who compiled the various versions of the bodhisattva's biography. Over time, both courtiers and monks contributed to this composition, which in contemporary Thai society has come to be viewed primarily as an entertaining adventure story and cultivated expression of classical poetry rather than as a religious text.

Paul Christopher Johnson examines Western and Thai perspectives on the biography of King Mongkut (r.1851–1868), who sought to fashion his own life to encompass both Western ideals of rationality and enlightenment philosophy and Theravāda notions of religious purification and emulation of the Buddha's life. Johnson engages in a critical examination of the processes by which Mongkut's biographical image is negotiated by various authors to become meaningful in terms of the polarities of Western modernity and Thai traditionalism.

The fourth group of essays analyzes biographical themes in ethnography and their interpretations in the local, culturally constructed contexts of Theravāda Buddhism. My essay explores local contexts, myths, other texts, and rituals associated with the Burmese Mahāmuni image. This icon is believed to be the Buddha's "living" double. Like contributions by Brown, Walters, and McGill, it examines—from the perspective of ethnography—the iconic and cultic extensions of Buddhist biography and indicates how this local complex functions as an indexical symbol within the broader Buddhist tradition and cosmology. The biographical modalities of the Mahāmuni complex make use of ritual, myths, and texts to shift referents, levels, and contexts of interpretation in numerous ways. The efficacy of the ritual creates the Buddha's presence in the local Burmese context and allows contemporary Burmese Buddhists to be immediate participants in his biography and pristine community. In this manner, Burmese Buddhists may project the karmic configurations of their own lives in local contexts onto the universal cosmology of the Buddha field that encompasses all sentient existence. The indexical symbolism of the Mahāmuni myth also makes implicit allusions to episodes in the *Dhammapada Commentary* that recount how the Buddha illuminated the cosmos and created his own living double during his exposition of the Abhidhamma. The biographical modalities of the Mahāmuni complex provide religious legitimation—in ritual, textual, and mythic forms—for Burmese Theravādins by enabling them to place their own lives within the karmic fields of the living Buddha.

James Taylor and Gustaaf Houtman explore relationships between biography, biographer, and context in the ethnographic study of contemporary Theravāda saints. Taylor focuses on complementary developments in textualization and contextualization of the ascetic tradition in Thailand. He chronicles transformations in the oral hagiography of a forest meditation teacher and the lineage of his disciples, describing the process by which oral hagiography—fashioned after salient features of the Buddha's biography—becomes a literary genre of national salience. In the contextualized extensions of this hagiographic process, popular fascination with this monastic hagiography is linked to a cult of relics that extends from the periphery to the center of elite power at the Thai capital. Taylor's observations are based on ethnographic research, but they speak directly to issues raised in other essays in this volume. An example of such congruence is Taylor's observation that the paths of Buddhist saints—as depicted in these hagiographies—typically encompass previous lives. Furthermore, Taylor remarks that the biographical process characteristically emphasizes the regeneration of pristine Buddhist ideals in the present. The "biographical imperative," in Woodward's terms, thus shapes the continuing interpretation of Buddhist biography in contemporary social, historical, and political contexts in Thailand and elsewhere in the Theravāda world.

Houtman's essay focuses on the biography of a Burmese lay meditation teacher. He discusses the use of established Burmese literary conventions to historicize and sacralize a modern, nontraditional biography in order to legitimize its significance within Buddhist hagiography. Houtman emphasizes that historical events, as defined by Western scholarship, are not necessarily significant or relevant elements in the construction of life accounts of Buddhist saints. He critically appraises the relationship of Burmese Buddhist biography and Western conceptions of life history. Like Strong, Johnson, and Walters, he emphasizes the need for a critical awareness of the Western, epistemological bias in the examination of Buddhist biography.

The reader will encounter additional trajectories that cut across the order of presentation in this collection of essays. For instance, Reynolds, Walters, and Woodward engage the Pāli version of the *Buddhavaṃsa* to construct perspectives on structural continuity, ritual performance, and philosophical discourse, respectively. Conversely, Strong, Ray, and Brown share common interests in the use of sacred biography in Sanskrit and other, non-Theravādin Buddhist traditions. Karmic cohorts or karmic life streams are taken up by Strong, Ray, and Woodward, while McGill and Ray both engage a focus on the future Buddha, Maitreya. Conceptual relations between Buddhist sacred biography and secularization are discussed by Hudak, Houtman, and Johnson, while issues concerning post-traditionalism and modernity are raised by Taylor, Johnson, Houtman, and Schober. Finally, a focus on the place of sacred biography in ritual is found in the essays by Brown, McGill, Walters, and Schober.

Conclusion

These essays go beyond historicist reconstruction to identify significant themes and processes of interpretation in Buddhist sacred biography that, as Reynolds states in this volume, have fundamentally shaped the development and dynamics of the tradition. Although further comparisons of analogous features in the biographical genre can be fruitfully added to the list of characteristics indicated here, a more productive method seeks to determine those aspects of Buddhist sacred biography that account for its powerful role within the tradition. How do we explain the fact that Buddhist sacred biography can simultaneously historicize mythic lineages, transform visual reliefs into icons of veneration, contextualize cultural formations and rituals, project local contexts onto universal cosmologies, and provide ritual means to bring Buddhists into the sacred presence of the living Buddha?

The interpretive plasticity of the Buddhist biographical genre becomes apparent only after we depart from the historicist epistemology that presumes biography to be defined by the unique events and circumstances of a single life spans of an individual actor captured in unilinear history. The contributions to this volume define a distinctly Buddhist epistemology derived from categories intrinsic to the tradition whereby the recurrent themes of sacred biography are interpreted in relation to other religious modes and categories—doctrinal, mythic, ritual, or cosmological—and against the shifting contexts of culture, society, and history.

In Buddhism, biographical episodes function as frames of reference that map thematic configurations onto divergent trajectories of time and space. In this manner, the themes of Buddhist biography are indexical symbols—as defined by Tambiah—that shift the interpretation of meaning to multiple levels, contexts, and referents. The characteristic ability of Buddhist biographies to shift narrative foci and interpretive contexts makes for a powerful, didactic tool, but does not in itself determine the content conveyed. A perspective on Buddhist sacred biographies as indexical symbols, however, enhances the multivocality and narrative shifts in the messages they convey.

The sacred biography of the Buddha is rooted in a distinctly Buddhist epistemology and encompasses analogous modes of path action throughout his many rebirths. Projecting the Buddha's biography onto other times and places legitimizes the belief in the universal efficacy of his dispensation and provides a model for its continuation in specific, local contexts. The biographical process proceeds through narrative patterns and indexical symbols that become salient and contextualized in the dialectical encounter of Buddhism and the cultures that participate in the development of the tradition. This can be discerned in the relationship between the biographer and biography and in the dialectic between biographical texts and the commentaries throughout the tradition. Buddhist sacred biography and the hagiographic traditions it engenders thus become central to the religious lives of the Buddhist community throughout the various schools, societies, and ages.

A pervading emphasis on sacred biography is not unique to Buddhism. Buddhism shares this concern with Christianity, Judaism, and Islam. Yet sacred biographies in those traditions do not share the same degree of interpretive plasticity, shifting referents, and contexts that lend such vitality to the Buddhist sacred biography. The disregard for linear history and its open-ended soteriology are two aspects of Buddhist epistemology that may account for this difference and distinguish it from epistemologies of other great traditions.

Acknowledgments

I am indebted to Frank Reynolds, Charles Hallisey, and Mark Woodward, who commented on various drafts of this essay. While I have benefited from their insights and suggestions, all mistakes are my own.

Notes

1. In "Text-Building, Epistemology, and Aesthetics in Javanese Shadow Theatre" (in *The Imagination of Reality: Essays in Southeast Asian Coherence Systems*, ed. A. L. Becker and A. A. Yengoyan, Norwood, N. J.: Ablex Publishing Corporation, 1979, pp. 211 ff.), A. L. Becker argues that modern philology rests on the notion that the meaning of a text is constrained by a set of relations, some of which are external to the text itself. He lists several constraints on the interpretation of texts, such as (1) hierarchy of textual units and their coherence within the text; (2) the relation of a text to other texts within the same genre or tradition; (3) relations of a text's content to the intentions of its creator(s) and audiences; and (4) the relation of units in the text to non-literary events (i.e., reference).
2. See Frank Reynolds, "The Many Lives of the Buddha" in *The Biographical Process: Studies in the History and Psychology of Religion*, Frank Reynolds and Donald Capps (The Hague: Mouton, 1976, pp. 37–66).
3. Although the contributions to this book examine some of the biographical instantiations, none of them speaks directly to the role of women in Buddhist sacred biography. The reader is therefore referred to excellent recent studies on the *Therīgāthā*, (Psalms of the Early Buddhists, C. A. F. Rhys-Davids [London: Luzac, 1964]), which contains biographical accounts of the mastery of the path by women in the early Buddhist community.
4. In his article on "Religion as a Cultural System" (in *The Interpretation of Cultures*, New York: Basic Books, 1973, p. 93), Clifford Geertz writes: "Unlike . . . nonsymbolic information sources, which are only models *for*,

not models *of*, culture patterns have an intrinsic double aspect: they give meaning, that is, objective conceptual form, to social and psychological reality both by shaping themselves to it and by shaping it to themselves" (emphasis in original).

5. The biography of this Theravāda monk, Acharn Mun, is taken up in James Taylor's essay in this book and has been the subject of several other studies.
6. Viz. Stanley Tambiah, *Buddhist Saints of the Forest and the Cult of Amulets* (Cambridge: Cambridge University Press, 1984, pp. 81–191), where he devotes lengthy discussion to the hagiography of Acharn Mun in text and context and to the symbiotic relations between biography and biographer.
7. Ibid., p. 4.
8. Frank Reynolds and Charles Hallisey's lucid and cogent assessment of the development of the biographical genre in Buddhism and of the scholarly work on this subject is found in an article entitled 'Buddha' in the *Encyclopedia of Religion*, ed. Mircea Eliade (New York: Macmillan, 1987), vol. 2, pp. 319–332.
9. Ibid., p. 323.
10. Erich Frauwallner, *The Earliest Vinaya and the Beginnings of Buddhist Literature* (Rome, 1956).
11. Alfred Foucher, *The Life of the Buddha According to the Ancient Texts and Monuments of India*, abridged translation from the French by Simone Boas (Westport, Conn.: Greenwood Press, 1963, 1972).
12. Étienne Lamotte, *History of the Indian Buddhism: From the Origins to the Sakka Era*, translated from the French by Sara Webb-Boin (Louvain-la-Neuve: Université Catholique de Louvain, Institut Orientaliste, 1988).
13. André Bareau, *Recherches sur la biographie du Buddha* (Paris: École française d'Extrême-Orient, no. 52, 2 vols., 1963).
14. Reynolds and Hallisey, "Buddha," p. 324.
15. Ibid., pp. 323–325.
16. Ibid.
17. An English translation of *The Jātaka: or Stories of the Buddha's Former Births* in 3 vols. and edited by E. B. Cowell was published by the Pāli Text Society, London, and reprinted most recently in 1990.
18. The reader is referred to John Strong's essay in this volume in which he discusses intersecting karmic streams in the Buddha's biography and the issue of proper segmentation in Buddhist biographical episodes.
19. This introduction by the Ceylonese commentator is translated into English in T. W. Rhys-Davids' translation of the *jātakas*, entitled *Buddhist Birth Stories* (London: Trübner & Co., Ludgate Hill, 1880). It has been reprinted by Arnopress, (New York, 1977).
20. A pertinent example of an independent biographical genre is the compilations of *Paññāsa Jātaka*, translated by I. B. Horner and Padmanabh S. Jaini, published by the Pāli Text Society, and distributed by Routledge and Kegan Paul (London, 1985).

21. For an example of this, see my essay in this volume, in which I discuss local myths about the Buddha's visits to sacred places in Burma.

22. Ruth-Inge Heinze, trans., *The Biography of Ahjan Man (1871–1949)*, compiled by Ahjan Bua (Taipei: The Oriental Cultural Service), *Asian Folklore and Social Life Monographs*, vol. 89.

23. Grant A. Olson, 'A Person-Centered Ethnography of Thai Buddhism: The Life of Rajavaramuni (Prayudh Payutto),' Ph.D. diss., Cornell University, 1989.

24. Gustaaf Houtman, "Traditions of Buddhist Practice in Burma," Ph.D. diss., University of London, School of African and Oriental Studies, 1990.

25. See Bonnie Pacala Brereton, *Thai Tellings of Phra Malai: Texts and Rituals Concerning a Popular Buddhist Saint* (Tempe: Monograph Series, Program for Southeast Asian Studies, Arizona State University, 1995).

26. Tambiah, *Buddhist Saints of the Forest*. pp. 81–194.

27. Charles Keyes, "Death of Two Buddhist Saints in Thailand," *Journal of the American Academy of Religion, Thematic Studies* 48, nos. 3 and 4 (1982), pp. 149–180.

28. Michael Carrithers, *The Forest Monks of Sri Lanka: An Anthropological and Historical Study* (Delhi: University of Oxford Press, 1983).

29. James L. Taylor, "From Wandering to Domestication: The Thai-Lao Forest Monastic Tradition," Ph.D. diss., Macquarie University, 1989.

30. Reginald Ray, *Buddhist Saints in India* (New York: Oxford University Press, 1993).

31. In this outstanding study, entitled *The Legend and Cult of Upagupta: Sanskrit Buddhism in North India and Southeast Asia* (Princeton, N.J.: Princeton University Press, 1992), Strong discusses stories and rituals concerning this saint in terms of themes central to the study of Buddhism in general, thus linking its Sanskrit textual tradition to vernacular Southeast Asian texts and rituals.

32. This book is published by Mosaic Press (New York and Oakland, Ont., 1988).

33. This book is published by Cambridge University Press (Cambridge and New York, 1988).

34. Alan Sponberg, epilogue, *Maitreya, The Future Buddha*, eds. Sponberg and Hardacre, p. 298.

35. Ibid., p. 293.

36. Reynolds, "The Many Lives of the Buddha," pp. 37–62.

37. See also Reynolds' discussion on the historical life of the Buddha and its extension through relics and teachings in the sacred histories of the Buddhist community in "The Many Lives of Buddha."

38. For a discussion of this paradigm, which became a model for subsequent Theravāda polities, see Stanley Tambiah's *World Conqueror and World Renouncer: A Study of Buddhism and Polity in Thailand against a Historical Background* (Cambridge: Cambridge University Press, 1977), pp. 54–72.

Part 1

Buddha Biography in Textual and Visual Narratives

Reynolds, Woodward, and Brown present a common focus on classical articulations of the Buddha biography in the textual and visual renditions of the Buddhist tradition and civilization. By focusing on the central role of the Buddha's own biography, this section begins the discourse at a juncture where previous studies and conventional understandings of the life of the Buddha meet innovative interpretations of the processes by which the Buddha biography becomes universalized across the tradition.

Reynolds' discussion of mythology in the Buddha's biography leads him to identify lineages that link the Buddha to his karmic past, to other Buddhas of the past and future, and to a genealogy of worldly rulers into which his last birth is placed. Reynolds shows how these lineages of the Buddha have been used to legitimate religious and civil institutions throughout the history of the tradition.

Woodward's emphasis on the biographical imperative in the Theravāda tradition relates the Buddha's biography and those of his fellow travelers to the philosophical tenets in the Theravāda tradition to illuminate correlations between biographical narratives about individuals and abstract conceptualizations of the path to enlightenment.

Brown's essay explores the role of visual and iconic representations of the Buddha biography in Indian and Southeast Asian religious architecture in order to expand our conventional understanding of their function as didactic tools and symbolic referents to the texts of the *jātaka* tales, the stories of the Buddha's former lives. He shows through evidence of the placement of these visual biographies, often partially hidden from view and out of narrative sequence, that these representations of the Buddha's biography served as objects of worship rendering more immediate the Buddha's presence within the architectural configuration of sacred space in these religious monuments.

Rebirth Traditions and the Lineages of Gotama: A Study in Theravāda Buddhology

Frank E. Reynolds

Buddhism, particularly in its Theravāda form, has often been presented as a religion in which mythology plays an insignificant role. The central Theravāda doctrines that affirm codependent origination as the basis for the coming-into-existence of worldly phenomena, the law of *karmic* reward and retribution as the regulating principle that determines the destinies of sentient beings, and the ineffability of the soteriological goal have all—so the argument goes—relegated mythic modes of expression to a secondary level.

This argument has a certain plausibility since the character of Theravāda teachings has, in fact, inhibited the development of certain kinds of mythology that have been prominent in more theistically oriented religions. For example, mythology associated with the gods in Theravāda Buddhism is far less developed than the parallel mythology in Hinduism. But the argument for the secondary role of mythology in the Theravāda context ignores the indisputable fact that the mythically constructed biography of the Buddha has, from the very beginning, played a fundamental role in the structure and dynamics of Theravāda religion.[1]

The mythically constructed biography of the Buddha, which has never been considered by Theravādins to be in conflict with any of the central teachings of the religion,[2] includes three interdependent and broadly overlapping components. The first component consists of mythic stories that trace the various lineages which culminate in the birth and life of the "historical" Buddha. The second component consists of accounts of events in the life of Gotama from the time of his descent from the Tusita heaven (his birth), through his Enlightenment at Bodh Gayā, to his *Parinibbāna* (his death) at Kusinārā. The third consists of stories that recount the fate of his teachings and his relics, often in the context of a sacred history composed by a particular segment of the Buddhist community.[3]

In the present essay I single out for attention the first of the three aspects of the Buddha biography. In so doing, I focus my discussion on various accounts of the three basic lineages that have established the background in relation to which the story of the "historical" life and the "extended" life of Gotama have traditionally been told.[4]

The Jātaka Lineage

The Buddha's *jātaka* lineage refers to the lineage that is constituted by a certain kind of stories of events, or of a series of events, that took place in his previous lives. In these events or series of events, the future Buddha is usually—though not always—the protagonist. In contrast to some other kinds of rebirth stories (discussed below), he carries on his action in a context where he has no contact with a Buddha or any other significant "field of merit." For the most part the future Buddha, who appears as an animal, as a human being, or (very occasionally) as a god, acts in a manner appropriate to the situation, and in so doing cultivates one of the virtues that will be manifest, in its fully developed form, when he attains his final rebirth as Gotama.[5]

The *jātaka* tradition in Buddhism is very ancient, extending back—in all probability—to the lifetime of the "historical" Buddha himself (somewhere between the sixth and fourth centuries B.C.E.). Certainly in the earliest strata of Buddhist texts that we possess, the foundations for the *jātaka* tradition are laid. For example, the basic legitimating charter for the *jātaka* tradition is found in the *Suttapiṭaka*—a "canonical" Theravāda collection of sermons attributed to the Buddha. In these *Suttapiṭaka* texts, the Buddha reports that he has succeeded, through the first of the three accomplishments that marked his accession to Buddhahood, in remembering all of his previous lives.[6]

In the context of the Enlightenment accounts, this attainment constitutes the first component in the breakthrough experience through which the Buddha claimed to transcend reality as it is ordinarily constituted. But, in addition to this specifically soteriological dimension, the Buddha's assertion that he had attained a full knowledge of his previous lives provided a firm epistemological basis for the credibility of references to previous lives that he had supposedly lived, and of accounts of particular incidents in which he had supposedly been involved.

The early tradition also contains specific *jātaka* stories that were attributed to the Buddha. Although we cannot be certain how the *jātaka* genre was delineated during the early centuries, it is significant that there is a reference to *jātakas* in a very early list of the literary forms in which the Buddha's teachings were being preserved. Moreover, there are *jātaka* stories that clearly conform to our understanding of the genre that are scattered throughout the *Suttapiṭaka*.[7] As in the case of other discourses contained in such texts, there is no way to determine for certain whether these *jātakas* were actually recounted by the Buddha himself, or whether they were incorporated into the tradition by the early community. However this may be, the presence of *jātaka* stories in the early strata of the remembered words of the Buddha proves that the genre cannot be lightly passed off as a development associated with a late "popularization" of the Buddha's original message.

This very early *jātaka* tradition, like many other aspects of early Buddhism, continued to develop in the centuries after the Buddha's death; and it took on a more definitive form in the period after the reign of King Aśoka (third century B.C.E.). The number of *jātakas* increased as a variety of folkloric stories of different kinds were incorporated into the tradition. In contrast to the earliest *jātakas* that we can identify, which depict the future Buddha as a king or sage living in a past era, the *jātakas* that were added to the tradition depict him in many different roles. In some cases he is portrayed as a human being, but in many others he is portrayed as an animal.

By the second century B.C.E. great *stūpas* (funerary mounds that usually contained relics of the Buddha) were being constructed which had, as an important component in their decor, sculptured depictions of *jātaka* stories. And by the beginning of the Common Era, at least two literary collections of *jātaka* stories were compiled and preserved in the Theravāda context, where they ultimately won a place among the texts that the tradition considered "canonical."

One of these two collections—the *Cariyāpiṭaka*—contains thirty-five stories, all told in verse.[8] Each story begins with the Buddha declaring that in one of his previous lives he had been a particular being living in a particular situation; it continues with a short story in which a particular perfection or the like is cultivated; and it concludes with a positive affirmation in which the Buddha identifies the particular aspect of Buddhahood that the story has highlighted.

In the first set of ten stories, the virtue the future Buddha cultivates is the perfection of selfless giving; in the second set of ten stories, the virtue he cultivates is the perfection of moral rectitude; and in the remaining fifteen stories the virtues he cultivates are the perfections of truth (six stories), of renunciation (five stories), of amity (two stories), of determination (one story), and of equanimity (one story).[9]

The second of the post-Aśokan *jātaka* collections that came to be accepted as "canonical" by the Theravādins was the one that became the core of their most extensive *jātaka* tradition. In fact, this "*Jātaka Book*"—which is constituted by a series of very enigmatic poetic verses—is now accessible to us only because of a voluminous commentary that was translated from Sinhala into (or back into) Pāli in the fifth or sixth centuries C.E. Known as the *Jātakaṭṭhakathā*, this commentary includes—apart from an attached "introduction" that will be discussed below—547 sets of verses each with its own extensive prose elaboration.[10] In Burma and Southeast Asia, variant versions of this collection have been disseminated, some containing 550 stories, others containing 500.

In this *Jātakaṭṭhakathā* strand of tradition, the format is quite consistent. The stage is set by a short "story of the present," in which the situation in which the Buddha supposedly recounted the *jātaka* in question is described. This is followed by the "story of the past," which constitutes the *jātaka* itself. After the story of the past is completed, the Buddha concludes by identifying certain characters as the "rebirth precursors" of himself, of particular members of his family, of particular disciples, or of other contemporaries.[11]

In the *Jātakaṭṭhakathā*, the *jātaka* stories are ordered in accordance with the number of "canonical" verses that each one contains. Thus the collection begins with shorter stories, many of which are only slightly or not at all related to specifically Buddhist themes. The *jātakas* that are located toward the end of the collection are much longer stories (often described by modern interpreters as "epics" and/or "romances") that contain many verses and exhibit a very distinctive Buddhist character.

According to the tradition, the entire collection of stories depicts the actions through which the future Gotama cultivated the ten perfections that are characteristic of Buddhahood. More specifically, it is affirmed that the last ten *jātakas* (which are often treated as a self-contained set) describe how the future Buddha successively cultivated each of these ten perfections. Finally, the two longest *jātakas* that are placed at the very end of the commentary tell how the future Buddha perfected what the Theravādins came to recognize as the two preeminent virtues of a Buddha, namely the virtue of practical wisdom (the *Mahā-Ummagga Jātaka*)[12] and the virtue of selfless giving (the *Vessantara Jātaka*).[13]

Given the preeminence that is associated with the perfection of the virtues of practical wisdom and selfless giving in the *Jātakaṭṭhakathā* and its variants (and in the Theravāda tradition more generally), it is not surprising that the two best known of the later collections of Pāli *jātakas* highlight stories in which these two virtues are emphasized. Both of these texts were composed in Southeast Asia, probably in the Chiangmai kingdom of northern Thailand. In both cases it is probable that the versions of the texts that we presently possess were given their present form during the middle centuries of the second millennium C.E.

The first of these texts is called the *Mahāpurisa* or *Great Person Jātaka.*[14] The author-compiler of this text has utilized the well-established *Jātakaṭṭhakathā* format (story of the present, story of the past, and concluding identification of the characters) to frame a composite text that contains elements from the *Mahā-Ummagga Jātaka*, several other *jātakas* taken from the *Jātakaṭṭhakathā*, and additional material drawn from the *nīti* (practical wisdom) tradition of Indian and Southeast Asian literature. Clearly the virtue the future Buddha is cultivating through the series of stories that are recounted in this text is the virtue of practical wisdom, a virtue that involves the utilization of a superior level of knowledge in order to achieve what would ordinarily be thought of as worldly success.[15]

The other late Southeast Asian Pāli collection that concerns us here is the so-called *Paññāsa Jātaka*, which contains fifty separate stories, each of which begins with a brief verse followed by a short "story of the present," a "story of the past" which is the center of attention, and a concluding identification of key characters.[16] A very few of these stories are altered or embellished versions of stories that appeared in earlier Theravāda collections. Some are versions of *jātakas* that can be identified in earlier Sanskrit texts, but a significant number of stories do not have any identifiable precursors.

The *Paññāsa Jātaka* collection includes several striking *jātakas* that recount stories of romantic love involving the separation (often because of shipwreck) and the subsequent reunion of the future Buddha and his wife. Although there are precursors to some of these stories, particularly in the Sanskrit tradition, the *jātakas* of this type that are included in the *Paññāsa* collection are extended accounts that are distinctive to the Southeast Asian milieu.

Although the *Paññāsa Jātaka* contains a number of stories that are of great individual interest, what is important to highlight in the present context is the emphasis that the author-compiler of the collection has placed on the future Buddha's cultivation of the virtue of selfless giving. There are several stories that provide accounts of selfless giving that closely parallel the accounts of selfless giving in the *Vessantara Jātaka* itself—accounts in which the future Buddha gives his kingdom, his wealth, his wife, and/or his children. In addition, many of the stories recount acts in which the Buddha sacrifices his own body for the benefit of others. All in all, more than half of the stories in the *Paññāsa Jātaka* collection depict, in one way or another, the future Buddha's practice of the perfection of selfless giving.

Finally, there is one additional extension of the *jātaka* tradition that deserves to be mentioned. In the Laotian cultural area, probably during the middle centuries of the second millennium C.E., a fascinating *jātaka* called *Phra Lak/Phra Lam* was composed.[17] In this very long and complex *jātaka*, the future Buddha is reborn as Rama (Phra Lam), a figure who had appeared in the earlier *jātaka* tradition as the protagonist in the relatively brief *Dasaratha Jātaka* that is included in the *Jātakaṭṭhakathā*, and in the Hindu tradition as the hero in many versions of the Ramayana. In the new Laotian Buddhist telling of the story, Rama—who is identified as a rebirth precursor of Gotama—is reborn, near the beginning of the present cosmic age, in order to reestablish the cosmic/social order that is being disrupted by Ravana. According to the narrative (which recounts many incidents that are directly parallel to incidents in Hindu Ramayanas), Rama succeeds in his mission of defeating Ravana and reestablishing proper order in the cosmos and society. Once this is accomplished, he goes on to establish—at the site of the present Laotian capital—the dynasty that was ruling there at the time that the text was written.[18]

The Lineage of Buddhas

According to the Theravādins, the Gotama Buddha had, in addition to his *jātaka* lineage, a Buddha lineage as well. This means that, as a Buddha, Gotama was the successor of a series of Buddhas (Great Beings who had attained full Enlightenment and undertaken the task of teaching the Dhamma they had discovered) that stretched far back into the past. In principle this Buddha lineage stretched back into infinity, but in fact the Theravādins have focused their primary attention on a set of Buddhas in which Gotama is the seventh and on a more extended set in which Gotama is the twenty-fifth.

Like the notion of Gotama's *jātaka* lineage, the notion of his Buddha lineage appeared in the very early years of Buddhist history. In fact, it is quite possible that it, too, had its origins in the teachings of the Buddha himself. It is clear that Gotama represented himself throughout the whole range of early Buddhist texts in which his teaching is supposedly recorded, not as one who had discovered a new Truth, but rather as one who had rediscovered a Truth that had been known in earlier times. Moreover, the *Mahāpadāna Sutta*—which is the "root text" from which the Theravāda notion of the Buddha lineage has developed—is a sutta that is included in the *Dīghanikāya* that has as much claim to antiquity as any of the other great suttas that are attributed to Gotama.[19]

Like the stories in the *jātaka* tradition, the stories recounted in the *Mahāpadāna Sutta* have their epistemological grounding in the ability to remember previous lives. According to the Buddha's testimony as reported in the text itself, he is able to activate his memory concerning previous Buddhas in two different but complementary ways. On the one hand, he is able to call to recollection significant things about previous Buddhas and their activities by utilizing his own clear insight into the principle of Truth. At the same time, he is able to confirm/enhance his knowledge of such matters by meditational attainments which enable him to gain access to the exalted realms of the cosmos. The divine inhabitants of these realms then provide him with information concerning what they have observed in their previous lives in which they have themselves been followers of these previous Buddhas.[20]

In the first segment of the *Mahāpadāna* text, the Buddha gives a brief, stereotyped account of the last seven Buddhas, himself included. In each case Gotama identifies the cosmic eon in which the particular Buddha was born, his social status (nobleman or brahmin), his family group (*gotta*), the normal life span during the period in question, the kind of tree under which he was enlightened, the names of his two chief disciples, the number of fully accomplished saints (*arhats*) who participated in the *bhikkhu* ("monastic") assemblies that he established, the name of his preeminent attendant *bhikkhu*, his father's name, his mother's name, and his place of birth.

In the second segment, Gotama recounts in considerable detail the life of Vipassī, the first in the series of seven Buddhas mentioned in the text. The story that is told is an amazing account that must be either a "model for" or a "model of" the biography that we presently know as the biography of Gotama himself. It includes most of the major events (and many of the accompanying details) that we now associate with Gotama's early and middle life. These include a descent from the Tusita heaven, a miraculous birth, a great renunciation, a quest that culminates in Enlightenment (into which is incorporated an extensive explication of the central Buddhist teaching concerning codependent origination and its reversal), a divine enticement that leads to a decision to preach the Dhamma, a first sermon in a famous Deer Park, a founding of the *bhikkhu* order, and a commissioning of the *bhikkhu* community to "Fare ye forth on the mission that is for the good of the many, for the happiness of the many, to take compassion on the world and to work profit and good and happiness to gods and men."[21]

The clear implication of the text is that the lives of the six subsequent Buddhas repeat, with variations of scale and minor variations of content, the exemplary model that is portrayed in the story of Vipassī. Thus Gotama Buddha (at least the Gotama Buddha of the text) depicts himself as having a distinguished lineage of Great Beings whose life story and saving message were virtually identical to his own.

The Theravāda tradition concerning the lineage of twenty-four previous Buddhas was—as best we can judge from the available texts—a somewhat later development. Expressed in a text called the *Buddhavaṃsa* that was one of the very last to be included in the Theravāda "canon,"[?] it both encompassed and adapted the lineage tradition associated with the *Mahāpadāna Sutta.* Although the *Buddhavaṃsa* has not received a great deal of serious attention from Buddhologists, the lineage of Buddhas that it established became one of the most basic and pervasive components in later Theravāda mythology.[22]

In the introductory chapter of the *Buddhavaṃsa,* the author-compiler describes an occasion that occurred at the very beginning of the Buddha's ministry. According to the account, Gotama perceives that the gods and human beings who populate the world at that time are quite unprepared to receive him and his teaching. Therefore, in order to show these rather dull-witted gods and human beings what a Buddha is really like, he creates a marvelous "walk in the sky, adorned with jewels." Pacing back and forth on this jeweled walk, he shows forth his glory and performs various miracles. Overwhelmed by the magnificent cosmic display, Sāriputta (one of the early disciples) asks the Buddha to describe the vow and the practice of perfections that enabled him to achieve the Enlightenment that brings with it this kind of supreme glory and power.

The Gotama of the text then recounts a lineage of twenty-four Buddhas (a set which includes, as the last six, the six previous Buddhas mentioned in the *Mahāpadāna Sutta*), telling in each case a story in which that previous Buddha plays a significant role. But, as the question to which Gotama is responding demands, the stories that are told differ drastically from the accounts that are given in the *Mahāpadāna* context. To be sure, each story contains an account (often very brief) that describes the specific characteristics and activities of the previous Buddhas in ways that are clearly reminiscent of earlier accounts of previous Buddhas. In the *Buddhavaṃsa,* however, the primary focus is on an encounter between the previous Buddha in question and Gotama in one of the previous lives in which he is moving toward his own attainment of Enlightenment.

The crucial *Buddhavaṃsa* story, which is by far the longest and provides the paradigm for all the others, is the first. It describes in considerable detail a series of encounters between the Buddha Dīpaṅkara and the future

Gotama who was at the time (which is said to be four incalculable ages and a hundred thousand eons in the past) a well-accomplished ascetic named Sumedha. In the series of encounters that the text describes, the future Gotama—inspired by Dīpaṅkara's person and message—makes his original vow to attain Buddhahood, as well as his original commitment to practice the ten perfections that are necessary prerequisites for the realization of that goal. Dīpaṅkara then predicts that Sumedha will eventually, in the far distant future in his final rebirth as Gotama, attain the goal of Enlightenment and become a Great Teacher for all mankind.

In each of the twenty-three stories that follow, another one of the previous Buddhas encounters the future Gotama in one of his ensuing rebirths. In each case the future Gotama is inspired to renew his vow and to reaffirm his commitment to the practice of the ten perfections; and in each case the Buddha in question predicts that in the future Gotama will achieve his goal.[23]

Thus the Gotama of the *Buddhavaṃsa* recounts a Buddha lineage that begins with the Buddha whom he knew when, in his far distant rebirth as Sumedha, he was first inspired to make his vow to attain Buddhahood and to commit himself to the practice of the ten perfections. This Buddha lineage is continued by the twenty-three other Buddhas under whom Gotama—in twenty-three of his own previous lives—renews his vow and his commitment that assures his continued progress toward the goal. Finally, this Buddha lineage is once again extended, this time through the future Buddha's own rebirth as Gotama and his own attainment of the Enlightened mind and the glorious body that are the necessary characteristics of all members of the set.[24]

It is difficult to overemphasize the importance that the lineage of Buddhas that we are able to glimpse in the *Buddhavaṃsa* has had in the later development of Theravāda Buddhology and sacred history. Most subsequent authors-compilers of various Theravāda biographical and "historical" texts have utilized some version or adaptation of this lineage of Buddhas as their entrée into the particular narratives that they are most concerned to relate.

One of the most interesting and influential examples of the use of the *Buddhavaṃsa* lineage in an obviously biographical context is the *Nidānakathā*, a text that was written to serve as an introduction to the Pāli translation of *Jātakaṭṭhakathā* (ca. sixth century C.E.). The *Nidānakathā*—which Buddhologists have often recognized as the first full-scale biography of the "historical" Buddha that the Theravāda tradition produced—begins with a recounting of the lineage of twenty-four previous Buddhas that is taken directly from the *Buddhavaṃsa*; and only when this narrative of the lineage of Buddhas is complete does the author move on to a narrative of the final life of Gotama. This second, more "historical" section of the *Nidānakathā* begins with Gotama's descent from the Tusita heaven and carries the story forward to the time when Gotama is settled in the Jetavana monastery where, according to the tradition, he recounts the stories that are recorded in the main body of the commentary.[25]

In its original setting as an introduction to the *Jātakaṭṭhakathā*, the *Nidānakathā* establishes the overarching temporal framework within which the classical *jātaka* tradition is framed. Viewed in the context provided by the *Nidānakathā* introduction, the *jātakas* of the *Jātakaṭṭhakathā* (and, implicitly, most other *jātakas* as well) are situated in a kind of *jātaka* time that extends from the era of Dīpaṅkara and Sumedha until the moment of the future Buddha's descent from the Tusita heaven to begin his final life as Gotama.

Moreover, the presence of the *Buddhavaṃsa* frame calls attention to the emphasis that is placed in the stories that constitute the *jātaka* collection on the physical, bodily transformations that result from the moral (and immoral) actions that are performed. Although the relationship between spiritual and moral attainment, on the one hand, and natural and physical changes, on the other, is less explicitly highlighted in the *Nidānakathā* than in the *Buddhavaṃsa*, the fact is that the theme of morally generated bodily and natural transformation pervades the stories that are recounted in the *jātaka* collection. Thus the *jātaka* collection provides further support for the notion that the Gotama Buddha—as a result of his cultivation of the ten perfections—attained not only spiritual Enlightenment, but acquired a marvelous and extraordinary physical body as well.[26]

With the passage of time, however, the *Nidānakathā* took on another function quite distinct from its role as an introduction to the *Jātakaṭṭhakathā*. It was taken over and incorporated into texts that provided much more extended Theravāda accounts of the "historical" life of the Buddha. These later and more "complete" biographies retained the *Buddhavaṃsa* account of the lineage of Buddhas pretty much intact, but added extensive materials concerning the Buddha's "historical" life (including materials about the later portions of his ministry and his *Parinibbāna*, or passing away) and the distribution and subsequent fate of his relics.[27]

The *Buddhavaṃsa* version of the lineage of Buddhas also became closely associated with the distinctively Theravāda genre that I have elsewhere characterized as the "biographical chronicle."[28] Biographical chronicles begin with one or more sections dealing primarily with lineages of Gotama. They include the lineage of Buddhas and his royal genealogy, as well as short accounts of events in his "historical" life, which often prefigure events that occur in later Buddhist history. And they then move into the main narratives, which are largely chronological accounts of the way in which the Buddha's influence (represented by the *Dhammic* teachings and the monks, on the one hand, and by relics and kings, on the other) persist from the time of his death and the distribution of his relics to the time when the chronicle in question is written.

The *Mahāvaṃsa*, the "classic text" of this genre, was written in Sri Lanka in the fifth century C.E. The *Mahāvaṃsa,* account begins with an introductory comment that is immediately followed by a brief listing of the twenty-four previous Buddhas, each one accompanied by a reference to their encounters with the future Gotama.[29] However in the *Jinakalamāli*, a fifteenth-century northern Thai text which represents a much later stage in the development of the genre, the lineage of Buddhas has undergone a considerable elaboration.[30]

In the *Jinakalamāli*, the narrative does not begin with the lineage of Buddhas described in the *Buddhavaṃsa.* In fact, it begins in a much more ancient era in which the future Gotama, without the benefit of the presence of a fully enlightened Buddha, makes a vow to attain the goal of Buddhahood. According to the story, the future Gotama is shipwrecked with his mother and carries her on his shoulders as he swims across the great ocean to safety. The god Brahmā, seeing this action, is greatly impressed; and through Brahmā's power, the future Gotama arouses within himself the thought, "I will become enlightened and enlighten others, I will become released and release others, I will cross over and take others across."[31]

After mentioning a great number of additional lives (the story of two are recounted at some length), the author-compiler of the *Jinakalamāli* turns to stories in which a previous Buddha encounters the future Gotama. The first of these is especially important, both because of its intrinsic interest and because it initiates the now vastly expanded lineage of Buddhas. The story goes as follows: a young woman (the future Gotama), who is a stepsister of the Buddha Purāṇa-Dīpaṅkara, makes a gift of mustard oil to a renowned Elder, who is named Pacchima-Dīpaṅkara. When she does this, she makes an accompanying mental resolve to eventually become a Buddha called Siddhattha, another name by which Gotama Buddha is often known. Despite the fact that she makes this resolve to attain Buddhahood, and despite the fact that (unlike her rebirth precursors who had made the same vow) she has the advantage of having personal contact with a fully enlightened Buddha, she still cannot—because of her gender—receive from him the prediction that her vow will be fulfilled. Instead, the Buddha Purāṇa-Dīpaṅkara predicts that the Elder to whom she has given the mustard oil will—in the far distant future—be reborn as the Buddha Dīpaṅkara, and that his stepsister will be reborn as the male ascetic named Sumedha. He goes on to affirm that the Buddha Dīpaṅkara will, at that time, give the prediction that will confirm that she (then reborn as Sumedha) will ultimately attain the goal to which she has committed herself.[32]

The *Jinakalamāli* then proceeds to affirm that, following the era of the Buddha Purāṇa-Dīpaṅkara, there were two very extended expanses of time totaling sixteen incalculable ages during which there were hundreds of thousands of previous Buddhas who encountered the future Gotama in hundreds of thousands of his previous lives. Then, with all of this new material in place, the author-compiler continues his version of the lineage of Buddhas in a way that is in close accord with the *Buddhavaṃsa* tradition. Thus he goes on to recount the stories of twenty-seven Buddhas who were mentioned in the *Buddhavaṃsa*: the three predecessors of Dīpaṅkara whose names appeared in the *Buddhavaṃsa* only in a formal list, and the twenty-four Buddhas whose stories constituted the main body of the text.[33]

The Royal Lineage

The third of the three lineages of the Buddha is a royal lineage that ultimately came to play an important role in the mythic system that the Theravādins developed. Since this third lineage tradition traces a line of kings that extends right down to the time of the Buddha himself (and has "branch lines" that continued after his lifetime), certain of the more recent segments of it have some claim to justification in the "historical memory" of the Buddhist community. But what is the epistemological basis for the knowledge of the phases of the royal lineage that are temporally more remote?

The answer to this question is never (to my knowledge at least) explicitly given. Nevertheless Buddhaghosa, in his famous and authoritative *Path of Purification*, provides a suggestive hint. In Buddhaghosa's text, the royal lineage is discussed in sections that deal with the same special power that was utilized in order to provide an epistemological basis for the authenticity of the *jātaka* lineage and the lineage of Buddhas, namely the capacity of Buddhas and great saints to remember their previous lives and to recall what they had done, seen, and heard in the course of those lives.[34]

In the very early Buddhist tradition, most of the key structural elements that were to be a part of the fully developed royal lineage tradition were already in place. These include the identification of Gotama's parents as the king and the queen of the Sakyā tribe, which ruled over a kingdom that controlled an area that extended along the present boundaries of India and Nepal. They include a reference in the *Ambaṭṭha Sutta*, which attributes the origins of the Sakyā tribe and its ruling dynasty to the exiled children of a famous ruler of long ago named Okkāka.[35] They also include an extremely important myth that is incorporated into the *Aggañña Sutta*'s famous account of the beginnings of the present cosmic eon, a myth that recounts the choice of Mahāsammata (the Great Elect) as king in order to bring peace and order into an otherwise degenerating social situation.[36]

In the Theravāda tradition, it is probable that a more fully elaborated royal lineage was included in the *Sīhalaṭṭhakathā-Mahāvaṃsa*, a relatively early (ca. beginning of the Common Era) text that has been lost but is referred to by later authors who deal with the subject.[37] However, it was not until the fourth to fifth centuries C.E. in Sri Lanka that we have Theravāda texts that are actually available to us in which the crucial connections are made and the basic pattern articulated. The *Dīpavaṃsa* (fourth century) and the *Mahāvaṃsa* (fifth century) recount an extended royal lineage that begins with Mahāsammata, the mythical founder of the institution of kingship. The royal lineage continues from Mahāsammata through a huge number of successors to Okkāka, and from Okkāka through a huge number of his successors to the parents of the Buddha himself. Later in the fifth century C.E., Buddhaghosa, in his *Path of Purification*, provides a very similar royal genealogy; but, in addition, he identifies Mahāsammata as a rebirth precursor of Gotama.[38]

In the much later phases of Theravāda development, minor emendations appear in many relevant texts. In the *Jinakalamāli*, for example, some changes and additions are made in the list of kings, and still another king in the royal, blood-lineage tradition is specifically identified with Gotama in one of his previous lives. This king is Vessantara, a near descendant of King Okkāka, whom the author-compiler of the *Jinakalamāli* specifically identifies with the Vessantara of the *jātaka* tradition.

In addition, a much more original development in the royal lineage tradition occurred in Laos with the composition of the *Phra Lak/Phra Lam* or *Rama Jātaka*. As we can deduce from the brief description of this text that has been provided above, the author attributes to Rama the crucial sociogonic role that Mahāsammata had played in the more mainstream Theravāda mythology. Although in the *Phra Lak/Phra Lam* context there is no direct reference to any royal genealogy that extends from Rama to Gotama, Rama had traditionally been one of the kings included in the genealogical lists of Gotama's royal ancestors. Thus it seems safe to assume that, in the *Phra Lak/Phra Lam* account, Rama (who is explicitly identified as a rebirth precursor of Gotama) is being presented not only as the founder of *Dhammic* kingship for our cosmic era, but also as the founder of Gotama's royal lineage.[39]

Conclusion

Thus far we have traced the development of the Theravāda accounts of the three primary lineages of Gotama. In order to round out our discussion, we must now adopt a more synthetic perspective and focus briefly on the justification, on the coherence, and on the practical importance of lineage and lineage-oriented mythology within the Theravāda tradition as a whole.

From the perspective of Theravāda doctrine, the authenticity of all three of the lineages of Gotama is justified on the basis of a central Buddhist epistemological contention—namely, the notion that the Buddha (and secondarily various divinities and other Buddhist saints) is able to remember his previous lives. The connection between the belief in the Buddha's capacity to remember his previous lives and the perceived authenticity of the *jātaka* stories is obvious. But our examination of relevant texts has suggested that this same capacity of the Buddha (and others) provides the epistemological grounds for affirming the authenticity of the stories that constitute the two other lineages as well.

In addition to the fact that the three lineages and the stories that constitute them are firmly integrated with basic Theravāda doctrine, it is also important to emphasize the fact that these stories cohere within a single temporal framework of mythic time. This temporal framework was given its classical expression in the *Buddhavaṃsa*. According to this text, the relevant mythic time began four incalculable ages and a hundred thousand cosmic eons ago when the future Gotama, in his birth as Sumedha, made his vow to attain Buddhahood. The basic mythological period, thus begun, continued—according to the *Buddhavaṃsa*—through to the time of Gotama himself.

In the course of subsequent Theravāda history, this basic temporal framework was modified in at least two major respects. First, it was taken much further into the distant past by the notion that, prior to his birth as Sumedha, Gotama had been aspiring to Enlightenment for a very extensive number of incalculable ages. Second, the framework was divided into two segments: an extremely long period that extended from the point at which the future Buddha had first become an aspirant to Enlightenment up until the beginning of the present cosmic eon, and a subsequent period that began with the devolution of the present cosmic eon and ended with the birth of Gotama.

The first segment serves as the temporal niche for the stories of the lives of Gotama before his birth as Sumedha, for the stories of the first twenty-one of the twenty-four Buddhas whose lives and encounters with the future Gotama are recounted in the *Buddhavaṃsa*, and for the great majority of *jātaka* stories in which the future Gotama cultivates the ten perfections. The second segment, which extends from the beginning of the present cosmic era to the time of Gotama, serves as the temporal niche for the stories of the last three Buddhas whose encounters with the future

Gotama are mentioned in the *Buddhavaṃsa*, for several *jātaka* stories that are considered to be relatively recent (for example, the story of Vessantara), and for the royal lineage from Mahāsammata (or Rama) to the time of Gotama.

Finally, it is important to highlight the central role that a whole range of lineage traditions have played in Theravāda community life and in Theravāda practice. In some cases, the lineages in question have been lineages that we have not discussed because they were initiated *by* Gotama. For example, Theravādins have traditionally recognized a lineage of spiritually advanced disciples who, by virtue of their high-level spiritual insight and attainment, have been identified as "sons of the Buddha." At a more institutional level, they have also recognized a closely connected lineage comprised of successive generations of monastic followers who have maintained a supposedly continuous tradition of proper monastic ordination and practice.

The Theravādins have, with at least equal consistency, emphasized and employed the three lineages *of* Gotama on which our discussion has focused. For example, the royal lineage has served, in many Theravāda contexts, as a legitimating mythology for Buddhist dynasties that have ruled in the post-Gotama age. The *jātaka* lineage has constituted a rich repository of stories that have been used to mold Buddhist popular culture and to inculcate Buddhist ethical teachings. And this *jātaka* tradition has, in addition, included a number of figures who have, in various local traditions, become associated with particular sacred places.

For its part, the lineage of Buddhas has provided Buddhist communities not only with an important sense of their cosmic-historical past, but with a highly relevant perspective on the cosmic-historical future as well. From a very early period in Buddhist history, Theravādins have affirmed that after the age of Gotama and his religion, there will—in the far distant future—be a successor Buddha named Metteya who will continue the same lineage of Buddhas. In Theravāda circles merit-making practices often have been (and often still are) carried on with the specific goal of facilitating rebirth at the time of Metteya's coming. In addition, a number of religio-political and millennial-type leaders in Theravāda contexts have been identified—either directly or indirectly—as the Metteya-who-has-come.[40]

From all of this, three important and closely related conclusions can be drawn. The first is that the Theravādins *did* develop a mythology that is systematic in its structure, rich in its content, and closely related to the dynamics of Theravāda life. The second is that this mythology is closely correlated with the distinctive context and limits that characterized traditional Theravāda doctrine. The third is that a significant segment of this mythology was expressed in and through a set of three quite different but closely intertwined lineages that were incorporated as foundational elements in the sacred biography of Gotama.

Acknowledgments

My thanks to Steven Collins, Charles Hallisey, and Jonathan Walters, who have all provided suggestions that have made this a better essay. In the title and throughout the text, I have not used diacriticals with words that have become commonplace in ordinary English usage.

Notes

1. In addition to the mythologies that are involved in the sacred biography of the Buddha, the Theravādins have other important mythologies as well, including some that are related more or less directly to the biographical tradition. I have discussed some of the other important mythological complexes in my essay "Multiple Cosmogonies and Ethical Order: The Case of Theravāda Buddhism" in *Cosmogony and Ethical Order: New Essays in Comparative Ethics,* ed., Robin Lovin and Frank Reynolds (Chicago: University of Chicago Press, 1985) and in an article on "Theravāda Eschatologie" in *Sehnsucht nach dem Ursprung*, ed., Hans Peter Duerr (Frankfurt: Syndikat, 1983).
2. During the modern period there have been a number of Theravāda Buddhists who have rejected certain aspects of the traditional Buddha biography that they have considered to be mythical in the sense of ahistorical and untrue. In many cases, those aspects of the traditional biography that are the focus of the present essay have been especially vulnerable. However, the kind of critique that has been mounted in modern times has not had significant premodern precedents. Nor has it seriously influenced the great majority of contemporary Theravāda adherents; nor has it significantly altered the structures of Theravāda practice that remain firmly grounded in the traditional accounts.
3. I have previously discussed the overall structure of the Theravāda renderings of the sacred biography of the Buddha; see "The Many Lives of Buddha" in *The Biographical Process*, ed., Frank Reynolds and Donald Capps (The Hague: Mouton, 1976).
4. In the discussion that follows, I trace the development of each of these three lineages through a series of texts that are widely separated in time. Each of the texts that I have chosen to highlight incorporates new elements that have accumulated over the centuries. Therefore, I do not mean to imply that the new developments that I discuss in relation to a particular text are necessarily the original contributions of its author or compiler.

5. The identification and differentiation of *jātakas* and related genres is a vexed question that has been approached differently by various scholars. The basic "solution" to the problem that I have adopted in this essay has been spelled out and defended by John Strong in his essay "Buddhist Avadānas and Jātakas: The Question of Genre," presented at the annual meeting of the American Academy of Religion held in Dallas, Texas, in December 1983.
6. For a discussion of the early accounts of the enlightenment, including their chronology and contents, see André Bareau, *Recherches sur la biographie du Buddha* (Paris: École française d'Extrême-Orient, no. 52, 2 vols., 1963).
7. Perhaps the best known and most interesting examples are the *Mahā-Sudassana* and *Mahā-Govinda Suttas* that are included in the *Dīghanikāya*; See T. W. Rhys-Davids, et al., trans., *Dialogues of the Buddha—Part II* (vol. 3 of the *Sacred Books of the Buddhist* series, reprint, London: Pāli Text Society, 1977), pp. 199–232 and 259–281.
8. I. B. Horner, trans., *Buddhavaṃsa: Chronicle of Buddhas and Cariyāpiṭaka: Basket of Conduct* (*Minor Anthologies*, vol. 3, London: Pāli Text Society, 1975).
9. Though a discussion of non-Theravāda forms of the *jātaka* tradition is beyond the scope of the present paper, it is still interesting to note that the *Cariyāpiṭaka* shares a great deal in common with the *Jātakamālā*, a later (ca. third to fourth century C.E.), non-Theravāda text that assumed a major role in various forms of Sanskritic Buddhism. More than a third of the thirty-four *jātakas* that are recounted in a highly sophisticated literary style in the *Jātakamālā* are stories that appear in simpler and cruder form in the *Cariyāpiṭaka*. Moreover, the *Jātakamālā*, like the *Cariyāpiṭaka*, begins with ten stories that are associated with the perfection of selfless giving, and follows with ten stories that are associated with the perfection of moral rectitude. Unfortunately, Peter Keroche, in his introduction to his excellent translation of the *Jātakamālā* (*Once the Buddha Was a Monkey*, published by the University of Chicago Press, 1989), makes no reference to the quite specific continuities which suggest that the *Cariyāpiṭaka* embodied a distinctive pattern of rendering the *jātaka* tradition that was later taken up and developed in a more sophisticated literary style by the teller of tales who composed the *Jātakamālā*.
10. E. B. Cowell, trans., *The Jātaka: or Stories of the Buddha's Former Births* (7 vols. in 3; London: Pāli Text Society, 1969).
11. Here and throughout the essay I have chosen to employ the rather cumbersome term "rebirth precursor" in order to avoid the inappropriate connotations conveyed by the word "incarnation," which is usually used in this context.
12. The adjective "practical" has been included to differentiate the perfection of wisdom as it is understood in the Theravāda tradition from the much more mystical notion of the perfection of wisdom that is often affirmed in the Mahāyāna context.

13. In some contexts the *Vessantara Jātaka* is interpreted as a story of the future Buddha's activities in which he is perfecting all ten perfections. See, for example, *Jinamahānidāna*, which has been published in Pāli with a Thai translation by the Fine Arts Department in Bangkok in 1987.
14. The *Mahāpurisa Jātaka* is sometimes identified by the name *Lokaneyyapakarana* (Treatise for the Guidance of the World). P. S. Jaini has chosen to use this alternate name in his edition published by the Pāli Text Society as number 175 in its Text Series (London, 1986). This edition includes a very helpful introduction.
15. Certain aspects of the *Mahāpurisa Jātaka* suggest that the text was written with a rather immediate polemic purpose in mind. For example, the author-compiler describes many of the future Buddha's antagonists in a way that suggests that he is alluding to Shaivite court brahmins who were competing with Buddhists for influence in several of the royal courts of mainland Southeast Asia during the period when the text was being crafted. It is also interesting that the text includes a denigration of a Buddhist monastic community and its leadership. In a series of episodes, the wisdom of the future Buddha is vividly contrasted with the lack of wisdom of the members of the then-existing Buddhist *Sangha*, including particularly its preeminent leader, the *Sangha-rāja*. (The presence of a specifically Buddhist community in the main segment of a *jātaka* story is virtually unique to the *Mahāpurisa* text.)
16. I. B. Horner and P. S. Jaini, trans., *Apocryphal Birth Stories*, 2 vols. (London: Pāli Text Society, 1985, 1986).
17. Satchidananda Sahai, ed., *Phra Lak/Phra Lam*, 2 vols. (New Delhi: Kansamphan Vatthanatham India, 1973).
18. For an in-depth discussion, see Frank Reynolds, "Ramayana, Rama Jataka and Ramakien: A Comparative Study" in *Many Ramayanas*, ed., Paula Richman (Berkeley: University of California Press, 1991).
19. Some scholars, including T. W. Rhys-Davids, who translated the *Mahāpadāna Sutta* and wrote an accompanying introduction (*Dialogues of the Buddha—Part II*, pp. 1–41), have considered the account that it provides, along with the conception of Buddhahood and the Buddha lineage that it conveys, to be an obviously late expression of Buddhism that ought to be considered as a degeneration of the teaching of the Founder and his earliest disciples. This view is, however, based on a now-outdated notion of an "original" and "pure" Buddhism to which mythic elements were foreign. Although it is not possible to date the *Māhapadāna Sutta* (or, for that matter, any of the other great suttas contained in the *Suttapiṭaka*) with any real precision, it is not insignificant that it is already recognized as authoritative by the author-compiler of the *Culla-niddesa*, a text that is included in the *Khuddakanikāya* section of the "canon" (see G. P. Malasekera, *Dictionary of Pāli Names*, vol. 2, [London, 1974], p. 525). It is also worth noting that the seven Buddhas mentioned in the *Mahāpadāna Sutta* are represented in the very early archaeological record.

20. Though the *Mahāpadāna Sutta* is characterized in the *Culla-niddesa* as a *jātaka*, it is clear that in terms of the definition I have adopted, it is not. It is probable that the author-compiler of the *Culla-niddesa* is using the term *jātaka* in a much broader sense to refer to any story that is associated with the Buddha's memory of his previous lives.
21. Rhys-Davids, "Introduction," *Dialogues of the Buddha—Part II*, p. 37.
22. Horner, *Buddhavaṃsa: Chronicle of Buddhas and Cariyāpiṭaka: Basket of Conduct.*
23. Extending the kind of genre analysis suggested above, the stories containing the main body of the *Buddhavaṃsa* should be classified as *apadāna*. That is to say, they are stories in which a religious personage (in this case the future Gotama) has a soteriologically efficacious interaction with a significant "field of merit" (in this case, a particular Buddha of the past).
24. The *Buddhavaṃsa* is often considered to be a text in which there is a definite move away from early Buddhist/Theravāda perspective in the direction of Mahāyāna. My own view is, on the contrary, that the *Buddhavaṃsa*, by recounting the story of other Buddhas in such a way that the focus of attention remains on Gotama, presents what was (and remained) a mainstream Theravāda orientation.
25. T. W. Rhys-Davids, *Buddhist Birth Stories* (Boston: Houghton Mifflin, 1880).
26. For an analysis that highlights the importance of this theme, see Arnold Aronoff's doctoral dissertation, "Contrasting Modes of Textual Clarification: The Jataka Commentary and Its Relationship to the Pali Canon" (University of Chicago, 1982).
27. The "received text" of the *Buddhavaṃsa* itself concludes with two short chapters that deal with the life of Gotama and with the distribution of his relics. However, as Steven Collins has pointed out to me, these two final chapters are—in all probability—later additions to the main body of the text.
28. Reynolds, "The Many Lives of Buddha."
29. Wilhelm Geiger, trans., *The Mahāvamsa or The Great Chronicle of Ceylon* (London: Pāli Text Society, 1964).
30. N. A. Jayawickrama, trans., *The Sheaf of Garlands of the Epochs of the Conqueror* (London: Pāli Text Society, 1978).
31. Ibid., p. 3. The prominence given to this story in the *Jinakalamāli* is clearly associated with the importance attached to filial piety. Certainly the story meshes nicely with the notion that sons should make merit for their parents (and especially their mothers) by entering the monkhood. It is especially significant to note that in many Theravāda traditions in Southeast Asia, young men were expected to undertake a temporary stay in the monkhood, and to do so with the specific purpose of making merit for their mothers. A different, Sinhalese version of the same story is presented and discussed by Richard Gombrich in "Feminine Elements in

Sinhalese Buddhism," *Wiener Zeitschrift für die Kunde Sudasiens* 16 (1972), pp. 67–93.

32. According to the Theravāda view that was embedded in the older texts, only a male can make a vow to attain Buddhahood and receive the confirming prediction from a Buddha that is held to be inseparably connected with the vow. By affirming the possibility of a long-term temporal separation between a future Buddha's vow to attain Buddhahood (which can be made by a woman) and the confirming prediction provided by an already awakened Buddha (which can only come when the aspirant to Buddhahood is a male), the author-compiler of the *Jinakalamāli* modifies the traditional position. Given his description of the process of attaining Buddhahood, it is clearly possible for a woman—despite the fact that she still remains at a definite soteriological disadvantage—to make an efficacious vow that involves the attainment of the highest goal. But it should be noted that this modification leaves intact the established Theravāda notion that once a future Buddha has made the vow and received the prediction, the possibility of any further rebirth as a woman is eliminated.

33. In the *Jinakalamāli* version of the lineage of Buddhas, the emphasis on the story of Dīpaṅkara and Sumedha has been significantly diminished. To be sure, Dīpaṅkara remains the Buddha who gives the future Gotaṃa the prediction that confirms that he will attain his goal. However, the story of Dīpaṅkara and Sumedha no longer stands at the beginning even of the subseries in which it is included (it is preceded by the stories of three preceding Buddhas who lived in the same era who are mentioned—but only mentioned—in the *Buddhavaṃsa*). What is equally striking, the story of Dīpaṅkara, which had been by far the longest and most detailed story in the *Buddhavaṃsa*, is rendered by the compiler-author of the *Jinakalamāli* in a space that is roughly equal to the space given to each of the stories of the other twenty-six Buddhas in the series. Clearly, the prominence given to the story of the future Gotama saving his mother (the first story in the text) and to the story involving the Buddha Purāṇa-Dīpaṅkara (the first story in the Gotama's Buddha lineage as we have defined it) has, as its counterpoint, a suppression of the prominence that had previously been given to the story of Dīpaṅkara and Sumedha.

34. Bhikkhu Nāṇamoli, trans., *Path of Purification* (Berkeley: Shambala, 1976), pp. 250–251 and 460.

35. T. W. Rhys-Davids, trans. *Dialogues of the Buddha—Part I*, vol. 2 of the *Sacred Books of the Buddhists* series (Reprint, London: Pāli Text Society, 1977), pp. 108–136. The fact that the Sanskrit form of Okkāka is Īkṣvāku raises an interesting question concerning the relationship between Okkāka and the Īkṣvāku, who plays a very important role in the Puranic traditions of the Hindus.

36. T. W. and C. A. F. Rhys-Davids, trans., *Dialogues of the Buddha—Part III*, vol. 4 of the *Sacred Books of the Buddhists* series (Reprint, London: Pāli Text Society, 1977), pp. 77–95.

37. In the *Mahāvastu*, which is an extant non-Theravāda text that was also composed in the centuries around the beginning of the Common Era, the three elements that have been mentioned, as well as a fourth element that so far as we can tell was not yet present in the Pāli tradition (the identification of Mahāsammata as a rebirth precursor of the Buddha) were already connected and correlated. See volume 1 of the three-volume translation done by J. J. Jones that was published as volume 16 of the *Sacred Books of the Buddhists* (London, 1949).

38. Ñāṇamoli, *Path of Purification*, p. 460. For a discussion that highlights the crucial importance of the figure of Mahāsammata in the history of Theravāda Buddhism, see Stanley Tambiah's article on "King Mahāsammata: The First King in the Buddhist Story of Creation, and His Persisting Relevance," *Journal of the Anthropological Society of Oxford* 20, no. 2 (1989), pp. 101–122.

39. The Theravāda practice of connecting the royal lineage of Gotama with the lineage of kings who ruled in the area where the text was being written is an old one that can be traced back to the early Sinhalese *vaṃsa* tradition. A break in this tradition seems to have occurred in some of the new Theravāda contexts that were established in Southeast Asia (for example, note the absence in the *Jinakalamāli* of any claim concerning a blood relationship between the Buddha's royal lineage and the ruling dynasties of northern Thailand). Since it is quite probable that this break was caused by the close connections that had already been established between the Mahāsammata lineage and the lineage of various Theravāda kings in Sri Lanka, it is not difficult to discern why it was that some Theravādins in Southeast Asia chose to replace Mahāsammata with a more dynastically malleable sociogonic hero.

40. The Metteya myth is sometimes related to, but is not identical with, the traditions concerning mystics operating on the fringes of Theravāda orthodoxy who have claimed (or been accorded) the status of "living Buddhas." For a discussion of one mode in which these fascinating mystical traditions have been expressed, see Juliane Schober's unpublished doctoral dissertation, "Paths to Enlightenment: Theravada Buddhism in Upper Burma" (University of Illinois, 1989), especially the section on "*Htwetyap pauk* Mysticism," pp. 251–350.

The Biographical Imperative in Theravāda Buddhism

Mark R. Woodward

The textual corpus of Theravāda Buddhism includes a rich and diverse body of sacred biography. While questions concerning the "historical Buddha" have figured most prominently in Western scholarship, there are numerous texts recounting the former lives of the Buddha Gotama [the *Jātaka, Nidānakathā* (ND), and the later *Paññasa-Jātaka* (PJ)], those of previous Buddhas [the *Mahāpadāna Sutta, Buddhavaṃsa* (BU), *Cariyāpitaka* (Cyp), and *Jinakalamālipakaranam* (JM)], and Bodhisattva who will attain Buddhahood in the future [*Dasabodhisattuppattikatha* (DB)]. There are also accounts of the lives of great disciples, *arhat* (P. enlightened disciples) [*Thera/Therīgāthā* (TT)], the inhabitants of the heavens [*Vimanavatthu* (Vv)], and even hungry ghosts [*Petavatthu* (Pv)]. The *Vinaya* and commentaries such as the *Dhammapadatthakatha* (DhA) also include vast stores of sacred biography.

This essay explores thematic interrelations in Theravāda biographical texts and the role of sacred biography in the larger Theravāda religious system. It focuses on three recurrent themes: (1) the legitimization of doctrinal and ecclesiastical teachings by associating them with the omniscience of Buddhas; (2) the characterization of Buddhism as an open-ended cosmological system that denies its own historicity; and (3) the portrayal of Buddhas and their associates as cohorts who move together through countless lives.

More generally, I am concerned with the implications of J. Bruner's distinction between paradigmatic and narrative thought for understanding the development of religious traditions. Bruner defines the paradigmatic thought as "attempts to fulfill the ideal of a formal, mathematical system of description and explanation. It employs categorization or conceptualization and the operations by which categories are established, instantiated, idealized and related one to the other to form a system."[1] The creative use of paradigmatic thought produces "good theory, tight analysis, logical proof, sound argument, and empirical discovery."[2] Applied to religious problems, it yields logically constructed doctrinal systems, of which the Theravāda Abhidhamma, and philosophical commentaries such as *Visuddhimagga* are examples. Narrative thought "deals with human or human like intention and action and the vicissitudes and consequences that mark their course. It strives to put timeless miracles into the particulars of experience and to locate experience in time and place."[3] Applied to religious phenomena, it locates timeless truths in individual lives and personal experience in cosmologically conceived times and places. Among its products are myth, religious art and ceremony, and sacred biography.

Bruner argues that neither mode can be reduced to the other. Each is a way of knowing reality and rendering experience meaningful. They are, however, complementary. As Bruner notes, each reinforces or legitimizes the other.[4] The contrast between philosophical discourse and sacred biography in Theravāda Buddhism indicates that both are essential components of religious traditions. Philosophical speculation is accepted only when it is linked to sacred biography. Biographical narrative explores the implications of abstract premises for the lives of individuals.

Buddhology and Buddhist Biography

Despite the extent of the Theravāda biographical corpus and its role in literature, art, and popular piety in Theravāda societies, it has long been viewed with suspicion by Western Buddhologists. Theravāda biographical texts are often described as only tangentially related to such core doctrines as *nibbāna* (P. enlightenment), *anicca* (P. impermanence), and *paticcasamuppada* (P. dependent origination). T. W. Rhys-Davids described the *jātaka* as "fairy tales, parables, fables, riddles and comic and moral stories," a theme which is echoed in M. Cunningham's more recent treatment of Theravāda sacred biography as literature.[5] Attempts by W. Rockhill, E. Thomas, and others to use Theravāda materials to reconstruct the historical biography of the man Gotama are important in their own right, but less than revealing concerning the ways in which he is understood from within the tradition.[6] H. Saddhatissa attributes the growth of a Theravāda biographical tradition, and particularly the veneration of future Buddhas, to a combination of Hindu and Mahāyāna Buddhist influences.[7] The view, most clearly articulated by

Edward Conze, that the Buddhist biography was intended as a "gospel for the busy householder," that "It has little to do with the fundamental teachings of Buddhism," and that only in Mahāyāna can householders be "Bodhisattvas, i.e. first-class Buddhists," rests on the assumption that the fundamentals of Buddhism are to be found in abstractly formulated doctrinal propositions combined with a psychologically tinged, reflective meditation focused exclusively on the attainment of enlightenment.[8]

While Conze's critique of the Buddhist biography can be understood as a Mahāyāna polemic, students of Theravāda Buddhism have offered similar interpretations. This is apparent in the contrast between Rhys-Davids' comments on the *Mahāpadāna Sutta* and *Maha Nidana Sutta*. Both suttas expound upon the doctrine of dependent origination. The *Mahāpadāna Sutta* attributes it to the Buddha Vipassī who taught ninety-one *kappa* ago. The *Maha Nidana Sutta* attributes it to the Buddha Gotama.[9] The *Mahāpadāna Sutta* is characterized as follows: "We find in this tract the root of that *Birana* weed which, growing up along the rest of Buddhism, went on spreading so luxuriantly that it gradually covered up much that was of value in the earlier teaching, and finally led to the downfall, in its home in India, of the ancient faith. The doctrine of the Bodhisatta, of the Wisdom Being, drove out the doctrine of the Aryan Path. A gorgeous hierarchy of mythological wonder-workers filled men's minds, and the older system of self training and self control became forgotten."[10] In contrast the *Maha Nidana Sutta* is described as "not only the whole of early Buddhism in a nutshell, but also just those points concerning which we find the most emphatic affirmations of Dhamma as Dhamma ascribed to Gotama."[11]

M. Weber offers a similar interpretation, attributing the origin of Buddhist biography to a combination of Hindu influences and a need to formulate a salvation cult rooted in "hagiolatry and idolatry," suitable for the untutored masses.[12] Unlike Rhys-Davids and Conze, Weber is not concerned with the authenticity of any variant of Buddhism, but with their ethical and economic consequences. He does, however, concur with the view that in its earliest form Buddhism was "the most radical form of salvation-striving conceivable."[13] He characterizes the biographical tradition as "mythologies swollen to fabulous dimensions."[14]

While the abstract, soteriological understanding of enlightenment and the path leading toward it promoted by Rhys-Davids and subsequent students of Theravāda Buddhism is a central component of the tradition, and one which, as M. Carrithers has observed, has strong appeal for Western and Westernized Buddhists, it does not exhaust it.[15] The central thesis of this essay is that owing to the ways in which Theravāda Buddhism defines enlightenment, Buddhahood, and the paths leading toward them, it is driven by a biographical imperative necessitating the formulation of a complex hagiographic corpus. I build on F. Reynolds' study of Theravāda sacred biography, which locates accounts of former lives of the Buddha and of Buddhas of the past in the oldest strata of the Theravāda canon.[16] It will be argued that biographical narratives describing the many lives of many Buddhas, their disciples, and opponents constitute the epic tradition of Theravāda Buddhism. Like other South Asian religious narratives including the *Puranas*, the *Mahabharata*, and the *Ramayana*, this epic is not intended as philosophical discourse. It is rather the sacred history that legitimizes and is at the same time informed by the philosophical, ecclesiastical, and ritual systems of the tradition. The growth of the biographical tradition is understood best not as that of a *birana* weed, but rather as the narrative rationalization of a founded religion.

Sacred Biography and Textual Authority

Buddhas are omniscient. In *Atthasalini* (A), Buddhaghosa characterizes the Buddha as the one "who knows all knowable things, discerns all discernable things, is the eye of the world, is the wisdom of the world."[17] In the sutta, Vinaya, and Abhidhamma texts, doctrinal teachings and monastic regulations are contextualized by references of events in the life of the Buddha Gotama, one of his contemporaries and/or precursors. The extensive use of biographical frames in doctrinal and philosophical texts suggests that paradigmatic speculation requires narrative legitimation and that Weber's "mythologies swollen to fabulous dimensions" were as important for his "cultured professional monks" as to the hagiolatrous laity.

All Theravāda texts are framed, directly or indirectly, by biographical narrative. The phrase "Thus I have heard" that introduces the sutta of the first four *nikāya* of the Pāli canon is a reference to the biography of the Buddha's personal servitor Ananda, to whom they were recited or repeated. Ananda's statement guarantees the authenticity of the text because, as is explained in TT, the Buddha ranked him foremost among his disciples for his ability to recall his precise words, and because of his promise to repeat to him all that was taught on those rare occasions when he was not in the Buddha's presence.[18] The introduction to the *Patika Sutta*, which concerns the magical powers of the Buddha and the conversion of ascetics, is a clear, but by no means extraordinary example: "Thus have I heard: The Exalted One was once staying among the Mallas, at Anupiya, one of their towns. Now the Exalted One, having robed himself in the early morning, put on his cloak and took his bowl, and entered the town for alms. And he thought: It is too early for me now to go through Anupiya for alms. I might go to the pleasurance where Bhaggava the Wanderer dwells, and call upon Bhaggava."[19]

In the Vinaya, biographical frames justify the imposition of particular rules of monastic conduct. The Vinaya allows monks a single begging bowl and states that "An extra bowl may be kept for at most ten days. For him who exceeds that (period), there is an offense of expiation involving forfeiture."[20] The text includes two sets of comments on this rule, one paradigmatic, the other biographical. The paradigmatic commentary explains the precise meanings of "extra," "bowl," and "forfeiture" in legalistic terms. The biographical commentary explains the purpose of the rule. It includes two parts, one justifying the limitation of monks to a single bowl and another legitimizing the ten-day grace period. The prohibition is justified by a tale of six monks who hoarded bowls and offended the laity. It states: "Now at that time the group of six monks made a hoard of many bowls. People engaged in touring the dwelling place and seeing (this hoard) looked down upon, criticized, spread it about saying: 'How can these recluses, sons of the *Sakyāns*, make a hoard of many bowls? Will these recluses, sons of the *Sakyāns*, do a trade in bowls or will they set up an earthenware shop?' " When this is reported to the Buddha, he establishes the prohibition. The grace period is explained by a story of Ananda and Sāriputta, one of the Buddha's great disciples. Ananda and Sāriputta were great friends. The text states: "Now at that time an extra bowl had accrued to Ananda, and the venerable Ananda became desirous of giving this bowl to the venerable Sāriputta; but the venerable Sāriputta was staying at Saketa. Then it occurred to the venerable Ananda: 'A rule of training laid down by the Lord is that an extra bowl should not be kept. And this extra bowl has accrued to me, and I am desirous of giving this bowl to the venerable Sāriputta, but the venerable Sāriputta is staying at Saketa. Now what line of conduct should be followed by me?' " When Ananda explains his concern to the Buddha, the prohibition is altered allowing Ananda to keep the bowl for the nine days until Sariputta's return.[21]

The contrast between the uses of the tale of the archheretic Devadatta in sutta, *jātaka*, and Vinaya texts is an example of the ways in which a single biographic narrative may be used for different purposes. Devadatta was among the early followers of the Buddha, but later grew jealous of the Buddha's fame and that of his great disciples. He conspired to assume leadership of the order and, when the Buddha refused, tried to kill him. When this failed, Devadatta attempted to cause a schism in the order. The biographical narrative is included in the Vinaya and the introduction to the *Culla-Hamsa Jātaka* and is discussed in the *Mahasaropama Sutta*. A summary of the version included in the Vinaya is also included in DhA. In the Vinaya and DhA the narrative is used to frame a discussion on the eschatological consequences of bringing about a schism in the order. Devadatta is described as an incurable heretic bound to spend an eon in hell because he has knowingly taught non-*dhamma* as *dhamma* and willfully caused a schism in the order.[22] The *Mahasaropama Sutta* uses the example of Devadatta to discuss the consequences of monks falling away from the path because of a desire for fame and honors, a subsidiary theme in the Vinaya account. The *Culla-Hamsa Jātaka* uses the narrative to extol the virtues of Ānanda, who risked his life for the Buddha by standing between him and the raging Nalagiri Elephant that Devadatta had sent to kill the Buddha.[23]

The *jātaka* and other explicitly biographical texts employ similar narrative styles. Episodes from the sacred biography of the Buddha Gotama and his great disciples are used as biographical frames for the stories of past lives and past Buddhas, creating a circle of biographical legitimation. In the *jātaka* a question arising at the time of the Buddha Gotama (*paccuppanna-vatthu*) frames a longer narrative concerning one of his former lives (*atita-vatthu*). The text begins in the present, moves to the past, in which the primary religious discourse is related, and returns to the present in which the Buddha identifies characters of the first section with those of the second (*samodhana*). There is not always a clear connection between events in the two sections of the *jātaka*. The *Vessantara Jātaka*, which is among the best known Theravāda narratives, is primarily concerned with the virtue of giving. The tale is, however, framed by two accounts of a magical rain shower. The *jātaka* is introduced by an account of a magical red rain during which "those who wished to be wet were wetted, but he who did not, had not even a drop fallen upon his body." The Buddha explains that: "This is not the first time, Brethren, that a great shower of rain has fallen on my kinsmen."[24] The tale concludes with Sakka, the king of the gods, sending a shower of jewels to Vessantara's city.

Like the *jātaka*, *Buddhavaṃsa* (BU) uses the biography of the Buddha Gotama to frame a discussion of the past. Here Gotama creates a jewel walk spanning ten thousand world systems to demonstrate the greatness of Buddhas before delivering his discourse on the nature of the path leading to Buddhahood and Buddhas of the past. DB, Vv, Pv, and TT include similar biographical frames as introductions. The introduction to TT is a short history of the Buddha's path to enlightenment beginning with his encounter with the Buddha Dīpaṅkara.[25] It appears to be based on NK.[26] Vv is described as having resulted from Moggallana's journey to the heaven of the thirty-three *deva*, while DB is described as an answer to Sāriputta's questions concerning the Buddhas of the future.[27] Many of the individual tales included in these texts are also provided with frame stories linking them to the life and teachings of the Buddha Gotama. Commentaries such as DhA use biographical narrative to establish the context for doctrinal texts lacking biographical introductions. The *Dhammapada* is among the most widely dispersed and often quoted Buddhist text.[28] It is an anthology of

423 sayings attributed to the Buddha and among the most precise statements of Theravāda doctrine and ethics. DhA provides biographical and mythological contexts for the points of doctrine included in the *Dhammapada* and draws heavily on the *jātaka* and TT.

In contrast, commentaries on biographical texts such as the *Madhuratthavilasini*, an exposition of BU, and *Paramatthadipani nama Petavatthu-atthakatha* (PvA), a commentary on Pv, do not add greatly to the store of sacred biography, but focus on grammatical, semantic, and doctrinal points.[29] Pv is a collection of ghost stories concerning the consequences of demeritorious action and the transfer of merit. The commentator explains his purpose as follows:

> It is due to a difference in the fruition of this and that deed done by *peta* in their previous births that this and that existence as a peta has been brought about for them. Clarifying this is that the teaching of the Buddhas that demonstrates the fruition of deeds, that particularly gives rise to agitation, and that is well founded on a thorough understanding (of the subject), namely, the *Peta* Stories that were rehearsed by the Great Masters in the *Khuddaka Nikaya*. Relying thoroughly thereon after the manner of their ancient commentary and at various places explaining the particular subject matter, Resolving quite clearly and without confusion, the subtle meanings in accordance with the views of the present residents of the *Mahavihara*, I will, as well as I am able, set forth an illuminating exposition of their meaning.[30]

The "illuminating exposition" includes discussions of concepts such as fields of merit, the ways in which the act of giving comes to fruition, path stages and their fruitions, and the characteristics of *arhats*.[31] It is clearly informed by an understanding of Abhidhamma and other doctrinal works.[32] Gehman describes Pv as a "base type of Buddhism." His thesis that it includes "numerous stories floating around orally in India" is probably correct.[33] The commentary, however, provides a sound Buddhist explanation of what many believed to be historical events, while the biographic frame stories link them to the omniscience of the Buddha Gotama. The result is the Pv is a Theravāda text, even if many of the narratives it includes are derived from South Asian folklore.

Sacred biography plays a part in even the most philosophical and abstract Theravāda texts. Philosophical texts such as *Patisambhidamagga* (The Path of Discrimination, Ps) and *Visuddhimagga* (The Path of Purification, Vsm) assume familiarity with the biographical corpus.[34] Vsm begins with a biographical fragment taken from the sutta literature in which a *deva* asked the Buddha Gotama: "The inner tangle and the outer tangle, this generation is entangled in a tangle. And so I ask of Gotama this question: Who succeeds in disentangling this tangle?"[35] In a consideration of knowledge about knowledge, Vsm distinguishes between trainers, who have acquired knowledge from teachers, and nontrainers, who have developed it through prior effort. Prior effort is "devotion to insight in the dispensations of former Buddhas."[36] It is characteristic of fully enlightened Buddhas, *Pacceka* Buddhas, and chief and great disciples. Ananda, the Buddha's personal servitor, and the lay devotees Citta, Dhammika, and Khujjutara are mentioned as examples of trainers. They are all described in the *Dhammapada* and other commentaries as teachers of the laity.[37] In a discussion of the recollection of death, Vsm teaches that one should compare one's own fate with those of great kings, rich men, and others of great merit as well as chief disciples, *Pacceka* Buddhas, and Buddhas. The examples cited, among them the treasurers Jotika, Jatila, and Mendaka and the chief disciples Moggallana and Sāriputta, are drawn from the *Dhammapada* and the *jātaka* and other biographical texts.[38] In a discussion of success through magical powers, Ps cites the treasurers Jotika, Jatilasa, Ghosita, and Mendaka as well as Universal Monarchs as examples of individuals who possess inexhaustible wealth because of previous meritorious deeds.[39] Vsm also includes direct quotations from the *jātaka* and TT.[40]

A more complex biographical method is used to legitimize the Abhidhamma, which most scholars, and in some instances the Theravāda tradition itself, believe to post-date the historical Buddha. Biographical frame stories are so common in sutta and Vinaya texts, that according to *Atthasalini* (A) "heretics" pointed to their absence from Abhidhamma texts as a sign that they were not truly spoken by the Buddha.[41] Buddhaghosa's argument is that while the Buddha is the source of the totality of the *dhamma*, portions of the sutta and Abhidhamma were compiled by his disciples. Sāriputta, for example, is recognized as the author of part of the sutta literature and as the compiler of the seven books of the Abhidhamma.[42]

Buddhaghosa provides biographical frames for the transmitters of the *dhamma* as well as linking it to the Buddha. Regarding the Abhidhamma, he states:

> But if a heretic should say, had the *Abhidhamma* been spoken by the Buddha, there would have been an introduction prefatory to it, just as in many thousands of the *Suttas* the preface generally runs as, "One Day the Blessed One was staying in Rajagaha," etc. he should be contradicted thus: "The *Jātaka, Suttanipata, Dhammapada*, and so on, have no such introductions, and yet they were spoken by the Buddha." O wise one, this *Abhidhamma* is the province of the Buddhas, their birth, their attainment of perfect wisdom, their turning of the Wheel of the Law, their

performance of the Twin Miracle, their visit to the *deva*, their preaching in the *deva* world, and their descent therefrom are all manifest. . . . There is, O wise one, no need for an introduction to the *Abhidhamma*.[43]

Buddhaghosa's point would appear to be the performance of the "twin miracle," in which the Buddha uses his magical powers to produce a double who asked him questions concerning the *dhamma*, his ascent to *Tavatimsa* heaven to preach to his mother, and his descent via the jeweled staircase accompanied by a host of *deva* provide the biographical frame for the entire Abhidhamma. The account of the twin miracle is most fully developed in DhA.[44] Buddhaghosa is, however, not content with this explanation and expounds at considerable length on the ways in which the Buddha sustained himself while preaching continuously for a lunar month and on the rays of various colors that emerged from his body as he preached the *Patthana*, the last and most complex book of the Abhidhamma. Buddhaghosa explains that while the Buddha was teaching the Abhidhamma to the *deva* in Tavatimsa heaven, Sāriputta also journeyed there to wait on the Buddha. He learned the Abhidhamma from the Buddha's preaching and subsequently organized it into seven books and taught it to 500 of his students, who in former lives as bats had heard it taught by disciples of the Buddha Kassapa.[45]

While this method seems to have satisfied Theravāda Buddhists that the "heretics'" claims were false, later texts, including *Kathavatthuppakarana* (K) and *Milindapana* (Mil), pose an additional problem. Both concern doctrinal controversies arising within the Buddhist community and clearly postdate the historical Buddha. K concerns debates between rival sects discussed at the third Buddhist council which, according to A, was held 218 years after the death of the Buddha.[46] In A and again in his commentary on K, Buddhaghosa explains that the Buddha "laid down the table of contents," which were filled in by Tissa at the time of the third council.[47] Tissa's apparent authorship of K and its position as a canonical, rather than commentarial, work is justified by the following prophecy, which Buddhaghosa attributes to the Buddha: "When in the future the turn for expounding K shall arrive, my disciple, the greatly wise Tissa, son of Moggali, having purged the blemishes that have arisen in the teaching and holding a Third Council will, seated in the midst of the Order, divide this compilation into a thousand discourses."[48]

Mil was compiled at least five centuries after the death of the Buddha Gotama. It is an account of the monk Nagasena's answers to questions posed by King Malinda. The introduction provides a biographical frame for Nagasena; King Malinda and the text, the construct. It explains that during the dispensation of the Buddha Kassapa, Nagasena is a monk and Malinda a novice. The future Nagasena beats the incipient king with a broom handle for neglecting to dispose of a heap of garbage. The novice, "throwing out the rubbish through fear," makes an aspiration: "Through this meritorious deed of throwing out the rubbish may I, wherever I am successively reborn until I attain *nibbāna*, be prompt in saying the right thing and prompt in answering questions."[49] Hearing this the monk aspires: "May I, wherever I am successively reborn until I attain *nibbāna*, be prompt in answering questions . . . and may I be able to unravel promptly and explain all the answers to the questions constantly asked me by this (novice)."[50] A prophecy attributed to the Buddha Gotama links Nagasena with Tissa and Mil with K: "And even as Moggali's son the Elder Tissa was seen by our Lord, even were these also seen, as it is explained: Five hundred years after I have attained complete *nibbāna* these will uprise (again) and, disentangling it and making it clear by asking it questions and by the use of similes, they will explain what was made abstruse by me when I taught *Dhamma* and Discipline."[51]

Theravāda tradition attributes the authorship or translation of the *Dhammapada* and the *jātaka* to the fifth-century scholar monk Bhadantacariya Buddhaghosa, who is also stated to be the author of Vsm, K, A, and numerous other commentaries.[52] It is, as Rhys-Davids and Burlingame have argued, unlikely that Buddhaghosa was the author or even the translator of all the works attributed to him. This does not, however, require us to accept their disparaging comments about the biographical commentaries, which as Burlingame puts it: "differ so widely in language and style from the genuine works of Buddhaghosa as to make it in the highest degree improbable that he is the author of either of them."[53] There are two issues in question here. First, as Ñāṇamoli observes, the attribution of all of the Sinhalese commentaries to Buddhaghosa should probably be understood as a statement concerning orthodoxy rather than authorship.[54] Second, the relationship between the philosophical and biographical commentaries is stronger than Burlingame and Rhys-Davids make it out to be. The use of biographical works, which are among the least philosophical of Theravāda texts, to provide context for and legitimize the Abhidhamma and philosophical commentaries and the use of abstract philosophical concepts in commentaries on works such as BU and Pv suggests that doctrine and sacred biography should be understood as interdependent components of a larger religious system. The mere attribution of a "paradigmatic" text like Vsm and the clearly "narrative" DhA to Buddhaghosa provides strong support for this position.

The Multiplicity of Buddhas and the Problem of History

In Vsm it is stated that "The path taken by Buddhas, *Pacceka* Buddhas, and the Great Disciples has to be taken by me."[55] The path to enlightenment is singular, the Buddhas and other who have trod it are plural. Buddhism is a "founded religion." While it makes universal claims and presents itself as the only path leading to salvation, it is grounded in the religious experience of a single individual. This presents a number of problems, among which is that of establishing the truth of the *dhamma* as prior to the person of the historical Buddha.

Theravāda Buddhism "solves" the problem of history by denying its own historicity. This is accomplished by epic narrative with mythological time depth rivaling or surpassing those of other Indian traditions. Just as the teachings of the Buddha and subsequent commentaries on them are legitimized by biographical narrative, the tradition as a whole is framed by biographies of past and future Buddhas. These narratives map the structure of the early Buddhist community onto the past and the future. As the tradition develops, it views the Buddha Gotama as but one of a series of individuals who have penetrated the truth and set the wheel of *dhamma* in motion.

According to the *Mahāpadāna Sutta*, which describes seven Buddhas, knowledge of previous Buddhas has two sources: (1) the ability of Buddhas to see indefinitely into the past and future; and (2) their conversations with beings of the *Brahma loca* who owe their positions to devotion to Buddhas of the past. The *Buddhavaṃsa* lists twenty-four Buddhas of the past. The *jātaka* commentary expands the list to twenty-seven. Later texts greatly expand the number of Buddhas. *Jinakālamālīpakaranam* (JM) mentions 387,000.[56] This expansion continues in DB where Gotama Buddha explains: "Sāriputta, there have been limitless and countless noble people in the world who have successively fulfilled the perfection, attained Buddhahood and, having completed a Buddha's duty, passed away at the end of their life-span."[57]

The *Mahāpadāna Sutta* explains that all Buddhas share certain physical characteristics, analogous life histories, and former lives. All Buddhas have personal servitors and a pair of chief disciples. Their conceptions and births are accompanied by the same miracles, including "a splendid radiance passing the glory of the gods," at the time of conception and showers of warm and cold water at birth.[58] All Buddhas are born with the thirty-three marks of the *Mahāpurusa* (P. great man). In each case the principle episodes in the life of the Buddha Gotama are repeated: the prediction that he will be either a Buddha or a World Monarch, the great renunciation, the practice of austerities, the discovery of the four noble truths and the doctrine of dependent origination, the attainment of enlightenment, and the founding of the *sangha* (monastic order).[59] This discourse is extended in BU in what Horner describes as "almost mathematical beauty in its unvarying regularity."[60] BU describes the eon (sometimes), number of penetrations, number of assemblies, who the Bodhisatta was then and of what kind was his act of merit he performed towards the Buddha, names of the Buddha's city, father and mother, duration of his household life, the names of his three palaces, the number of women attendants (in the palaces), the means of conveyance by which he departed on the Great Renunciation . . . the length of time he spent in striving . . . the turning of the Wheel of Dhamma, the names of the chief disciples, of the (monastic) attendant, of the chief women disciples, of the Bodhi-Tree, of the chief (lay) attendant, first the men and then the women, the height of the Buddha's physical frame, his lustre (if any), the duration of his life-span, his complete or final *nibbāna*.[61]

The *Mahāpadāna Sutta* relies on analogical reasoning to explain the links between Buddhas and their dispensations. Subsequent texts (BU, the *Nidānakathā*, and DhA) describe an interconnected lineage of Buddhas. The paradigmatic example is the story of the Buddha Dīpaṅkara and the Brahmin/ascetic Sumedha found in the *Buddhavaṃsa* and *Nidānakathā*.[62] Sumedha was a wealthy Brahmin who renounced the world to become an ascetic and a religious teacher. He is overjoyed to learn that there is a Buddha in the world. He performs a great act of merit, throwing himself in the mud in front of the Buddha and 400,000 monks, takes a vow (P. *katab-hiniharena mahasattena*) to become a Buddha himself, and receives in return a prophecy that his wish will be realized. Buddha Dīpaṅkara states that "Innumerable eons from now he will be a Buddha in the world." He also mentions the Buddha Gotama's name, as well as those of his parents, his chief male and female disciples, personal attendant, and lay followers.[63] DhA explains that the episode of the vow and the prophecy is repeated during the lifetime of each of the following twenty-three Buddhas.[64] JM pushes Gotama's biography even further into the past, describing the Bodhisattva's resolve to attain enlightenment prior to birth as Sumedha. Here distinctions are drawn between a desire for enlightenment and a statement by a Buddha that it will be attained and an aspiration made during a life, meeting the necessary conditions for a prophetic reply to an aspiration and one in which a Buddha is capable of responding only indirectly. The future Gotama makes his initial mental resolve to attain enlightenment in a period in which there are not Buddhas. Consequently JM explains that "on account of the absence of a personal meeting with an Enlightened One, it is not taken into reckoning."[65] In a subsequent existence he is born as the stepsister of the Buddha Purāṇa-Dīpaṅkara. During his dispensation the future Buddha Dīpaṅkara received a prophecy that he would obtain Buddhahood. The future Gotama presented him with a gift of mustard oil, making a mental resolve "in consequence of the outflow of merit from the gift of mustard oil, when I become an Enlightened One, let me have the name Siddhattha."[66] The future Dīpaṅkara relays this resolve to the Buddha, who responds with a prophecy that during the time of the Buddha Dīpaṅkara his stepsister will receive her prophecy. JM continues that it was because of the "incongruity of sex" that the future Gotama did not receive a prophecy from Purāṇa-Dīpaṅkara.[67]

Although these texts are primarily concerned with the former lives of the Buddha Gotama, they also introduce the concept of future Buddhas. They presume a lineage of Buddhas stretching indefinitely into the past and future. For those of the Buddha Dīpaṅkara's time, Sumedha was a future Buddha, whereas at the time of the future Gotama's mental resolve, Dīpaṅkara was himself a future Buddha. The *Nidānakathā* (ND) uses this narrative to comment on the religious significance of the Buddha to be. When they hear of Buddha Dīpaṅkara's prophecy, his unenlightened followers rejoice, thinking "The hermit Summedha, it seems, is an embryo Buddha, the tender shoot that will grow up into a Buddha. For thus they thought, 'As a man fording a river, if he is unable to cross to the ford opposite him, crosses to a ford lower down the stream, even so we, if under the dispensation of Dīpaṅkara Buddha we fail to attain the Paths and their fruition, yet when thou shalt become Buddha we shall be enabled in thy presence to make the Paths and their fruition our own.' "[68]

Metteya is the only future Buddha mentioned in the Pāli canon. According to the *Cakkavatti-Sihanada Sutta*, he will be the last of the five Buddhas of this *kappa*. Sinhalese and Southeast Asian texts identify Metteya with the monk Ajita. Gotama Buddha is said to have identified him as Metteya on the occasion of his donation of two pieces of cloth.[69] DB, which circulated throughout mainland Southeast Asia, identifies ten future Buddhas, seven of whom are identified with figures in the Pāli canon. At the end of each section of DB, Gotama informs Sāriputta that those who have not attained *nibbāna* in the past will long for coming dispensations, extending the narrative of BU and ND.

The "mathematical beauty" of BU can also be found in accounts of the lives of past and future Buddhas. Theravāda Buddhism presumes the existence of an infinity of bodhisattvas who proceed through analogous series of lives. Malalasekara observes that certain conditions must be meet for a vow to attain Buddhahood to be effective. One must be "1. a human being, 2. male, 3. sufficiently developed to become an *arhat* in that very birth, 4. a recluse at the time of the declaration, 5. he should declare his resolve before a Buddha, 6. should be possessed of attainments such as *jhanas*, 7. be prepared to sacrifice all, even life, and 8. his resolution should be absolutely firm and unwavering."[70] All bodhisattvas cultivate the ten perfections required for Buddhahood in a long series of lives.

Following his encounter with the Buddha Dīpaṅkara, Sumedha contemplates the *dhamma* and the path to enlightenment, causing the entire world to shake. Buddha Dīpaṅkara reassures the populace, stating "have no fear of this earthquake. He of whom I declared today that he will be a Buddha in the world is reflecting on the *Dhamma* that was followed by former Conquerors. The *Dhamma* reflected on by him is the entire plane [perfection of a Buddha] of Buddhas."[71] This theme is repeated in the Bodhisattva's encounter with each of the subsequent Buddhas.

Just as the *Mahāpadāna Sutta* establishes analogies between the life of Gotama and those of previous Buddhas, accounts of the former lives of former Buddhas draw heavily on *jātaka* texts. The *jātaka* are tales of the Buddha Gotama's former lives.[72] They are thought to follow the Bodhisattva's encounter with the last of the twenty-seven previous Buddhas. In addition to these lives, the text refers to thousands of others, at least one of which was lived in Hell. Like the list of Buddhas, the *jātaka* tradition is an "open text." Other *jātaka* texts circulate in Southeast Asia.[73] There are also "*jātaka*" tales of the former lives of past and future Buddhas. Many of these draw on the *Vessantara Jātaka*. The *Vessantara Jātaka* concerns the perfection of giving and is the last of the 547 stories. The Bodhisattva (King Vessantara) gives away the magical white elephant that ensure the prosperity of his kingdom and finally his wife and children. This completes his cultivation of the perfection. The extent gift is even more strongly stated in stories concerning former and future Buddhas. In *Madhuratthavilasini* (MV), a commentary on BU, Mangala, the third of the twenty-four Buddhas, gives his children to a demon who devours them.[74] DB describes the great gift of the future Buddha Narada in similar terms.[75] In every case the gift of children is made in the Bodhisattva's penultimate human existence. Commentarial texts point to the gift of children as a general feature of the Bodhisattva path. MV states that Mangala made the gift during "an individuality resembling Vessantara's," while in Mil Nagasena explains: "All Bodhisattvas, sire, give away their wife and children."[76] Together these data indicate the life histories as well as the perfection of Buddhas and Bodhisattva are analogous.

Cohorts of the Buddhas and the Irony of Kamma

Bodhisattvas do not journey to *nibbāna* alone. Every Buddha has parents, a wife, a son, disciples, chief disciples, a personal servitor, and chief male and female lay donors who follow him on the path to enlightenment. These communities begin to form as the bodhisattva practices the perfection. Their structures are among the subsidiary themes of BU, the *jātaka*, DhA, and TT. Moggallana and Sāriputta are the Buddha's chief disciples. Sāriputta is the wisest of the Buddha's disciples. Moggallana is the master of magic. Ananda is his personal servitor. Each made a vow to a previous Buddha to attain his position in a future life. The future Sāriputta and Moggallana resolve to become great disciples at the time of the Buddha Anomdassin, the seventh Buddha of BU. DhA explains that Sāriputta could have attained enlightenment at this time, but is distracted by his disciple Nisabha, who is described as having "reached the pinnacle of the perfection of knowledge capable of attainment by a disciple."[77] He then makes a resolve to become a chief disciple, which is followed by a prophecy that it will be fulfilled during the time of the Buddha Gotama. The future Sāriputta then convinces his friend, the future Moggallana, to entertain Buddha Anomdassin and his disciples and to resolve to become the second great disciple.[78] Ananda resolved to become the personal servitor of a Buddha at the time of Buddha Padumuttara, the tenth Buddha of BU. While entertaining the Buddha, he was greatly impressed by his attendant and made a resolve to become one in a future life.[79]

These accounts indicate that there are lineages of great disciples corresponding to the lineage of the Buddhas. Each is mentioned in numerous *jātaka* stories: Ananda in 147, Sāriputta in 90, and Moggallana in 57. In some cases the narrative structure of these stories parallels episodes from the life of the Buddha. Ananda is often a personal servant, Sāriputta the wisest companion of the Bodhisattva, and Moggallana a master of magical power. In others they are friends and associations of the Bodhisattva.

Accounts of the former lives of Devadatta indicate that the cohorts of the Buddhas include great schismatics and heretics as well as great disciples. As the result of his sins against the Buddha and the *sangha*, Devadatta is swallowed by the earth and tormented in the Avici Hell. While there is no record that he ever expressed a resolve to suffer this fate, accounts of his former lives parallel those of Gotama. He is mentioned in sixty-seven *jātaka*, in which he is described a treacherous, ungrateful, drunk. In three of these, he is swallowed by the earth. Devadatta is, however, more than the Theravāda manifestation of evil. He serves as the most extreme example of the compassion of Buddha. The account of his death and torment is of great soteriological significance, demonstrating that the possibility of enlightenment is open to even the most evil beings. As he is being swallowed by the earth, Devadatta takes refuge in the Buddha. At this point the Buddha ordains him, so that "it will be possible for him to look forward with confidence to future existence," and predicts that in the future he will become a *Pacceka* Buddha.[80]

Future Buddhas will have similar communities. Presumably they have already begun to form. Sinhalese texts discussed by H. Saddhatissa mention the names of great disciples of the future. JM states that the members of Metteya's community were formerly Sinhalese kings and queens.[81] There is no record that anyone has claimed to be the Devadatta of a future Buddha's dispensation. This is not surprising.

The lives of great beings and their struggles over incalculable periods to attain enlightenment as Buddhas or great disciples is the major theme in Theravāda sacred biography. There are, however, also texts concerning the paths of beings of lesser stature and, in a more general sense, the ways in which seemingly insignificant acts may have enormous soteriological consequences. A related body of texts concerns particular events in the life of the Buddha Gotama and the ways in which Buddhas differ.

Vimanavatthu (Vv) and *Pettavatthu* (Pv) result from Moggallana's visit to heaven and his conversations with hungry ghosts. Vv describes the types of deeds that result in rebirth in heavenly abodes, Pv those which lead to states of suffering. The point of both texts would appear to be that all human acts have enduring cosmological consequences. The commentary on Vv states: "One day this reasoning occurred to the venerable Moggallana the great. . . . What if I were to make a deva tour and ask the devatas at first hand what was the deed of merit of which they now experience the fruit. If I then told the matter to the Blessed One he might conduct a teaching on Dhamma based on these Mansion stories. It would be for the good, the welfare, the happiness of devas and men."[82]

Many of the tales included in these texts are thematically related to episodes in the lives of the Buddhas and other prominent figures in the biographical corpus. The "Story of the Peta with a Putrid Mouth" concerns the consequences of promoting disharmony in the *sangha*. Its theme is similar to that of the biography of Devadatta, that is, that causing discord within the *sangha* leads to states of woe. It concerns a *peta* who was a monk at the time of the Buddha Kassapa, the twenty-fourth Buddha of BU. The monk's "evil disposition" led him to covet the donations of an entire village and to drive out other resident monks by backbiting and slander. He soon died and was reborn in the Avici Hell and at the time of the Buddha Gotama was still suffering the consequences of his actions, having been reborn as a *peta* whose mouth was constantly being devoured by worms and which emitted a putrid odor.[83]

Many of the "mansion stories" concern the rewards of charity and, in this sense, are related to the *Vessantara Jātaka*. In Vv, Moggallana asks each of the *devi* and *deva* what act of merit led to rebirth in the heavenly abode. The most common replies are the presentation of alms to the Buddha or a monk and the observance of the five moral precepts incumbent on lay Buddhists.

Theva/Therīgāthā (TT) is a collection of verses attributed to male and female *arhat* of the Buddha's community. The biographical frames of monks and nuns differ significantly. The nuns' tales all refer to acts of merit and devotion performed during the times of previous Buddhas. Those of the monks are concerned primarily with the final path stages. The nuns' verses are framed by accounts of births in the times of previous Buddhas. The verse of the unnamed nun who utters the first of the verses is more detailed than most, but in other respects typical: "How was she reborn? Long ago, a certain daughter of one of the clans became a fervent believer in the teaching of the Buddha Konagamana, and entertained him with hospitality. She had an arbour made with boughs, a draped ceiling, and a sanded floor, and did him honour with flowers and perfumes. And all her life doing meritorious acts, she was reborn among gods, and again among men when Kassapa was Buddha, under whom she renounced the world. Reborn in heaven till this Buddha-dispensation, she was finally born in a great nobleman's family at Vesali."[84]

There are also frames referring to alternating positive and negative action. Addhakasi was a nun at the time of the Buddha Kassapa and well established in the moral precepts. But because she referred to another nun, who was already an *arhat*, as a prostitute, she was unable to obtain enlightenment and was reborn in a state of woe. She was herself reborn as a prostitute at the time of the Buddha Gotama, but she entered the order and attained enlightenment.[85]

Although there are exceptions like Sukka, who was "Learned, proficient in the doctrine, and a ready speaker" at the time of four previous Buddhas, most of the nuns reach the final path stages by keeping moral precepts and obtain enlightenment through insight following an encounter with the Buddha or one of the great disciples.[86] As C. Rhys-Davids has observed, monks are much more likely to attain enlightenment through solitary forest meditation, the exercise of magical powers, and mastery of doctrine. Others become *arhat* after leaving non-Buddhist ascetic orders. While many reach enlightenment through insight, it is often preceded by austerities and the cultivation of other meditative states.

Monks are more frequently portrayed struggling against the world and their own passions than are nuns. With few exceptions the monk's biographical frames begin with the phrase "Reborn in this Buddha age." The tale of Kulla is illustrative of the way in which these motifs are combined:

> Reborn in this Buddha age at Savatthi in the family of a landowner, and named Kulla, he was converted by faith, and was ordained by the Master. But he was often seized by fits of lustful passion. The master, knowing his tendencies, gave him the exercise on foul things, and bade him often meditate in the charnel field. And when even this sufficed not, he himself went with him and bade him mark the process of putrefaction

and dissolution. Thus, as Kulla stood with heart disinfatuated, the Exalted One sent out a glory, producing in him such mindfulness that he discerned the lesson, attained first jhana, and on that basis developed insight, won arahantship.[87]

Comparison of nuns' and monks' verses indicate that men and women move toward enlightenment in different ways. A monk's path employs many of the elements found in the lives of the Buddha and is one of self-cultivation, although generally aided by the teaching of the Buddha. A nun's path is one of lay piety and devotion leading to the sudden development of insight in her final existence. Hers is a path of piety and devotion, whereas that of a monk is one of struggle against the world and himself. This distinction also helps to clarify anomalies in the biography of Ananda. Malalasekera argues that it was because of Ananda's attachment to the Buddha Gotama that he was unable to attain *arhatship* until after his master's death. Ananda was also the strongest advocate of women in the Buddha's community, convincing him to allow female ordination after thrice refusing.[88] It is perhaps significant that the monk who most strongly champions the cause of women is one whose own path to enlightenment most closely resembles their own.

Despite the "mathematical beauty" of BU, Buddhas are not the same in all respects. MV states that they differ with respect to life span, height, family, time required for striving, the extent of rays, vehicle used in the great renunciation, the tree under which enlightenment is obtained, and the size of the cross-legged meditation posture.[89] There are also particular events in the lives of some Buddhas that do not occur in others. These are the result of *kamma*, which must be expiated in the Buddha's final existence. The *apadāna* includes verses explaining the *kammic* basis for unpleasant aspects of Gotama's last life. Several of these concern his encounters with Devadatta. Malalasekera describes them as follows: "Once, greedy for wealth, he killed his stepbrothers, hurling them down a precipice; as a result, Devadatta attempted to kill him by hurling him down a rock. Once, as a boy, while playing on the highway, he saw a Pacceka Buddha and threw a stone at him, and as a result, was shot at by Devadatta's hired archers. In another life he was a mahout, and seeing a Pacceka Buddha on the road, drove his elephant against him; hence the attack by Nalagiri." Gotama's six years of striving are explained as the consequence of a disparaging remark he made concerning the enlightenment of the Buddha Kassapa.[90]

Comparing these events in the former lives of the Buddha with the ghost stories of Pv and even the tales of the former lives of nuns included in TT illuminates the irony of *kamma*. A nun who speaks ill of another and a monk who causes dissension within the order suffer for enormous periods. A Bodhisattva who kills his relatives and assaults a *Pacceka* Buddha with an elephant is assaulted—unsuccessfully—by the forces of a schismatic who is swallowed by the earth. While all actions of those who remain in *saṃsāra* have consequences, Bodhisattvas, by virtue of their goal, are exempt from rebirth in the eighteen inauspicious states, including those of *peta* and the Avici Hell.[91]

Conclusion: Theravāda Buddhism and the Terror of History

In the final chapter of the *Myth of Eternal Return*, Mircea Eliade speaks of the "terror of history," which he describes as the existential position of modern, post-religious humanity.[92] This terror is, in part, the knowledge that systems of meaning are products of human imagination rather than repetitions of eternal archetypes. This awareness is the product of the Enlightenment, the growth of science as a way of knowing, and of "higher criticism," which demythified Christian scripture. Among the reactions to the religious problems posed by these realizations were quests for the historical Jesus and the formulation of a psychologically oriented Christianity in which religious experience rather than myth, rite, and sacred biography define the fundamentals of faith. The search for rationalized, individualist alternatives to Christian religiousness was another.

I would not go so far as P. Almond, who sees "Buddhism" as a creation of Victorian discourse about the mysterious Orient.[93] The depiction of early Buddhism as a radically individualistic quest for personal salvation may, however, be understood as both a response to and an attempt to escape from the terror of history. This is accomplished by substituting a newly discovered "rational" faith for a discredited mythic Christianity. This is apparent in C. Rhys-Davids' comparison of Buddhism and Christianity, in which she sees both as ethical religions emphasizing human conduct instead of sacrifice. Her view is that in Buddhism:

> the New Word saw the way out as different. It saw it only in the man himself. No external methods as such can help. The man must find the way. In himself must each seek salvation. . . . The man in our day is no longer the man of the day when Sakya began, any more than he was man of the day when Sakya was becoming what we call Buddhism. In the earlier day the man meant he who had within, latent, yet astir, the very Divine, the Highest, the Most. This self it was, and no external deity, on whom man was thrown back, to whom man was referred, to follow whom was the way out. It is of the first importance that this be realized; the ignoring of it, the substitution for it of the later Buddhist limited view of the man, the self, and of our own limited view of the man, the self, is ever vitiating modern treatment of Buddhist teaching.[94]

The "truth" of Buddhism and escape from the terror of history are, therefore, to be found in the paradigmatic doctrines of the historical Buddha. As Carrithers notes, the movement was often one from Christianity to Romanticism, combined with nontheistic piety to Buddhism.[95] It is, in Eliade's terms, a journey from the archetype of Christ to that of the Buddha. By understanding Buddhism as a personal salvation quest, the journey preserves Cartesian individualism and rationalism—the intellectual hallmarks of modernity—while escaping the terror of history. Given this perspective, it is not difficult to understand the characterization of Theravāda biographical narrative as a "*birana* weed." But to characterize Buddhism as a religion of radical individual autonomy is possible only on the basis of a selective reading of the textual tradition, and it is possible only from the perspective of the doctrine of autonomous personhood and the related concept of individual religious experience, which are themselves products of the terror of history.

Although the terror of history may be the existential condition of modernity, it is not an exclusively modern phenomena. Buddhism, Christianity, Islam, and other founded faiths are confronted with the problem of establishing themselves as eternal truths in the face of competing claims of older, established religions. Christianity and Islam accomplish this by appropriating portions of Judaic scripture and by presenting themselves as the culmination of a lineage of prophets. Theravāda Buddhism maps the biographical lineage of the Buddha Gotama onto Buddhas of the past and the future. It remains, however, a doctrinally conservative tradition. Even though there are many Buddhas, there can be only one at a time. Buddhas are human, not divine. There is nothing in the Theravāda epic that recalls Mahāyāna Buddhology, with its implicit denial of the teaching of impermanence and the equation of *saṃsāra* and *nirvāṇa*. As stated in DB, Bodhisattvas attain enlightenment as Buddhas and "pass away having completed a Buddha's duty."[96] The expansion of the biographical tradition in the early centuries of the common era suggests that development of Theravāda Buddhology parallels, but is not necessarily a response to, that of the Mahāyāna tradition. It also parallels the development of the paradigmatic component of the Theravāda tradition. The importance of the *jātaka*, DhA, and other biographical narratives in contemporary Theravāda societies is illustrative not of the debasement of a pristine, paradigmatic tradition, but rather of the centrality of narrative thought in religious life. The emergence of the narrative tradition saved Theravāda soteriology, including the proximate goal of a better existence, as well as the ultimate end of *nibbāna*, from the terror of history. The further development of biographical narrative keeps it at bay.

Notes

1. J. Bruner, *Actual Minds Possible Worlds* (Cambridge, Mass.: Harvard University Press, 1986), p. 12.
2. Ibid, p. 13.
3. Ibid.
4. Ibid, p. 11.
5. T. W. Rhys-Davids, *Buddhist Birth Stories* (London: Trübner and Co., 1880), p. i; M. Cummings, *The Lives of the Buddha in the Art and Literature of Asia* (Ann Arbor: Michigan Papers on South and Southeast Asia, Center for South and Southeast Asian Studies, The University of Michigan, no. 20, 1982).
6. W. Rockhill, *The Life of the Buddha and the Early History of His Order Derived from Tibetan Works in the Bkah-Hgyur and Bstan-Hgyur* (London: Trübner's Oriental Series, 1884); E. Thomas, *The Life of the Buddha as History and Legend* (London: Routledge and Kegan Paul, 1927).
7. H. Saddhatissa, *The Birth-Stories of the Ten Bodhisattas and the Dasbodhisattuppattikatha. Being a Translation and Edition of the Dasbodhisattuppattikatha* (London: Pāli Text Society, 1975), p. 1, hereafter cited as DB.
8. E. Conze, *Buddhism: Its Essence and Development* (New York: Harper and Row, 1975), p. 87.
9. T. W. and C. A. F. Rhys-Davids, trans., *Dialogues of the Buddha—Part II* (London: Luzac and Co., 1910), pp. 23–28 and 50–70.
10. Ibid, p. 1.
11. Ibid, p. 44.
12. M. Weber *The Religion of India* (Glencoe: The Free Press, 1958), p. 222.
13. Ibid, p. 206.
14. Ibid, p. 249.
15. M. Carrithers, *The Forest Monks of Sri Lanka: An Anthropological and Historical Study* (Delhi: Oxford University Press, 1983), pp. 26–45.
16. F. Reynolds, "The Many Lives of the Buddha: A Study of Sacred Biography and the Theravada Tradition," in *The Biographical Process. Studies in the History and Psychology of Religion*, ed. F. Reynolds and D. Capps (The Hague: Mouton, 1976), pp. 37–62.
17. Pe Maung Tin, trans., *The Expositor (Atthasalini) Buddhaghosa's Commentary on the Dhammasagani, the First Book of the Abhidhamma Pitaka* (London: Pāli Text Society, 1976), p. 7, hereafter cited as A.
18. C. A. F. Rhys-Davids, trans., *Psalms of the Early Buddhists* (London: The Pāli Text Society, 1913), vol. 2, pp. 350–351, hereafter cited as TT.
19. T. W. and C. A. F. Rhys-Davids, trans., *Dialogues of the Buddha Translated from the Pali of the Digha Nikaya* (London: Oxford University Press, 1921), p. 7.
20. I. B. Horner, trans., *The Book of Discipline* (*Vinaya-Pitaka*), vol. 2, *Suttavibhanga* (London: Oxford University Press, 1940), pp. 113–117.
21. Ibid, p. 114.

22. Ibid., pp. 259–290. E. Burlingame, trans., *Buddhist Legends Translated from the Original Pali Text of the Dhammapada Commentary* (Cambridge, Mass.: Harvard University Press, 1921), vol. 1, pp. 230–242, hereafter cited as DhA.
23. H. Francis, trans., *The Jataka or Stories of the Buddha's Former Births* (London: Cambridge University Press, 1905), vol. 5, pp. 175–185.
24. E. Cowell and W. Rouse, trans., *The Jataka or Stories of the Buddhha's Former Births* (London: Cambridge University Press, 1907), vol. 6, pp. 264–305.
25. TT, vol. 1, pp. 3–8.
26. Rhys-Davids, *Buddhist Birth Stories*, pp. 2–131.
27. I. B. Horner (assisted by N. A. Jayawickrama), *The Minor Anthologies of the Pāli Canon*, Part 4, *Vimanavatthu: Stories of the Mansions* (London: Pāli Text Society, 1974), p. xxvii; DB, p. 54.
28. M. Müller, trans., *The Dhammapada: A Collection of Verses. Being One of the Canonical Books of the Buddhists* (Oxford: Clarendon Press, 1898).
29. I. B. Horner, trans., *The Minor Anthologies of the Pāli Canon* Part 3, *Chronicle of Buddhas (Buddhavaṃsa) and Basket of Conduct (Cariyāpiṭaka)* (London: Pāli Text Society, 1975), pp. 1–99, hereafter cited as Bc and Cyp; I. B. Horner, trans., *The Clarifier of Sweet Meaning (Madhuratthavilasinī) Commentary on the Chronicle of the Buddhas by Buddhadatta Thera* (London: Pāli Text Society, 1978); hereafter cited as MV; H. Gehman, trans., *The Minor Anthologies of the Pāli Canon*, Part 4, *Petavatthu: Stories of the Departed* (London: Pāli Text Society, 1974), hereafter cited as Pv; U. Ba Kyaw, trans., *Elucidation of the Intrinsic Meaning so named The Commentary on the Peta-Stories (Paramatthadipani nama Petavatthu-atthakatha by Dhammapala)* (London: Pāli Text Society, 1980), hereafter cited as PvA.
30. PvA. p. 3.
31. Ibid., pp. 9–11, 258–263.
32. G. P. Malalasekera, *Dictionary of Pāli Proper Names* (London: Routledge and Kegan Paul, 1974), vol. 1, pp. 296–297; p. 1146 states that Dhammapala, the author of PvA, also wrote a commentary on Buddhaghosa's Vsm.
33. Pv, p. xii.
34. B. Ñāṇamoli, trans., *The Path of Purification (Visuddhimagga)* (Berkeley: Shambhala, 1976), hereafter cited as Vsm; Ñāṅamoli, trans., *The Path of Discrimination (Patisambhidamagga)* (London: Pāli Text Society, 1982), hereafter cited as Vsm.
35. Vsm, p. 1.
36. Ibid., p. 487.
37. Malalasekera, *Dictionary*, Vol. 2, pp. 719, 865–866, and 1154; DhA, vol. 1. pp. 228, 282, 292, vol. 2, pp. 12, 144, 194, vol. 3, p. 183.
38. Vsm, p. 250–251.
39. Ps, p. 384.

40. See Pe Maung Tin, *The Path of Purity: Being a Translation of Buddhaghosa's Visuddhimagga* (London: Pāli Text Society, 1975), pp. 39, 264–268. Pe Maung Tin provides citations to Cowell's edition of the *jātaka* for quotations included in Vsm.
41. A, p. 37.
42. Malalasekera, *Dictionary*, vol. 2, pp. 1116–1117.
43. A, pp. 37–38.
44. DhA, vol. 3, pp. 35–56.
45. A, pp. 20–21.
46. A, p. 6.
47. B. C. Law, trans., *The Debates Commentary* (*Kathavatthuppakarana—Atthakatha*) (London: Pāli Text Society, 1940), pp. 1–2, hereafter cited as K.
48. Ibid., p. 1.
49. I. B. Horner, trans., *Malinda's Questions* (London: Luzac and Company, 1969), p. 4, hereafter cited as Mil.
50. Ibid., p. 5.
51. Ibid.
52. For discussions of the problems surrounding the authorship of the *jātaka, Dhammapada*, and Vsm, see Burlingame, *Buddhist Legends*, vol. 1, pp. 59–60; and Ñāṇamoli, *Path of Discrimination*, pp. xv–xxvi.
53. Burlingame, *Buddhist Legends*, pp. 59–60.
54. B. Ñāṇamoli, trans., *The Minor Readings* (*Khudakapatha*) (London: Pāli Text Society, 1978), pp. x–xv.
55. Vsm, vol. 1, p. 137.
56. N. Jayawickrama, trans., *The Sheaf of Garlands of the Epochs of the Conqueror* (London: Pāli Text Society, 1978), p. 12.
57. DB, p. 53.
58. Rhys-Davids, *Dialogues*, pp. 8–18.
59. For a discussion of the characteristics shared by the Buddhas, see Malalasekera, *Dictionary*, vol. 2, pp. 296–297.
60. Horner, *The Minor Anthologies of the Pali Canon*, Part 3, p. xx.
61. Ibid. pp. xxii–xxiii.
62. BU, pp. 9–25. The story of Sumedha is repeated in many other accounts of the lives of the Buddha Gotama, including the *Nidānakathā* (Rhys-Davids, *Buddhist Birth Stories*, pp. 2–18), hereafter cited as ND.
63. BU, pp. 16–17.
64. DhA, vol. 1, p. 194.
65. JM, Jayawickrama, *Sheaf of Garlands*, p. 2.
66. Ibid., p. 7.
67. Ibid.
68. ND, p. 15; BU (p. 16) includes a shorter variant of the narrative.
69. See Saddhatissa (*Birth Stories*, pp. 31–33). This identification is significant for understanding esoteric Buddhism in contemporary Theravāda societies because it shows that it is possible for a monk to be a Bodhisattva.

70. Malalasekara, *Dictonary*, vol. 1, pp. 322–323.
71. BU, p. 24.
72. Only the verse elements of the *jātaka* tales are held to be canonical. The prose sections are commentaries explaining the verses. Reynolds ("The Many Lives of the Buddha," p. 42) has argued that despite the fact that the collection of 547 stories did not assume its final form until the fifth century C.E., the *jātaka* are among the oldest elements of the Theravāda biographical tradition. The fact that carvings of some of the ten great *jātaka* are found on second- and third- century monuments is one line of argument for this position. Another can be found in the texts themselves. The *Khandha-vatta Jātaka* (no. 203) mentions the seven Buddhas. The tale itself is of minor importance. It is about charms for warding off snake bites. The fact that it mentions seven Buddhas may be taken as evidence that the text is older than the *Buddhavaṃsa*.
73. P. Jaini, ed., *Paññasa-Jātaka or Zimme Pannasa.* (London: Pāli Text Society, 1983).
74. MV, p. 206.
75. DB, p. 72.
76. MV, p. 206; Mil, p. 95.
77. DhA, vol. 1, p. 214.
78. Ibid., p. 216.
79. The account of Ananda's resolve is found in the *Theṅgāthā Commentary*, cited in Malalasekera, *Dictionary*, vol. 1, pp. 265–266.
80. DhA, vol. 1, p. 240.
81. DB, p. 40; JM, p. 81.
82. Vv, Horner, *The Minor Anthologies of the Pali Canon, Part 4*, p. xxvii.
83. Pv, pp. 4–5.
84. TT, p. 9.
85. Ibid., pp. 25–26.
86. Ibid., pp. 40–41.
87. Ibid., pp. 211.
88. Malalakasekara, *Dictionary*, vol. 1, pp. 257–258.
89. MV, p. 425.
90. Malalasekara, *Dictionary*, vol. 1, p. 808.
91. Ibid., vol. 2, p. 323.
92. M. Eliade, *The Myth of Eternal Return or, Cosmos and History* (Princeton: Princeton University Press, 1971), pp. 141–162.
93. P. Almond, *The British Discovery of Buddhism* (Cambridge: Cambridge University Press, 1988).
94. C. A. F. Rhys-Davids, *Sakya or Buddhist Origins* (London: Kegan Paul, Trench, Trübner and Co., 1928) pp. 9–10.
95. Carrithers, *The Forest Monks of Sri Lanka*, p. 44.
96. DB, p. 54.

Narrative as Icon: The Jātaka Stories in Ancient Indian and Southeast Asian Architecture

Robert L. Brown

The *jātakas* are stories, often very good ones, filled with what makes stories interesting (action, intrigue, romance, love, death, the marvelous) and constructed around plots that have the twists and turns and unexpected events to keep the listener or reader fascinated. Each deals with a past life of the Buddha by narrating various individuals' actions described in a chronological sequence. The listener or reader mentioned just above implies a spoken, or possibly a written, text. But the *jātakas* were frequently represented visually in the art of India and Southeast Asia, and placed within architectural contexts. It is some of these representations that I wish to discuss here.

Scholars make certain assumptions with regard to the visual representations of the *jātakas*, or more broadly, to visual representations of stories, and I wish to challenge some of these assumptions. One assumption is that the same things (the narrative content, the story line) hold the attention of the viewer of the *jātakas* and the attention of the listener/reader. Does the narrative content of the stories interest the worshiper, and if so, how does the story content relate to the written text and to the image? And, can assumptions regarding the nature and function of the word texts be applied to the visual texts of the *jātakas*?

I wish to argue that considering the visual representations of the *jātakas* on certain ancient Southeast Asian and Indian monuments as illustrated versions of the word stories is incorrect. These visual images, in my opinion, are not present on the monuments to tell stories at all, but are there with an iconic function. The *jātakas* were considered as units, functioning within the context of the monument as a whole and with particular non-narrative roles defined by their locations and uses.

The Indian Monuments

I want to begin with some comments on Buddhist narratives on Indian monuments. An article on the topic of Buddhist narrative in early Indian art, Vidya Dehejia's "On Modes of Visual Narration in Early Buddhist Art,"[1] quickly focuses some of the issues for us. Dehejia has used for her analysis Indian art that dates from Bhārhut (ca. 100–80 B.C.E.) to Ajaṇṭā (ca. 460–480 C.E.), and includes both sculpture and painting. Her categorization divides the way narrative content is visualized by analyzing its artistic organization, such as monoscenic narratives, synoptic narratives, conflated narratives,[2] and so forth. There is one basic verbal or textual story, but it can be told in a number of different artistic modes. As she bases her identification of visual narrative forms in Indian art on scholarship of narrative in Western art, one might initially ask how it relates to Indian art. Perhaps visual narrative types are universal, but even so, one might wonder if similar formal arrangements indicate similar intentions or meanings in Indian and Western art. At least we might anticipate the possibility of explicating visual narrative types in Indian, not Western, terms.

For example, Dehejia uses the Ajātaśatru pillar from Bhārhut (see fig. 1), which has three life-scenes of the Buddha stacked one above the other to illustrate what she calls "static monoscenic narration, diachronic mode."[3] The arrangement of the scenes is the miracle of Śrāvasti at the bottom, next the descent at Sāṅkāsya, and at the top, the preaching in Indra's Heaven. Dehejia's main assumption in explicating the arrangement of these three scenes is that they would have been "read" diachronically as if mimicking a verbal or written narrative sequence. Indeed, that the visual should be read as if illustrating a verbal narrative is the major assumption of her article. If the Ajātaśatru pillar scenes are put into a chronological narrative order, the events begin at Śrāvasti (bottom), then move to Indra's Heaven (top), and end at Sāṅkāsya (middle), so that Dehejia suggests that the "viewer must move" from the bottom to the top panel and "end with the central panel." She feels that because the Sāṅkāsya and Śrāvasti panels have a similar composition (crowds of worshipers centered on a tree above a throne), "in isolation, [the Indra's heaven scene] would present problems of identification,"[4]

Figure I. *Ajātaṣatru pillar (with scenes from bottom: Miracle of Śrāvasti, Descent at Sāṅkāsya, and Preaching in Indra's Heaven). Stone. From Bhārhut (India). Indian Museum, Calcutta. (Photo from Vidya Dehejia, "On Modes of Visual Narration in Early Buddhist Art,"* The Art Bulletin *72, no. 3 [September 1990].)*

and that the identification of the top scene of the preaching in Indra's Heaven would rely on the viewer's visual familiarity with the other two scenes and the knowledge of the chronology of the three events. If we accept her interpretation, it makes the relationship of the three artistic scenes (chronologically from bottom to top to middle) something of a puzzle.

There are, however, principles of narrative organization at Bhārhut that are not based on telling a story through time. One principle is the association of events in spatial or geographical terms. For example, the descent at Sāṅkāsya is placed below the scene in Indra's Heaven because the descent down the ladders to Sāṅkāsya from the Heaven is visualized as below Heaven. The two upper scenes can thus be considered as a unit in space. A second principle used to organize the narrative at Bhārhut centers on notions of cause and effect. The Śrāvasti miracle scene is placed together with the preaching and descent group because the miracle is the event (cause) that leads to the preaching/descent (effect). They are events that all Buddhas repeat, and here Śākyamuni Buddha's miracle at Śrāvasti leads inevitably to the other two events. In other words, the organization of the three scenes has, to my mind, little to do with the narrative as a story told through time.

We may look at a second example that Dehejia illustrates, the great departure of Śākyamuni on the east gateway at Sāñcī (fig. 2), which she uses as an example of continuous narration. She correctly notes that this relief is a "classic instance" of continuous narration, one in which successive

Figure 2. Great Departure (detail on east gateway). Stone. Sāñcī (India). (Photo: Robert L. Brown)

episodes of a story are placed within a single artistic frame with the protagonist repeated in each. The departure is depicted with the riderless horse moving from left to right across the space in four images from the gates of Kapilavastu to before the Buddha's footprints at the far right, and then, just below, in a single image returning to the palace, a sequence that mimics the narrative sequence. Nevertheless, Dehejia does not mention that in the center of the picture-space is a tree surrounded by a fence and with attendants. The tree is a *jambu* tree, and it is there for both of the reasons mentioned above regarding the "Indian" organization of the Bhārhut scenes. It is there because it was in the vicinity of Kapilavastu that the young Prince Śākyamuni sat under the *jambu* tree in his first meditation (associated, therefore, geographically with the departure) and because it was during this first spontaneous meditation that the prince began to have the initial thoughts regarding the pain and sorrow of the human condition (cause) that eventually led to his decision to abandon his princely life (effect). In other words, the organization of the narrative has to do with concerns other than the attempt to "tell" a linear story.

Dehejia discusses in relation to continuous narration the method of worship we associate with *stūpa* worship, circumambulation, as the narrative reliefs at Bhārhut and Sāñcī are on the fences and gates that surround the *stūpas*. In this regard, she speaks of circumambulation moving the worshiper in a clockwise rotation, and thus with regard to the scroll-like space of the Sāñcī architraves, the passing worshiper would read the narrative from right to left as he or she passed it from the front, or from left to right if circumambulating on the inner *pradakṣiṇāpatha* (circumambulation path), and thus seeing the architrave from the "back."[5] The artist therefore would, supposedly, move the narration linearly across the artistic space in either right to left or left to right directions, depending on the location of the relief and the approach of the viewer. Dehejia, however, immediately notes in her discussion that the *Vessantara Jātaka* relief does not follow this organization, leading her to state: "It would appear that the sculptor carved one face of the architrave, and then commenced the inner face at the end he had just completed, apparently disregarding the manner in which the circumambulating viewer would experience the story. In any event, the viewer must perforce abandon the general movement of circumambulation if he wishes to experience this story in its entirety."[6] But the most obvious point to make here is that, unless the viewer is on a ladder or using a telephoto lens or binoculars, the *jātaka* relief at Sāñcī cannot be seen in any detail at all from the ground as (at over five meters above the ground) it is simply too high up (fig. 3). The viewer would not be called upon to abandon circumambulation to experience the story in its entirety because he or she could not have experienced any of it in the first place.

Figure 3. Stūpa I, south gateway. (Compare size of figure to gate and height of architraves.) Sāñcī (India). (Photo: Robert L. Brown)

What about the scenes on the Ajātaśatru pillar from Bhārhut? These are on an upright of the *stūpa* fence and are more accessible to the viewer, but even here the bottom panel is only about twenty centimeter from the ground. Although a person in circumambulation can see the panel, it requires kneeling, squatting, or bending to see it well. Remember that Dehejia has talked about the viewer moving from panel to panel, by which I assume she means moving one's body and eyes, if not one's feet.

All of this is to say that Dehejia is assuming that the reliefs are being read by the viewers and that their interest is to recreate the story in its chronological sequence from the images. Here she is very explicit. In discussing the monoscenic narratives, for example, she says "a single, easily identifiable scene . . . is presented to stimulate the viewer's recognition of the story," but "having given enough information to identify the tale, the artist leaves the viewer to narrate the story himself."[7] Or when later discussing the monoscenic narratives again she writes that they "must . . . contain sufficient narrative content to stimulate the story-telling process in the mind of the observer."[8] How might this work? Are we to imagine the worshiper stopped in front of the image going through the story in detail in his or her mind? How long might this take? If the worshiper were a monk with the story familiar to him in some detail, would he recreate the story from start to finish, pausing for ten, twenty, or more minutes silently telling himself the story?[9] What would he be doing with his eyes, with the art, with the monument during this "silent read"?

Dehejia's discussion of the narrative scenes (again the Buddha's life stories and *jātakas*) in the Ajaṇṭā paintings is also grounded on the assumption that the paintings were read as a linear narrative. Again, there are problems, as the paintings are on the whole extremely complicated in their organization, so much so that their identification and explication by scholars is an ongoing question. Dehejia's response is that "it appears that only an intimate knowledge of the Buddhist texts popular in the fifth century would enable one to unravel these tortuous sequences."[10] She speaks a little later of the absence of what she considers key scenes in a painting of the *Vessantara Jātaka* in Cave 17 as "strange."[11] Surely that the sequence is "tortuous" or the subject choice is "strange" is in the eyes of the modern scholar, not of the artist or the contemporary worshiper. And the use of the paintings is dealt with in a similar fashion to that of the Bhārhut and Sāñcī reliefs: "When lit only by flickering oil lamps, the murals would have required 'strong eyes, great persistence and an excellent retentive memory' in order to follow the narrative course. As a purely practical matter, one wonders if any viewer was inclined to put in so much effort. Yet, the sense of the narrative must have been clear to him through familiarity with the subject."[12] In other words, the murals were there to be read and a story told, yet Dehejia recognizes that many factors (the organization of the paintings, the scenes chosen, the placement within a dark cave) made the viewing process difficult or practically impossible.

My own suggestion is that the paintings were not there to be read or to tell a story. The paintings were there for worshipers, not for viewers, and the choice of "viewer" as the way to characterize most often the person relating to the Indian art is to "art historicize" the material, to make it an issue between art historian and object. Instead, the issue for me is between worshiper and deity. The paintings at Ajaṇṭā are part of the overall adornment of the caves, which included, according to Varāhadeva's inscription in Cave 16, "windows, doors, beautiful picture-galleries, ledges, statues of the nymphs of Indra and the like . . . [and] beautiful pillars and stairs," all of which were intended to make the cave resemble "the palaces of the lord of gods [that is, Indra]."[13] The picture-galleries are listed here along with such items as doors and ledges as adorning the cave. At least Varāhadeva is not singling the paintings out as of greater importance, which might give us pause when assessing their intended purpose.

The same inscription mentions that the cave "has a temple of the Buddha inside."[14] Inside the cave, which is a *vihāra*, there is an enormous Buddha seated with his legs pendant (*pralambapādāsana*) and his hands turning the wheel of the law (*dharmacakramudrā*) (fig. 4).[15] The image is placed at the center rear of the cave in a shrine.[16] This image, in its particular seated posture and wheel-turning gesture, is among the first such images in Indian iconography, a type that quickly spread throughout northern India in the second half of the fifth and sixth centuries.[17] Specifically, the gesture of wheel-turning was introduced at this time,[18] and although it has been associated with the Buddha delivering the First Sermon at Sārnāth and is frequently so indicated by the inclusion of deer and the wheel below the image, the Cave 16 Buddha lacks these symbols. Nevertheless, the gesture is one of teaching.

Also perhaps introduced at Ajaṇṭā, or at this same time, is the placement of the rock-cut Buddha image within the *vihāra* in what amounts to an enlarged and elaborated monk's cell. The image was thus brought into the monk's residence to worship, and this appears to coincide with the "falling off" of worship in the *caitya* halls with their focus on the *stūpa*.[19] There is no reason, however, not to suppose that monks had portable Buddha images—in bronze, stone, or wood—that they had been worshiping in the context of the *vihāra* earlier. The difference is thus of *permanently* installing an image. There seems little doubt that the image in the cell was worshiped, by the monks and probably by lay people as well.[20] I would like to shift, however, the focus somewhat away from the image as a focus for worship. Gregory Schopen, in his article "The Buddha as an Owner of

Figure 4. Cave 16 Buddha image. Stone. Ajaṇṭā (India). (Photo: Robert L. Brown)

Property and Permanent Resident in Medieval Indian Monasteries,"[21] has used the Cave 16 inscription, among others, to argue that the image was considered the actual person of the Buddha in residence in the *vihāra*, his central cell called the Perfume Chamber (*gandhakuṭī*). If this is correct, we can see why the Buddha image was permanently installed in the cell. At the same time that it made the cell into a shrine, it also, and perhaps more importantly and most obviously, installed the Buddha in his residence cell within the monastery, which he shared with the other monks. The Buddha was in residence—a fellow monk—and, as when he resided with his monks and followers during his "human" existence, he taught them the doctrine. Thus the introduction of the wheel-turning gesture indicates his teaching of the law to the monks and lay people within the context of the monastery.

Now returning to the Ajaṇṭā paintings of the *jātakas* and life scenes of the Buddha, it may be possible to interpret them as bringing his presence into this context. They are there to indicate, to make "actual," the Buddha through his life and history. They do this simply by being there, and perhaps are best seen as allowing the Buddha through his "history" to participate with the monks and lay worshipers. The purpose is to make the Buddha's presence felt, his forms and teachings manifest. Indeed, the manifestation of the Buddha—in terms of his form, voice, and knowledge—are according to Andrew Rawlinson, the very essence of the Mahāyāna.[22] It is the vision of the Buddha (*buddha-darśana*), hearing his voice (*buddha-śabda*), and immersion in his knowledge (*buddha-jñāna*) that brings about "nothing less than direct contact with the Buddha."[23] Rawlinson makes it clear that the contact itself is sufficient to transform the worshiper, be it contact with the form of the Buddha or with the sound of his teaching: "forms (*rūpa*) display a truth just by being seen. They are thus just as much a language as the sounds which are encountered in *samādhi* and which transmit a truth just by being heard."[24] For our purposes, these notions (derived by Rawlinson from texts) fit with Schopen's conception of the Buddha image as a "living" Buddha in medieval Indian monasteries (derived by Schopen from inscriptions), and they support the point that "truth" can be realized instantly and spontaneously through physical contact with the Buddha. The painted and plastic imagery of the Buddha's past lives must have worked in this fashion to deliver the truth through contact with the worshiper. It is unlikely that the Ajaṇṭā *jātakas* were used as didactic devices by the monks, something like illustrated Sunday school texts, that were worked through episode by episode.

Thus the imagery was not "read," or even looked at in any logical or analytical fashion. This is not to say that we cannot learn from attempts to order the paintings, to identify the textual relationships, and so forth, or that the Ajaṇṭā artists and monks had no "logic" to the way they organized and chose the scenes. It is to say that they did not organize the paintings as a silent narrative.

Finally, we can return to the reliefs from Bhārhut and Sāñcī and ask what was their purpose, if we conclude that they were not there to produce a narration within the heads of the worshipers. For the reliefs on the Sāñcī gates, many of which are too high to be seen by the worshiper, there can really be no argument for their use to tell a story. We need not argue that the artist was uninterested in organizing the images in a coherent chronological narrative sequence (seen or otherwise), but I have already suggested that, although a portion of the chronological sequence of the departure scene (fig. 2) is indicated through continuous narration, there are "Indian" principles other than a chronological sequence that were used to organize the events of the story within the artistic space. In other words, a story can be told visually in ways not available to the verbal or textual telling. While a word text can move back or ahead in time, it must always keep the chronology of the events in the story manifest to avoid confusion. The visual text begins with the knowledge of the story.[25] In a sense, this frees the visual text to rearrange the events in the narrative, to make new connections that are not narrative in nature, to arrange the events by principles other than a telling through time. The artist can bring into the Sāñcī departure scene, for example, the *jambu* tree and the story of the first meditation, making a statement not found in any word text.[26]

The purpose of the relief depictions on the fence and gates of Bhārhut and Sāñcī must, I think, be seen in relation to the *stūpas* which they surround.[27] As with the Ajaṇṭā murals, the *jātaka* reliefs at Bhārhut and Sāñcī were intended to historicize and manifest the presence of the Buddha. The notion of manifestation of Hindu deities is widely accepted. Underlying the idea is that the deity is normally in an unmanifest form, and he or she takes a manifest form (as in an image) for the benefit of the worshiper.[28] In the context of the Hindu temple, the notion has been particularly used for Śaivite temples, as the *liṅga* in the central shrine (*garbhagṛha*) is Śiva's most unmanifest visual form that is then more specifically revealed in anthropomorphic images on the walls of the temple.[29] I believe that something similar is involved with the Buddha images. The *stūpa*, in its unmanifest nature at the center with the figurative representations on the surrounding gates and fences, at least suggests a relationship of unmanifest to manifest. The organization of Borobudur, discussed below, very strongly places the Buddha into a continuum of unmanifest to manifest, with the *stūpa* being the unmanifest and the anthropomorphic forms the manifest. How the manifestation of the Buddha and that of Hindu deities differs needs to be analyzed in detail, but in part the Buddha manifests himself in terms of a history, a biography (and this includes the *jātaka* tales) much more strongly than do the Hindu deities, who manifest themselves in mythic terms, often of a cosmic nature.

The Southeast Asian Monuments

I want to argue now along similar lines with regard to the depictions of the *jātaka* stories on four Southeast Asian monuments.[30] In each case the depiction of the *jātakas* is a significant part of the visual decoration, yet in no case were they intended to be read as stories. Indeed, in two instances the *jātaka* reliefs were not intended to be seen in any detail at all, reminding one of the inaccessibility of the Sāñcī gateway reliefs. The specific reason why the *jātakas* are depicted on the monuments and the way in which they are shown vary with each, as the *jātaka* representations did on the Indian monuments, yet they share the lack of a narrative intent (that is, the telling of a story) and any overriding didactic purpose. After discussing the Southeast Asian monuments, I will conclude by suggesting that these *jātaka* "pictures" function more as icons than as narrative illustrations, and ask how this may affect our view of the Buddha's sacred biography.

Chula Pathon Chedi, Thailand (ca. eighth century)

Chula Pathon Chedi[31] is located in Nakhon Pathom in Thailand. As Chula Pathon is called a *chedi* (P. *cetiya*, S. *caitya*), the assumption is that the monument is a *stūpa*, but it is unlike *stūpas* (as we shall see) in India.[32] It was first excavated by Pierre Dupont and Luang Boribal Buribhand in 1939 and 1940, and Dupont's discussion of it was published posthumously in 1959 in his book *L'archéologie Môṇe de Dvāravatī*.[33] Although Dupont recognized that the brick monument was built in several stages, he did not know that under the decoration on its base were covered reliefs of *jātakas*. These reliefs, in stucco and terracotta, were discovered accidentally in 1968 when a section of the monument was inadvertently bulldozed.

The Fine Arts Department undertook an excavation, but due to the broken and incomplete nature of the finds, many questions remain unanswered. My concern is to ask: What is the narrative nature of the reliefs, and second, how do they fit into the conception of the monument as a whole? The reliefs, each a panel placed in a shallow niche of about a square meter, are simple compositions with few figures depicted. Figure 5 is a typical example, showing a turtle on whose back ride two men. Piriya Krairiksh identifies the scene as the *Kacchapāvadāna*, in which the Buddha born as a turtle saves 500 merchants from drowning. His identification is based on comparison with similar depictions of this birth story in such distant places as

Figure 5. Buddha in birth as a turtle (Kacchapāvadāna). Stucco. From Chula Pathon Chedi (Thailand). The National Museum, Phra Pathom Cedi. (See fig. 6 for original placement.) (Photo: Robert L. Brown)

Borobudur (Java) and Kizil (Central Asia), examples that date from the ninth and the fourth/fifth centuries, respectively.[34] Although the significance of such comparisons can be variously interpreted, we know at least that because these various places participated in a shared Buddhist oral and textual tradition,[35] they also shared in an artistic tradition. This tradition involves the reduction of the narrative to a few figures, the turtle and just two (of the 500) merchants in the *Kacchapāvadāna* scene at Chula Pathon Chedi.

It is misleading, perhaps, even to describe it as a reduction of the narrative, as the narrative is clearly not the focus in these visual depictions. Such reductions of stories into a single scene are presumed to be like freezing a particularly significant or identifiable frame from a motion picture, so that the viewer (who has "seen" the film before) can recall the story both before and after the frozen frame. While Dehejia makes this assumption in her discussion of "monoscenic narratives" in Indian art, she interestingly divides the monoscenic narratives into "being in a state" and "being in action," categories borrowed from Meyer Schapiro.[36] Those scenes in action fit closely my analogy to a frozen frame of a motion picture. Dehejia says: "The monoscenic mode centers around a single event in a story, one that is generally neither the first nor the last, and which introduces the theme of action. Such a scene is usually an easily identifiable event from a story, and it serves as a reference to the narrative. . . . Monoscenic narratives must, of course, contain sufficient narrative content to stimulate the story-telling process in the mind of the observer."[37] In contrast, scenes in a state have "the narrative content . . . sharply reduced, and the reliefs represent scenes in which the action has already taken place." And, referencing Schapiro, she says that the "static depictions were regularly used in situations where theological concerns were predominant."[38] The examples she uses to illustrate the two types of monoscenic narratives in Buddhist art are very interesting, because those in action are all *jātakas* and those in a state are all Buddha's life stories. I wonder if the artistic organization in sculpted reliefs of the two categories of Buddha's biography, in which the life-scenes tend to have the Buddha (or his symbols) centralized, lends a static feeling to the life-scenes not found in the (usually) more snapshot-like *jātaka* scenes? I do not feel, in any regard, that there is more or less narrative content in the two types of monoscenic depictions, as neither attempts to create a narrative.[39] They certainly refer or relate to stories, but their recognition by the worshiper is not to allow them to be read but to make the monument meaningful by clearly manifesting the Buddha. Thus the answer to the first part of my question posed above (What is the narrative nature of the Chula Pathon Chedi *jātaka* reliefs?) is that they have little narrative function; they are not illustrations to a story. Rather, they are aspects of the Buddha's history or nature that are being recorded on the *chedi*.

Which brings up the second part of my question: How do the *jātaka* reliefs fit into the monument as a whole? Unfortunately, this is difficult to answer precisely. The panels were located around the base of the *chedi*, where there are a total of seventy-two niches for panels, of which forty-eight contained *jātaka* scenes (fig. 6). But less than half of the *jātaka* panels

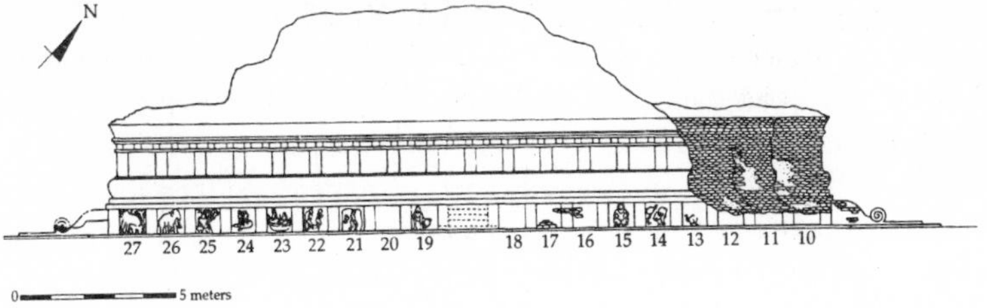

Figure 6. Chula Pathon Chedi, southeast face (Thailand). (Figure 5's original location is noted as 24.) (Drawing after Piriya Krairiksh, Buddhist Folk Tales Depicted at Chula Pathon Cedi *[Bangkok, 1974].)*

are extant, and many of these are fragmentary. Furthermore, the attempts to identify even those that are extant have not been entirely successful, and there are a number of other controversies regarding their dates and the ways in which they have been reconstructed.[40] And finally, the superstructure of the *chedi* itself is largely in ruins. There is not, therefore, sufficient information to piece together the identification, order, and organization of the *jātaka* panels and how they relate to the iconography of the rest of the monument.[41] Nevertheless, they are placed around the base, while the upper levels of the monument, although badly damaged, appear to have been a stepped or pyramidal structure with niches for images of the Buddha.[42] The significance of this (*jātakas* below or "first" with Buddha images above or "second") will come up again.

Borobudur, Java (late eighth–first half of the ninth centuries)

Borobudur dates perhaps a century later than Chula Pathon Chedi.[43] It is a much more elaborate monument than Chula Pathon Chedi and has been the focus of an enormous amount of scholarship, without, however, producing any consensus as to its meaning or use.[44] I want first to give my thoughts regarding a general organization that appears to have been at play at Borobudur, based on the manifestation of the Buddha that we have been discussing. It is within this framework that I place the Borobudur *jātaka* reliefs. I pose the same two questions I asked in regard to the Chula Pathon Chedi reliefs: What is the narrative nature of the *jātaka* reliefs, and how do they fit into the conception of the monument?

As at Chula Pathon Chedi, the Borobudur *jātaka* reliefs are placed around the base of the monument (fig. 7). They are not the lowest reliefs, this is true, but those that are "below" the *jātaka* reliefs are completely covered by an enormous stone foot and thus cannot be seen. The overall sculptural and architectural organization of Borobudur is extremely complicated, and some notion of this organization is needed to understand the meaning and nature of the *jātaka* illustrations. Borobudur is essentially a flat-topped pyramid with three circular terraces and a large, closed *stūpa* on top. Starting from the bottom, there is the added foot that covers the earlier base. This base was largely finished, with carved moldings and a series of relief panels, before being covered. Above the foot are four galleries. Access to these and then to the upper circular terraces is from four directional stairways. The four galleries make up the "steps" of the pyramid, with each gallery having an outer balustrade wall and an inner wall made up of the sides of the solid monument, with carved reliefs on both the inside of the balustrades and on the inner walls (which include the *jātaka* reliefs). There is no roof and the galleries are open to the sky. Decorating the outside of the balustrades at each level are Buddha images

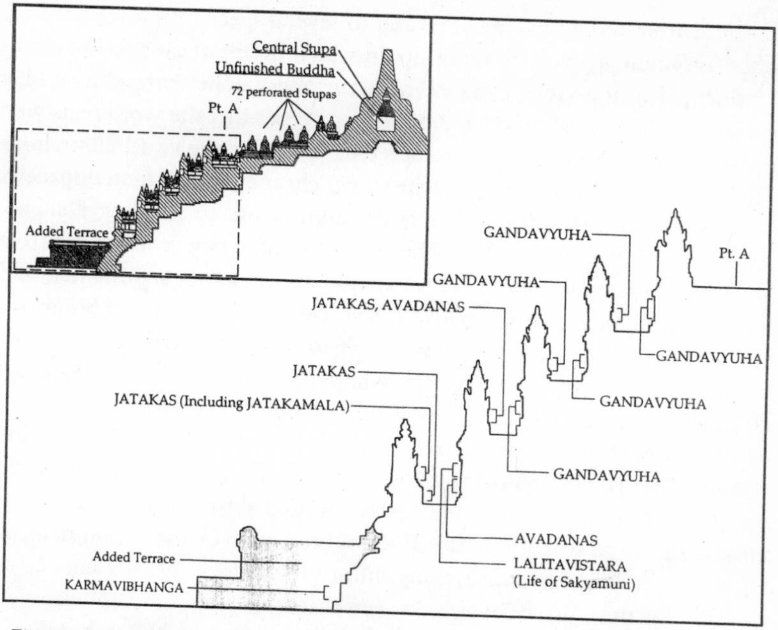

Figure 7. Borobudur, cross section (Indonesia). (Drawing after John Miksic, Borobudur: Golden Tales of the Buddha *[Boston, 1990].)*

and miniature *stūpas.* As there is a balustrade around the open area between the end of the top gallery and the first circular terrace, there are five balustrades altogether decorated with Buddha images and *stūpas.*

Thus one can circumambulate the monument in the four galleries and at four different levels. From the fourth and top gallery, one walks out into an area on which are located the three circular terraces and the central *stūpa.* Unlike in the galleries, a person is not enclosed on this top area; you can see all the circular terraces at once and the surrounding countryside. On these circular terraces are perforated *stūpas,* each containing a Buddha image. There are a total of seventy-two of these perforated *stūpas,* thirty-two on the lower terrace, twenty-four on the next, and sixteen on the top. Finally, centered at the top is the closed *stūpa,* which, however, is not solid. Within this *stūpa* originally was the famous unfinished Buddha image.[45]

The decoration of the monument can be organized into three categories: reliefs, *stūpas,* and Buddha images. The reliefs begin on the original base that is today covered. These covered reliefs consist of 160 panels and can be identified as illustrating the results of people's *karma,* that is, their actions that result in either good or bad situations, usually in a future life; thus the Buddha is not represented in them. These reliefs have long been identified as illustrating a specific Indian text, the *Karmavibhaṅga.* Indeed, the reliefs at Borobudur have been related to several specific Indian texts in an often astoundingly close relationship, in which details of the text are clearly represented in the visual image. The often one-to-one correspondence in details between visual image and word text argues that the word texts were used as sources that the artists attempted to "copy" in the visual illustrations. Furthermore, the reliefs often tell the stories chronologically in multipaneled formats. In sum, the Borobudur reliefs come close to fulfilling Dehejia's assumption that the visual should be read as if mimicking a verbal narrative.

It is important to pause here to reiterate that I am not arguing that such a visual telling of a verbal narrative never happened in the art of South and Southeast Asia.[46] I am restricting myself to *jātaka* illustrations on certain Buddhist architectural monuments, where such telling, although unusual, does exist (as here at Borobudur). What I am suggesting, rather, is that even when it does exist, it is not there to elicit a mental telling of the story in a viewer. That is, even when the visual images are organized to reflect the narrative nature of a verbal text (events related through time), the visual images are there to express the Buddhistic nature of the monument, to locate the Buddha and his teaching, not to tell a story. What evidence do we have for this? We have already seen that frequently the very elaborate and carefully produced images on the Indian monuments (the architraves of Sāñcī, the paintings at Ajaṇṭā) were not intended to be seen in any detail. Indeed, the *Karmavibhaṅga* reliefs at Borobudur bring home with stunning force the inability to see and read the visual images: they were covered over shortly after their installation and cannot be seen at all. The makers of Borobudur did not feel it necessary even to see the (detailed and text-specific[47]) reliefs for the proper functioning of the monument.

A possible Indian reference that helps explain the Borobudur *karma* reliefs can be found in Buddhaghosa's ca. fourth-century *Sārattha-pakāṣinī*:

> There are Brahmin sectaries whose general name is Nakha. They having a (movable or portable) picture-gallery made, roam about with it, exhibiting thereupon (apparently upon the outer faces of the four piece-boards serving as walls) the various kinds of representation of happy or woeful states of existence according to good or bad destinies, and causing the labels to be inscribed to the effect:
>
> "Having done this deed, one attains to this state."
>
> "Having done that, one attains to that state."
>
> Thus showing different destinies, they wander about with these pictures.[48]

The organization of these pictures, showing the positive or negative results of certain acts, is exactly that of the Borobudur reliefs, and the pictures' labels reflect the organization of the *Karmavibhanga* text. The wandering Nakha's exhibition of these *karma* pictures was, apparently, pitched toward a nonsectarian popular audience (that of the marketplace) and was how the showmen earned their living. The popular interest in how one's actions would manifest themselves in the future is reflected as well in the widespread Indian practice of showmen displaying pictures on cloth of the Brahmanical god of death, Yama, allotting rewards and punishments to people, according to their accumulated actions, upon their deaths. Mair traces these displays from Mauryan (ca. 323 to 185 B.C.E.) to modern times.[49] Mair also gives an eighth-century reference in a Jain context to a cloth scroll painting depicting the cycle of transmigration (*saṃsāra-cakra-paṭa*), which essentially deals with similar *karmic* issues.[50] In short, one's *karmic* destiny was of intense popular concern and was presented in visual narratives, probably because this made them vividly real. The *Karmavibhanga* reliefs of Borobudur appear to relate to this Indian visual tradition of *karmic* narratives. While there was some transference of such imagery onto Indian temples,[51] it was extremely limited and certainly not in the extensive fashion as at Borobudur. Yet, as I have said, the Borobudur reliefs were covered over, with no attempt to remove them first in order to display them elsewhere. We must conclude that the Borobudur *Karmavibhanga* panels were not intended to be the focus of a spoken or mental narrative, unlike the Indian painted cloth *karma* images.

Returning now to the organization of the reliefs at Borobudur, we move into the first gallery, where there are two rows of relief panels on both the inside of the balustrade and on the inner wall. The *jātaka* and *avadāna*[52] reliefs occupy the balustrade and the lower row (120 panels) on the inner wall. The upper 120 wall panels are scenes from the life of the Buddha and, as with the hidden base reliefs, are closely related to an Indian text, this time the *Lalitavistara*.[53] This text and the reliefs end with the Buddha's first sermon at Sārnāth. The *jātakas* and *avadānas* continue onto the balustrade of the second gallery, now with a single row of reliefs, but the remainder of the panels (488 panels) on both the walls and the balustrades of all the remaining galleries are devoted to illustrations related to a single Indian text, the *Gaṇḍavyūha* (and the attached *Bhadracarī*).[54] The large number of *Gaṇḍavyūha* reliefs alone indicates the importance of this text for Borobudur. The text tells the story of Sudhana, a merchant's son, who undertakes a search for spiritual wisdom. The search involves his interviewing a vast array of people and gods, and the reliefs usually show him seated before these different teachers, frequently bodhisattvas, talking to them in his pursuit of spiritual understanding. Sudhana ends his quest by interviewing the Bodhisattva Samantabhadra and reaching a region of spiritual attainment of that of a Buddha.

The other two categories of decoration, the Buddha images and the *stūpas*, can be considered together as they are organizationally and iconographically linked. Both decorate the outside of the five balustrades and can be seen from the ground before the monument, as well as when walking in the galleries. The Buddha images are set in niches, each niche being topped by three *stūpas*, with a single *stūpa* between each niche. The four galleries with their balustrades have on each side (and thus in one of the four cardinal directions) Buddha images performing the same gestures. Assuming the traditional naming, these Buddhas are:

Akṣobhya	East	*bhūmisparśamudrā* (earth-touching gesture)
Ratnasambhava	South	*varadamudrā* (boon-giving gesture)
Amitābha	West	*dhyanamudrā* (meditation gesture)
Amoghasiddhi	North	*abhayamudrā* (fear-not gesture)

There are ninety-two Buddhas on each side, with a total of 368 images. The top or fifth balustrade has sixty-four Buddha images (sixteen on a side), all of which perform the same gesture, that of exposition (*vitarkamudrā*). The identification of this Buddha is controversial, but following van Louhizen-de Leeuw,[55] I identify him as Samantabhadra, that is, the Buddha form of the bodhisattva from whom Sudhana in the reliefs of the top gallery took the vow of bodhisattvahood. The seventy-two perforated hollow *stūpas* on the three circular terraces each contain a seated Buddha making yet a sixth gesture, the turning of the wheel gesture (*dharmacakramudrā*), and can be identified as a sixth Buddha, Vairocana. Finally, the unfinished Buddha makes the earth-touching gesture, and as with the ninety-two earth-touching Buddhas in the eastern balustrade niches, could be Akṣobhya, although Śākyamuni Buddha is also, in my opinion, a (not mutually exclusive) possibility.[56]

With this organization of Borobudur in mind, we can ask how the notion of the Buddha's manifestation might help to explain it, and how the *jātaka* reliefs fit in. Borobudur as a manifestation of the Buddha was intended to bring the devotee to the Buddha and the Buddha to the devotee. The devotee is, like Sudhana, a pilgrim on a quest for spiritual truth. Each individual must begin by working himself or herself up, starting from this world of desires (represented on the monument on a level with the earth, but covered and left behind, just as it is actually left behind by the devotee). Then, by circumambulating the monument and moving upward, he or she first retraces the steps of Śākyamuni, participates with Śākyamuni in his past lives, then his last earthly life just to the point that Śākyamuni reaches Buddhahood and gives his first sermon. The sequence ends (as it does in the *Lalitavistara*) with the sermon and does not continue to recount the last forty years of Śākyamuni's life up until his death (*parinirvāṇa*). The last forty years were not essential to the devotee, because it was Śākyamuni's moment of Buddhahood and then sermon, the essential goal achieved and advice and teaching given, that the devotee must know. The devotee then goes beyond this, by retracing Sudhana's steps, participating with Sudhana on his quest, which involves apparently the devotee's own vow of bodhisattvahood, paralleling that of Sudhana.

Perhaps Samantabhadra's own transition from a bodhisattva to a Buddha is implied by the transition from the bodhisattva form depicted in the reliefs of the fourth gallery to the Samantabhadra Buddha images in *vitarkamudrā* just above in the niches of the top balustrade.[57] In any regard, a very high spiritual state is implied at the level of the top balustrade. At this level the devotee enters out onto the plane of the circular terraces, a world of perfected form. It is seen in terms of the Buddha image and, primarily, the *stūpa*. The perforated *stūpas* reveal but glimpses of the Buddhas inside. The two symbols are becoming one, with the closed *stūpa* on top "filled" with the unfinished Buddha image. The *stūpa* must represent the ultimate image of spiritual realization.

That the makers of Borobudur intended spiritual perfection to be seen in perfection of form is also seen in the use of geometric shapes. The perforations on the *stūpas* go from diamonds on the two lower terraces to squares on the top terrace. The closed *stūpa* is circular. We have diamond to square to circle, an apparent refinement of perfection in geometric shapes. Likewise, the circular terraces themselves show a similar geometric development. The two lower terraces are not exactly circular (as they are almost always incorrectly shown on drawings), but are like bulging squares with rounded corners. Only the top terrace is perfectly round, with the closed *stūpa* in the center. Thus in geometric forms the makers of Borobudur attempted to show a building toward a perfection and absolute indicated by a perfect circle.

But the manifestation of the Buddha is also shown in the opposite direction, downward from the absolute world of perfected form and spirituality to the world of humans. From the hidden and not fully created Buddha in the top *stūpa*, to the completed but only partially seen Buddhas in the perforated *stūpas*,[58] to the fully visible Buddhas of the balustrades, the Buddhas manifest themselves in ever easier to apprehend and more numerous forms for the benefit of the devotee on earth.

Most of these ideas are not new,[59] nor are they presented here as the only meaning of the monument, but they help us create a likely context for the *jātaka* reliefs. As with the *Karmavibhaṅga* reliefs, the *jātaka* reliefs at Borobudur can sometimes be clearly related to texts, but not in such a comprehensive fashion. Indeed, except for one text, Āryaśūra's fourth-century *Jātakamālā*, no other extant text has been identified as being used at Borobudur, and the *Jātakamālā* series is only thirty-four stories comprising 135 reliefs out of a total of 720 reliefs depicting *jātakas* and *avadānas*. Bernet Kempers says another twenty-five stories, comprising 136 reliefs, have been identified, leaving some 449 *jātaka* and *avadāna* reliefs (in fact, the majority of them) still unidentified.[60]

For our purposes, we need to ask if the reliefs were intended to be read as if they were a word text. The issue of being able to see the reliefs is, surprisingly, at play because the lower series of 120 panels on the inner wall of the first gallery is difficult to see clearly by a standing adult (the top of the panel comes to about 115 cm. from the floor), while the lower panels of the balustrade are impossible to see clearly without bending or kneeling down (the top of the panel comes to about 75 cm. from the floor) (fig. 8). How do we imagine these reliefs being used if we assume they are being read like a text? It is difficult to envision monks and pilgrims on their hands and knees, well-thumbed *jātaka* texts in hand, following the narrative of the lower balustrade reliefs.

If this seems unlikely, there is other evidence that the reliefs were not intended to be read. The one text thus far identified that is depicted among the *jātaka* reliefs is the *Jātakamālā*. As with the *Karmavibhaṅga*, one may read the *Jātakamālā* and follow the stories while looking at the reliefs.[61] But the number of reliefs dedicated to each of the thirty-four stories varies considerably, going from one relief for story 16 to eight for story 32 (see the table).[62]

In terms of the stories' lengths, story 16 is much shorter than story 32 (53 versus 184 lines), relating perhaps in some rough way "amount to be said" to number of panels. But story 32 is in no way the longest of the *Jātakamālā* stories. A glance at the chart shows that there are several stories of about the same length, and nine stories that are considerably longer.[64] One of the longest, story 22 with 358 lines, gets only four panels, the same number that the just prior story, 21, received with 145 lines of text, and that story 4 received with only 84 lines. The sheer length of the story needs not be the criterion used for choosing the amount of detail and number of panels shown in the visual depiction, although I cannot propose, after reading the stories along with viewing the panels, what criteria were used. Nevertheless, the lack of correspondence between the length of the text (in words) and the length of the images (in space) would force our hypothetical pilgrim, assuming he or she was "reading" the images (with the *Jātakamālā* in hand or head), to stand before some panels for a long period of time, while moving rapidly from panel to panel at other times. In short, the vision of people moving in fits and starts along gallery one, at times standing, at others bending, kneeling, or crawling, fits that of visiting modern tourists and scholars, but does not appear to fit that of monks and pilgrims in worship. I can best see the reliefs used by the worshiper as the (very differently organized) Ajaṇṭā paintings were, to manifest and make real the Buddha and his history for the worshiper, but who, in the context of Borobudur, was on his or her own parallel spiritual quest in what Sylvain Lévi calls "la prodigieuse gestation qui prépare un Bouddha."[65]

Figure 8. First gallery. (Compare figure's size and relation to rows of relief carvings, two rows on the inside wall and two on outer balustrade.) Borobudur (Indonesia). (Photo from A. J. Bernet Kempers, Ageless Borobudur *[Wassenaar: Servire, 1976].)*

Jātakamālān Reliefs. Ananda Temple, Pagan, Burma (ca. 1100 A.D.)

story no.	*no. of relief panels*	*no. of lines in Sanskrit text*[63]
1	4	132
2	5	201
3	5	105
4	4	84
5	4	120
6	2	152
7	3	182
8	7 (?)	268
9	4	393
10	4	145
11	4	77
12	1(?)	89
13	5	183
14	3	176
15	2	71
16	1	53
17	3	123
18	2	84
19	5	175
20	4 (?)	141
21	4	145
22	4	358
23	5	316
24	3	172
25	5	116
26	5	203
27	3	154
28	5	256
29	4	194
30	4	183
31	4	421
32	8	184
33	5	77
34	3	103
Total	134	

There remain two Southeast Asian *jātaka* series to discuss, both of which are major elements of architectural decoration. In the case of the Ananda Temple at Pagan, there are 912 small *jātaka* plaques of glazed terracotta on the temple, but they are situated on the roof with no access and are far too high up to be seen (except as small articulated squares) from the ground (fig. 9). In the case of the Sukhothai monument, Wat Si Chum, there are some 100 stone relief panels of *jātakas* embedded in the ceiling within an extremely narrow, almost completely dark, stairway of the mondop, making the reliefs very difficult, and at times impossible, to see clearly. In my discussion of the two series of *jātakas*, I want to suggest (briefly) how they fit into the significance of their respective monuments. But the point is already made that the series of *jātaka* images cannot be seen easily (Wat Si Chum) or at all (Ananda) and could not have been used for telling (mentally, orally, or textually) stories.

The Ananda Temple at Pagan was built by King Kyanzittha (r. 1084–1113 C.E.), probably around 1105.[66] It is perhaps the most well known of the literally thousands of temples at Pagan and is still in active worship today. It is often seen by modern scholars as something of a culmination of the Pagan artistic tradition, and it is usually tied directly to Kyanzittha in terms of his personality and professed ideology. As with most notions regarding Pagan, we must turn to the writings of Gordon Luce for the development of the Ananda. While I feel that much of what Luce suggests is helpful, I want nevertheless to argue against one of his fundamental assumptions regarding the Ananda and Kyanzittha's motivations in building it, which is that it was—above all—used to teach Buddhism to the unconverted masses.

Luce's notion that the Ananda was something of a giant textbook for use in proselytizing must be contextualized within his general interpretations of early Pagan Buddhism and monuments. He feels that the first Pagan kings—Aniruddha (r. ca. 1044–1077), Saw Lu (d. 1084), and Kyanzittha—were attempting to convert their subjects to Theravāda Buddhism, which had been brought to Burma from Ceylon, and that they used art to teach the people and to proselytize this new Sinhalese Buddhism. Aniruddha, already a Buddhist (but apparently of some type of Mahāyāna or Tantric Buddhism, reflecting the current Buddhism in eastern India[67]), spent much of his reign attempting to obtain copies of the texts of the Tipiṭaka and relics of the Buddha Śākyamuni. That Aniruddha was focused on these dual preeminently Theravādin concerns of texts written in Pāli and relics of the historical Buddha may seem strange, given his Mahāyāna background, and indeed this problem is never addressed by Luce. It is perhaps important to realize that the evidence for this focus is not really in question, although it comes primarily from later Theravādin chronicles and as such may be exaggerated.

Luce identifies the Pahtothamya Temple as the first monument at Pagan that reveals a knowledge of the Buddhist (Sinhalese) Tipiṭaka and, dating to ca. 1080, is when "the pendulum of purpose will swing from Devotion to Instruction."[68] Indeed, Luce finds the eleventh century a period of crisis for Buddhism in Southeast Asia, with Pagan one of the few

Figure 9. View of the Ananda Temple showing the jātaka plaques in rows on the levels of the roof. Pagan (Burma). (Photo: Robert L. Brown)

places remaining where Buddhism existed.[69] In such an atmosphere, it is King Kyanzittha who will unite Burma under the flag of Theravādin Buddhism by creating "mass religious enthusiasm"[70] through a program of teaching and proselytizing. The Pahtothamya is the earliest temple to be used for "Instruction," built just before Kyanzittha came to the throne, and has on its walls paintings with ink-glosses that are literally the texts made visible. There was undoubtedly an attempt to record carefully in visual form the Buddhist doctrine, but it is curious to me that Luce felt these were used for teaching. The paintings are almost entirely high up on the walls. Luce writes that "Climbing with difficulty these dark high coigns, Col. Ba Shin and I could do little but try and read the broken lines of frittered gloss."[71] Tottering on their ladders in the pitch darkness, it is surprising, perhaps, for them to conclude that the paintings were part of a didactic program.

The Ananda Temple is the culmination, according to Luce, of the interest in religious education begun in the Pahtothamya. The amount of visual imagery associated with the Ananda Temple is overwhelming. The *jātaka* plaques on the roof, visible only as rows of regular indentations from the ground, are a series of the Sinhalese recension of 547 *jātakas* arranged in two parts, the first 537 *jātakas* each depicted on an individual plaque and a second set, placed above the first on the roof, depicting in 375 plaques the last ten *jātakas*, the *Mahānipāta*. There is, in addition, a series of 552 plaques showing Māra's army and a procession of gods around the plinth of the temple.[72] Inside the temple, the sheer number of images is tremendous as well, with over 1,500 stone images and, although today they are white-washed, once extensive wall paintings. It will not surprise the reader to learn that many, if not most, of these stone images cannot be seen clearly, if at all (see fig. 10). But if Kyanzittha's motive was not to produce such detail and number to teach the ignorant and illiterate,[73] what might it have been?

While the question deserves careful and lengthy discussion, I want here at least to suggest an alternative to the didactic theory. Kyanzittha was concerned with the purity and completeness of the Buddhism he professed. Indeed, the power of Theravādin Buddhism lies in its accuracy and authenticity judged in its approximation to the Buddha, his teachings, and his monks. Although Kyanzittha certainly saw himself as teaching the Buddhist doctrine to his people, he was also, in his role as upholder of the Law, purifier and recorder of the doctrine: "(He) [Kyanzittha] shall purify (and) make straight, write down (and) establish all the Holy Scriptures. (He) shall proclaim (and) voice the Law, which is even as a resounding drum. (He) shall arouse all the people that are slumbering carelessly. (He) shall stand steadfast in the observance of the commandments at all times."[74] I think the Ananda Temple had to do with the goals of the first sentence of this excerpt from one of Kyanzittha's inscriptions: to purify, make straight, write down, and

Figure 10. Corridor in Ananda Temple with niches, reaching to the ceiling, in which stone sculptures are placed. Pagan (Burma). (Photo: Robert L. Brown)

establish. Kyanzittha was aiming toward completeness and correctness in the iconographical program of the Ananda. Just as having the complete Tipiṭaka in written form was important, not to be read but to be kept, so was having the Ananda as a complete visual form of the doctrine important.[75]

Kyanzittha's interest in completeness and correctness can be argued in several ways. For one, he undertook the extraordinary elaboration of the Śākyamuni Buddha iconography, as seen in the careful numbering and labeling of the *jātaka* plaques, so that a complete set is depicted, and then one must consider the incredibly detailed elaboration of the last ten *jātakas*. These *jātaka* plaques, each about thirty-five centimeters square, are very simply and repetitively organized, with from one to three figures, minimal props, and the Mon label and number across the bottom (fig. 11).[76] They

Figure 11. Jātaka plaque. Inscription reads "cūḷajanaka jāt 52." Ananda Temple, Pagan (Burma). (Photo and reading from Gordon H. Luce, Old Burma—Early Pagan [Locust Valley, N.Y., 1970].)

are, in other words, stripped of most narrative content and context and would, in most instances, be impossible to identify without the label.

This elaboration of iconography, coupled with the lack of narrative content, is true for the stone images inside the temple as well. Luce characterizes the stone reliefs in terms of Kyanzittha's personal taste, which included an insistence on symmetry, an emphasis on the figure of the Buddha with any identification of the narrative scantly placed in the predella, and a use of architectural and geometric backgrounds to lock the figures into place (fig. 12). Luce finds, however, that "though the total effect . . . may please, or even move the devout, it gets monotonous. If the architectural background forced some unity in design, it also numbed movement, life and action. . . . The tendency has been to petrify religious sculpture in a lifeless, hieratic groove."[77] Again, I wonder why Luce felt this type of petrified, lifeless sculpture (that he says may move the *devout*) would have been chosen in order to teach the ignorant. I feel that these formal characteristics may, instead, indicate Kyanzittha's desire to purify, make straight, write down, and establish the doctrine. They are an interesting attempt to use formal means to situate the iconography in strict, regular, clear formats, to lock in and regularize the imagery and its meaning so that it is, like the Tipiṭaka, the complete, correct, final, and here quite literally unshakeable (visual) doctrine.

Wat Si Chum, Sukhothai, Thailand (fourteenth century)

The plaques on the Ananda Temple are the most extensive depictions of the *jātakas* in Burmese architecture. The most extensive series in Thailand, used in conjunction with architecture, is at Wat Si Chum at Sukhothai. The Wat Si Chum series consists of some one hundred stone plaques enigmatically embedded in the ceiling of an extremely narrow tunnel-like passageway in the walls of the mondop that encloses a fifteen-meter-high Buddha image. One enters the passage to the left of the entrance into the mondop and then, by a series of stairways, goes up and around behind the huge Buddha image, and ends by emerging onto the roof on its left side (fig. 13). The narrowness of the tunnel (about fifty centimeters wide), the almost total lack of light, the panels' placement in the ceiling where they are very difficult to see, and the delicacy of the linear incised relief carving (see fig. 14) have led scholars to suggest that the plaques were not intended to be placed in the dark passage, but were at some point moved from another location and monument, one in which they could have been easily seen.[78] The mystery has then been to explain why they were placed in such an inaccessisble setting. Most scholars have followed George Coedès' suggestion that the plaques were placed in the

Figure 12. Śākyamuni standing between his horse and his groom. Stone. Ananda Temple, Pagan (Burma). (Photo: Robert L. Brown).

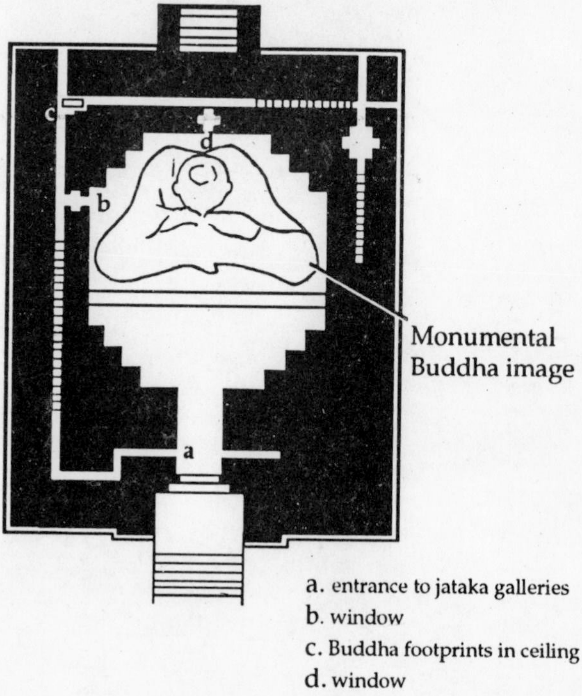

Figure 13. The galleries of the mondop, plan. Wat Si Chum, Sukhothai (Thailand). (Plan after Jean Boisselier, Thai Painting *[Tokyo, 1976].)*

passage for safekeeping.[79] Only Betty Gosling has argued that there was a doctrinal reason for "hiding" them, basically that *jātakas* became less acceptable to the increasingly orthodox Theravādin Buddhist in the second half of the fourteenth century.[80]

Both suggestions are based on the assumption that the panels were made to be displayed clearly, were then removed from their original site, and placed in the passage to be hidden, no longer seen, and no longer used. Based on the discussion in this essay, it may be that these are wrong assumptions, as we need not assume that the inaccessible areas were places art was not displayed and used. What use might the passage with the *jātakas* have had? There are two small windows that look out from the passage into the inside of the mondop (fig. 13 b and d). Window d is centered behind the neck of the Buddha image and was, it is thought, used to make the Buddha speak. That the Wat Si Chum Buddha could speak is still a legend in the area, and the small window would have allowed a monk to speak with the voice of the Buddha without being seen. The second window

Figure 14. Bhojājānia Jātaka. Stone. (enhanced) From Wat Si Chum, Sukhothai (Thailand). National Museum, Bangkok. (Photo from Jean Boisselier, Thai Painting *[Tokyo, 1976].)*

(b) could, I think, have been used by the monks to hear and see the worshiping petitioners below and in front of the image (see figure 15). The inside of the mondop would have been very dark with the now-lost wooden roof, and this second window, high up on the dark wall, would not have been seen from below, or perhaps was masked by cloth hangings.

However, if the monks wished merely to trick the devotees into believing that the Buddha could speak, it appears a rather overly elaborate physical arrangement. A ladder directly behind the image would have sufficed. Indeed, the doorway to the passage, which is very small (about 35 × 53 cm.), does not appear to be hidden, but comes directly off of the entrance into the mondop. In other words, the speaking Buddha may be linked to the passage and its *jātaka* decoration in an overt fashion.

The *jātaka* plaques are arranged in more or less the order of the Pāli text, we can at least say that the arrangement is not haphazard and is intended to follow the chronological order of the Buddha's past lives. Someone moving through the passage would be tracing these lives while also moving up, as at Borobudur. Indeed, each stair step is more or less coordinated with two panels above, and then the panels are set one after the other in the level passageways as well, as if marking the steps of the person walking below (fig. 16). This notion of (re)tracing the steps of the Buddha is, as I have argued elsewhere, a popular imagery during the Sukhothai period, with the footprints and images of the walking Buddha and his *bhiksus*.[81] That the imagery

Figure 15. Looking down from the small window inside the mondop (marked b on fig. 13) to the lap and area in front of the monumental Buddha image. Wat Si Chum, Sukhothai (Thailand). (Photo: Robert L. Brown)

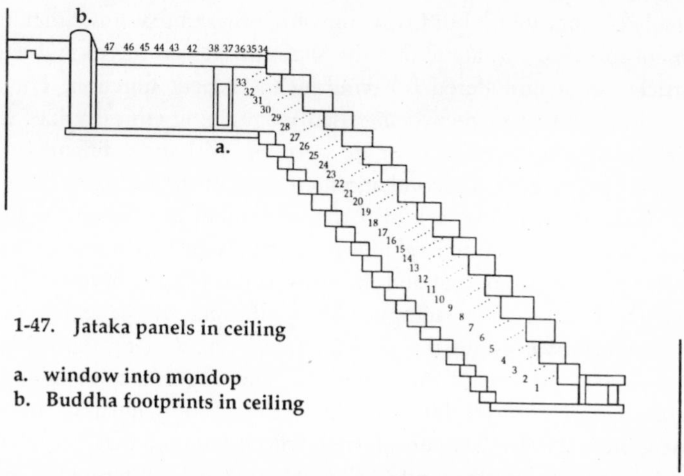

Figure 16. Figure 16. The southern gallery of the mondop, cross section. Wat Si Chum, Sukhothai (Thailand). (Plan after Jean Boisselier, Thai Painting *[Tokyo, 1976].)*

is intended to be seen with the Wat Si Chum *jātaka* plaques is supported by the actual implantation of the Buddha's footprints in the ceiling among the panels (fig. 13 c). It appears to me, therefore, that a monk walking through the passage was on a spiritual journey, one that may have prepared him (among other things) to speak authoritatively and authentically for the Buddha.

Conclusion

Before making some final comments on the narrative functioning as icons, I want briefly to bring up the issue of the didactic purpose of the *jātaka* images we have discussed. That the *jātaka* stories were (and are) used for teaching Buddhist moral and ethical values and lessons has been stressed by many scholars. Almost one hundred years ago Max Müller advised us "to look upon these Birth-stories as homilies used for educational purposes and for inculcating the moral lessons of Buddhism."[82] The stories' often didactic purpose cannot be denied, but the assumption that images of the *jātakas* have a similar purpose is not at all clear. Religious visual imagery is often regarded from the dual commonsense view that "a picture is worth a thousand words" and that a visual image is more accessible to the uneducated masses than the word text. The *jātaka* images seem to fit the didactic purpose so perfectly: the narratives are teaching morals that the images make immediately accessible to the (uneducated) pilgrim. The issues raised are in reality extremely complicated,[83] but I want only to point out that it is difficult after the discussion above to argue that the *jātaka* images on the monuments in this article can be considered as having such a didactic function. The most obvious impediment to their being used for teaching ethical values is that they frequently cannot be seen, or are seen only with great difficulty.

There is, however, a second argument against their didactic function, which has to do with the lack of narrative content of most of the images we have discussed. A moral value can be expressed in a narrative in two ways, in terms of its content and in terms of the process of its telling and hearing (or writing and reading). The significance of content is usually fairly straightforward, and the *jātakas* often even sum up explicitly the moral lesson at the end of the narratives. The importance of telling and hearing a narrative for teaching morality is perhaps less apparent, but I am following such scholars as Lynne Tirrell, who has argued that "storytelling, because of its narrative structure, is an aid to moral epistemology and so moral development. It is not the product [i.e., content], but rather the *process* of articulation that is of the first significance."[84] In both content and process the narrative nature of the *jātaka* images (and visual images as a whole) differ from that of word narratives. Images do not "tell" stories. As I have said, the story or narrative must be known if the images illustrating the story are to make sense (at least in terms of the word story). There is no way anyone could ever, even after seeing all the visual depictions extant of any particular *jātaka* story, be able to tell what the names of the characters are, what their exact relationships are, the exact sequence of their interactions, and the sometimes surprising moral point being made,[85] without having read the text or heard the story; in other words, no one could look at the images and sit down and write a story that would be close to the actual word text. In order for the image to be "an aid to moral epistemology and so moral development," it would have to function as Dehejia has suggested, as a switch to turn on the word narrative in the viewer's head. If this is accurate, the image is, except for the initial reminder, completely extraneous to the process. As I do not believe this is what took place between image and worshiper, I do not feel the images were intended to teach Buddhist morality.

The term *icon* is loaded with implications. I intend it in a specifically Indic religious sense, simply as a form of the deity that is the focus of reverence and worship.[86] The form here is highly diverse. Although we tend to think of it in terms of an image, it has a much broader and inclusive meaning because of the notion that deities can manifest themselves in a variety of forms. This is most apparent with Hindu deities, but the concept of manifestation is, as I have said above, seen in Buddhism as well.

Daniel Boucher speaks of "one of the ongoing struggles within the Buddhist tradition: to maintain the presence of the all-too-absent Buddha."[87] He continues: "the Buddhist tradition has since the death of the Buddha, or perhaps more precisely, because of the death of the Buddha, wrestled between two tendencies: to locate the Buddha in his corporeal body, especially as left behind in his relics; or to locate the 'true' Buddha in the *dharma*, his teachings."[88] Boucher places this struggle between the cults of the *stūpa*/relic and the *dharma*. He shows that the *dharma*, essentialized in the *pratityasamutpādagāthā* and further shortened to a four-line verse (the often-called Buddhist creed),[89] becomes in medieval India "synthesized" with the *stūpa*/relic presence of the Buddha. But whether in terms of the *stūpa*/relic or the *dharma*, both are to identify and locate the Buddha for the worshiper. Boucher's discussion is of particular interest for us because it illustrates a process by which the *dharma* (given in words) has become iconized, reduced to a short formula that can easily be inscribed (made into an object) and worshiped, one which "became a manifestation of the Buddha's real presence at cultic centers . . . in the same way as relics were thought to infuse the living presence of the Buddha in *stūpas*."[90] We have thus the manifestation of the Buddha in an image composed of a brief verse, a verse that refers to a much longer word text, and ultimately to the complete teachings (*dharma*) of the Buddha. The *jātaka* illustrations we have been discussing are iconized word texts similar in some ways to the iconized *dharma*. Both are visual images;[91] both are references to (longer) word texts; both are placed within the context of the Buddha's biography; both are used in conjunction with architectural monuments;[92] and both manifest the presence of the Buddha. Even such an obvious difference between these images of the Buddha as that one is in words and one is in plastic figural forms is blurred in the examples of the *jātakas* from Pagan, where the naming and numbering are often given equal weight to the plastic figures.[93]

The relationships between word text and plastic image are central to my discussion. I have shown that the *jātaka* illustrations on the monuments I have discussed cannot be considered merely illustrations of a word text; they are not reminders to start a mental telling of what is (considered by scholars as) really important, the narrative stated in words; and they were not used to teach others. Rather, the examples I have discussed, however varied they are artistically, all share meanings and uses rooted in the context of the monuments with which they are associated. In other words, although other scholars have sought the meaning of the *jātaka* illustrations in the context of the word texts, I believe it is found in the context of the monuments.

Considered in these terms, the *jātakas* on the monuments worked as icons, units of meaning and reverence, expressions of an aspect of the Buddha's nature and life that is (more) fully expressed by the entire monument. One might say that a story is being told on these monuments, but it is told in a different way than through a narrative as read from a word text. It is told in terms of the presence of the Buddha, his manifestation being produced through a visual (re)presentation of his history. Although his biography is being "told," it is not in terms of a "heard" imagery, but through the worshiper's physical encounter with the monument as part of what Gustav Roth calls "the habit to be near the physical presence of the Buddha, and to look at his body."[94] I believe that the Buddha has a visual biography, but it must be judged in terms separate from those used for his textual biography.

Notes

1. Vidya Dehejia, "On Modes of Visual Narration in Early Buddhist Art," *The Art Bulletin* 72, no. 3 (September 1990), pp. 374–392. Because I use Dehejia's paper only to contrast with my own views, I do not discuss here those aspects of her argument with which I agree. In spite of my disagreements, I feel that her paper is an important contribution toward organizing the narrative sculpture.
2. Monoscenic narrative is when only a single narrative event is used to identify the entire story; synoptic narrative is when "multiple episodes from a story are depicted within a single frame, but their temporal sequence is not communicated with regard to either causality or temporality" [ibid., p. 382]; and conflated narrative is similar to synoptic except that rather than the protagonist being repeated, the protagonist is conflated into a single figure in the scene.
3. Ibid., pp. 380–381.
4. It is not clear to me why the Śrāvasti miracle would be more easily identifiable than the Indra's Heaven scene.
5. Dehejia, "On Modes of Visual Narration in Early Buddhist Art," pp. 385–386.
6. Ibid., p. 386. Likewise, the departure relief she has just discussed, and which I discuss above in the text, would not hold for her theory, as the action is predominantly left to right, whereas the circumambulating worshiper would be reading it from right to left.
7. Ibid., p. 374.
8. Ibid., p. 378.
9. The Pāli *Vessantara Jātaka* runs to about one-hundred pages in the English translation. To tell this story mentally in any detail would take a very long time indeed. For the English translation, see Margaret Cone and Richard F. Gombrich, *The Perfect Generosity of Prince Vessantara* (Oxford: Oxford University Press, 1977).
10. Dehejia, "On Modes of Visual Narration in Early Buddhist Art," p. 388.
11. Ibid., p. 390.

12. Ibid., p. 392. The quotation is from Richard Brilliant, *Visual Narratives: Storytelling in Roman and Etruscan Art* (Ithaca: Cornell University Press, 1984), p. 63.
13. V. V. Mirashi, *Inscriptions of the Vākāṭakas, Corpus Inscriptionum Indicarum,* vol. 5 (Ootacamund: Government Epigraphist for India, 1963), p. 111.
14. "*[ni]veśitābh yantaracaityamandiram*" (ibid., p. 109, verse 20).
15. See Walter M. Spink, "Ajaṇṭā's Chronology: The Crucial Cave," *Ars Orientalis* 10 (1975), pp. 143–170, for a discussion of Cave 16 and illustrations.
16. See ibid., text fig. 1, for ground plans.
17. Ibid., p. 166.
18. See Sheila L. Weiner, *Ajaṇṭā: Its Place in Buddhist Art* (Berkeley: University of California Press, 1977), pp. 57–63.
19. Of the twenty-three Mahāyāna caves (that is, fifth-century caves) at Ajaṇṭā, only two are *caitya* halls.
20. The development of the Buddha image within the shrine in fifth- and sixth-century Buddhist caves can be traced from their appearance (as in Cave 16) in the center of the cell so that the image can be circumambulated, to being placed against the back wall of the shrine, to being moved along with the entire shrine into the center of the *vihāra* itself. That lay people worshiped the image is indicated most graphically by the placement of stone lay "donors" in eternal adoration before the image, perhaps most impressively in Cave 3 at Aurangabad.
21. Gregory Schopen, "The Buddha as an Owner of Property and Permanent Resident in Medieval Indian Monasteries," *Journal of Indian Philosophy* 18 (1990), pp. 181–217.
22. Andrew Rawlinson, "Visions and Symbols in the Mahāyāna," in *Perspectives on Indian Religion: Papers in Honour of Karel Werner*, ed. Peter Connolly (Delhi: Sri Satguru Publications, 1986), pp. 191–214.
23. Ibid., p. 191.
24. Ibid., p. 204.
25. Dehejia also argues that there has to be a knowledge of the story in order to read the image, but she confines the visual merely to reminding the viewer of this remembered narrative, to acting like a switch to turn on the mental recording.
26. The association of the first meditation under the *jambu* tree with the departure occurs in other examples in the art of India. It appears, for example, in a third-century C.E. relief fragment from Andhra Pradesh now in the Los Angeles County Museum of Art (see Pratapaditya Pal, *Indian Sculpture* [Los Angeles: Los Angeles County Museum of Art, 1986], vol. 1, pp. 205–206, fig. S82) and in a second Andhra example now in the British Museum (see *Masterpieces of Buddhist and Hindu Sculpture from the British Museum* [n.p.: The British Museum, Asahi Shimbun, 1994], no. 7).
27. The fence and single remaining gate at Bhārhut have been removed from the site and are now mostly in the Indian Museum, Calcutta.

28. Precisely what this manifestation entailed is, however, subject to a variety of interpretations, focusing on whether the image is considered the deity or is a symbol of the deity. See Richard Davis, "Enlivening Images: The Śaiva Rite of Invocation," in *Shastric Traditions in Indian Arts*, ed. Anna Libera Dallapiccola (Stuttgart: Steiner Verlag Wiesbaden 1989), vol. 1, pp. 351–359.

29. Stella Kramrisch may be the writer who has argued this dynamic most influentially. See, for example, her discussion of the Śaiva cave at Elephanta in *The Presence of Śiva* (Princeton: Princeton University Press, 1981), pp. 443–468. Compare Richard Davis: "Because in form the liṅga is without parts (*niṣkala*), it is the most appropriate support for Śiva in his highest, encompassing, undifferentiated aspect. This aspect of Śiva is similarly non-partitive, with the most human-like bronze images of Śiva, with parts (*sakala*), correspond to the encompassed, differentiated manifestations of Śiva as he has acted on earth" ("Loss and Recovery of Ritual Self Among Hindu Images," *Journal of Ritual Studies* 6, no. 1 [Winter 1992], pp. 49–50).

30. These four monuments were chosen primarily because they are among those with the most extensive representations of *jātaka* stories. Certainly other monuments could be added, particularly the many *stūpas* in Burma that include *jātaka* representations, but this would involve a much too lengthy essay. The four monuments I discuss are Chula Pathon Chedi (Thailand), Borobudur (Indonesia), Ananda Temple (Burma), and Wat Si Chum (Thailand).

31. The monument is also called Wat Pra Pathon.

32. *Cetiya* appears to be the Pāli word-equivalent for *stūpa*. See Gregory Schopen, "The Stūpa Cult and the Extant Pāli Vinaya," *Journal of the Pāli Text Society* 13 (1989), pp. 83–100.

33. Pierre Dupont, *L'archéologie Mône de Dvāravatī* (Paris: École française d'Extrême-Orient, 1959), pp. 65–98.

34. I am using the dating (earlier than the traditional dating) proposed by Angela F. Howard, "In Support of a New Chronology for the Kizil Mural Paintings," *Archives of Asian Art* 44 (1991), pp. 68–83.

35. The case of the *Kacchapāvadāna* is particularly intriguing, as this particular *jātaka* occurs only in one extant collection in Sanskrit, which is unlike most *jātakas* that occur in a variety of textual sources, thus arguing for some specific connection. See Jan Fontein, "Notes on the *Jātakas* and *Avadānas* of Barabuḍur," in *Barabuḍur: History and Significance of a Buddhist Monument*, ed. Luis O. Gómez and Hiram Woodward, Jr. (Berkeley: Asian Humanities Press, 1981), p. 101.

36. Dehejia, "On Modes of Visual Narration in Early Buddhist Art," pp. 378–382.

37. Ibid., p. 378.

38. Ibid., p. 380.

39. Word texts tell the story themselves. They may have illustrations included in the actual physical text, and often do in the Indian tradition, but these illustrations relate to the text in a number of complicated ways that must

be looked at in the context of each specific text. We are not dealing with these examples here, however, as I am speaking of images on monuments, which are not included within written texts.

I am not arguing that visual images are never used in the telling of stories. They are, of course, but the examples of which I am aware are paintings or drawings used in oral tellings or in conjunction with written texts. The images in the context of monuments that I am discussing *could* be used as props for telling the story, and undoubtedly were used as such at times, just as today the *jātaka* and life story reliefs at Borabudur are used by the many local Muslim guides to tell tourists the biography of the Buddha. I cannot argue categorically that monks were not doing exactly the same thing with pilgrims at Borobudur in the ninth century C.E., although I doubt it (as I will elaborate below). Nevertheless, my point is that the *jātaka* images on the monuments discussed here were part of an overall schema that empowered the entire monument with the Buddha's presence, and only make sense in that context.

40. Articles in which these issues are discussed, presented in chronological order, include: Jean Boisselier, "Récentes recherches à Nakhon Pathom," *Journal of the Siam Society* 58, part 2 (July 1970), pp. 55–65; Piriya Krairiksh, *Buddhist Folk Tales Depicted at Chula Pathon Cedi* (Bangkok: privately published, 1974) (text in Thai and English); M. C. Subhadradis Diskul, "Porāṇgatī-Vicāraṇa," *Archaeology* 5, no. 3 (August 1974), pp. 315–320 (in Thai); and Nandana Chutiwongs, "On the Jātaka Reliefs at Cula Pathon Cetiya," review of Piriya Krairiksh, *Buddhist Folk Tales Depicted at Chula Pathon Cedi*, in *Journal of the Siam Society* 66, part 1 (January 1978), pp. 133–151.

41. Jan Fontein has pointed out that the total number of possible *jātaka* panels at Chula Pathon Chedi (48) is the same as the number of *jātakas* at the Choir Cave at Kizil, which "suggests the possibility that there existed in the kingdom of Dvāravatī a *jātaka* collection very similar to that which was illustrated at Qyzil" (Fontein, "Notes on the *Jātakas* and *Avadānas* of Barabuḍur," p. 101. But compare Chutiwongs, "On the Jātaka Reliefs at Cula Pathon Cetiya," p. 141). Piriya Krairiksh has suggested that the additional twenty-four panels on the base (out of the total of seventy-two)—that apparently contained images of elephants, lions, and several mythical creatures—are there to suggest the *chedi*'s symbolism as Mount Sumeru, although he makes no attempt to integrate the *jātaka* panels into this imagery (Krairiksh, *Buddhist Folk Tales Depicted at Chula Pathon Cedi*, pp. 11–12 [in Thai] and p. 7 [in English]).

42. See Dupont, *L'archéologie Mône de Dvāravatī*, for possible reconstruction of the superstructure.

43. While the date of Borobudur is generally agreed upon by scholars, the date of Chula Pathon Chedi is less certain, complicated by the fact that there were several rebuildings of the *chedi*, one of which, of course,

involved the covering up of the *jātaka* reliefs. The *jātaka* reliefs were part of the initial stage of the monument, and date, in my opinion, roughly to the eighth century. See discussions in the references cited in note 40 above.

44. See my comments in Robert L. Brown, "Recent Stūpa Literature: A Review Article," *Journal of Asian History* 20 (1986), pp. 223–228. For bibliographies on Borobudur, see N. J. Krom, *Barabuḍur: Archaeological Description* (The Hague: Martinus Nijhoff, 1927); and Gómez and Woodward, *Barabuḍur: History and Significance of a Buddhist Monument.*

45. The image, after years sitting under a large tree at ground level (perhaps reflecting the acceptance of its not being originally in the solid *stūpa*), has been moved to the new site museum (perhaps reflecting its acceptance as original). It has been the focus of extensive debate as to whether it was or was not originally in the central *stūpa*. J. E. van Lohuizen-de Leeuw has argued, convincingly to me, for its originality in "The Dhyāni-Buddhas of Barabuḍur," *Bijdragen tot de Taal-, Land- en Volkenkunde* 121 (1965), pp. 389–416.

46. For example, it is clear that portable paintings were used as props for story-telling in ancient India and Southeast Asia. The best introduction to this topic is Victor H. Mair, *Painting and Performance: Chinese Picture Recitation and Its Indian Genesis* (Honolulu: University of Hawai Press, 1988). One point that comes out of reading Mair, however, is that the storyteller in the Indian context, with few exceptions, was considered socially inferior, ranked with entertainers such as dancers, singers, mimes, wrestlers, conjurors—individuals Mair would call showmen. The purpose of the pictures and stories was entertainment, and they seem in this regard far from the supposed revered images on the Buddhist monuments we have been discussing. Nevertheless, what the audience found in the paintings may tie them to the monument images.

47. Jan Fontein says "the first 85 reliefs of the *Karmavibhaṅga* series represent, in all probability, the most meticulous and detailed, word-for-word illustration of a text in the entire Buddhist world" (Jan Fontein, *The Law of Cause and Effect in Ancient Java* [Amsterdam: n.p., 1989], p. 75).

48. Quoted in Mair, *Painting and Performance*, p. 33.

49. Ibid., pp. 25–26. The significance of the Yama depictions within this picture-telling tradition is reflected in contemporary Bengal, where the picture scrolls, painted today on paper, often end with a depiction of Yama, no matter what the story being told, and have the storyteller sing: "Oh hearken you sinners! The righteous will be led to heaven by the messengers of Krishna, but the sinners will be dragged to hell by the messengers of Yama (Death), who will punish them for their misdeeds. They will push an adulteress down a spiky date palm; force a man who has refused drinking water to another to drink out of a cesspool; pull the tongues out of the mouths of liars and dissemblers and those who fail to sing the name of God. God's name cleanses all sin" (K. G. Subramanyan,

"The Comic-strip of the Bengal Village," in *India* [Bangkok: Media Transasia, 1985], p. 50).

50. Mair, *Painting and Performance*, pp. 28–29.

51. I am thinking specifically of the Buddhist *bhavacakra* painted in the veranda of Ajaṇṭā Cave 17, which appears to relate (in theme but not format) to the Jain *saṃsāra-cakra-paṭa* mentioned in the text; see Jean Przyluski, "La Roue de la Vie à Ajaṇṭā," *Journal Asiatique* 16, no. 2 (October–December 1920), pp. 313–331.

52. *Avadānas* are stories of previous births that include individuals other than the Buddha, but they function like *jātakas* and need not be differentiated for our purposes.

53. See N. J. Krom, *The Life of Buddha on the Stūpa of Barabuḍur according to the Lalitavistara* (The Hague: Marinus Mijhoff, 1926).

54. See Jan Fontein, *The Pilgrimage of Sudhana: A Study of Gaṇḍavyūha Illustrations in China, Japan and Java* (The Hague: Mouton, 1967).

55. van Louhizen-de Leeuw, "The Dhyāni Buddhas of Barabuḍur."

56. A similarly incomplete Buddha image in the earth-touching gesture, identified as Śākyamuni, was the primary icon according to myths at Bodhgaya in India. See Robert L. Brown, "Bodhgaya and South-East Asia," in *Bodhgaya: The Site of Enlightenment*, ed. Janice Leoshko (Bombay: Marg, 1988), pp. 118–119.

57. The identification of the *vitarkamudrā* Buddha as Samantabhadra is, however, only a possibility. The problem is that Samantabhadra as a supreme Buddha (Ādibuddha) is represented in art, as far as I know, in royal garb only.

58. The *stūpas* here are literally dissolving to reveal the fully formed Buddhas, while the two, Buddha and *stūpa*, will be placed side by side on the balustrades.

59. Studying Borobudur, one has the particular frustration of discovering in subsequent readings that an ("original") insight has already been suggested. The biblography is too extensive even to begin to reference here these various ideas, but A. J. Bernet Kempers has discussed Borobudur in the framework of a similar overall conception: "The major mystery expressed in Barabuḍur . . . is the meeting of the Holy and Mankind, enacted by the descent of the Holy—of Ultimate Reality, Totality—and the ascent of Man" (A. J. Bernet Kempers, "Barabuḍur: A Buddhist Mystery in Stone," in *Barabuḍur: History and Significance of a Buddhist Monument*, ed. Gómez and Woodward, p. 112); see also his *Ageless Borobudur* (Wassenaar: Servire, 1976).

60. Bernet Kempers, "Barabuḍur: A Buddhist Mystery in Stone," p. 107.

61. See Krom's *Barabuḍur: Archaeological Description* for illustrations.

62. The *Jātakamālā* has been translated into English. See J. S. Speyer, *The Jātakamālā or Garland of Birth-Stories of Āryaśūra*, Sacred Books of the Buddhists, vol. I (London: Henry Frowde, 1895; reprint: Delhi: Motilal Banarsidass, 1982); and Peter Khoroche, *Once the Buddha Was a Monkey: Ārya Śūra's Jātakamālā* (Chicago: University of Chicago Press, 1989).

63. I am using Hendrik Kern's edition published in the Harvard Oriental Series, vol. I: *The Jātaka-Mālā or Bodhisattvāvadāna-Mālā by Ārya-Śūra* (Cambridge, Mass.: Harvard University, 1891).
64. Stories 2, 8, 9, 22, 23, 26, 28, 29, and 31.
65. Sylvain Lévi, "Les Jātaka: Étapes du Bouddha sur la Voie des Transmigrations," in *Mémorial Sylvain Lévi* (Paris: Paul Hartmann, 1937), p. 39.
66. In truth, that Kyanzittha built the Ananda Temple is not stated overtly in any inscriptons, but is based largely on art historical arguments, although there seems little doubt that he was its patron.
67. His interest in Mahāyāna Buddhism, for example, is shown by his preference for Lokanatha.
68. Gordon H. Luce, *Old Burma—Early Pagan* (Locust Valley, N.Y.: J. J. Augustin, 1970), vol. 1, p. 304. See also his references on pp. 9, 26, 49, and 62.
69. Ibid., p. 27.
70. Ibid., p. 64.
71. Ibid., p. 309.
72. The actual number of plaques is confusing to determine from the published sources. Just a survey of three authors (Shorto, Strachan, and Luce) produces these descrepancies (in fact, Luce offers different counts in the same source) as to numbers of plaques in the three series (H. L. Shorto, "The *Devatā* Plaques on the Ananda Basement," in *Essays Offered to G. H. Luce by His Colleagues and Friends in Honour of His Seventy-fifth Birthday*, vol. 2 [Ascona: Artibus Asiae, 1966], pp. 156–165; Paul Strachan, *Pagan: Art and Architecture of Old Burma* [Whiting Bay: Kiscadale, 1989]; and Luce, *Old Burma—Early Pagan*:

	plinth (Māra's army)	*roof (numbered jātakas)*	*roof (Mahānipāta)*	*total*
Shorto	552	537	389	1,478
Strachan	554	537	375	1,466
Luce (p. 79)	552	532*	375	1,459
Luce (p. 359)	552	537	375	1,464

*(I assume this is a typographical error.)

73. Luce writes that Kyanzittha "was a devotee of Buddhism. But he knew that his common people, still illiterate and animist, were only skin-deep Buddhists. Many passages in his inscriptions prove that both he and his *mahāthera Arahan* made popular religious education their prime concern" (*Old Burma—Early Pagan*, p. 381).
74. *Epigraphia Birmanica*, vol. 2, part 2, p. 141.
75. It is perhaps the history of the Emerald Buddha, now in Bangkok, with its various chronicles and stories that traces best the complementarity of the

written and visual forms, and the necessity of having them kept together. Remember that it was Aniruddha who instigated the travels of the Emerald Buddha from Ceylon along with a full set of the Tipiṭaka. See Frank Reynolds, "The Holy Emerald Jewel: Some Aspects of Buddhist Symbolism and Political Legitimation in Thailand and Laos," in *Religion and Legitimation of Power in Thailand, Laos, and Burma*, ed. Bardwell L. Smith (Chambersburg, Penn.: Anima, 1978), pp. 175–193.

76. The size of the plaques actually decreases as they go up, increasing the illusion of the temple's height when seen from the ground. The numbers on the plaques cease at 754, with those of the final three *jātakas* without numbers. The *Mahānipāta* plaques are discussed and illustrated in *Epigraphia Birmanica*, vol. 2, parts 1 and 2 (by Charles Duroiselle, they are separately titled *The Taliang Plaques on the Ananda*).

77. Luce, *Old Burma—Early Pagan*, p. 364.

78. The only scholar I know who has suggested that the plaques were made for the site is Jean Boisselier, although his suggestion is very brief, just a few sentences, and without any argument. See Jean Boisselier, "Récentes recherches archéologiques en Thailande," *Arts Asiatiques* 12 (1965), p. 128; and Jean Boisselier, *Thai Painting* (Tokyo: Kodansha, 1976), p. 75.

79. George Coedès, *Recueil des Inscriptions du Siam. Première partie: Inscriptions du Sukhodaya* (Bangkok: Bangkok Times Press, 1924), p. 177.

80. Betty Gosling, "Why Were the *Jātakas* 'Hidden Away' at Wat Sīchum?" *Journal of the Siam Society* 72, parts 1 and 2 (1984), pp. 14–18. Also see Betty Gosling, "Once More, Inscription II—An Art Historian's View," *Journal of the Siam Society* 69, parts 1 and 2 (1981), pp. 13–42; Michael Wright, "Note on Betty Gosling's Article: Why Were the Jātakas 'Hidden Away' at Wat Si Chum?" *Journal of the Siam Society* 73, parts 1 and 2 (1985), pp. 226–234; and Betty Gosling, "Betty Golsing's Reply to Michael Wright's Note 'Why Were the *Jātakas* 'Hidden Away' at Wat Sī Chum?' " *Journal of the Siam Society* 74 (1986), pp. 199–206.

81. Robert L. Brown, "God on Earth: The Walking Buddha in the Art of South and Southeast Asia," *Artibus Asiae* 50, nos. 1 and 2 (1990), pp. 73–107.

82. In the editor's preface to Speyer, *The Jātakamālā or Garland of Birth-Stories of Āryaśūra*, p. xiii.

83. The literature discussing the two notions is extensive, although it deals almost exclusively with Western art.

84. Lynne Tirrell, "Storytelling and Moral Agency," *The Journal of Aesthetics and Art Criticism* 48, no. 2 (Spring 1990), p. 118 (emphasis in original).

85. These points come at the end of the story and often, at least to me, seem extremely contrived with little relation to the narrative.

86. I perhaps should bring up the terms *iconic* and *aniconic* used by Indian art historians, particularly in writing about the early Buddhist art of India, as my use of *icon* here is not intended to relate to this dialectic. In Indian art historical scholarship, the terms *iconic* and *aniconic* are used to indicate the

presence (iconic representation) or absence (aniconic representation) of the anthropomorphic image of the deity. Although aniconic art can mean in art-historical writing nonfigurative art, in early Buddhist art it means only the absence of the human-figured Buddha; otherwise, the art is fully figurative.

87. Daniel Boucher, "The *Pratītyasamutpādagāthā* and Its Role in the Medieval Cult of the Relics," *The Journal of the International Association of Buddhist Studies* 14, no. 1 (1991), p. 1. It was not only the Buddhists who saw the absent Buddha as a problem, but also their rivals. Glenn Yocum, for example, notes how Buddhists were defeated in a debate with Śaivas in seventh-century Tamilnadu on a challenge as to "how the Buddha can receive the homage of his devotees and reward their worship, if in his case the five *khandhas* have been destroyed and he is no longer present" (Glenn E. Yocum, "Buddhism through Hindu Eyes: Śaivas and Buddhists in Medieval Tamilnad," in *Traditions in Contact and Change: Selected Proceedings of the XIVth Congress of the International Association for the History of Religions*, ed. Peter Slater and Donald Wiebe [Waterloo, Ontario: Wilfrid Laurier University Press, 1980], p. 150).

88. Boucher, "The *Pratītyasamutpādagāthā* and Its Role in the Medieval Cult of the Relics," p. 1.

89. The verse (*dhammapariyāya*) in Pāli is:

> *ye dhammā hetuppabhabvā tesāṁ hetuṁ tathāgato*
> *āha tesāñ ca yo nirodho evaṁvādī mahāsamaṇo 'ti*

Boucher's English translation:

> Those *dhammas* which arise from a cause
> The Tathāgata has declared their cause
> And that which is the cessation of them.
> Thus the great renunciant has taught (ibid., p. 6).

90. Ibid., p. 15.

91. The *pratītyasamutpādagāthā* as a "visual image" may not at first seem obvious, and Boucher does not argue its importance in these terms. Nevertheless, the *ye dharmā* . . . verse was created to be inscribed on objects, and was so used to inscribe literally thousands of objects throughout the Buddhist world, evidence for which is thoroughly presented by Boucher. The point was to create an object (to function like the "concrete" relics) out of the more "abstract" *dharma* ("concrete" and "abstract" are Boucher's terms). The central importance of the verse as an object is shown by the *many* instances in which the verse cannot be read: it is written in Sanskrit or Pāli (in areas where or periods when these languages are not known); in a foreign (and unreadable) script; in forms that are not clear and cannot be read (as with many of the stamped votive tablets); or in forms that showed "that this so-called creed was

frequently inscribed by 'someone who did not know what he was writing' " (ibid., p. 15; Boucher is quoting Maurizio Taddei, "Inscribed Clay Tablets and Miniature Stūpas from Gaznī," *East and West* n.s. 20 [1970], p. 76).

92. See Boucher (ibid.) for discussions of the *pratītyasamutpādagāthā* in the context of the Buddha's life and architectural monuments.

93. And of course the *pratītyasamutpādagāthā* is usually inscribed on an object that also has or is a plastic form.

94. Gustav Roth, "The Physical Presence of the Buddha and Its Representation in Buddhist Literature," in *Investigating Indian Art*, ed. Marianne Yaldiz and Wibke Lobo (Berlin: Museum für Indische Kunst, 1987), p. 298.

Part 2

Extensions of the Buddha Biography in Texts

In this section, Strong, Ray, and Walters illuminate textual sources across a variety of Buddhist traditions. Their essays illustrate the ways in which salient characteristics of the Buddha biography were extended to encompass the lives of other enlightened beings and religious communities or "karmic collectivities."

In his examination of the path to enlightenment practiced by the Buddha's family, Strong challenges conventional presumptions of biography and argues that meaningful sequences in Buddhist sacred biography encompass longitudinal and lateral extensions that transcend individual life spans.

Ray similarly observes that the hagiographic model of Buddhist saints across several branches of the tradition characteristically involves extraordinarily long life spans. By examining longevity as a marked characteristic in Buddhist hagiography, Ray uncovers structural commonalities in the path to sainthood that are pervasive throughout the tradition.

Walters' essay focuses on the constructions of the Buddha's biography among the religious community of the post-Aśokan empire. His descriptions of merit-making rituals centered on the celebration of the Buddha biography draw on epigraphic, art historical, and textual evidence to argue that the fundamental conception of the Buddha's biography was already present during the period immediately following Aśoka.

A Family Quest: The Buddha, Yaśodharā, and Rāhula in the Mūlasarvāstivāda Vinaya

John S. Strong

Almost every introductory textbook on Buddhism recounts, in one fashion or another, the touching Theravāda tale of the Buddha's farewell to his sleeping wife and his newborn son on the night of his Great Departure. Disgusted by the sight of the drooling denuded damsels of his harem, Gotama resolves to leave, but on his way out, he pauses at his bedroom door: "At that moment a lamp, fed with sweet-smelling oil, was burning dimly in the inner chamber. The mother of Rāhula was asleep on a bed strewn with many jasmine flowers, and resting her hand on the head of her son. Stopping with his foot on the threshold, the Bodhisat[tva] thought, 'If I lift her hand to take my son, she will awake; and that will prevent my going away. I will come back and see him when I have become a Buddha.' And he left the palace."[1]

The older strata of the Pāli canon know nothing of this postcanonical story; in most suttas that recount the Great Departure, there is no reference at all to the Buddha's wife or child, and instead, as André Bareau has pointed out, he is portrayed as leaving behind his sobbing mother and father.[2] Nonetheless, the commentaries' tale of the Buddha's attempted farewell to the son he had just called a "fetter" (*rāhula*) did find fortune among Western Buddhologists who have sought to analyze it, anthologize it, and impart it to their students.[3]

This in itself is not surprising, for the story is not only psychologically poignant, but it reflects and reinforces what might be called our bias toward individualism in the study of sacred biography. This is the assumption that the life stories of religious founders, saints, and followers are chiefly concerned with recounting the religious quests of individually significant selves. To be sure, these "selves" are thought to interact with other "selves," but generally speaking, the major thrust of their biographies is seen to be their own separate spiritual journeys and independent accomplishments.

This individualistic bias may be mitigated somewhat by the realization that Buddhist (as indeed most Indian) sacred biographies do not properly begin and end with a single person's lifetime but incorporate a whole karmic history, including previous lives and future existences as "other" beings. Thus the biography of the Buddha, for example, is commonly "extended" to comprise not only his "historical" life as Gotama, but also his previous births (*jātakas*) as a great variety of personae (animal, human, and divine), as well as the saga of his ongoing presence in his relics and in his teachings.[4]

But such longitudinal extensions of individual biographies over many lifetimes run the risk of merely reinforcing a sense of self, if they are not complemented by lateral expansions. Karma is not only individual, it is collective as well, and as a result, karmic biographies treat not only of the "histories" of identifiable karmic continua over a series of lives, but also of ongoing karmic nexuses. In this light, the individuals involved in biographies may sometimes cease to be the significant biographical units, and instead, the focus of the story may shift to a different level to explore and state the multiple and collective dimensions of certain common biographical events.[5]

In what follows, I illustrate this by reexamining the story of the Bodhisattva's Great Departure and its aftermath, not only as it affected him, but also as it interacted with the lives of two of his karmic companions: his wife, Yaśodharā, and his son, Rāhula. To do this, I focus on the tale as it is presented not in postcanonical Pāli texts, but in the *Sanghabhedavastu* section of the Sanskrit *Mūlasarvāstivāda Vinaya*[6] and corroborative sources.[7] The *Sanghabhedavastu*, in fact, is much richer than the Pāli tradition with regard to both Rāhula and his mother, and shows a remarkably different version of their early relationship to the Buddha.

To begin with, it makes no mention of the Bodhisattva's touching farewell to his sleeping wife and son. The reason for this is not hard to find: in this tradition, Rāhula has not yet been born. Indeed, the night of the Great Departure marks not the birth but the conception of the Buddha's son, for far from not waking his wife on his way out the door, the Bodhisattva decides to make love to her. The *Sanghabhedavastu* is explicit about this: "Lest others say that the prince Śākyamuni was not a man (*apumān*—a eunuch) and that he wandered forth without 'paying attention' to Yaśodharā, Gopikā, Mṛgajā, and his other sixty thousand wives, [the Buddha entered his bedchamber]. And thinking 'let me now "pay attention" to Yaśodharā,' he did so, and Yaśodharā became pregnant."[8]

Obviously, psychologically, this presents a rather different picture of the Bodhisattva at this crucial moment. Instead of turning away in disgust from sexuality and abandoning the family life, the Bodhisattva here, in his last act as a prince, affirms the householder's state and fulfills his sexual duty by engendering a son.

As a result, we are told, that night, various people in the Śākya household had various dreams. Mahāprajāpatī, the Bodhisattva's stepmother, subconsciously delighted that her daughter-in-law was with child, dreamt four auspicious dreams: she saw the moon eclipsed by Rāhu, the sun rising in the East, and a great crowd of people bowing down before her, and smiling at her.[9]

The Bodhisattva, on the other hand, had five dreams. These are said to have been presages of his imminent attainment of Buddhahood, but psychologically speaking, they are perhaps also interesting reflections of his new sense of himself as a "great male" (*mahāpuruṣa*). Having just impregnated his wife, the Bodhisattva dreamt he was lying on his back with the whole of the earth as his bed, Mount Meru as his pillow, his left arm in the Eastern Ocean, his right arm in the Western one, and his two feet in the Southern one. An upright reed grew up out of his navel and reached as far as the sky.[10] Big birds (*śakunaka*), which were all white with black heads, stood at his feet and came up to his knees. Other birds of different colors (*varṇa*) came from the four directions and, standing in front of him, became one color. Finally, he dreamt he walked back and forth over a mountain of feces.[11]

As interesting as all this may sound, the *Sanghabhedavastu's* real focus here is on Yaśodharā's dreams, which seem to have been much less auspicious and, fairly clearly, may be viewed as straightforward expressions of her underlying anxiety. Yaśodharā had eight dreams: she dreamt that her own maternal lineage (*mātṛkāvaṃśa*) was cut off, that her magnificent couch was broken, that her bracelets were broken, that her teeth fell out, that the braid of her hair was undone, that happiness departed from her house, that the moon was eclipsed by Rāhu, and that the sun rose in the East but then set there again.

Waking up, she told the Bodhisattva of her dreams, but he, seeking to comfort her, explained them away: "You say your maternal lineage was broken, but is it not established? You say your couch was broken, but look, it is standing. You say your bracelets were broken, but you see they are not. You say your teeth fell out, but you yourself know they haven't. You say

·the braid of your hair was undone, but it is itself, look. You say 'happiness has left my house,' but for a woman a husband is happiness, and I am right here. You say the moon was eclipsed by Rāhu, but is that not the moon over there? You say the sun rose in the East and then set again, but it is now midnight, the sun has not yet risen, how then can it set?"[12]

This intimate moment between husband and wife is rather touching and gives us a rare glimpse of the Buddha as a family man. Yaśodharā, however, is only partially comforted. She ponders her husband's words in silence and then, still worried, extracts a promise from him: "Lord," she requests, "wherever you go, take me with you." And the Bodhisattva replies: "So be it. Wherever I go, I will take you."[13]

By morning, however, the Bodhisattva is gone, and Yaśodharā has been left behind. The text explains that his promise to her had been made, thinking that he would take her along with him—not physically on his Great Departure—but spiritually to *nirvāṇa*. This explanation could be interpreted as a little piece of prevarication, but it seems to me to be deeper and more significant than this; it reflects the fact that in this tradition the Buddha is not alone in his quest for enlightenment. Instead, as we shall see, both he and Yaśodharā, each in their own way, embark on their quest together, and the symbol of that quest is their son Rāhula. In the *Sanghabhedavastu*, Rāhula, engendered by the Buddha on the night of his Great Departure, is not born until the day of his enlightenment at Bodhgaya, and Yaśodharā thus bears him in her womb for six full years.

This assertion understandably raised at least two important questions, within the tradition: How did it happen that Rāhula remained unborn, in the womb, for so long, and *did* it happen? Was the Buddha really Rāhula's father, or was this story of a six-year gestation period an attempt to cover up the fact that Yaśodharā had been unfaithful to her husband during his quest? The answers to these questions form the framework for the rest of the *Sanghabhedavastu*'s story, and so we shall deal with them in turn.

Six Years in the Womb

Yaśodharā's extended pregnancy is unusual but not unique in the Buddhist tradition.[14] Basically, two types of explanations are given for it, karmic and naturalistic ones.

The karmic explanations take the form of *jātaka* tales that focus either on the deeds that Yaśodharā did that resulted in her extended pregnancy, or on the deeds that Rāhula did that brought about his being the one who stayed so long in her womb. In the *Sanghabhedavastu*, both types of tale are found.

In the first case, long ago, we are told, there were two cowherdesses, a mother and a daughter, who were in the habit of carrying their milk to the market in heavy pails. One day the daughter, who was dishonest, told her mother to take her milkpail for a bit, as she had to relieve herself by the side of the road. The daughter then hid in the bushes and deliberately did not catch up with her mother, who in this way was forced to carry the extra milk for a distance of six leagues (*krośa*). The daughter, however, eventually reaped the bad merit of her tricky ways: reborn as Yaśodharā, she had to carry her child not for six leagues, but for six years.[15]

In the second case, long ago, not far from Benares, there were two brothers, Sankha and Likhita, who lived as *ṛṣis* in a forest hermitage. Sankha, the elder, was the teacher, and Likhita, the younger, was his pupil. One day Sankha filled his pot with drinking water, and then, leaving it at the hermitage, he went off into the forest to gather roots and fruits. During his absence, Likhita, who had been off on his own expedition, came back. Thirsty, he saw his elder brother's waterpot and proceeded to drink it dry. When Sankha returned and found his pot empty, he exclaimed: "What thief has taken my water?" Likhita, ashamed, replied, "Master, I am that thief; I drank it; punish me!" Sankha, however, forgave him, saying he wasn't really a robber, he was his brother, his pupil. But Likhita insisted that he pay for his bad deed, and finally, in exasperation, Sankha told him: "I can't punish you, if you want to be punished, go see the king." So off Likhita went to Benares to find King Brahmadatta; he told him what he had done, and insisted on being punished for it. Brahmadatta, however, said that drinking water was no crime and dismissed the charge against him. But then, distracted by other business, he was called away from the court. Telling Likhita to wait—he would be right back—he stepped outside. However, one thing led to another, and Brahmadatta, forgetting about the whole affair, never did come back and instead went off on a hunting expedition for six days. Upon his return, he found Likhita still standing there, waiting for him. Because of this, Brahmadatta, who was eventually reborn as Rāhula, had to wait himself, in the womb, for six years.[16]

These karmic explanations of Yaśodharā's extended pregnancy are noteworthy but not at all unusual. More interesting, for our purposes, is the *Sanghabhedavastu*'s additional claim that the development of Rāhula in her womb was retarded not by *karma*, but as the natural result of her practice of austerities, austerities which in every way paralleled those of the Bodhisattva. In this regard, it is important to realize that in this tradition, when the Bodhisattva leaves his home to go out on his quest, his family remains very much aware of what he is doing and keenly keeps track of his progress. For example, in the *Sanghabhedavastu*, the five mendicants who join the Bodhisattva in his ascetic practices and to whom he later preaches his First Sermon at Sārnāth, are not simply fellow *śramaṇic* questers, but are attendants (*upasthāyaka*) who were sent by the Bodhisattva's father,

King Śuddhodana, and by his maternal grandfather, Suprabuddha, to look after him.[17]

Moreover, Śuddhodana and Suprabuddha also send a team of 500 spies (news-carriers, *vārtāvāhaka*) who report back daily to the Śākyan court on the Bodhisattva's activities: "The bodhisattva is carrying out such and such an austerity. He is eating a meal of one sesame seed; one grain of rice; one jujube; one pulse pod; one kidney bean; one mungo bean. He makes his bed on darbha grass," etc. Hearing this, we are told, Yaśodharā "was overcome with sorrow for her lord, and, her face wet with tears, her ornaments and garlands cast aside, despondent, she too undertook austerities. She too began to eat just one sesame seed, one grain of rice, one jujube, one pulse pod, one kidney bean, one mungo bean. And she made her bed on straw (*tṛṇa* grass)."[18]

As a result of these ascetic practices, Yaśodharā, like the Bodhisattva, becomes very thin, and her pregnancy is unnoticed. Worse, the life in her womb is threatened, for gradually, as the text puts it, her "foetus wasted away" (*garbho layaṃ gataḥ*). Upon hearing this, King Śuddhodana grows concerned for the fate of his unborn grandson and potential heir. "If," he reflects, "Yaśodharā continues to hear news of the bodhisattva, and thereby to be stricken with sorrow for her husband and to persist miserably in her penance, she will not be able to bear this foetus. It will perish."[19] Śuddhodana, therefore, undertakes measures to ensure that Yaśodharā be told no more news of the Bodhisattva.

Śuddhodana's news blackout is effective; Yaśodharā, no longer able to emulate her husband, recommences eating more substantial meals, and the interrupted growth of Rāhula in her womb resumes. What is interesting is that, in the text, this corresponds to the end of the Bodhisattva's fast as well. Realizing that the extreme of asceticism is getting him nowhere, Gotama abandons his austerities and accepts Nandā and Nandabalā's offering of milkrice.[20] These two sisters, in the Sanskrit tradition, play the role of Sujātā, whose gift of milkrice, it will be remembered from Pāli sources, was a votive offering intended for a tree spirit and connected to her desire to give birth to a son.[21]

In any case, in the *Sanghabhedavastu*, fortified by his resumption of eating, the Bodhisattva proceeds with his quest; and Yaśodharā, fortified by the resumption of her eating, proceeds with her pregnancy. Nothing can now stop these joint processes, which will end in enlightenment at Bodhgaya and birth in Kapilavastu.

The final scenario, in fact, goes out of its way to stress this parallelism. The Buddha is at Bodhgaya, where he defeats Māra under the Bodhi tree, but the latter, in a final spiteful gesture of nastiness, sends some of his godlings to Kapilavastu to announce that the Buddha, as a result of his intense austerities, has died before attaining enlightenment. Learning this, Yaśodharā (who has heard nothing about her husband since Śuddhodana's news blackout) falls on the ground in a faint and is revived only to recommence wailing and wasting away. Because of her grief, she is literally in danger of losing her child and dying herself, when, fortunately, some other divinities who have faith in the Buddha (in one version of this story, this is the deity inhabiting the Bodhi tree) arrive and contradict Māra's devastating message. "The bodhisattva Śākyamuni is not dead," they announce, "but he has attained to highest knowledge."[22]

Yaśodharā's reaction is immediate; from the depths of despair, she goes to highest happiness and promptly gives birth to a son. He is called Rāhula because, at that very moment, the moon was being eclipsed by Rāhu. Simultaneously, it might be added, Amṛtodana's wife (the Buddha's aunt) gives birth to a child who is given the name Ānanda because of the family's great "joy" (*ānanda*) at the news of the Buddha's accomplishment.[23]

Proofs of Paternity

Rāhula's birth is a joyous occasion for Yaśodharā, but coming as it does six years after her husband's departure, it not surprisingly raises certain questions in the minds of her in-laws, the Śākyas. Before long, the maligners among them start asking: Can this really be Gotama's son or has Yaśodharā been unfaithful to her husband?

In this regard, it is important to realize that Rāhula's birth, despite his long gestation period, was considered to be an ordinary birth and not a miraculous or virginal one. Indeed, at least one version of the story is quite careful to point out that, unlike Bodhisattvas and unlike *cakravartins* who are born not as a result of the intercourse of their father and mother but by "spontaneous generation" (*aupapāduka*), from their own merits, Rāhula is not so born.[24] Thus, despite the karmic and physical explanations for the extended pregnancy given above, Yaśodharā soon feels pressured to offer graphic proof of her son's legitimacy and her own fidelity.

The first of these proofs comes not long after Rāhula's birth. Yaśodharā takes her child and sits him on top of the Bodhisattva's old exercise stone (*vyāyāmaśilā*), which she then has thrown into a nearby pond, with her son still on it. "Then, undertaking an act of truth, Yaśodharā solemnly declared: 'If this be the son of the bodhisattva, may he [and the stone on which he is sitting] not sink.' And, instantly, he remained afloat. Then she said: 'Let him now go from this shore to the other shore and back again.' He did so and everyone was amazed. Yaśodharā then said: 'Sirs, I have demonstrated to you that this is the child of the bodhisattva; I have not gone astray!' "[25]

Crossing over a body of water to the "other shore" and then returning back to this side is, of course, symbolically significant in the Buddhist context, where it foretells Rāhula's transcendence of *saṃsāra* followed by his remaining in this world.[26] Here, however, it more immediately acts as a miraculous confirmation of the Buddha's paternity.

But this is not the only way in which this paternity is demonstrated. In an immediate sequel to this story, the *Sanghabhedavastu* recounts the tale of Rāhula's recognition of the Buddha upon his return to Kapilavastu six years after his enlightenment.[27] The anecdote is complicated by the attempt of Yaśodharā to win back her husband; hoping to bewitch him, she gives Rāhula an aphrodisiac sweetmeat (*vaśīkaraṇamodaka*) and tells him to take it to the Buddha, thinking he will not refuse something offered to him by his own son. The Buddha, however, knowing the calumnies that Yaśodharā has suffered, turns this into another occasion to clear her good name by demonstrating to the assembly Rāhula's legitimacy. Using his magical powers, he creates there in the midst of the hall 500 identical replicas of himself. But a true son always knows his real father, and thus Rāhula is not confused by this; he quickly passes by the 499 false clones and gives the aphrodisiac to the real Buddha, thereby proving his sonship.[28]

This story is dramatic enough to warrant, in our text, a *jātaka* tale that seeks to explain it karmically. Like many *jātakas*, this is a Buddhist reworking of a well-traveled piece of folklore. In Herodotus' *Persian Wars*, it appears as the story of the Treasure of King Rhampsinitus. In a previous life, we are told, the Buddha was born as a great thief (*mahācora*) who repeatedly tricked a king, eluding all the traps that were set for him and always getting away with his booty. Finally the king decides to lure the thief with his own daughter. He sets her on a boat planted with all kinds of vegetation—a sort of floating raft-garden—in the middle of the Ganges, and he tells her to cry out should anyone try to rob her or molest her. He then stations guards hidden on either bank to lie in wait. But once again, the master thief outwits him. Going upstream, he repeatedly throws empty pots into the river; the guards, suspicious at first, smash these to pieces when they approach the boat-island. Eventually, however, they tire of breaking these always empty pots and start ignoring them. This, of course, is the moment the thief has been waiting for. Slipping a pot over his head, he floats downstream and climbs on board the boat. There he threatens the princess and rapes her. By the time she can sound the alarm, he is long gone and she has been impregnated. Nine months later, she gives birth to a baby boy.

This, however, gives the king one last chance to catch the thief. He has an immensely large assembly hall built—it takes him six years—and to it, on a given day, he convokes the entire population of his kingdom. He then gives a garland to his little grandson, telling him to go and give it to his father. The boy, despite the fact that he has never met his father, has no difficulty in recognizing him—the master thief—in all the crowd. The latter is immediately arrested, but instead of having him executed on the spot, the king decides to give him his daughter in marriage, having gradually over the years come to admire his cleverness and skill.[29]

What this tells us about the relationship of the Buddha to his wife I am not quite certain, but in this story, the identifications are clear: the Bodhisattva was the rapist thief, Yaśodharā was the princess, and Rāhula the little boy. Just as in that life, he had no trouble recognizing the father he had never seen, so too in this one, he is able to deliver to the Buddha the aphrodisiac sweetmeat intended for him.

The plot in this lifetime, however, backfires. For, although in the *jātaka* the Bodhisattva is captured and forced to stay with the mother of his child, in the *Sanghabhedavastu* that does not happen. Indeed, instead of consuming the sweetmeat offered him, the Buddha gives it back to Rāhula, and Rāhula eats it and is utterly captivated by his father, so much so that when the Buddha leaves the assembly hall, Rāhula goes with him and is soon ordained into the *sangha*. Yaśodharā, instead of regaining her husband, has now lost her son.[30]

She makes one more attempt to get them back, however. Inviting the Buddha to come and eat in the inner apartments of the palace, she uses the occasion to try to seduce him, an attempt that has its karmic precedent in the tale of the unicorn hermit Ṛṣyaśṛnga, which is told in our text as a justificatory *jātaka* but which is so well known that we shall not recount it here.[31] It need hardly be said that in this second attempt Yaśodharā fails again. This time, however, utterly depressed and filled with hopelessness, she tries to commit suicide by jumping off the palace roof. Fortunately, the Buddha, ever mindful, saves her with his magical powers.[32]

But the point has been made: Yaśodharā has reached the depths of suffering (*duḥkha*), and from those depths there can be only one refuge, the Buddha. The latter, therefore (after a quick *jātaka* to explain how he had once saved her in a previous life when he was a *kinnara* and she a *kinnarī*), preaches to her the four noble truths, and Yaśodharā, upon hearing his sermon, immediately becomes enlightened, and wandering forth from the household life herself, she is ordained as a nun. The Buddha proclaims her to be the foremost in modesty of all his female disciples who are *bhikṣuṇīs*.[33]

As for Rāhula, he, in the Sanskrit tradition, goes on to become an important elder who outlives his father. According to the *Ekottarāgama* and the *Śāriputraparipṛcchā*, he is one of four *arhats* whom the Buddha, prior to his *parinirvāṇa*, asks to prolong their lifetimes and remain in this world as guardians of the Dharma until the coming of the future Buddha Maitreya.[34] It is no surprise, then, to find him included in later Chinese listings of the sixteen or eighteen *arhats* (*lo-han*) who do much the same thing, and in Burmese schemes of eight *arhats* who abide geographically in the eight directions.[35] Nor should we be astonished to read, in Hsüan-tsang, a story of an encounter of a wealthy Buddhist with a strange old monk with bushy eyebrows and white hair who affirmed that, in his day, the water which he used to clean the Buddha's bowl was tastier than the wonderful repast he had just been given. Upon inquiry, the monk (before mysteriously vanishing from sight) revealed himself to be none other than Rāhula, the Buddha's son, still in this world, preserving the Dharma and enhancing the faith of devotees.[36]

Conclusion

I have tried to suggest that the story of the Bodhisattva's Great Departure was not universally, in the Buddhist tradition, treated as the solo quest of a solitary seeker after enlightenment; it was also, at least in part, a family affair. The Buddha's renunciation is, of course, genuine; whatever his feelings, he wanders forth, abandoning his family and the householder's life, and his Great Departure, even today, provides a mythic model for the ordination of Buddhist monks. But such a renunciation is not his alone. It has repercussions in the lives of others; it is an act not only for the abandoner, but for those who are abandoned, those who are left behind in the householder's state. I have pointed to these parallelisms throughout this article, but at this point, it may be helpful to summarize them in tabular form:

Bodhisattva/Buddha	*Yaśodharā/Rāhula*
Buddha impregnates Yaśodharā	Yaśodharā conceives a son
Buddha's confident dreams of accomplishment	Yaśodharā's anxious dreams of downfall and abandonment
Buddha comforts Yaśodharā, promising to take her with him (to *Nirvāṇa*)	Yaśodharā desires to go wherever Buddha goes
Buddha wanders forth	Yaśodharā stays at home
Buddha practices austerities, becomes thin: no progress in spirituality	Yaśodharā practices austerities, becomes thin: no progress in pregnancy
Buddha eats milkrice of maidens desiring to bear children and regains wholesome body.	Yaśodharā resumes eating, foetus resumes growth, and pregnancy becomes apparent

Buddha blamed and abandoned by five companion-ascetics (sent by Śākya clan)	Yaśodharā blamed and abandoned by Śākya clan
news sent by Māra that Buddha is dead	Yaśodharā collapses
news sent by deities that Buddha is alive and attained enlightenment	Yaśodharā revives and gives birth to Rāhula
Buddha decides to stay in *saṃsāra* and preach	Yaśodharā has Rāhula cross over pond on rock and return
Buddha returns to Kapilavastu	Yaśodharā tries to regain her husband, and Rāhula, his father
Buddha converts and ordains Rāhula and then Yaśodharā	Rāhula becomes a monk, Yaśodharā becomes a nun; both are enlightened

What the parallels on this chart further reveal is that the act of the Buddha's Great Departure is at least a double deed. It makes for achievements in both the homeless and the householder's states. Indeed, in achieving the goal of renunciation—enlightenment—the Buddha also achieves the goal of lay life—fatherhood. But conversely, and just as importantly, in achieving the goal of motherhood, Yaśodharā makes possible the goal of renunciation. This story, then, could serve as a soteriological model not just for monks and nuns at the time of their "wandering forth" but also for laypersons (both female and male) who, willy-nilly, choose the family life. It implies a parallelism and balance between at least two Buddhist paths, both of which lead to enlightenment: a *śramanic* one involving ordination and a stay-at-home one for householders.

In this light, the question "for whom is the Great Departure—or, in present-day ritual terms, for whom is Buddhist ordination—religiously significant?" becomes an important one. The assumption of traditional approaches to sacred biography is that it is primarily significant for the individual quester. The *Sanghabhedavastu*, however, suggests we should expand on that answer.

Anthropologists, of course, have long been aware of the fact that Buddhist ordination is at least as significant an event for the ordained's family as it is for the ordinand himself.[37] Generally speaking, however, they have asserted or assumed that there are two types of "significances" involved here, that, by virtue of his ordination, a new monk is engaging upon a *nibbānic* quest, while his relatives, who remain lay householders, seek to accumulate large amounts of *kammatic* merit by sponsoring the ceremony and giving up their sons.[38] In recent times, however, such clear-cut distinctions between two types of Buddhist soteriology have increasingly been challenged by scholars who have highlighted both the *kammatic* aspects of meditation and the *nibbānic* dimensions of merit-making, whether by laypersons or monastics.[39]

The evidence of the *Sanghabhedavastu* recounted in this paper would tend to support this more integrated view. Yaśodharā, as a pregnant laywoman, experiences some of the same intense austerities, uncertainties, and breakthroughs as her Bodhisattva-husband. Of course, there are differences between their paths: he leaves a wife, she loses a husband; he gives birth to bodhi, she gives birth to a son; he emphasizes Dharma, she emphasizes rūpa. But in the final analysis, the broad themes of their questing remain the same, for she too, along with her son,[40] is on a path that involves the realization of the truth of suffering and the consequent attainment of *nirvāṇa.*

Notes

1. T. W. Rhys-Davids, *Buddhist Birth Stories* (London: Trübner and Co., 1880), p. 82. Cf. *The Jātaka*, ed. V. Fausbøll (London: Kegan Paul, Trench, Trübner, 1877–1896), vol. 1, p. 62, herafter cited as J. See also *Madhuratthavilāsinī*, ed. I. B. Horner (London: Pāli Text Society, 1946), p. 282 (English trans., I. B. Horner, *The Clarifier of the Sweet Meaning* [London: Pāli Text Society, 1978], p. 404), hereafter cited as MV; *Dhammapadaṭṭhakathā*, ed. H. Smith and H. C. Norman (London: Pāli Text Society, 1906–1915), vol. 1, p. 85 (English trans., E. W. Burlingame, *Buddhist Legends* [Cambridge, Mass.: Harvard University Press, 1921], vol. 1, p. 195), hereafter cited as DhA.
2. André Bareau, "La jeunesse du Buddha dans les sūtrapiṭaka et les vinayapiṭaka anciens," *Bulletin de l'École française d'Extrême-Orient* 61 (1974), pp. 248–250. The same is true in the sutras and vinayas of almost all of the other schools; only the *Mahīśāsaka Vinaya* develops the harem women scene (which it models on the story of the wandering forth of Yaśas), but it too fails to mention the Buddha's son and wife (see ibid., pp. 251–253). Note that in these texts, the Buddha's mother is portrayed as still being alive at the time of his Great Departure. On this, see also André Bareau, "Un personage bien mystérieux: l'épouse du Buddha," *Indological and Buddhist Studies in Honour of Professor J. W. de Jong*, ed. L. A. Hercus, F. B. J. Kuiper, T. Rajapatiran, and E. R. Skrzypczak (Delhi: Satguru Publications, 1982), pp. 31–59.
3. See, for example, Henry Clarke Warren, *Buddhism in Translations* (Cambridge, Mass.: Harvard University Press, 1922), p. 62. For a recent demythologization (or remythologization) of the tale, see David J.

Kalupahana and Indrani Kalupahana, *The Way of Siddhartha* (Lanham: University Press of America, 1987), pp. 61–66.

4. For one example of such a treatment, see Frank E. Reynolds, "The Many Lives of the Buddha," in *The Biographical Process*, ed. Frank E. Reynolds and Donald Capps (The Hague: Mouton, 1976), pp. 37–61. Obviously such extended lives reflect complex interactions of myth and history, doctrine and ritual, local and pan-regional pilgrimage traditions.
5. Much the same point may be found, albeit in a very different context, in Ranjini Obeyesekere and Gananath Obeyesekere, "The Tale of the Demoness Kālī: A Discourse on Evil," *History of Religions* 29 (1990), pp. 318–334.
6. *The Gilgit Manuscript of the Sanghabhedavastu, Being the 17th and Last Section of the Vinaya of the Mūlasarvāstivādin*, ed. Raniero Gnoli (Rome: Istituto Italiano per il Medio ed Estremo Oriente, 1977), vol. 1, pp. 81–83, 106–111, 119–121; vol. 2, pp. 30–44 (partial English trans., John S. Strong, *The Experience of Buddhism* [Belmont: Wadsworth, 1995], pp. 10–18), hereafter cited as SBhV. Partial translations and synopses of the relevant portions of the Chinese and Tibetan versions of the SBhV may be found in Bareau, "Un personage bien mystérieux," pp. 42–46; Etienne Lamotte, *Le traité de la grande vertu de sagesse* (Louvain: Institut Orientaliste, 1949–1980), pp. 229n and 1003n; and W. W. Rockhill, *The Life of the Buddha* (London: Kegan Paul, Trench and Trübner, 1907), pp. 28–33, 53–58.
7. These include the *Mahāsanghika Vinaya*, the *Mahāvastu*, the *Mahāprajñāpāramitā śāstra*, and such Buddha biographies as the *Abhiniṣkramaṇasūtra*. For references, see Lamotte, *Traité*, pp. 1001–1002. The story has been curiously neglected in the English-speaking world, although in its general outline, it has been known at least since the publication of Samuel Beal, *The Romantic Legend of Śākya Buddha* (London: Trübner and Co., 1875), see pp. 359–366. Etienne Lamotte, in his *Histoire du bouddhisme indien* (Louvain: Institut Orientaliste, 1958), pp. 733–736, highlighted it as an example of the way in which Buddhist legends develop.
8. SBhV, vol. 1, p. 81.
9. Ibid., vol. 1, p. 82. The reference to Rāhu here is significant because, as we shall see, in the Sanskrit tradition, the origin of Rāhula's name is connected not to the word for "fetter" but to the name of the mythological being Rāhu, who, in Indian astrology, is thought to create eclipses by swallowing the sun or the moon.
10. In the *Mahāvastu*, ed. E. Sénart (Paris, 1882–1897), vol. 2, p. 137 (English trans., J. J. Jones, *The Mahāvastu* [London: Pāli Text Society, 1949–1956], vol. 2, p. 131), hereafter cited as Mtu, this is specified as a reed with milky sap (*kṣīrikā*). Note also, here, the possible parallelisms with the image of *Viṣṇu* reclining on the waters.
11. SBhV, vol. 1, pp. 82–83. These dreams of the Bodhisattva are well known from various sources, e.g., the Mtu (vol. 2, pp. 136–137; English trans.,

Jones, vol. 2, pp. 131–132), the *Lalitavistara* (French trans., Ph. Ed. Foucaux, *Le Lalita Vistara* [Paris: E. Leroux, 1884], pp. 173–174), and the *Abhiniṣkramaṇasūtra* (English trans., Beal, pp. 128–129).

12. SBhV, vol. 1, p. 83.
13. Ibid. Contrast these dreams to those recounted in the *Mahāvastu* (English trans., Jones, vol. 2, pp. 129ff.), the *Lalitavistara* (French trans., Foucaux, pp. 172–173), and in the *Abhiniṣkramaṇasūtra* (English trans., Beal, 126–129). In the latter text, Yaśodharā has twelve dreams, and the Bodhisattva makes love to her after she wakes up frightened in order to allay her fears and suspicions.
14. Compare the case of Sīvalī, who spent seven years in his mother's womb. For references, see G. P. Malalasekera, *Dictionary of Pāli Proper Names* (London: J. Murray for the Pāli Text Society, 1937–1938), vol. 2, p. 1163.
15. SBhV, vol. 2, p. 42. The same story may be found in the *Abhiniṣkramaṇasūtra* (English trans., Beal, p. 363) and in Kṣemendra's *Avadānakalpalatā*, ed. P. L. Vaidya (Darbhanga: Mithila Institute, 1959), p. 484, hereafter cited as AvK.
16. SBhV, vol. 2, p. 43. The Sankha and Likhita story is a variant of the more commonly found *jātaka* of the two ascetics Sūrya (the Buddha) and Candra (Rāhula), versions of which may be found in Beal, p. 363; Jones, vol. 3, pp. 167–170; Édouard Chavannes, *Cinq cents contes et apologues extraits du Tripiṭaka chinois* (Paris: Imprimerie Nationale, 1934), vol. 1, pp. 197–201; and Lamotte, *Traité*, p. 1006. For a fuller bibliography, see Lamotte, *Traité*, p. 1006, n. 1, to which should be added AvK, p. 482.
17. SBhV., vol. 1, p. 99. These five were chosen from among 500 sent to the Bodhisattva. Three were from the paternal side and two from the maternal one.
18. SBhV, vol. 1; p. 106.
19. Ibid.
20. Actually, in the SBhV, vol. 1, p. 107, the Bodhisattva first eats an "unpalatable meal" (the excrement of newborn calves who have been separated from their mothers). He then lies down next to a corpse in a graveyard and is pelted with clods of dirt by the local village boys and girls, who mistake him for a ghoul (*piśāca*). Then he recommences eating. Then his five companions desert him; then he accepts Nandā and Nandabalā's offering.
21. See sources in Malalasekera, *Dictionary*, vol. 2, p. 1186. In the SBhV, Nandā and Nandabalā are asked what they would like to obtain from their meritorious offering; they reply that they have heard that the Śākyan prince will become a *cakravartin* king and they hope to be his wives.
22. SBhV, vol. 1, p. 119. See also Lamotte, *Traité*, p. 229.
23. SBhV, vol. 1, pp. 119–120. See also vol. 2, p. 30. The tradition of Amṛtodana (Pāli Amitodana) as Ānanda's father is also known (along with others) in Pāli sources. See Malalasekera, *Dictionary*, vol. 1, p. 148.
24. Mtu, pp. 145, 153–154 (English trans., Jones, vol. 1, pp. 115, 121–122).

25. SBhV, vol. 1, p. 120 and vol. 2, p. 312. See also Lamotte, *Traité*, p. 1003n. For a similar tale, more influenced perhaps by the story of Rāma and Sītā, see Chavannes, *Cinq cents contes*, vol. 3, pp. 136–137. There, the Śākyas force Yaśodharā to enter a blazing fire. She, swearing that she has remained pure and loyal, invokes the Buddha's aid: the inferno is transformed into a cool pond, in the midst of which Yaśodharā is found to be sitting on a lotus blossom with her son in her arms.
26. See discussion in text below.
27. The story of the Buddha's encounter with Rāhula upon his return to Kapilavastu is also known in Pāli tradition. According to the Vinaya, on this occasion, Rāhula, acting on instructions from his mother, goes up to the Blessed One and asks for his inheritance. The Buddha responds by giving his son his "true inheritance," the Dharma, and he more or less shanghais Rāhula into the *sangha* by conferring on him the *pabajjā* ordination and thus making him into the first Buddhist novice. See *Vinayapitaka*, ed. H. Oldenberg (London: Williams and Norgate, 1879), vol. 1, p. 82 (English trans. T. W. Rhys-Davids and Hermann Oldenberg, *Vinaya Texts* [Oxford: Oxford University Press, 1882], vol. 1, pp. 208–209). For other versions, see Bareau, "Un personage bien mystérieux," p. 33. Beyond this, the Pāli canon has little more to say about Rāhula: a few verses are attributed to him in the *Theragāthā*; the Buddha preaches a few sermons to him in the *Majjhima Nikāya* (one of which even gets mentioned in Aśoka's Bhabra Edict), and in the *Anguttara Nikāya*, he is proclaimed the "foremost among those disciples who are anxious for training (*sikkhākāma*)." For references, see Malalasekera, *Dictionary*, vol. 2, pp. 737–740. Even less is said about his mother, the Bodhisattva's wife, who in the Pāli tradition is identified here and there under various names, but who for the most part is presented anonymously as "Rāhulamātā" (see ibid., p. 741).
28. SBhV, vol. 2, p. 31–32. See also Lamotte, *Traité*, pp. 1003–1005. The same story is found in the Mtu, pp. 142–143 (English trans., Jones, vol. 3, pp. 137–138) without, however, the detail of the Buddha's multiplication of his body. See also Bareau, "Un personage bien mystérieux," pp. 42–44.
29. SBhV, vol. 2, pp. 32–36. See also Herodotus, *The Persian Wars*, English trans., George Rawlinson (New York: The Modern Library, 1942), pp. 174–177; and Edouard Huber, "Le trésor du roi Rhampsinite," *Bulletin de l'École française d'Extrême-Orient* 4 (1904), pp. 704–707.
30. SBhV, vol. 2, pp. 32.
31. Ibid., pp. 38–40. See also Heinrich Lüders, "Die Sage von Ṛṣyaśṛnga," *Nachrichten von der königlichen Gesellschaft der Wissenschaften, Göttingen, Philologisch-historicsche Klasse* (1897), pp. 87–135, and (1902), pp. 28–56; and Wendy Doniger O'Flaherty, *Asceticism and Eroticism in the Mythology of Śiva*, (Oxford: Oxford University Press, 1973), pp. 42–52.
32. SBhV, vol. 2, pp. 40–41. Here too a *jātaka* is told to show that this is not the first time that the Buddha has saved Yaśodharā in this way. For

another version of the suicide story and its *jātaka,* see also AvK, pp. 386–410.

33. SBhV, vol. 2, p. 41.
34. Sylvain Lévi and Edouard Chavannes, "Les seize arhat protecteurs de la loi," *Journal asiatique* 8 (1916), pp. 192–194. See also Ernst Leumann, *Maitreya samiti, das Zukunftsideal der Buddhisten* (Strasbourg: Karl J. Trübner, 1919), p. 250.
35. On this, see John S. Strong, *The Legend and Cult of Upagupta* (Princeton: Princeton University Press, 1992), pp. 237–241.
36. Thomas Watters, *On Yuan Chwang's Travels in India* (reprint, Delhi: Munshi Ram Manohar Lal, 1961), vol. 2, p. 43. Hsüan-tsang also mentions that in Māthurā, Rāhula's shrine was especially revered by novices; see ibid., vol. 1, p. 302.
37. In present-day Theravāda countries, this is especially true for the parents of a new monk, but in ancient India, it may also have been the case for his wife and children.
38. The terms were popularized by Melford E. Spiro, *Buddhism and Society* (Berkeley: University of California Press, 1982).
39. See, most recently, Russell F. Sizemore and Donald K. Swearer, eds., *Ethics, Wealth and Salvation: A Study in Buddhist Social Ethics* (Columbia, S.C.: University of South Carolina Press, 1990).
40. More investigation would also show here a further coordination with the spiritual development of the Bodhisattva's stepmother, Mahāprajāpatī (who later becomes a leader of the community of nuns), and with that of his father, Śuddhodana.

Nāgārjuna's Longevity

Reginald A. Ray

The Buddhist master Nāgārjuna (second–third century)[1] is one of the greatest and most celebrated of all Indian Buddhist saints. He is identified as the founder of the Madhyamaka school, author of numerous important texts, guru of a number of important figures, and even, in some accounts, the first propounder of Mahāyāna Buddhism itself.[2] Yet in spite of his important and well-documented presence within Indian Buddhism, Max Walleser, Jan Yün-hua, and other scholars who have taken up "the problem of Nāgārjuna" agree that he remains an enigmatic figure, described in a hagiography that is rampant with difficulties.[3] Prominent among perplexing elements of Nāgārjuna's story is the extraordinary life span attributed to him, in some sources several centuries, in others specified as 600, 629, or 700 years. The *Mañjuśrīmūlakalpa*, for example, says, "This is a prediction of the *tathāgata* himself—that [Nāgārjuna] will reach the grade (*bhūmi*) of *pramuditā*, live six hundred years, obtain the charms of the Mahāmayūrī; after having thrown off his body he will re-appear in Sukhāvatī."[4] Another Indian text, the *Caturaśītisiddhapravṛtti* (Csp)[5] or *History of the Eighty-four Siddhas* by Abhayadatta, similarly attributes to Nāgārjuna a longer than normal (but unspecified) lifespan.[6] In the Csp account, one finds two additional motifs, the significance of which will presently become clear: first, he is a *bodhisattva*—the enlightened ideal of the Mahāyāna—and his exclusive motivation during his long life is compassion for others; second, he finally dies because he is, in effect, asked to do so: the god Brahma asks Nāgārjuna for his head and, seemingly because he is a *bodhisattva* and therefore unable to refuse any being's request,[7] the saint accedes.

The Indian affirmations of Nāgārjuna's long life and manner of death are repeated in Tibetan sources. Tāranātha, for example, in his *History of the Seven Special Transmissions* (*bka'.babs.bdun.ldan* [Kbdd]) (written in 1600), says that Nāgārjuna, practitioner of the long-life *mantra* of Amitāyus and possessor of the elixir of longevity,[8] was predicted to live 600 years but fell short of this venerable age by seventy-one years owing to the following circumstances. A certain southern Indian king, Nāgārjuna's disciple, was also very long-lived because his life span was tied to that of the Ācārya. His eldest son, desirous of gaining the throne, knew that by bringing about Nāgārjuna's death he could also cause his father's, so he went to the saint and asked for his head. Nāgārjuna did not refuse and, when the prince was not able to sever his head, even obliged by performing the deed himself.[9] As in Nāgārjuna's life in the *History of the Eighty-four Siddhas*, so here we find the theme of the *bodhisattva* who has the power of longevity, but whose ability to exercise it is somehow bound up with the wishes and requests of sentient beings.

Scholars have attempted to explain the origin and significance of Nāgārjuna's longevity by reference to historical idiosyncracies of his biography. Nalinaksha Dutt,[10] in an extended discussion of Nāgārjuna's long life,[11] explains that the well-known second-century Buddhist figure known as Nāgārjuna was followed some six hundred years later by the appearance of another Nāgārjuna, this time a Tantric author to whom are attributed many works in the Tenjur.[12] Dutt states that the *Mañjuśrīmūlakalpa* (Mmk), reflecting this same time period and followed by later Buddhist tradition, has taken these two Nāgārjunas "to be a single person [and] his span of life has been supposed to be of 600 years." Thus "the *Mañjuśrīmūlakalpa*, belonging to a date prior to the ninth century A.D., has very probably mixed up the traditions relating to more than one person bearing the name of Nāgārjuna."[13] Other scholars discussing Nāgārjuna's longevity have tended to accept Dutt's explanation.[14]

The Indian and Tibetan sources cited above all post-date the rise of Tantric Buddhism in India, and would seem to support or at least not to contradict Dutt's theory. However, there are two problems with Dutt's explanation. First, it is not possible to have any confidence in the dating of the *Mañjuśrīmūlakalpa*, and particularly the section in which the prediction of Nāgārjuna is given, to such a late time as the one suggested by Dutt.[15] There is, in fact, no sound reason for believing that the text would be in any position to confuse two authors of the same name, one living in the second or third century and the other six hundred years later, when Tantric Buddhism was already in a mature form in India. Second, and even more decisive, two Chinese works discussing Nāgārjuna's life, Hsüan-tsang's seventh-century report and Kumarājīva's early fifth-century biography

(402–417), both non-Tantric sources and both preceding the time of the so-called second "Tantric Nāgārjuna," provide similar indications of Nāgārjuna's longevity and the manner of his death. Hsüan-tsang, in his account of his trip to India, tells us that Nāgārjuna lived for "many hundreds of years" and recounts a story of his passing that closely resembles Tāranātha's [Kbdd], including the theme that Nāgārjuna ended his life owing to the request from an ambitious prince.[16] Elsewhere, Hsüan-tsang attributes to Nāgārjuna a lifespan of 700 years.[17] Kumārajīva's biography, revealing similar themes, tells us that there was a certain Hīnayāna dharma master who was always angry. When Nāgārjuna was close to death, the saint asked the "Hīnayānist," "Would you like me to remain for a long time in this world?" He replied, "Truthfully, I do not wish it." Thereafter, Nāgārjuna passed away.[18]

This story contains two interesting implications: first, that Nāgārjuna could have lived "a long time" had the Hīnayānist wished it; second, that Nāgārjuna passed away because the Hīnayānist did not wish it. The existence of references to Nāgārjuna's longevity prior to the time postulated for the "second, Tantric Nāgārjuna" and its presence in non-Tantric evidence more or less undercuts the attempt to explain Nāgārjuna's long life by reference to a confusion of pre-Tantric and Tantric figures. This brings us back, then, to the question of the origin and significance of Nāgārjuna's longevity. In what follows, we address this question not by referring to peculiarities of Nāgārjuna's individual history as Dutt and others have tried to do, but rather by taking a different tack, attempting to see Nāgārjuna within the large and multifaceted tradition of Buddhist saints in India, within which he was a primary actor.

The Longevity of Saints in the Vajrayāna

In the Tantric *History of the Eighty-four Siddhas* [Csp], it is not only Nāgārjuna who lives to an unnatural age, but many other *siddhas* as well who are either said to live a long time or are assigned specific life spans. Bhikṣana[19] [61], for example, is said to have lived "many years," as are Mekhalā [66] and Kanakhalā [67]. The Csp tells us that Gorakṣa [9] is still alive at the time of the text's composition such that the sound of his ritual drum (*ḍamaru*) can be heard by those pure in heart.[20] Śāvaripa [5] is given a truly stupendous life span, for he "will remain in Jambudvīpa in this very body until the coming of Maitreya."[21] Many other *siddhas* have specific life spans attributed to them: Kaṅkana [29] lived for 500 years, Kucipa [35] worked for the benefit of beings for 700 years, Mahipa [37] taught beings in Magadha for 300 years, and so on. The following list summarizes the information on the longevity of the eighty-four *siddhas*, as provided in the Csp.

100 Years	*600 Years*
Bhusuku (Śāntideva) [41]	Sarvabhakṣa [75]
Gorura [55]	*700 Years*
300 Years	Kucipa [35]
Mahipa [37]	Jayānanda [58]
Acinta [38]	Dhahuli [70]
400 Years	Kirava [73]
Nalina [40]	*800 Years*
500 Years	Panaha [79]
Kaṅkana [29]	*2000 Years*
Kapalapa [72]	Nāgabodhi [76]
Putali [78]	

Excluding those *siddhas* for whom a more than natural longevity is not unequivocally stated,[22] we find that fifteen or nearly one-fifth of the eighty-four *siddhas* are connected with longevity of an unusual duration, with an average age (excluding Śāvaripa, because of his vast life span, and Nāgārjuna, because the term of his longevity is not specifically stated) of between 600 and 700 years (669 to be exact), right in the neighborhood of the specific ages ascribed to Nāgārjuna in our sources. So far, in his longevity, Nāgārjuna is not idiosyncratic, but rather a typical *siddha*.

In gaining a view of the *siddhas*' life spans in the Csp, it is also pertinent to ask what purpose this longevity is supposed to serve. The answer nearly always given is that the *siddhas* are acting out of compassion and that they spend their time working for the welfare of sentient beings.[23] This purpose is sometimes articulated in instructions given by the guru to the newly realized disciple. More often, the *siddhas* are simply said to spend their time helping beings, providing instruction, and bringing blessings to them.[24] The central role of this theme is seen in the fact that of the thirteen *siddhas* whose longevity is given a specific term, in every case the *siddha* is either instructed to spend his time acting compassionately for the benefit of beings or is said to have spent his life in such activities.

The story of Nāgabodhi [76] sheds some further light on the text's understanding of saintly longevity. Nāgabodhi's guru, who happens to be Nāgārjuna, tells him "You should remain on Śrī Parvata itself, accomplishing the welfare of beings (*'gro.don.gyis.shig*)."[25] "It is said," the story continues, "that he will remain there for 2,000 years."[26] This story exhibits a theme seen in the life of Nāgārjuna himself, namely that the longevity of the saint is somehow dependent upon the wishes and requests of others. Whereas in Nāgārjuna's case the saint dies in fulfillment of someone's request, in this case the *siddha* is asked to remain on Śrī Parvata accomplishing the welfare of beings, and so he lives on. The longevity of the *siddhas*, then, reveals the same threefold structure already observed in Nāgārjuna's life: (1) the *siddhas*, as realized saints, have the power to extend their lives to great lengths; (2) the explicit purpose of this longevity is to enable the *siddhas* to act compassionately for the welfare of sentient beings; and (3) the *siddhas'* prolongation of their lives is sometimes dependent upon others' requests.[27] This, then, provides a partial answer to the problem of Nāgārjuna's longevity. One reason that Nāgārjuna lives a long time is because this is typical and anticipated behavior from a Tantric saint.

Longevity among Saints in the Mahāyāna

At the same time, however, we saw above that intimations of Nāgārjuna's longevity are found in pre- and non-Tantric materials, and this raises the question of whether it is only Tantric saints who are believed to have the power to live a long time. In fact, a variety of evidence suggests that the power of longevity is also commonly attributed to Mahāyāna saints with no explicit connection to the Vajrayāna, including the three most important classes of Mahāyāna saints: *arhats*, *bodhisattvas*, and *buddhas*.

A fairly detailed discussion of the longevity of *arhats*, seen from a Mahāyāna viewpoint, is found in the *Nandimitrāvadāna* (Nma), an Indian Mahāyāna text (at least in its final form[28]) preserved in both Tibetan and Chinese,[29] which enjoyed particular popularity among the followers of Ch'an Buddhism in China and Zen Buddhism in Japan, and among Mahāyāna Buddhists in Tibet.[30] The Nma presents itself as spoken by the great *arhat* Nandimitra who lived in Sri Lanka "800 years after the *nirvāṇa* of the Buddha,"[31] a chronology which, if followed, would place Nandimitra in or about the fourth century.[32] In any case, the text was in existence sometime prior to the seventh century, at which time it was translated into Chinese by Hsüan-tsang.[33] According to the Nma, when the Buddha was about to enter *parinirvāṇa*, he entrusted his *dharma* to sixteen great *arhats* and their entourage, and commanded them to protect it and preserve it from extinction. Among these *arhats* were Piṇḍolabhāradvāja as first and chief of the group, and also Kanakavatsa, Kanakaparidhvaja, Subinda, Nakula, Bhadra, Kālika, Vajraputra, Śvapāka, Panthaka, Rāhula (name of the Buddha's son), Nāgasena, Iṇgada, Vanavāsi, Ajita, and Cūḍapanthaka.[34] According to the Nma, the Buddha asked these sixteen saints to protect the *dharma* and to make themselves available to the laity as fields of merit, so that the laity, by making donations to them, might earn great reward. In order to fulfill the Buddha's request, the sixteen *arhats*, by means of magical power, have extended their lives indefinitely. Thus we read, "Because [the sixteen *arhats*] have received the command of the Buddha, owing to the power of their supernatural penetrations, they have prolonged the duration of their own lives. And as long as the correct *dharma* of the Blessed One endures . . . they will constantly protect and maintain it, and will act as a veritable field of merit so that their benefactors will obtain great reward."[35] The sixteen *arhats* have taken up abodes in mysterious and out of the way places, including certain mountains known for meditating hermits, the major continents of the world, semimythical lands, and even the realms of the gods. From these places, if properly supplicated, they will come among ordinary folk, singly and anonymously, presenting themselves as alms seekers. How long will be the life spans of these *arhats*? The *Nandimitrāvadāna* tells us that they will stay in the world through a decrease and then an increase in the ordinary human life span. When humans will live for 70,000 years, the *dharma* will disappear from the world forever. At that time, the sixteen great *arhats* will gather together, erect a great *stūpa* containing all the relics of Buddha Śākyamuni and, after praising it effusively, will ascend into the air, burst into flame, and spontaneously cremate themselves.[36] These events will be a prelude to the coming of Maitreya, who will arrive when the duration of human life will have reached 80,000 years.[37] Thus it is that the sixteen *arhats* will live nearly to the end of the *kalpa*.[38] The longevity of the sixteen *arhats*, then, exhibits the same threefold structure that we have already seen in the biography of Nāgārjuna and among the eighty-four *siddhas*: (1) the *arhats* are able to greatly extend the lengths of their lives; (2) their motivation is compassion, for they would protect the *dharma* and be fields of great merit for sentient beings; and (3) their ongoing presence in the world is bound up with their being asked to remain—in this case, it is the Buddha who asks them to delay their *parinirvāṇas*.[39]

The Mahāyāna also knows of another longevity, this time of future *buddhas*, the *bodhisattvas*, who achieve longevity through their power to control the length of their lives. The *Daśabhūmika Sūtra*,[40] for example, tells us that when the *bodhisattva* attains the eighth *bhūmi* known as *acalā* or "the immovable," he develops the ten *vaśitā*. Among these is included *āyur-vaśitā*, or the power over life span enabling one to prolong one's life according to one's wishes.[41] The text explains this as the ability to live up to an immeasurable number of *kalpas*.[42] This characterization is, of course, found quite widely among Mahāyāna *sūtras*[43] and *śāstras*.[44]

Finally, the Mahāyāna, particularly in its *sutra* literature, speaks of the longevity not only of *arhats* and *bodhisattvas*, but also of *buddhas*. One example is provided by the *Daśabhūmika Sūtra* just mentioned, where it is assumed that every *buddha* has already gained the power of longevity as a *bodhisattva* at the eighth *bhūmi*. The *Sukhāvatīvyūha Sūtra* states that, based on the power of his meditative attainment, the Tathāgata could, if he wishes, live for "a whole *kalpa* . . . or for a hundred *kalpas*, or for a thousand *kalpas*, or for a hundred thousand *kalpas*, to a hundred thousand *niyutas* of *koṭis* of *kalpas*, nay, he could live beyond."[45] And we are told that "the length of the life of the Bhagavat Amitābha, the *tathāgata*, is immeasurable, so that it is not easy to know its length, so as to be able to say (that it comprises) so many *kalpas*, so many hundreds of *kalpas* . . . so many hundred thousands of *niyutas* of *koṭis* of *kalpas*."[46] Further, the Mahāyāna *Mahāparinirvāṇa Sūtra*, has the Buddha saying "you cannot count the length of my life."[47] The text further remarks, "the length of life of the *tathāgata* is uncountable . . . he is the first of all eternal things. . . . How could it not be that he can live for half a *kalpa*, a *kalpa*, a hundred *kalpas*, a hundred thousand *kalpas*, or innumerable *kalpas*. Because of this know that the *tathāgata* is an eternal and unchanging existence."[48] The Mahāyāna commentarial traditions follow these themes, as in the *Ratnagotravibhāga Śāstra*, which confirms the ten *vaśitās*, with longevity as the first item, as a defining feature of the *tathāgata* as a type.[49] A more cultic glimpse of the *buddha*'s longevity is provided by Śāntideva's *Bodhicaryāvatāra*. In the context of an account of the classical "sevenfold service," we read,

> *With folded hands, I beseech*
> *The conquerors who wish to pass away*
> *To remain for countless kalpas*
> *And not to leave the world in darkness.*[50]

Note the themes of *buddhas* who can extend their presence nearly indefinitely, whose presence is bound up with the help they provide to the world, and (implicit in this passage) who are able and willing to respond to sentient beings' requests that they remain. Therefore, in the Mahāyāna discussions of the longevity of *bodhisattvas* and *buddhas*, we find the same three interconnected beliefs seen above in the longevity of Nāgārjuna, the *siddhas*, and the sixteen *arhats*: (1) that saints have the power to greatly extend their life spans; (2) that they do so in order to benefit sentient beings; and (3) that requesting them to remain is somehow pertinent to their doing so.

The Longevity of Saints in Nikāya Buddhism

The longevity of Buddhist saints is also an important theme in Nikāya Buddhism, in Theravāda, Sarvāstivāda, and Mahāsāṇgikan traditions. In accord with all other Buddhists, the Nikāya schools maintain that Buddha Śākyamuni, like all *buddhas*, has the power of long life.[51] Thus the Sarvāstivādins held that the Buddha could have lived for a *kalpa*,[52] the Mahāsāṇghikas that his life is unlimited,[53] and the Theravādins that the length of his life cannot be conceived.[54]

The Nikāya traditions also exhibit beliefs in the longevity of *arhats*.[55] There is evidence, for example, that the Sarvāstivādins engaged in the cult of the sixteen *arhats.*[56] In addition, one finds other evidence of cultic traditions among the Theravādins closely resembling the cult of the sixteen *arhats*. Maung Kin,[57] for example, tells us that the Burmese cult of the Buddhist master Upagupta (Upagutta or Upagutta Nāga[58]) (for which the *Lokapaññati* is an important textual source) involves the belief that the saint has prolonged the life of his body through the power of *ṛddhi* (P. *iddhi*) gained through his meditation and realization. Upagupta now lives in a palace hidden in the depths of the southern ocean and will remain alive there, protecting the *dharma*, as long as it shall survive upon earth. A second example, from the northwestern texts recounting the legend of Aśoka [the *Aśokāvadāna*, contained in the *Divyāvadāna*[59] and the *Aśokarājāvadāna* (C. *A-yü-wang-chuan*[60])], is that of Piṇḍolabhāradvāja. In the *Aśokāvadāna* version, this saint suddenly and miraculously appears before King Aśoka to occupy the place of honor at a great feast offered by the king to the Buddhist *saṅgha.*[61] Aśoka's guru has previously told the king of Piṇḍola's miraculous longevity, that this saint was alive in the time of Buddha Śākyamuni himself, and that it is only he who may occupy the place of honor at the feast. Piṇḍola arrives, exhibiting the marvelous body of a *pratyekabuddha*, with white hair and heavy eyebrows. When the king asks whether Piṇḍola has in fact seen the Buddha, the saint replies that he has, and goes on to give a long, detailed, and evocative description of some of his experiences of seeing the Blessed One. These two examples are interesting because, taken together with the Mahāyāna cult of the sixteen *arhats*, they reveal a very specific type of Buddhist saint quite independent of sectarian divisions.

A different kind of the longevity of *arhats* within Nikāya Buddhism is found in the variety of legends surrounding Mahākāśyapa, a close disciple of the Buddha and, according to Sarvāstivāda and Mahāsāṇghika sources, his principal lineage holder. Mahākāśyapa's unique status is embodied in the Buddha's *pāṃśukūla* or mendicant's robe, which the Buddha has entrusted to him, asking him to keep it until the coming of Maitreya, the future *buddha*. When this latter arrives upon earth, Mahākāśyapa is to pass it on to him, thus symbolizing the continuity of lineage from the Buddha to Mahākāśyapa to Maitreya. In the *Aśokarājāvadāna*, in the chapter describing the *nirvāṇa* of Mahākāśyapa, we read that one day while he is in Rājagṛha, this saint realizes that his work is now complete and the time of his final passing close at hand. He transmits his lineage to Ānanda and makes a final pilgrimage to adore the relics of the Buddha. Mahākāśyapa's devotees, both human and divine, realize that the end of their master is near, and they exhibit sorrow and lamentation. Soon Mahākāśyapa quits Rājagṛha and ascends Mount Kukkuṭapāda, where he will enter *nirvāṇa*. In the middle of three peaks, he sits down in meditation posture, reflecting that his body is now clothed in the *pāṃśukūla* that the Buddha gave him, which he will wear until the coming of Maitreya. The earth now quakes in six ways and Śakra and his retinue of deities arrive, showering offerings of celestial flowers and perfumed powders on the saint. Then Mahākāśyapa passes into the trance of cessation (*nirodha-samāpatti*) and the mountain closes over his body. King Ajātaśatru, the saint's principal royal patron, arrives along with Ānanda, Mahākāśyapa's lineage holder, and in accordance with a prediction previously made by Mahākāśyapa, the mountain opens allowing the king to see and venerate him. However, when the king suggests a cremation, Ānanda tells him that Mahākāśyapa is not dead, but plunged in meditation and he must not be burned, but allowed to remain intact so that he can fulfill his mission when Maitreya arrives. Thus Mahākāśyapa remains and shall remain, abiding in *nirodha-samāpatti* until the future Buddha walks upon earth.[62] In the evidence of Mahākāśyapa's longevity, we thus see the same threefold pattern: (1) Mahākāśyapa has the power to prolong his life—in his case, through his meditation in *nirodha-samāpatti*; (2) his doing so is an expression of his compassion for sentient beings—here, he accomplishes great benefit for the world by providing continuity from Buddha Śākyamuni to Maitreya; and (3) he prolongs his life because he has been asked to do so, in this case, by the Buddha himself. In concluding our discussion of Mahākāśyapa, it may be noted that Mahākāśyapa's type of longevity is not entirely idiosyncratic for, in fact, a number of specific themes connected with it are found elsewhere. For example, Hsüan-tsang reports that the *bodhisattva* Bhāvaviveka, deeply desiring to see the Buddha Maitreya, was instructed to make supplication to Vajrapṇi at his shrine at the "Asura's Palace" in a certain cliff near Dhānyakaṭaka. As a result, the cliff would open, whereupon he would be able to enter and there, like Mahākāśyapa, await the coming of Maitreya. Bhāvaviveka follows these instructions and, after three years, the cliff opens and he passes in along with six others.[63]

The foregoing analysis shows, then, that Nāgārjuna's longevity is not an idiosyncratic phenomenon, nor even restricted to the Vajrayāna and Mahāyāna but is rather one example of a widespread pattern within Indian Buddhism. Longevity is often attributed to the Buddhist saints as such, irrespective of sectarian affiliation, be they *arhats, bodhisattvas, siddhas*, or *buddhas*, and regardless of the tradition with which they are associated.

The Longevity of the Buddha

The preceding discussion is based on texts dating from the common era, and this leaves unanswered a crucial question: To what extent do the Buddhist saints and their longevity reflect early Buddhism, and to what extent do they represent a later development? Étienne Lamotte, in his *Histoire du Bouddhisme indien*, has suggested the commonly accepted interpretation. The Buddha, Lamotte says, originally taught a philosophico-mystical doctrine to his close disciples[64] and was originally understood by them as a human being, with all the limitations implied thereby.[65] In time, owing largely to pressure from the laity, Buddhism changed from a philosophy into a religion[66] and, as part of this transition, began to develop more grandiose notions of its enlightened ones, for, as Lamotte puts it, "nothing could prevent the Buddhists from also having their saints."[67] According to this explanation, found variantly in the works of Bareau,[68] Pachow,[69] and many others, the extravagant beliefs about the Buddhist saints and the cult that surrounds them are relatively late phenomena and do not represent early Buddhism.

Let us reconsider this issue by seeing what, if any, role our theme of the longevity of the Buddhist saints may play in older texts. As an example, we can consider the *Mahāparinirvāṇa Sūtra* (Mps) (P. *Mahāparinibbāna Sutta*), which, in its older sections, is believed by Frauwallner[70] and others to stand at the beginnings of Buddhist literature itself. In chapter three of the Pāli version, we in fact find an extended discussion of the Buddha's longevity.[71] The Pāli Mps relates how one day the Buddha, after seeking alms in Vaiśāli, walks with Ānanda to the Cāpāla Cetiya.[72] Sitting down there, he comments to Ānanda that "Whosoever has thought out, developed, practised, accumulated, and ascended to the very heights of the four paths to *iddhi* (*iddhi-pāda*), and so mastered them as to be able to use them as a means of (mental) advancement, and as a basis for edification, he, should he desire it, could remain in the same birth for a *kalpa*, or for that portion of a *kalpa* which had yet to run.[73] In order to understand this passage, we need to know that the *iddhi-pāda* (Skt. *Ṛddhi-pāda*) are four *samādhi* or meditative attainments,[74] which are classically understood to lead to facility in the six *abhiññā* (Skt. *abhijñā*) or supernatural powers.[75] Thus the Buddha is here saying that the meditator who has perfected the *iddhi-pāda* and is therefore in possession of the supernatural powers can indefinitely extend his life span, even to that unimaginably distant time when all worlds shall end.[76] Then, in order to clarify his meaning, the Buddha continues, "Now the *tathāgata* has thought them out, and thoroughly practiced and developed them [in all respects as just more fully described], and he could, therefore, should he desire it, live on yet for a *kalpa*, or for that portion of the *kalpa* which has yet to run.[77] Here we have the claim of extraordinary longevity made by the Buddha for himself: because of his attainment, he is not subject to the usual operation of death, but may live indefinitely, until the end of the *kalpa*. It is important to note that this claim—as presented in this passage—is understood to apply not just to Śākyamuni, nor to any one class of saints (e.g., *buddhas*), but is to be gained by anyone, as the text says, who has the requisite attainments. This ends up being a claim, on the part of the Mps, that realized saints, as such, have the power of longevity, even to the end of the *kalpa*.

The Mps has already told us that the Buddha's longevity is not automatic: he will live on only if he wishes to do so (*ākaṅkhamāna*). But under what conditions will he wish to do so? The answer is provided in the following section of the text. The Buddha, presumably because he is himself without personal desire, must be supplicated to remain in *saṃsāra*, otherwise he will not do so. In fact, the Mps tells us, the reason why the Buddha brings this subject up to Ānanda in the first place is to prod him to make the necessary request. However, the text continues, "even though a suggestion so evident and a hint so clear were thus given by the Blessed One, the venerable Ānanda was incapable of comprehending them; and he besought not the Blessed One."[78] It is very interesting that the Mps then tells us *exactly* what Ānanda should have said: "he besought not the Blessed One saying, 'Vouchsafe, Lord, to remain (*tiṭṭhatu*) during the *kalpa*! Live on through the *kalpa*, O Blessed One! for the good and the happiness of the great multitudes (*bahujana-hitāya . . . bahujana-sukhāya*), out of pity for the world (*lokānukampāya*), for the good and the gain and the weal of gods and men (*atthāya hitāya sukhāya deva-manussānan*)!' "[79]

And why did Ānanda not ask the Buddha to live on? The Mps says that his heart was possessed by Māra.[80] In fact, Māra has already previously asked the Blessed One to die now, and Ānanda not intervening, Māra's request remains in force.[81]

Here, then, in this ancient Buddhist text, we find a belief in the power of longevity not only of Buddha Śākyamuni, the paradigmatic Buddhist saint, but of realized saints as such. In the attribution of this power to Buddha Śākyamuni, we also find the same threefold pattern: (1) Śākyamuni Buddha possesses the power to live up to the end of the *kalpa*; (2) if he did so, it would be "for the good and the happiness of the great multitudes, out of pity for the world, for the good and the gain and the weal of gods and men"; and (3) his activation of this power is dependent upon the wishes and explict requests of sentient beings—if Ānanda had asked him to live on, he would have. Since Ānanda did not, the Blessed One accedes to Māra's request for a speedy entry into final *nirvāṇa*.[82] The set of beliefs taking shape in the tradition of Nāgārjuna's longevity, then, is not only one example of a set of beliefs concerning the longevity of realized persons commonly held in Indian Buddhism, but also one dating back to early times.[83]

However, more yet can be said. Bareau, as a result of his extensive analysis of the *Mahāparinirvāṇa Sūtra*, concludes that the text as it now exists in its six extant versions was composed over a long period of time, the earliest sections dating from soon after the passing of the Buddha, the latest sections being completed shortly before the beginning of the common era.[84] It is significant that the section dealing with the Buddha's longevity occurs in that part of the Mps judged by Bareau to be the oldest, and it also occurs in all six versions of the text, further suggesting its relative antiquity, even within this oldest part.[85] This implies, of course, that the belief in the longevity of the Buddha (and other saints) stands close to the initial composition of the Mps itself, thus pushing this belief back toward the beginnings of Buddhist literature. However, one may perhaps go a bit further yet. Not only is this belief found in the earliest sections of this text, but it can be demonstrated that the Mps actually presupposes the Buddha's longevity and other features of the Buddhist saints, and constructs many of its arguments as responses to these.[86] In light of this, it would not be unreasonable to hypothesize that the specific belief in the longevity of the Buddhist saints, as defined in this essay, actually predates the initial composition of the Mps itself.

Conclusion

We may conclude by summarizing our findings and suggesting some of their more obvious implications.

Nāgārjuna's longevity is clearly not an idiosyncratic phenomenon of the individual history of a particular saint, but rather one example of a very widespread pattern within Indian Buddhism. Longevity is often ascribed to the Buddhist saints as such, whether *buddhas*, *arhats*, *bodhisattvas* or *siddhas*. Moreover, this belief is found in each of the major Indian traditions—Nikāya, Mahāyānist, and Tantric—and from the earliest days of Buddhism in India down to its latest manifestations.

The longevity of each of these saints, throughout the various traditions and periods of Indian Buddhist history, is conceived in a remarkably similar manner, containing three relatively consistent features. First, the Buddhist saints have the power to greatly extend their lives. Second, this extension is intimately bound up with their compassion for sentient beings—they live longer than normal, specifically in order to help those still entrapped within *saṃsāra*. And third, the longevity of the Buddhist saints is closely connected with the wishes and explicit requests of others. This threefold pattern, then, provides a kind of relatively stable and enduring structure that was integral to the way in which Buddhist saints were identified, defined, and understood in India.

However, this threefold pattern, although relatively uniform within Indian Buddhist tradition, is at the same time able to make room for considerable diversity, suggesting that it was able to provide an accommodating framework within which various and changing ideas of Buddhist sainthood could take shape and develop. As one example of this diversity, we may consider the way in which the factors bringing about the saints' longevity are discussed. Our evidence identifies three, often cooperating causes, (1) accomplishment in meditation; (2) the explicit requests and wishes of others; and (3) the commitment of the saint to remain. In relation to the first cause, it is a fundamental assumption of Indian Buddhism that accomplishment in meditation is accompanied by the attainment of various supernatural abilities (*ṛddhi*), including the power of longevity, and as we have seen, from the days of the Mps onwards, longevity is an assumed power of the saints, whether or not they exercise it.[87] Sometimes our sources explicitly link meditation and longevity, as in the case of Mahākāśyapa. At other times, this linkage is implicit, as in the *Daśabhūmika Sūtra*, where a great deal of meditational attainment (in the lower *bhūmis*) precedes the attainment of this power. At still other times, it functions more as an assumed background, in the sense that to be a *buddha*, *arhat*, high-level *bodhisattva* or *siddha* implies realization, and this in turn implies meditational attainment. In this context, it may also be observed that the kind of meditation that results in the power of longevity is somewhat tradition-specific. Thus the *arhat* attains realization through the early classical practice of mindfulness and the *dhyānas*, the *bodhisattva* joins these practices with those of compassion, while the *siddhas* follow more tantric methods. Here Nāgārjuna, in the tantric sources, is an apt example with his practice of the longlife *mantra* of Amitāyus and his attainment of the eight *siddhis*, among which is included the elixir of long life. But if the sources agree on the central role of meditation, they present varying descriptions on exactly how it works. In the majority of cases—e.g., the Buddha, the sixteen *arhats*, the high-level *bodhisattvas*—one is in possession of the power simply by virtue of having attained realization. Alternatively we are told that it is while one is actually in the state of realized meditation itself that longevity is achieved. Thus Mahākāśyapa seems to attain his longevity by virtue of entering into the "trance of cessation" (*nirodha-samāpatti*).[88]

The second cause of longevity, the requests and wishes of others, makes it possible, as we have seen, for the saints to activate the power they possess. Here, as noted, the connection between the longevity of the saint and the wishes and requests of sentient beings takes one or another of three possible forms: (1) the saint is asked to live a long time, and does so (the *arhats*, *siddhas*, *buddhas*); (2) he is not specifically asked to live a long time, and so he dies (Śākyamuni Buddha after Ānanda's failure); or (3) he is explicitly asked to bring his life to an end (the Buddha, Nāgārjuna), and he complies. It is interesting that all three of these possibilities are already implicitly acknowledged in the *Mahāparinirvāṇa Sūtra*, for the possibility of the Buddha's living on is stated (1), Ānanda fails to make the necessary request (2), and Māra specifically asks him to die (3). Significantly, these variations provide an explanatory framework that can accommodate differing circumstances. Thus the belief in the saints' longevity can be retained not only when that longevity is believed to have been achieved, but also when a saint dies an untimely death or lives out a merely normal life span: he died because he was not asked to remain, was not asked in the prescribed manner, desired to die or was explicitly asked to do so. This framework can also account for how a saint, who is in possession of extraordinary supernatural power, can be killed by a malefactor. This explanatory schema is interesting additionally in the way in which it stresses two important Buddhist doctrines. First, it makes it possible to retain the idea of the great powers of the saint while at the same time affirming that the actual longevity of a saint is not independent of causes and conditions. Second, it provides a firm basis for the Buddhist cult of saints, without at the same time falling into the pitfall (from the Buddhist viewpoint) of denying individual responsibility. The saints may from one viewpoint be all-powerful, but from another the suppliant's own awareness and actions are critical, and ordinary beings bear major responsibility for the saint's ability to remain in the world and teach.

The third cause of the saints' longevity, the commitment (or vow) to remain in *saṃsāra* that is frequently associated with the saint's longevity, also shows variations. In the Buddha's case, this commitment (along with the power to do so) is assumed, and thus the Mps must offer some explanation as to why he appears not to have seen this commitment through. In the cases of Mahākāśyapa and the sixteen *arhats*, the commitment arises specifically at the request of the Buddha. In the case of the *bodhisattva*, the commitment is part of the saint's vow to save sentient beings. In the *siddhas*' "lives," the vow to remain is assumed and only occasionally explicated. Particularly interesting is the fact that the vow to remain in *saṃsāra* and its association with compassion, which is usually associated by modern scholarship specifically with the *bodhisattva* and the Mahāyāna, is revealed by our evidence to be a much more general phenomenon within Indian Buddhism, and in fact it is associated with *buddhas*, *arhats*, *bodhisattvas*, and *siddhas*. This, of course, has important implications for correctly understanding the place of the Mahāyāna ideal within the larger Indian Buddhist context.[89]

Our fourth conclusion is that differences such as these raise an obvious question: Do we in any sense have to deal here with distinct traditions of longevity within the larger frame of the general Buddhist belief in the longevity of its saints? Some hints in this direction are perhaps provided by the interesting fact that, within our evidence, one can discriminate several distinct and different ways of conceiving the precise temporal span of the saints' longevity. First, there is the type of longevity described in the Mps, wherein any meditator who has attained the *iddhi-pādas* has the power to live until the end of the *kalpa*.[90] As a variation of this type (if not understood as identical to it) is the longevity wherein a saint lives either until the coming of Maitreya or as long the *dharma* shall survive upon the earth. This fantastic but ultimately limited type of longevity clearly had considerable cultic importance, for we find it turning up not only in the Mps, but also in the Mahāyāna cult of the sixteen *arhats*, the Burmese cult of Upagupta, the Mahāyāna doctrine of the *bodhisattva*, and the tradition of *siddhas*, as seen in the example of Śavaripa in the Csp. As perhaps a special subclass of this type is the notion that the saint is residing within a mountain (or *stūpa* or temple), and in Mahākāśyapa's case abiding in *nirodha-samāpatti*, from which he will arise at the time of Maitreya's coming, a pattern connected with both Mahākāśyapa and Bhāvaviveka. A second type of longevity is that found predominantly among the *siddhas*, where a specific number of years is assigned to each saint. This longevity, although extravagant by normal standards, is still far closer to an ordinary human scale than the "end of the *kalpa*" type, with its vastly longer time spans. The "relatively human" scale of the *siddhas*' longevity is perhaps also reflected in the fact that we are typically told that, during their long sojourns in this world, they remained on earth instructing sentient beings. This stands in contrast to the first kind of saint who, although living so long, is no where depicted as residing in or among people. Finally, a third way of thinking about longevity ascribes to the saint a life span of indefinite length. This tradition seems specifically associated with the *buddhas* and with those high-level *bodhisattvas* who are approaching the status of a *buddha*.[91] These three ways of conceiving longevity are not always distinct, as in the case of Mahākāśyapa and Bhāvaviveka who, like the long-lived *arhats*, have a vast life span but, like the *siddhas*, seem to have a corporeal longevity: their physical forms remain here, if enclosed within their mountain fastnesses.

A fifth and final conclusion concerns the particular context of religious life in which the longevity of Nāgārjuna and the other Buddhist saints was important. Many contemporary scholars of Buddhism would have it that the Buddhist saints and their cults, whether of Nikāya, Mahāyāna, or Vajrayāna Buddhism, are primarily a reflection of popular (lay) as opposed to elite (monastic) Buddhism.[92] At least in terms of the evidence examined here, such a position would seem difficult to maintain. For example, Hsüan-tsang, Abhayadatta, and Tāranātha, energetic in their reports of Nāgārjuna's longevity, represent the elite among the elite of their respective traditions. In a similar vein, the *Daśabhūmika Sūtra*, Vasubandhu's *Abhidharmakośa*, Asaṅga's *Bodhisattvabhūmi*, and Śāntideva's *Bodhicāryāvatāra*, all of which maintain the longevity of the Buddhist saints, can hardly be thought of primarily as expressions of popular religion. Further, the cult of the sixteen *arhats* was clearly developed and practiced by monks and elite meditators. We see this both in the actual content of the text itself, which reflects monastic concerns, and also in the central role of this cult in China and Japan among the elite of Ch'an and Zen Buddhism.[93] Finally, the *Mahāparinirvāṇa Sūtra* stands right at the heart of early elite monastic Buddhism, the initial formation and justification of which, Frauwallner has convincingly argued, is reflected in the text.[94] Clearly, then, the longevity of the Buddhist saints is a matter of extreme importance to the elite of Buddhist tradition, both monastic and yogic, of virtually every period of Indian Buddhist history and can hardly be restricted to or perhaps even primarily located in the sphere of lay or popular Buddhism.[95] We began this essay with a single, small, and seemingly simple problem: Why is such an extraordinary life span attributed to Nāgārjuna? Our search for an answer led to a surprisingly wide field of evidence and to conclusions that have bearing on the history of Indian Buddhism as a whole and, within that, on the identity of the Buddhist saints and their role within the tradition. This suggests what is (by now) the obvious point, that there is much that can be learned from an examination of Buddhist masters within the larger context of the Buddhist saints in India. Beyond trying to see these figures as specific individuals bound up with particular historical circumstances, texts, and schools, it is informative to consider the elements of their biographies in relation to the ascetic, hagiographic, and cultic conventions of the Buddhist saintly traditions as a whole, of which the belief in the saints' longevity is clearly a good example.

Acknowledgments

I would like to thank Gregory Schopen for reading a draft of this essay and providing a number of useful suggestions.

Notes

1. Cf. discussions of Nāgārjuna's dates in D. S. Ruegg, "The Literature of the Madhyamaka School of Philosophy in India," in *A History of Indian Literature*, vol. 7, fasc. 1, ed. Jan Gonda (Wiesbaden: Otto Harrassowitz, 1981), pp. 4–5 n. 11; and Étienne Lamotte, *Le Traité de la Grande vertue de Sagesse* (Louvain-la-neuve: Institut Orientaliste, 1981), vol. 3, pp. ff. See also Richard Robinson, *Early Mādhyamika in India and China* (Madison: University of Wisconsin Press, 1967), pp. 25–26; and Étienne Lamotte, *L'Enseignement de Vimalakīrti* (Louvain: Université de Louvain, 1962), pp. 70–77.
2. The principal Buddhist sources for the life of Nāgārjuna include:

   In Sanskrit: (1) the *Laṅkāvatāra (Sagāthakam)*, ed. P. L. Vaidya, *Laṅkāvatāra* (*Buddhist Sanskrit Texts*, no. 3) (Darbhaṅga: Mithila Institute, 1963), vol. 118, pp. 165–166 (D. T. Suzuki, *The Laṅkāvatāra Sūtra*

[London: Routledge and Kegan Paul, 1932], pp. 239–240); (2) the *Mañjuśrīmūlakalpa*, ed. Gaṇapati Śāstri, *Mañjuśrīmūlakalpa (Trivandrum Sanskrit Series*, vols. 70, 76, and 84)(Trivandrum: Government Press, 1920–1925), pp. 616–617, hereafter cited as Mmk; (3) a Sanskrit biography of the *siddhas*, G. Tucci, *Animadversiones indicae*: 6, "A Sanskrit Biography of the Siddhas and Some Questions Connected with Nāgārjuna," *Journal and Proceedings of the Asiatic Society of Bengal*, vol. 26 (1930), pp. 138–155 (S. Lévi, "Un nouveau document sur le bouddhisme de basse époque dans l'Inde, *Bulletin of the School of Oriental and African Studies* 6 [1930–1932], pp. 417–429); (4) Bāṇa's *Haṇacarita*, Parab, *Bāna's Harṣacarita* (Bombay, 1946); subsequently edited with copious notes by P.V. Kane, *The Harshacarita of Bāṇabhaṭṭa (Text of Uchchhvāsas I–VIII)* (Delhi, 1965), 137.20 ff. and 612; and (5) *Rājataraṅgiṇī of Kalhaṇa*, Vishva Bandhu, *Rājataraṅgiṇī of Kalhaṇa* (Hoshiarpur, 1963), I.173 and I.177; cf. also M. A. Stein, *Rājataraṅgiṇī of Kalhaṇa* (Westminster, 1900), 2 vols. (English trans., M. A. Stein, *Kalhaṇa's Rājataraṅgiṇī; A Chronicle of the Kings of Kashmir* [Delhi, 1961], 2 vols. (introduction, translation, commentary, and appendixes) (originally published, Westminster, 1900, 2 vols.), vol. 1, pp. 76 and book 1, verses 173 and 177. (6) Nāgārjuna is also mentioned in the *Bṛhatkathāmañjarī* (XVI.392–407) and the *Kathāsaritsāgara* (Kane, *The Harshacarita*, p. 612).

In Chinese: (1) the biography of Nāgārjuna attributed to Kumārajīva (T.50.184a–185b and T.50.185b–186c) (in this essay, I follow an unpublished translation of Roger Corless, for the use of which I thank the translator); and (2) the biographical account in Hsüan-tsang's Hsi-yü-chi (T.2087), 929a–930a (Samuel Beal, *Si-yu-ki, Buddhist Records of the Western World* [Delhi: Motilal Banarsidass, 1981], vol. 2, pp. 97 ff; Thomas Watters, *On Yuan Chwang's Travels in India* [New Delhi: Munshiram Manoharlal, 1973], vol. 2, pp. 200–208).

In Tibetan: (1) Abhayadatta's *Caturaśītisiddhapravṛtti* (translated into Tibetan as *grub.thob.brgyad.cu.rtsa.bzhi'i.lo.rgyus*), ed. Sempa Dorje, *The Biography of the Eighty-four Saints* (Sarnath: Central Institute of Higher Tibetan Studies, 1979), pp. 65–74 hereafter cited as Csp; (2) Bu.ston's *chos.'byung*, E. Obermiller, trans. (Heidelberg: Otto Harrassowitz, 1932); (3) Tāranātha's *bka'.babs.bdun.ldan* [hereafter cited as Kbdd], in Tseten Dorji, *Five Historical Works of Tāranātha* (Arunachal Pradesh, India: Tibetan Nyingmapa Monastery, 1974) and his *chos.'byuṇg* (Lama Chimpa and Alaka Chattopadhyaya, *Tāranātha's History of Buddhism in India* [Simla: Indian Institute of Advanced Study, 1970]); and (4) Sum.pa.mkhan.po's *dPag.bsam.ljon.bzang*, S.C. Das, *dPag.bsam.ljon.bzang* (Calcutta: Presidency Jail Press, 1908). Tibetan tradition contains other works on Nāgārjuna which, when investigated, will undoubtedly reveal information pertinent to the development of his biography in India and Tibet. Biographies in Hindu and Jain traditions may also be mentioned, the latter being the subject of a study by Phyllis Granoff, "Jain Biographies of Nāgārjuna:

Notes on the Composing of a Biography in Medieval India," in *Monks and Magicians: Religious Biographies in Asia*, ed. Phyllis Granoff and Koichi Shinohara (New York: Mosaic Press, 1988), pp. 45–66.

3. Cf., e.g., Jan Yün-hua, "Nāgārjuna, One or More? A New Interpretation of Buddhist Hagiography," *History of Religions* 10, no. 2 (1970), p. 139. Étienne Lamotte remarks that, of figures in Buddhism, "the *bodhisattva* Nāgārjuna . . . is one of the most enigmatic" (*Le Traité*, vol. 1, p. x). Some representative discussions of the life of Nāgārjuna, listed in chronological order of appearance, include: S. C. Das, "Life and Legend of Nāgārjuna," *Journal of the Asiatic Society of Bengal* 51, pt. 1 (1882), pp. 115–120; Max Walleser, "The Life of Nāgārjuna from Tibetan and Chinese Sources," *Hirth Anniversary Volume* (London: Probsthain and Co., 1922), pp. 421–455; Tucci, *Animadversiones indicae*, (Lévi, "Un nouveau document"); L. La Vallée Poussin, "Madhyamaka," *Encyclopedia of Religion and Ethics*, vol. 8 (1908–1926), pp. 235–237 and *Le dogme et la philosophie du Bouddhisme* (Paris, 1930), pp. 113–118; Th. Stcherbatsky, *Conception of Buddhist Nirvāṇa* (Leningrad: 1927; reprint, Delhi: Motilal Banarsidass, 1968), pp. 35–39; N. Dutt, "Notes on the Nāgārjunikoṇḍa Inscriptions," *Indian Historical Quarterly* 7 (1931), pp. 633–653; M. Winternitz, *History of Indian Literature* (Calcutta: University of Calcutta, 1933), vol. 2, pp. 341–348; Lamotte, *Traité*, vol. 1, pp. x–xiv; V. W. Karambelkar, "The Problem of Nāgārjuna," *Journal of Indian History* 2 (1952), pp. 21–33; Sunitikumar Pathak, "Life of Nāgārjuna (from the Pag-Sam-Jon-Zang)," *Indian Historical Quarterly* 30 (1954), pp. 93–95; Prafulla Chandra Ray, *History of Hindu Chemistry* (Calcutta, 1956), pp. 116–119; K. V. Ramanan, *Nāgārjuna's Philosophy as Presented in the Mahā-Prajñāpāramitā Śāstra* (Rutland, Vt.: Charles E. Tuttle, 1966), pp. 25–37; Robinson, *Early Mādhyamika*, pp. 21–27; Jan, "Nāgārjuna," pp. 139–155; Ruegg, *The Literature of the Madhyamaka*, pp. 4–9; and Frederick Streng, "Nāgārjuna," *Encyclopedia of Religion*, ed. Mircea Eliade (New York: Macmillan, 1987), vol. 10, pp. 290–293.

4. *Mañjuśrīmūlakalpa*, p. 440.

In addition, other texts give predictions concerning Nāgārjuna including: (1) *Laṅkāvatāra (Sagāthakam)*, passage discussed by J. Takasaki, "Sources of the Laṅkāvatāra and Its Position in Mahāyāna Buddhism," *Indological and Buddhological Studies: Volume in Honour of Professor J.W. de Jong on His Sixtieth Birthday* (Canberra: Faculty of Asian Studies, 1982), p. 550. The *Laṅkāvatāra* prophecy reveals similar themes to those of the *Mañjuśrīmūlakalpa* without, however, mentioning Nāgārjuna's long life:

dakṣiṇāpatha-vedalyām bhikṣuḥ śrīmān mahāyaśāh/
nāgāhvayaḥ sa nāmnā tu sadasatpakīadārakaḥ // (165)
prakāśya loke madyānaṃ mahāyānam anuttaram/
āsādya bhūmiṃ muditāṃ yāsyate 'sau sukhāvātīm// (166)

In Vedalī, in the southern part, a bhikṣu most illustrious and distinguished [will be born];

his name is Nāgāhvaya, he is the destroyer of the one-sided views based on being and non-being (165).
He will declare my Vehicle, the unsurpassed Mahāyāna, to the world; attaining the stage of Joy he will go to the land of bliss (166) (Suzuki, The Laṅkāvatāra Sūtra, *pp. 240–241).*

(2) *Mahāmeghasūtra*, cited in the *Madhyamakāvatara*, Tibetan ed. by La Vallée Poussin (St. Petersburg, 1912), p. 76 (translation, *Le Muséon*, [1910], p. 274); Chinese translation by Dharmarakīa, Taishō 387, k. 5, 1099–1100; examined by P. Demiéville, "Sur un passage du Mahāmeghasūtra," *Bulletin de l'École française d'Extrême Orient* 24 (1924), pp. 227–228; mentioned by Bu.ston, *chos.'byung*, vol. 2, p. 129; and

(3) the *Mahāmāyasūtra*, Taishō 383, k. 2, 1013c; discussed by J. Przyluski, *Légende de l'empereur Aśoka* (Paris: Paul Geuthner, 1923), pp. 163–164. Cf. Lamotte, *Le Traité*, vol. 1, p. xi, n. 4–7 for additional references.

5. T: *grub.thob.brgyad.cu.rtsa.bzhi'i.lo.rgyus.*
6. One of his pupils revisits him after an interval of 100 years [Csp, pp. 65–74].
7. See n. 15, where this is made explicit.
8. Kbdd, p. 365.
9. Ibid., pp. 369–370. Tāranātha gives essentially the same account in his *chos.'byung* (*History*, p. 110), written in 1608, eight years after the Kbdd.
10. Dutt, "Notes," pp. 633–653.
11. Ibid., pp. 636–639.
12. Other scholars believe that there were as many as three or four separate Nāgārjunas, for which cf. Tucci, *Animadversiones indicae*, pp. 138 ff.
13. Dutt, "Notes," pp. 636–637.
14. Benoytosh Bhattacharyya gives essentially the same explanation of Nāgārjuna's longevity (*Introduction to Buddhist Esoterism* [Varanasi: Chowkhamba Sanskrit Series Office, 1932], pp. 67–68), as does Lal Mani Joshi, *Studies in the Buddhistic Culture of India* (Delhi: Motilal Banarsidass, 1977), p. 262. See also Ramanan, *Nāgārjuna's Philosophy*, p. 366, n. 5, who appears to follow the essentials of Dutt's explanation. Most scholars dealing with Nāgārjuna's life, however, have subsequently tended to bypass his longevity, lumping it in with other similar "magical elements," and have moved on to examine other features of his life.
15. Cf. Matsunaga's discussion of some issues involved in the attempt to date the Mmk (Yūkei Matsunaga, "On the Date of the *Mañjuśrīmūlakalpa*," *Tantric and Taoist Studies in Honour of R.A. Stein*, vol. 3 [*Mélanges chinois et bouddhiques*, no. 22], ed. M. Strickmann [Brussels: Institut Belge des Hautes Études Chinoises, 1985], pp. 882–894). In an analysis accepted by Matsunaga, Przyluski had previously determined that the Mmk may be divided into two parts, chapters 4 and following, which were composed at an earlier time, and chapters 1–3 composed at a later time. Significantly, the

prediction regarding Nāgārjuna is found in the part of the text deemed by Przyluski to be the earlier one. Matsunaga has examined the Sanskrit text in relation to translations into Tibetan and Chinese and—extending and refining the work of Przyluski—hypothesizes that the Mmk originated gradually over a long period of time, during which relatively independent compositions were added to the text. Through his analysis, Matsunaga is able to make some initial hypotheses concerning the times of origin of certain sections of the text. However, he shows that a great deal of further analysis is needed before any firm conclusions can be drawn regarding the dating of these various sections of the text. Matsunaga thus dismisses scholars' (rather uncritical) dating of this text, including both those proposing a late date for the text as a whole, e.g., the one assumed by Dutt in the article cited here, as well as those proposing an early date, e.g., by Bhattacarya who holds for a first–second century composition. For an earlier discussion of the text's dating, cf. Ariane Macdonald, *Le Maṇḍala du Mañjuśrīmūlakalpa* (Paris: Adrien-Maisonneuve, 1962), pp. 3–20.

16. Hsüan-tsang reports that Nāgārjuna, upon being asked for his head, replied that "my constant vow [as a *bodhisattva*] has been not to oppose the desires of living things" (Beal, *Si-yu-ki*, vol. 2, pp. 212–214).

17. Jan, "Nāgārjuna," p. 129. Similarly Tao-shih (seventh century) [Jan, ibid., pp. 148–149]. The Korean pilgrim Hui-ch'ao also believed that Nāgārjuna died at the age of 700 years (Jan, ibid., p. 149).

18. Corless, unpublished translation, p. 12.

19. In citing the names of the *siddhas*, I follow the spelling in Sempa Dorje's edition of the Csp, in spite of the fact that, as in the present case (as often in Tibetan transliterations if not in the Indian original), the spelling violates the rules of classical Sanskrit orthography.

20. Caurāṅgi [10] should not be included among those to whom an extraordinary lifespan is attributed. In Robinson's translation of the Csp we read of "the immortal Caurāṅgi" (James B. Robinson, *Buddha's Lions, The Lives of the Eighty-four Siddhas* [Berkeley: Dharma Press, 1979], p. 56). However, the Tibetan reads "*'chi.med.brnyes.pa'i.cauranggi*" (Sempa Dorji, *Biography of the Eighty-four Saints*, p. 45), "Caurāṅgi who acquired the deathless," a common enough epithet of the *siddhas*, referring simply to their realization and not necessarily intending any reference to their life spans.

21. *byams.pa'i.bstan.pa.ma.shar.gyi.bar.du.sku.'di.nyid.kyis. 'dzam.bu'i.gling.'dir.bzhugs.so* (Csp 26.12–3). For additional remarks on Śāvaripa, cf. n. 37.

22. Those said to live many years, those given a life span of 100 years, and Gorakṣa.

23. The typical phrase is, as in Kapalapa's story, [72], "*(lo.lnga. brgyar).'gro.don.mdzad*" (Csp 225:12).

24. This compassionate activity receives further specification in the various examples. Of these, their activities include generally "accomplishing the

benefit of beings," recounting one's realization (i.e., in the Tantric context, providing teaching *dharma*), and bringing down great blessings.

25. Csp, 239.

26. Ibid.

27. This understanding of the *siddhas'* longevity seems to have been the prevalent one in the Indian Vajrayāna and is commonly found in other Tantric texts either deriving from India or Tibet in composition but basing themselves on Indian texts or traditions. Thus, to mention just a few prominent authors, 'Gos.blo.tsā.ba (G. N. Roerich, trans., *Blue Annals* [Delhi: Motilal Banarsidass, 1976]); Bu.ston's *chos.'byung* (E. Obermiller, trans. [Heidelberg: Otto Harrassowitz, 1932]); Padmakarpo (*Chos.'byung*, xyl., sPungs.thang edn. sixteenth century); and Tāranātha (Kbdd, and *History*), in their treatment of Indian saints, all depict a key role played by longevity.

28. In this text, for example, we find an early summary of Indian Mahāyāna canonical literature.

29. Chinese, *Ta A-lo-han Nan-t'i-mi-to-lo so chouo fa tchou ki*, T. 2030; Tibetan, *'phags.pa.dga'.ba'i.bshes.gnyen.gyi.rtogs.pa.brjod.pa*, Peking *bstan.'gyur*, vol. 127, vol. 8 of *'dul.ba'i.'grel.pa*, 299b–306a. Text no. 4146 of the *sde.dge.bstan.'gyur*, Nyingma edition (Berkeley, 1980), vol. 91, vol. su, 240a, 1. 4–244 b, 1. 2. Chinese text translated into French in Sylvain Lévi and Édouard Chavannes, "Les seize *arhat* protecteurs de la loi," *Journal Asiatique* 8 (1916), pp. 205–275, and into English in Shan Shih, *The Sixteen Arhants and the Eighteen Arhants* (Peking: Buddhist Association of China, 1961).

30. M. W. De Visser, *The Arhants in China and Japan* (Berlin: Oesterheld and Co., 1922–1923), pp. 105 ff.

31. Lévi and Chavannes, "Les seize *arhat* protecteurs," p. 6.

32. Paul Williams mentions a Nandimitra who plays a chief role in the *Ajitasena Sūtra* (*Mahāyāna Buddhism: The Doctrinal Foundations* [London: Routledge, 1989], pp. 26–27). Williams remarks that this sūtra, found in a mound near Gilgit early in this century, "is undoubtedly much earlier in origin" and indicates "a stage of proto-Mahāyāna, a stage of Mahāyāna prior to its own self-awareness as 'Mahāyāna'" (p. 26). The Nandimitra of this text is a great *śrāvaka* (*mahāśrāvaka*), a disciple of the Buddha whom the Buddha sends as a spiritual friend (*kalyāṇamitra*) to King Ajitasena (pp. 26–27).

33. Lévi and Chavannes, "Les seize *arhat* protecteurs," p. 5.

34. Lamotte's rendering (*Histoire du bouddhisme indien, 769;* Shan Shih, *The Sixteen Arhants,* p. 9).

35. Lévi and Chavannes, "Les seize *arhat* protecteurs," pp. 9–10; Shan Shih, similarly, *The Sixteen Arhants*, p. 9. The Tibetan (see n. 29 above) reads "[the sixteen *arhats*] were commanded by the Blessed one to extend their livespans by means of the blessing (*byin.gyis.brlabs*) [of their lives] [effected] by the power (*bala*) of their *ṛddhi* (supernatural abilities), *rdzu.'phrul.gyi.*

stobs.kyis.tshe.byin.gyis.brlabs.te.bsrings.nas.bcom.ldan.'das.kyis.bka'.gnas.pa.yin.no. (300b). A comparison of the translations from the Chinese with the Tibetan text suggests that there are a number of differences, some important, between the two versions.

36. During their stay, the *arhats* will see several stages of human history. First, the life span of ordinary humans will decline to ten years, when Buddhism will temporarily disappear from the earth. The *arhats* will continue to remain until the human life span has increased again to 100 years, at which time they will again spread the *dharma* abroad, teaching, converting beings, and bringing blessings to all. These *arhats* will continue to remain until the human life span will have increased to 60,000 years, when the *dharma* will be propagated throughout the world. When the length of human life has reached 70,000 years, the *dharma* will disappear forever, and the *arhats* will pass beyond.

37. As we saw above, in the Csp, the *siddha* Śāvaripa is predicted to live "in this very body" until the coming of Maitreya. Among the eighty-four *siddhas*, Śāvaripa's enormous longevity is unique. However, the present discussion reveals that Śāvaripa embodies a common though different type of longevity, namely that of the long-lived *arhat*.

38. Evidence of the belief of the longevity of *arhats* in China considerably precedes evidence of the cult of the sixteen *arhats*. For example, one may cite the first Buddhist literature translated into Chinese, reflecting Indian Buddhism in the middle of the first century A.D. (Rev. Soyen Shaku, *Sermons of a Buddhist Abbot*, translated from the Japanese by Daisetz Teitaro Suzuki [New York, 1971], pp. 3–21; see p. 3). In this work, we find a description of the four classes of *āryas* or Buddhist holy persons. Of the *arhat* we read, "The *arhant* is able to fly through space and assume different forms; his life is eternal and there are times when he causes heaven and earth to quake" [ibid., p. 5]. In other words, in this text, the *arhat* is defined chiefly by his magical powers, among these are mentioned two classic Buddhist *ṛddhi* and, right with them as a chief defining feature of the *arhat*, the power of longevity.

39. The cult of long-lived *arhats* is found not only in scriptural evidence such as the *Nandimitrāvadāna*, but also in other evidence of Buddhist cultic life in India. A significant body of this sort of evidence is provided by Lévi and Chavannes and by De Visser in examples of the cult of *arhats* in China and Japan, which must, to an extent difficult to specify, reflect Indian usages (Lévi and Chavannes, "Les seize *arhat* protecteurs," p. 79 and De Visser, *The Arhants in China and Japan*, pp. 105 ff). An intriguing glimpse of the cult is provided by Hsüan-tsang's description of the cult of Rāhula, one of the sixteen *arhats*. Thus the pilgrim tells us that one day, when he was passing through a certain village, he chanced upon the dwelling of a wealthy and eminent Brāhman. By his house, this worthy had constructed a shelter for wandering mendicants, and he would beg them to stop and stay there for a period of from one up to seven days in length. Some time

not long before the pilgrim's visit, a certain *śramaṇa*, with thick eyebrows and a shaven head, had accepted the Brahman's invitation to stay awhile. When in the morning the Brahman gave him some food, the *śramaṇa* took a bit, sighed, and returned the remainder to the donor. Distressed, the Brahman asked if his offering were in some way amiss. The *śramaṇa* replied, "When I sighed, it was not on account of your offering of rice; for during many hundreds of years I have not tasted such food. When [the] *tathāgata* was living in the world, I was a follower of his when he dwelt in the Veṇuvana-vihāra, near Rājagṛha; there . . . I washed his *pātra* in the pure stream of the river—there I filled his pitcher—there I gave him water for cleansing his mouth; but alas! the milk that you offer now is not like the sweet water of old! It is because the religious merit of *devas* and men has diminished that this is the case!" (Beal, *Si-yu-ki*, vol. 2, pp. 42–43). Astounded, the Brahman then asked his guest if he meant to say that he had, in fact, seen the very Buddha himself. The *śramaṇa* replied, "Have you never heard of Rāhula the Buddha's own son? I am he! Because I desire to protect the true law I have not yet entered *nirvāṇa*." Having said this, the saint suddenly disappeared, and the amazed Brahman made a shrine out of the place he had stayed and, in Hsüan-tsang's words, "placed there a figure of him, which he reverenced as though he were present" (ibid.).

40. *Daśabhūmika Sūtra*, P. L. Vaidya, ed., *Buddhist Sanskrit Texts*, no. 7 (Darbhaṅga: Mithila Institute, 1967), hereafter cited as Dbs; Chinese: T. 278, 279, 285, 286, 287; Tibetan: *sde.dge bka'.'gyur*, 44:31 (Nyingma edition, Oakland, Calif., 1980). English translation from the Sanskrit by M. Honda, *Annotated Translation of the Daśabhūmika Sūtra*, in *Studies in South, East, and Central Asia*, ed. Dennis Sinor, *Śata-Piṭaka Series* 74 (New Delhi: International Academy of Indian Culture, 1968).

41. The ten *vaśitā*, including *āyur-vaśitā*, are powers that are ascribed to fully enlightened *buddhas*. For an enumeration, see Kenjiu Kasawara, F. Max Müller, and H. Wenzel, eds., *Dharma-saṃgraha* (Oxford: Oxford University Press, 1885), sec. 74.

42. DbS, p. 46; Honda, *Annotated Translation*, p. 227; Har Dayal, *Bodhisattva Doctrine in the Buddhist Sanskrit Literature* (London, 1932; Delhi: Motlal Banarsidass), p. 140; cf. Nalinaksha Dutt, *Aspects of Mahāyāna Buddhism and Its Relation to Hīnayāna* (London: Luzac and Co., 1930), p. 281.

43. E.g., *Laṅkāvatāra Sūtra*, p. 1:6. Also important in the *Avataṃsaka Sūtra*, *Gaṇḍavyūha* section, discussed in D. T. Suzuki, *Studies in the Laṅkāvatāra Sūtra* (London: Routledge and Kegan Paul, 1930), pp. 230 and 234.

44. Asaṅga, *Bodhisattvabhūmi*, pp. 38, 240. Cf. also Jikido Takasaki, *A Study of the Ratnagotravibhāga (Uttaratantra)* (Rome: Istituto Italiano per il Medio ed Estremo Oriente, 1966), p. 214. In addition, it may not be irrelevant in this context to point out that the high-level *bodhisattvas* achieve what amounts to a kind of longevity within the world through their intentional rebirths within the six realms of *saṃsāra* over countless eons, as they journey on

toward complete and perfect enlightenment (*anuttara-samyak-saṃbodhi*). This quasi-longevity, based on their vow before a *buddha* and motivated by compassion for sentient beings, allows the *bodhisattvas* to maintain a continual presence within *saṃsāra*, with no more than periodic gaps when they die and take rebirth. It may be argued that this does not really constitute "longevity" in the strict sense of the term, since *bodhisattvas* die and then take rebirth. Although this argument is not without merit, it should at the same time be pointed out that in general structure and also in many details, this process among the *bodhisattvas* closely parallels the other types of longevity being discussed in this essay. To provide one example, the *bodhisattva*'s presence is, in effect, not as different from that of the sixteen *arhats* as might first appear. As we have seen, these *arhats* live in far off places, including the realm of the gods, from which they come periodically among humans. Interestingly, the theme of the anonymous coming characterizes not only *arhats* but also *bodhisattvas* (cf. Asaṇga, *Bodhisattvabhūmi*, pp. 40 ff. This theme of the *bodhisattva* who comes anonymously among men to teach them is found already in a mature form in the *Mahāparinibbāna Sutta* (*Dīghanikāya*, hereafter cited as Dn), edited by T. W. Rhys-Davids and J. E. Carpenter (London, 1890–1911), xvi.3.21–3 (T. W. Rhys-Davids, *Buddhist Suttas, Sacred Books of the East*, vol. 11 [Oxford: Oxford University Press, 1881], vol. 3, pp. 21–23).

45. F. Max Müller, "The Larger *Sukhāvatī-vyūha Sūtra*," in F. Max Müller, ed., *Buddhist Mahāyāna Texts*, part 2, *The Sacred Books of the East*, vol. 49 (Delhi: Motilal Banarsidass, 1972), p. 5.
46. Ibid., p. 32.
47. Kosho Yamamoto, *The Mahāyāna Mahāparinirvāṇa Sūtra* (Ube City, Japan, 1973), vol. 1, p. 61.
48. Ibid., vol. 1, p. 69.
49. Takasaki, *A Study of the Ratnagotravibhāga (Uttaratantra)*, p. 178 and p. 178 n. 45.
50. *nirvātukāmāṃśca jinān yācayāmi kṛtāñjaliḥ // kalpānanantāṃstiṣṭhantu mā bhūdandhamidaṃ jagat* (Bodhicarya vatāra 38, v. 5 [Marion Matics, *Entering the Path of Enlightenment* (New York: Macmillan, 1970), 153]).
51. Discussed in Padmanabh S. Jaini, "Buddha's Prolongation of Life," *Bulletin of the School of Oriental and African Studies* 21 (1958), pp. 546–552.
52. Louis de La Vallée Poussin, *L'Abhidharmakośa de Vasubandhu* (Brussels: Mélanges chinois et bouddhiques, 1971), vol. 2, pp. 120–121.
53. André Bareau, *Les sectes bouddhiques du petit véhicule* (Saigon, 1955), p. 260. This does not mean, however, that the Buddha lives forever, but rather that, in Dutt's words, "Buddha's length of life (*āyus*) is unlimited on account of his past accumulated merits. Buddha lives as long as the sentient beings live" (Nalinaksha Dutt, *Buddhist Sects in India* [Calcutta: Mukhopadhyay, 1970], p. 79).
54. One of the four *acinteyyas* of the *Aṇguttara-nikaya*, ii.80, cited by La Vallée Poussin, *L'Abhidharmakośa de Vasubandhu*, vol. 2, p. 83, n. 3. Cf. F. L.

Woodward, *Gradual Sayings* (London: Luzac, 1951–1955), vol. 2, pp. 89–90 (vii. 77).

55. Both cultic, as we are about to see, and scholastic. As an example of this latter, Vasubandhu, in his *Abhidharmakośa*, discusses the ability of *arhats* to prolong their lives (La Vallée Poussin, *l'Abhidharmakośa de Vasubandhu*, vol. 2, pp. 120–121).
56. For example, a group of Uighur-language fragments, almost certainly Sarvāstivādin, makes explicit reference to Piṇḍola-bhāradvāja and the rest of the sixteen *arhats*, within a cultic frame of reference (texts published by F.W.K. Müller, Uigurica II, 7 and 8, [Sitzungsberichte der Bayerischen Akademie der Wissenschaften, Phil.-Hist. Klasse, 1910, pp. 76–89; and W. Bang and A. von Gabain, Türkische Turfan-Texte IV, A and B (Sitzungsberichte der Bayerischen Akademie der Wissenschaften, Phil.-Hist. Klasse, 1930, pp. 432–450)] [referred to by APAW, SPAW, Jan Nattier, unpublished manuscript in possession of the author]).
57. Maung Kin, "The Legend of Upagutta," *Buddhism*, vol. 1 (1903), pp. 219–242.
58. Ibid., 219.
59. P. L. Vaidya, ed., *Divyāvadanam, Buddhist Sanskrit Texts*, no. 20 (Darbhaṅga, 1959), pp. 216–282.
60. Przyluski's translation, *Légende de l'empereur Aśoka*, pp. 264 ff. This text, a translation of a no longer extant Sanskrit original (with the likely title of the *Aśokarājāvadāna*) and a version of the legend of King Aśoka in many ways quite different from the version contained in the *Divyāvadāna*, was translated into Chinese in about 300 A.D. by Fa-ch'in. For a discussion of these and the two other major recensions (partial and complete) of the legend of King Aśoka, cf. ibid., pp. xi–xv.
61. John Strong, *The Legend of King Aśoka* (Princeton: Princeton University Press, 1973), pp. 260–264.
62. The tradition of Mahākāśyapa's longevity receives treatment in a number of other texts, for a summary of which cf. Lamotte, *Histoire*, pp. 226 ff. As in the case of the sixteen *arhats*, we have a variety of evidence indicating that the tradition of Mahākāśyapa's longevity was a matter not only of textual, but also of living, cultic importance in India. The *Aśokāvadāna*, for example, shows King Aśoka coming to the mountain and addressing Mahākāśyapa, who is considered to be alive and present at the place, ready to receive offerings and veneration (*Divyāvadana*, p. 90 [Strong, *Legend*, pp. 253–254]). The Chinese pilgrims Fa-hsien (Samuel Beal, *The Travels of Fah-hian and Sung Yun* [London: Susil Gupta, 1869], pp. 132–133) and Hsüan-tsang (Samuel Beal, *Si-yu-ki*, vol. 2, pp. 142–144) both provide similar insights into the cult of Mahākāśyapa, as carried on at Mount Kukkuṭapāda.
63. Watters, *On Yuan Chwang's Travels in India*, vol. 2, pp. 214–216.
64. Lamotte, *Histoire*, pp. 712–713.
65. Ibid., p. 765.

66. Ibid., pp. 712–713.
67. Ibid., p., 756.
68. A. Bareau, "The Place of the Buddha Gautama in the Buddhist Religion During the Reign of King Aśoka," in *Buddhist Studies in Honour of Walpola Rahula* (London: Gordon Fraser, 1980), pp. 1–9.
69. W. Pachow, "Gautama Buddha: Man or Superman," in *Malalasekera Commemoration Volume* (Colombo, 1976), pp. 257–269.
70. Erich Frauwallner, *The Earliest Vinaya and the Beginnings of Buddhist Literature* (Rome: Is. M. E. O., 1956).
71. Jaini has discussed some of the doctrinal debates in Nikāya Buddhism concerning longevity generated by this passage in the *Mahāparinibbāna Sutta* (Jaini, "Buddha's Prolongation of Life," pp. 546–552).
72. This episode is found in all six surviving versions of the Mps (Bareau, *Recherches sur la biographie de Buddha* vol. 1, p. 147). Within this section Bareau discerns a "primitive" core, and later additions (ibid.). Among the different versions, the Pāli shows signs of being particularly close to the primitive version (ibid., vol. 1, p. 149).
73. Rhys-Davids, *Buddhist Suttas*, pp. 40–41 (chap. 3, sec. 3). *Yassa kassaci Ānanda cattāro iddhipādā bhāvitā bahulī-katā yāni-katā vatthu-katā anuṭṭhitā paricitā susamāraddhā, so ākankhamāno kappaṃ vā tiṭṭheyya kappāvasesaṃ vā* (Dn xvi.3.3). Franklin Edgerton believes that the term *kalpāvaśeṣam* (Skt. equivalent of *kappāvasesaṃ*) means "more than a *kalpa*" rather than "for that portion of a *kalpa*" (*Buddhist Hybrid Sanskrit Dictionary*, hereafter cited as BHSD [Delhi: Motilal Banarsidass, 1970], p. 173), a position with which Jaini agrees (Jaini, "Buddha's Prolongation of Life," p. 547). At the same time, as we shall presently see, certain Pāli commentaries would like to claim for the Buddha a no more than normal human life span (see note 76). Owing to this interpretation, they must understand *kappāvasesaṃ* after the fashion of Rhys-Davids' translation, "for that portion of a *kalpa* [ordinary human life span] which had yet to run." This does not say, however, that other Pāli materials, or the Sanskrit tradition, may not have understood the matter as Edgerton suggests.
74. These include the *samādhis* of intention (*chanda*), energy (*viriya*), consciousness (*citta*), and investigation (*vīmaṃsā*) (Nyanatiloka, *Buddhist Dictionary: Manual of Buddhist Terms and Doctrines* [Kandy: Buddhist Publication Society, 1980], pp. 76–77). Cf. also Edgerton, BHSD, pp. 151–152, s.v., *ṛddhi-pāda*.
75. Edgerton, BHSD. The six supernormal powers include (in Pāli) (1) the various miraculous physical abilities (*iddhi*), (2) divine ear (*dibba-sota*), (3) penetration of the minds of others (*parassa ceto-pariya-ñāṇa*), (4) remembrance of former existences (*pubbenivāsānussati*), (5) divine eye (*dibba-cakkhu*), and (6) extinction of all cankers (*āsavakkhaya*) (Nyanatiloka, *Buddhist Dictionary*, pp. 2–3).
76. Buddhaghosa (*Sumaṅgalavilāsinī*, P.T.S., vol. 2, p. 554) and the *Milinda-pañha* (ed. Trenckner [London: Pāli Text Society], p. 141) both provide a

different interpretation of the word *kalpa*, claiming that it should be understood to refer to the normal span of a person's life. Figuring this life span as, at best, 100 years, according to these texts, the Buddha is here not relinquishing a vast life span, but really only a few years. However, this interpretation must be judged a later, polemical one. Bareau points out, for example, that this interpretation of the term *kalpa* occurs only in these two relatively late texts. Moreover, it does not occur in the two Chinese versions of the *Milinda-pañha*. This leads him to conclude that this interpretation was not the one in the minds of the authors of the Mps, "bien qu'elle paraisse beaucoup plus raisonnable et acceptable que l'autre" (*Recherches sur la biographie du Buddha dans les Sūtrapiṭaka et les Vinayapiṭaka anciens, vol. 2, Les derniers mois, le parinirvāṇa et les funérailles* [Paris: École française d'Extrême-Orient, 1970], vol. 1, p. 152 n. 1. Jaini, writing earlier, comes to similar conclusions. According to Jaini, unlike the Mahāsāṅghika and Sarvāstivāda, the Theravāda rejected the idea that a saint could prolong his life through meditation. They were for that reason forced to conclude that the Buddha could not have lived beyond what was understood as the natural human life span, and therefore chose to reject the obvious meaning of the Mps in favor of an obscure and idiosyncratic one (Jaini, "Buddha's Prolongation of Life," pp. 548–552). However, this led to certain inconsistencies in their interpretation of the events of the Mps (p. 549). In addition, the Theravādin sources themselves are not consistent in the interpretation of *kalpa* as an ordinary human life span, and even the *Milinda-pañha* contradicts itself on this point (ibid).

77. Rhys-Davids, *Buddhist Suttas*, pp. 40–41 (chap. 3, sec. 3). *Tathāgatassa kho Ānanda cattāro iddhipādā bhāvitā bahulī-katā yāni-katā vatthu-katā anuṭṭhitā paricitā susamāraddhā. So ākaṅkhamāno Ānanda Tathāgato kappaṃ vā tiṭṭheyya kappāvasesaṃ vā 'ti* (*Dīghanikāya*, xvi.3.3).
78. Dn xvi.3.4 (R III.4, 41).
79. Ibid.
80. Ibid.
81. Just how important the themes of the Buddha's power of longevity and its activation are to the authors of the Mps is seen in the fact that both of the quoted passages occur several other times in chapter 3 of the text. The passage concerning the Buddha's longevity (Dn xvi.3.3), for example, occurs no less than five additional times in the Rhys-Davids edition (Dn xvi.3.40, 41, 44, 45, 47 [R III.54, 56, 59, 60, 62]). In these occurrences of the passage, either the Buddha is reminding Ānanda that he could have lived for a *kalpa*, if only he had been asked (Dn xvi.3.41, 44, 45, 47 [R III:56, 59, 60, 62]) or Ānanda is repeating to the Buddha what the Buddha had previously said to him concerning the Buddha's ability to live for a *kalpa* (Dn xvi.3.40 [R III:54]). The closely aligned formula for supplicating the Buddha to remain and not pass away, also occurs—in addition to Dn xvi.3.4—five other times in this chapter (Dn xvi.3.38, 39

[two occurrences], 40, and 41 [R III.49, 51, 52, 55, and 56]). At Dn xvi.3.38, for example, when Ānanda has come to realize the tragic mistake he has made, he implores the Buddha to live on, employing exactly the supplication just quoted and repeating it three times (Dn xvi.3.38–39 [R III.49–52]). However, the Buddha tells him that the time for making this request is past. The Buddha then asks Ānanda why he has put this request to the *tathāgata* three times. Now Ānanda repeats the words the Buddha had uttered to him previously, "Whoever has thought out, Ānanda, and developed, practised, accumulated . . . should he so desire it, could remain in the same birth for a *kalpa*" (Dn, xvi.iii.40 [R III.54]). Then the Buddha says that had Ānanda, on the early occasion, uttered the appropriate supplication two times the Buddha might have refused to grant it, but had he uttered it a third time, the Buddha would have granted the request (Dn xvi.iii.41 [R III.55]). The second occurrence of this passage at Dn xvi.iii.41 (R III.56) communicates the same information. These occurrences tell us something about the use of this passage: the Buddha's desire to live on can only be roused when the supplication is repeated in precisely the right way, i.e., three times.

82. The Mps exhibits other themes noted in one or another of the texts examined above. For example, it is the Buddha's accomplishment as a meditator that has brought him his supernatural powers, and prominent among these is the power of longevity.

83. Gregory Schopen comments "for the Mps passage, see the very early stele from Amaravati—2nd B.C.—on which this incident is represented and labelled. The label contains something like a paraphrase of the text. All of this indicates the age and wide currency of the episode" (A. Ghosh and H. Sarkar, "Beginnings of Sculptural Art in South-east India: A Stele from Amaravati," *Ancient India* 20–21 (1964–1965), pp. 168–177; Schopen, personal communication.

84. On this, cf. André Bareau, "Les récits canoniques des funérailles du Buddha et leurs anomalies: nouvel essai d'interprétation," *Bulletin de l'École française d'Extrême-Orient*, 62 (1975), pp. 151–189.

85. Bareau, in his analysis of six versions of the Mps (one version each in Pāli [P] and Sanskrit [S], four in Chinese [Ch. A–D]), tells us that this episode is recounted in all six versions, suggesting its antiquity ("Recherches," vol. 1, pp. 147–156). Five texts (P, S, Ch. A, B, and C) place this episode near the end of the Buddha's stay in Vaiśāli, while Ch. D places it at the very beginning of the sūtra, after the words *evaṃ mayātśrutam* (ibid., vol. 1, 147).

86. This point is developed in my *Buddhist Saints in India: A Study in Buddhist Values and Orientations* (New York: Oxford University Press, 1994), pp. 358–367.

87. Jaini's discussion of doctrinal disputes arising in the Nikāya schools concerning the Buddha's longevity makes it clear that for most Buddhist commentators (Theravāda commentators excepted), the longevity of saints is a result of their meditation, either through prolonging the life span of

the present body or through creating an entirely new body altogether (Jaini, "Buddha's Prolongation of Life").

88. Adikaram has brought forward similar themes in relation to the cult of *arhats* in Sri Lanka; cf. Adikaram, *Early History of Buddhism in Ceylon* (Migoda: D. S. Pusmella, 1946). Along similar lines, *pratyekabuddhas* ("solitary *buddhas*") become invulnerable to death by entering into *nirodha-samāpatti*; e.g., cf. Dhammapāda Commentary (5 vols., H. Smith and H. C. Norman, eds., [London: L. S. Tailang, 1905–1915], vol. 1, pp. 224–226 [Burlingame, trans., *Buddhist Legends* (London: Luzac, 1969, first published, 1921), vol. 1, pp. 290–291]).

89. A study of sectarian views of the Buddhist saints reveals discontinuity and tension: the Nikāya schools contested with one another concerning the status of *arhats*; the Mahāyāna denigrated the *arhat* ideal; the Vajrayāna criticized both *arhats* and conventional *bodhisattvas* for their limitations; and so on. Such polemics often leave us with the impression that the Buddhist schools were quite separate from one another and their enlightened ideals quite different. A contrasting viewpoint is afforded by our examination of the longevity of the Buddhist saints. Here we have seen that similar claims of realization, power, and long life are made of the saints, they all share a compassionate motivation, and their dependence upon the requests of others is equally insisted upon. Whatever the schools may say, even the brief glimpse of the saints offered here suggests that, in important respects, the Buddhist saints are much more equivalent figures than their various designations, doctrinal definitions, and sectarian affiliations, as articulated by their various proponents and detractors, would lead us to believe. When we scholars think historically about Buddhism in India in terms of relatively discrete orientations we call Hīnayāna, Mahāyāna, and Vajrayāna, it may be that as much as anything else we are playing into polemical hands.

90. The text explicitly applies this to the *buddha*, but by saying "anyone who," it clearly intends to include in this statement other kinds of saints also attained through meditation; in the context of the Mps, this includes the other two types of saints central to the thought of this text, the *arhats* and *pratyekabuddhas*.

91. To this, one may wish to add the interesting case of the *bodhisattva* who maintains a "long-lived" presence within *saṃsāra* through intentionally taking death and rebirth, over and over, for vast periods of time. The Tibetan savant Lama Tāranātha (b. 1575) mentions yet another mode of longevity, namely the resurrection of the body. His account of Nāgārjuna describes the death of the saint through the severing of his head from his body. Tāranātha then proceeds to tell us that when Maitreya arrives, Nāgārjuna's head will be joined with his body, and the saint will live once more (Kbdd, pp. 369 ff.).

92. Cf. Lamotte, *Histoire*, pp. 765–775. Cf. Maung Kin, "The Legend of Upagutta," pp. 219 ff. On the famous passage in the Mps that supposedly

restricts monks in regard to the *stūpa* cult ("Hinder not yourselves, Ānanda, by honouring the remains of the Tathāgata," Dn xvi.5.10–11 [R V.24–26 (91–2)]), cf. Gregory Schopen, "Monks and the Relic Cult in the Mahāparinibbānasutta: An Old Misunderstanding in Regard to Monastic Buddhism," in *From Benaras to Beijing: Essays on Buddhism and Chinese Religion in Honor of Jan Yün-Hua*, ed. G. Schopen and K. Shinohara (Toronto, 1990). In this illuminating article, Schopen argues, first, that the passage in question does not refer to the worship of relics, but rather to the cultic reverence of the body of the Buddha, after his death but prior to his cremation and thus clearly prior also to the existence of relics and the building of *stūpas*, a cultic pattern that is found widely in the early evidence in reference not only to the Buddha but also to other saints. Second, Schopen argues that the injunction to Ānanda does not apply to all *bhikṣus*, but rather specifically to Ānanda: while this ritual action is proscribed in the case of Ānanda, it is in fact appropriately carried out by the great *arhat* Mahākāśyapa (Ānanda is not enlightened at this point). This shows that it is not the action itself that is problematic, but rather the action as performed by Ānanda. These two points lead Schopen to conclude that the interpretation of this passage that monks are prohibited from the worship of relics is a completely inaccurate reading.

93. De Visser, *The Arhants in China and Japan*, pp. 105 ff.

94. We have seen that, in later times, the belief in the longevity of the Buddhist saints cannot be classified as a feature primarily of popular religion, but is equally if not more important to the elite of the tradition. The passage in the Mps referred to above (note 92) has seemed to many as a text advocating the worship of the Buddha's relics as a particularly lay phenomenon (cf. Schopen, "Monks and the Relic Cult"). Not fully appreciated, however, is the fact that the Mps nowhere repudiates the phenomenon of the Buddhist saint, and nowhere denies that he has great attainment and power, including that of longevity. Again, Weber, Frauwallner, and others have suggested that the elite monastic community behind a text like the Mps rather simply wants to shift the central authority for the religious life away from the Buddhist saints as such toward the more stable and regularized foundation provided by the textual *dharma* and the vinayas.

95. We can in this context question the status of the widespread scholarly categorization of Buddhist phenomena as either "elite" or "popular." One of the reasons that scholars, beginning with T. and C. Rhys-Davids and continuing down to the present (as seen in the works of Lamotte, Bareau, Pachow, and many others), have been so strongly attracted to Buddhist studies as a field is that Buddhism itself often appears to speak with a remarkably contemporary voice, one that is urbane, learned, and reasonable. Whatever else it may reveal, scholarly insistence on relatively clear divisions between elite monastic Buddhism on the one hand and

popular Buddhism on the other has one interesting result: it enables the maintenance of the reasonability of Buddhism (elite Buddhism) in the face of so much that is not reasonable by any known standard (popular Buddhism). However, we have just seen that one of the more outlandish aspects of Buddhism, namely its belief in the enormous longevity of its saints, is characteristic of every period and every level of Indian Buddhist religious life. It cannot be relegated to the sphere of popular religion. If this conclusion is accepted, then I suppose we have to begin to rethink what Buddhism in India really was, and whether—in any of its manifestations—it was really as reasonable as we want it to be.

Stūpa, Story, and Empire: Constructions of the Buddha Biography in Early Post-Aśokan India

Jonathan S. Walters

In "The Many Lives of Buddha: A Study of Sacred Biography and Theravāda Tradition," Frank Reynolds sketched out a dynamic conception of the Buddha biography in which Buddhist life stories are viewed, not as comparatively accurate or inaccurate reflections of the events in "the historical Buddha's" life, but as a locus for creativity and change within the streams of Buddhist history.[1] In this essay I want to develop Reynolds' view that Buddhist biographies both reflected and shaped the historical situations in which they were composed, by examining a set of three biographical texts in Pāli verse that were produced in Buddhist India during about the second century B.C. Reynolds has already pointed to two of these texts—*Cariyāpiṭaka* and *Buddhavaṃsa*—as especially important for a historical reconstruction of the cultural role that Buddhist biography played in the early post-Aśokan period.[2] Adding a third, closely related text called *Apadāna*, I intend to nuance Reynolds' account of this particular period within the general framework that he sets out. Specifically, I shall analyze these three texts in light of what Reynolds calls "the most crucial problems which are amenable to future investigation," namely, the issues that "cluster around the identification of the various levels or stages in the development of the biographical tradition, the question of the structure of the various biographical fragments and texts, and the role which these fragments and texts have played within the broader tradition."[3]

These texts, in and of themselves, cannot reveal the historical situation that is to be reconstructed. They are poems about inconceivably ancient periods of time, not scientific histories. I make this fairly obvious point because it is not always grasped in Buddhology. The tendency in Buddhological studies to weave history directly out of literary remains, as though the authors of sacred texts were trying to describe objectively the times and places in which they lived, has elicited a devastating critique, in various forms over the last ten years, by Gregory Schopen, who has challenged fundamental pillars of the Buddhological construct—including various distinctions between monks and layfolk[4] and the origin of the Mahāyāna[5]—with an appeal to epigraphic evidence that can be dated centuries earlier than the notoriously recent extant textual manuscripts. With good reason Schopen has insisted that, except for certain ancient manuscript finds mostly from Central Asia, epigraphy and archaeology provide us with the only objects for reconstructing the first two millennia of the Buddha era that actually survive intact from the periods they are supposed to be talking about.

I agree with Schopen that epigraphy must now take the lead in a critique and new construction of ancient Buddhist history; but I am equally convinced that epigraphy cannot do without the textual evidence entirely.[6] Among other things, these texts have been vital to the project of reconstructing epigraphic languages and dating and identifying the kings in whose reigns the epigraphs were incised. Schopen's critique starts to reach fruition only when the epigraphs bring new questions to bear on the texts and, it is important to add, when the texts are then enabled to raise new questions about the epigraphs.[7] Together, the work of epigraphers and historical linguists allows us to identify certain epigraphs and textual compositions as coeval; both textual and epigraphic studies are reenergized when we can see particular texts as products of particular ages that can be reconstructed on the basis of (epigraphic and archaeological) evidence that is partially external to the texts themselves. As Schopen's work so clearly shows, situating textual studies within epigraphic history opens whole new frontiers for Buddhology. This paper follows Schopen's lead in its attempt to situate the texts in question within the history that can be reconstructed on the basis of "hard" evidence. In fact, Schopen himself has treated the *Apadāna* and related *jātaka* texts as potentially valuable for the epigraphic and archaeological study of early post-Aśokan India.[8]

The three biographical texts that I shall discuss in this essay are especially well suited to the development of both Reynolds' and Schopen's methodological projects. In terms of Buddhist life stories, they are the only comprehensive canonical tellings of the Buddha biography that contain descriptions of previous lives in addition to the present life, a completeness that remained the *sine qua non* for all Buddhist biography until the nineteenth century, and that still remains dominant in large parts of the Buddhist world today. These texts constituted, in other words, the first crucial transformation of the Buddha biography in its long and varied history; these texts constituted the rules for post-Aśokan Buddhist anthropology. From the perspective of epigraphy, the period in which these texts were written is extremely rich: well over two thousand epigraphs from the last two centuries B.C., inscribed in varieties of the early Brahmī script that adapted Aśoka's Mauryan alphabet to new purposes, and discovered throughout the ancient Indic world, from Sri Lanka to Śrāvasti, have been published. As the *Cariyāpiṭaka, Buddhavaṃsa*, and *Apadāna* eked out what was to become the foundation for all subsequent Buddhist biography, so the early Brahmī inscriptions of Sāñchi and Sārnāth, Aṇurāhapura and Amarāvatī, effected the first major transformation—political as well as palaeographical—of that discourse in stone that, inaugurated by India's first emperor, Aśoka, was to dominate all subsequent Indian imperial practice.

But Buddhist India just after Aśoka is especially important for the light it potentially can shed on the *overlap* of textual and epigraphic/archaeological histories. Here more than anywhere else in the vast world of Buddhology, the work of epigraphers and textual specialists has closely overlapped for more than a century. The discovery of the labeled carvings at Bhārhut merely confirmed what had been obvious even to the earliest Orientalists: the Buddhist monuments from which the inscriptions come contain illustrations of biographical stories that are also told, always in greater detail, in the texts. Moreover, the language of the inscriptions and that of the texts is so close that until recently it was standard practice among epigraphers to call most inscriptional Prakrits "Pāli." The result has been an enormous industry in all countries that host Indological studies, an industry that has attempted to describe the carvings and interpret the inscriptions on the basis of the texts, on one hand, and that has attempted to describe the development of the textual tradition on the basis of the carvings and inscriptions, on the other.

Ironically, it is a rare thing that Reynolds and Schopen should consider the *Cariyāpiṭaka, Buddhavaṃsa*, and/or *Apadāna* especially important for a reconstruction of early post-Aśokan Buddhist history. The enormous industry that I just described has in fact largely ignored the texts that historical linguists actually date to the period under discussion. Almost without exception these texts remain unmentioned in the works of even the best scholars concerned with this period, including the likes of Alexander Cunningham, Ananda Coomaraswamy, Albert Foucher, John Marshall, and Paul Mus. Instead, texts that postdate the early Brahmī inscriptions by centuries have been treated as though they had been the sources for the carvings that the inscriptions label: the most prominent texts cited in the scholarly discourse on the great *stūpas* and their carvings have been *Divyāvadāna* and *Lalitavistara* (ca. first century A.D.), *Mahāvastvavadāna* (ca. second century A.D.), *Jātakamāla* and (ca. fourth century A.D.), and *Jātakaṭṭhakathā* and *Dhammapadaṭṭhakathā* (after the fifth century A.D.).

This anachronism between text and epigraph obscures the historical position of the various biographies that Reynolds has called for scholars to reconstruct. For the early period, we are left with a catalog of biographical fragments cut off from the framework(s) in which they have meaning (for even if we accept that the narrative details belong to some timeless oral tradition,[9] we surely cannot look to the later texts for the *ideological* frameworks of the earlier period). In terms of the later biographies, too, the project is undermined: the interpretations and ideologies that they exhibit are treated as though they belong, not to the times and places in which the actual texts were written, but to the timelessly ancient oral tradition! Despite these epistemological difficulties, to this day only the later texts have been examined for the reconstruction of the Buddha biography as portrayed in the earlier carvings.

There are two main reasons that this anachronism in the Buddhological construct has gone unnoticed, except by Reynolds (in an analysis of the development of biographical tradition) and Schopen (in an analysis of the relationship between literary and epigraphic remains). First, the biographical texts that date to the time of the inscriptions—*Cariyāpiṭaka, Buddhavaṃsa*, and *Apadāna*—do not tell the Buddha biography with all the sumptuous detail that is found in the later texts and that scholars like to see in the ancient carvings as well.[10] The later texts have been privileged because only they tell the stories with enough detail to make the identification of the carvings believable.

A second major reason for the absence of the *Apadāna* and related texts in the vast scholarship on early post-Aśokan Indian Buddhism has to do with certain prejudices and scholarly presuppositions that have dominated the history of Pāli studies. Since the time of T. W. Rhys-Davids, founder of the Pāli Text Society (PTS), there has been widespread disdain for the texts in question. Their inclusion in the canon seems to mar an otherwise purely rational, secular humanist corpus. "The historical Buddha" is obscured, the standard argument runs, by the submission to "popular" needs for fairy tales, magic, ghosts, gods, and demons. The *Apadāna* and related texts represent the beginning of the end of the pristine "early Buddhism" that scholars of Theravāda have until recently been exclusively interested in reconstructing. As a result, the *Buddhavaṃsa* and *Cariyāpiṭaka*—although among the earliest PTS publications and available in translation for years—seldom appear in the extensive secondary work on the canonical period to which, in the eyes of the traditions that preserved that canon, they rightfully belong. The *Apadāna* has never been translated into a Western language, and the PTS (Roman script) edition of the Pāli is long out of print and hopelessly confused.[11] Dating these texts to the post-Aśokan period has had the effect of driving Pāli specialists to ignore them as late corruptions, rather than driving them to situate the texts in light of what else is known about the post-Aśokan period. Nonspecialists for whom the texts might prove relevant—such as epigraphers and art historians—are denied access to them as a result of their dependence on the work of textual specialists.

I hope to reconcile this anachronism by addressing the cotemporaneity of the texts (*Apadāna, Buddhavaṃsa, Cariyāpiṭaka*; henceforth "the ABCs") and the epigraphic and archaeological remains (of the first stages in the development of the major Buddhist *stūpas* during the early post-Aśokan, i.e., Śunga and early Sātavāhana, period). This essay is, to this end, an extended demonstration of the fact that Reynolds and Schopen both were right in their suppositions about the relevance of the ABCs: there is a complex and remarkable correspondence between the two bodies of evidence, textual and archaeological, which my narrative will clarify in some detail. But my primary aim is to reconstruct the nature and cultural context of Buddhist biography in about the second century B.C., and to demonstrate that epigraphy and textual studies together provide an exciting basis for that reconstruction.

Picturing the Path

The *stūpas* (huge dome-shaped monuments that enshrine the corporeal relics of the Buddha and his most famous disciples) are well known, even outside professional scholarly circles, and they need little initial introduction from me. I shall focus upon the *stūpas* of Madhya Pradesh (especially Sāñchi and Bhārhut) and Andhra Pradesh (especially Amarāvatī), which, perhaps constructed originally by Emperor Aśoka himself, survive as the most important evidence of early post-Aśokan sculptural and architectural excellence. Descriptions and photographs of these sites abound in even the most general studies of Indian art. The texts, however, as I have already stated, remain neglected in the scholarly tradition. So I shall begin with a few general words about the ABCs as a foundation for my discussion of their relationship to the epigraphic and archaeological remains.

There has been a consensus among scholars, who have studied the traditional accounts of the ABCs, their vocabulary, their grammatical and metrical structures, and their philosophical and mythological content, that these texts postdate Aśoka.[12] Indeed, the *Apadāna* makes reference to the *Kathāvatthu*,[13] which is held by Theravādins to have been composed only at the Third Great Council, during the time of Aśoka. *Apadāna* incorporates verse after verse from pre-Aśokan works, including *Sutta-Nipāta*,[14] *Dhammapada*[15] and *Thera-Therīgāthā*,[16] and even quotes large segments from other post-Aśokan texts, including *Buddhavaṃsa* and *Cariyāpiṭaka*.

In fact, there seems to be a direct line of appropriation and expansion from *Cariyāpiṭaka* to *Buddhavaṃsa* to *Apādāna*. *Cariyāpiṭaka* is a *jātaka* text, or biography of the Buddha that focuses almost exclusively upon his actions during (here thirty-five) previous lives. The colophon[17] describes *Cariyāpiṭaka* as *Buddhāpadāni[ya]* (a "Great Story" or "legend biography" of the Buddha). Many of its *pādas* are incorporated into *Buddhavaṃsa*; *Apadāna* then quotes the concluding verses and colophon of *Cariyāpiṭaka*[18] while it also quotes from *Buddhavaṃsa* extensively.[19]

This line of appropriation and expansion is not simply a matter of plagiarized verses and borrowed names. A central ideological theme was being appropriated and reworked in the process. I have already remarked that *Cariyāpiṭaka* is the earliest known complete biography of the Buddha on a cosmic scale, that is, the first that understands the Buddha's present life as the result of actions performed in a series of previous lives. Whichever view scholars take on the ultimately unanswerable question of whether *jātakas* preexisted this period or not,[20] *Cariyāpiṭaka* is the earliest definite evidence we have that Buddhists conceived of the Buddha biography in such cosmic terms. The concluding verses of *Cariyāpiṭaka*, which reappear in *Apadāna*, state succinctly the single revelation that the whole text makes *in extenso*: during the Buddha's previous lives, he cultivated some of the Ten Perfections (*dasapāramī*)[21] that fully developed, constituted in the present life his ultimate liberation.

This revelation was the answer to a major question that emerged for Buddhists only after the Aśokan impetus to universalism had created the new, cosmopolitan atmosphere that characterized post-Aśokan India. In the pre-Aśokan tradition, as far as we can know about it at all on the basis of the texts preserved in the rest of the Pāli canon, the paradigmatic Buddha biography, and the parallel early saints' biographies (as in *Thera-Therīgāthā*), were conceived in noncosmic, this-life-only terms.[22] The paradigmatic biography begins with renunciation of the world, continues with religious exertion, and concludes with the attainment of *nirvāṇa*. While such a biography is paradigmatic for renunciates (and lay people whose own religiosity is predicated on serving them), it leaves unaddressed the soteriological potential of most human beings, who will not renounce the world in this life and attain the goal, but will instead continue to transmigrate in a time conceived according to a devolutionary cosmology. Surely if the Buddha's teaching was true, the Path he guided humanity along is wide enough to include more than the handful of humans who are already near its end; it must be wide enough for universal society to stand upon. And by a remarkable logic—that if the Buddha's present life is paradigmatic for being at the end of the Path, then his previous lives must be paradigmatic for being at the beginning of the Path—*Cariyāpiṭaka* starts to chart out this widened, cosmicized soteriology. It reveals that the Buddha, long ago when he was still just a king or a Brahmin or a trader (or even an animal), turned his lives into opportunities for cultivating, in increasingly profound ways, the Ten Perfections that, when fully cultivated, are equivalent to the end of the Path. And the concluding verses drive the point home: the Buddha's advice (*buddhānusāsanī*) is that everyone start doing the same thing.[23]

Buddhavaṃsa investigates the implications of this central revelation. It opens with a very familiar scene: the Buddha is beneath the Tree of Enlightenment and Brahmā Sahampati is there, begging him to preach the Dharma for the sake of those who have "little dust in their eyes." The Buddha consents, but wishing to show just how powerful a *buddha* is, he does not, as in the familiar early story, get up, seek out his teachers, find that they are dead, then proceed to Sārnāth in order to Turn the Wheel of Dharma.[24] Instead, the Buddha magically creates an enormous gem walkway (*ratanacaṃkama*) that spans all of space, and he walks up and down on it without the passing of time. A magnificent festival ensues, in which all the beings in the universe praise the Buddha with songs, dances, perfume, musical instruments, flowers and, above all, delirious happiness. Those with little dust in their eyes, for whom the Buddha preached the Dharma, are not merely renunciates at the end of the Path. The Buddha preached his Dharma for everyone in the universe.

Sāriputta arrives and asks the Buddha to explain what the gem walkway symbolizes. The answer is that this universal soteriology is the cosmic Buddha biography itself: the Buddha proceeds to elaborate a cosmic autobiography along the lines of *Cariyāpiṭaka*, but greatly expanded. He reveals that he first took refuge in Buddhism one hundred thousand *kalpas* (eons) ago (*Cariyāpiṭaka* concerns only the present *kalpa*),[25] and that in the process of his transmigration across this unfathomable amount of time he participated in twenty-four previous Buddhisms before becoming Buddha and starting his own, which is the twenty-fifth "Buddha lineage" (*Buddhavaṃsa*). *Buddhavaṃsa* gives the biography of each previous Buddha in whose Buddhism "our" (*amhākaṃ*) Gotama Buddha performed acts that cultivated the Ten Perfections and culminated in his Enlightenment at Bodh Gayā, the setting in which the *Buddhavaṃsa* is supposed to have been revealed. The Buddha's own biography becomes the most recent of a type. All Buddhas live for a certain period, attain *nirvāṇa* in certain ways, initiate certain numbers of people into various stages of Path-life, are treated postmortem in particular fashions, etc. The categories have become so stereotyped by the time *Buddhavaṃsa* gets around to Gotama's recapitulation of this paradigmatic biographical structure that they are referred to in a shorthand which is extremely cryptic unless one has already read the biographies of the previous twenty-four Buddhas.

Buddhavaṃsa, in the process of drawing this map of cosmic time, reveals with far greater specificity what the *Cariyāpiṭaka* revelation of Buddha's cosmic biography means for humanity. It is not just that people must cultivate the Ten Perfections now, in small ways, if they hope to achieve the fulfillment of the Ten Perfections at some future point in their transmigrations. That cultivation must occur within a specifically Buddhist context: the Buddha in the *Buddhavaṃsa* gives alms to Buddhists and worships Buddhas. It is this specifically Buddhist action that patterns people for cultivation of the specifically Buddhist achievement, *nirvāṇa*.

There are two levels of soteriological potential at work in *Buddhavaṃsa*. On the one hand, we are all still living in a Buddha era, a period in which a Buddha and his Buddhism are known and can be practiced, worshiped, and admired. Specifically, Buddhist acts performed in the present will bear fruit in the time of future Buddhas, just as Gotama's actions in the time of previous Buddhas culminated in his present Buddhahood. In the penultimate chapter, *Buddhavaṃsa* reveals that the next of these Buddhas, Metteya (Maitreya), has already been predicted by Gotama.[26] On the other hand, it is not only Gotama Buddha and the present Buddhism that are populating the soteriological march across cosmic time. All Buddhas reveal a *Buddhavaṃsa* and declare soteriology universal. People who entered the Path but did not attain its end in the times of previous Buddhas, too, may achieve the *summum bonum* in the time of Metteya. In fact, the two classes overlap: many people in the present, especially those who connect themselves with the Buddha and his dispensation, must already have been practicing Buddhists during previous eons (that will be remembered only after the end is achieved).

The Buddha of *Buddhavaṃsa* is quite explicit about the fact that his Buddhism, like all those previous ones, will eventually disappear. But, like those previous Buddhisms, this one will disappear only after the Path has been pointed out for "countless crores of other" beings who, transmigrating now, will attain the fruit of their Buddhist practices in the future.[27] A universally accessible teleology intersects the devolutionary cosmology at those rare moments in time—twenty-five of them in one hundred thousand eons—when a Buddha has been born in the world; the universe brims with soteriological potential as a result. The *Buddhavaṃsa* was composed during such a rare moment in time.

The *Apadāna* utterly presupposes *Buddhavaṃsa*, for its actual verses as well as for its map of cosmic time, its Buddha biography, and its attempt at describing the specifically Buddhist acts that lead to eventual enlightenment. Here the expansion of the central *Cariyāpiṭaka* revelation is carried in new directions. The "Great Story" tells not only the biographies of the Buddhas, nor only of the Buddhas and *Pacceka* Buddhas. Those are tiny fragments compared to the entire corpus of five hundred-odd biographies of monks and about forty of nuns. These saints' life histories, which incorporated and revised the verses of *Thera-Therīgāthā*, allowed the *Apadāna* author(s) limitless room for expansion of the *Buddhavaṃsa*'s (meager) catalog of *which* specifically Buddhist acts have *which* specifically Buddhist results. *Apadāna* provides such a catalogue, *in extenso*, with a completeness unknown in any other text of the period or earlier. The actual content of the biographies is fairly limited—most of the monks and nuns are known only by their acts, i.e. "Rev. One Lamp," "Rev. Stūpa Worshiper," "Rev. Bowl Filler," "Rev. Flag Raiser," etc.—it is the acts themselves that are elaborated, explored, explained, and valorized.

Apadāna begins with the *Buddhāpadāna*, named from the colophon of *Cariyāpiṭaka*. Here too we find a Buddha who enters the Path unfathomably many eons ago, cultivates the Ten Perfections, then attains the goal in the present and advises everyone else to do the same thing. But this time his original, root act, of which all the subsequent perfection is ultimately the fruit, is a simple imaginative endeavor: in an unfathomably previous life the Buddha thought about a universe populated with countless Buddhas and saints all interacting with each other.[28] The fruit of this mental action (*manasā patthanāphalaṃ*)[29] is realized when the Buddha, under the Tree of Enlightenment at Gayā, actually becomes part of this wonderful universe he had imagined so long ago. And this act is precisely what any thinking person does when he or she hears the *Buddhavaṃsa* (or the remainder of the *Apadāna*); imagining in one's own mind the revelation of previous Buddhas and Buddhisms and their mutual interconnection is itself the ultimately salvific act. Those who are familiar with *Buddhavaṃsa* or who hear the *Apadāna* have already performed that act.

Additionally, the *Apadāna* listener—the texts are directed at a plural "you" enjoined to listen[30]—learns in the process of listening that this mental action is only the first among many diverse kinds of specifically Buddhist and extremely efficacious acts that are possible so long as there exists a Buddha or the memory of him and his teachings, or his relics, or his monks and nuns. The texts assure listeners in no uncertain terms that all seeds of *karma* will bear the appropriate fruit in the future,[31] an assurance proved in the biographies of each monk and nun who attained the goal in the dispensation of Gotama as the fruit of actions performed eons earlier. And in all the *apadānas*, we find that this extremely gradual Path is at least pleasant: in the intermediate eons, the performers of pious acts revel in heavenly palaces, rule the gods or are married to the rulers of gods, and likewise are born as human Wheel-Turning Monarchs, time and time again.

In *Apadāna* the Buddha biography has become a full-blown revelation of universal soteriology. The Path that it pictures cuts across all of time; the acts that it catalogues occur throughout the Indian world and are performed by people of all castes, occupations, ages, sexes, social statuses; by animals and gods and demons as well as humans. The *Apadāna* demonstrates biographically what the Buddha's "Gem Walkway" demonstrates symbolically: Buddhism is not only for renunciates; the Buddha's life made it possible to direct every conceivable walk of life toward attainment of the soteriological goal, *nirvāṇa*.

Buddhas of Bricks

It is here that we begin to see the overlap between the ABCs and the famous *stūpas* of early post-Aśokan India. The *Apadāna* is replete with specific descriptions of *stūpa* construction and relic worship,[32] always conceived within this cosmic soteriological framework, which to my knowledge are found nowhere else in the Pāli canon, yet which clearly parallel the actual practices at *stūpas* in early post-Aśokan India, as I shall demonstrate below. The inscriptions in turn are replete with indications that the patrons of these elaborate *stūpas* mirrored the universality of the *Apadāna*: kings and śūdras, artisans and Brahmins, householders and millionaires, men and women, young and old, monks and nuns contributed to the creation of these magnificent works of art. And the *stūpas* themselves are ornamented with the central conception that underlies the ABCs: carvings that illustrate a cosmic Buddha biography.

But the case is not so simple as it may appear. We cannot assume that the texts objectively reflect actual practice any more than we can assume that actual practice was a transparent enactment of the stories in the texts. The texts are traces of a particular way of thinking about the Buddha biography; the inscriptions and carvings are traces of particular human actions. The ideology and practice presuppose each other—why write a text about *stūpas* unless they exist, or build a *stūpa* without an idea of why that is a good thing to do?—and I have been trying to reconstruct the situation(s) in which they were, simultaneously, produced/used/thought about. In the present section I want to develop a few themes about the process by which several post-Aśokan *stūpas* came to be constructed, which have emerged in my study of the early Brahmī epigraphs and which have special importance in this attempt of mine to reconstruct the context in which these biographical texts and those actual *stūpa* practices coexisted.

The first important topic that needs to be reconsidered is that of historical agency. It is well known that the inscriptions record information about donors, which has made possible analyses of the people who built and ornamented the early post-Aśokan *stūpas*: Bareau has talked about their sectarian orientation,[33] Schopen has talked about their religious status,[34] Chakravarti has talked about their social status.[35] But an analysis of the individual donors as individual donors only takes us so far. It cannot explain, for example, how all these donors of such diverse backgrounds came together to donate sculptures, pillars, or carved friezes that happen to match each other precisely, that even form links in a single stone railing. Nor can it explain the process by which the donors enabled themselves to make the donations (even extremely rich people belong to families, polities, and economic organizations that constrain the flow of wealth). In both these instances, it is useful to posit the existence of what R. G. Collingwood calls "complex agency," an agency that involves groups of people joining together for some common goal.[36]

Many of the inscriptions make this complex agency apparent: the donors of certain objects are not individuals but networks of friends and families,[37] guilds,[38] committees,[39] villages[40] and mercantile towns,[41] of which single individuals were often the representatives but certainly not the sole agents. Many of the monastic donors, too, were standing as representatives of such social groups.[42] And these are only the donors who recorded the fact that they gathered together their friends, relatives, or whomever in order to finance the donation (which is a very common trope in *Apadāna* stories about *stūpa* worship);[43] we have no way of knowing how many of the supposedly individual donors also participated in complex agencies that were not mentioned in the epigraphic record.

Even this broader vision of the complex agency that erected and decorated the *stūpas* at Sāñchi, Amarāvatī, or Bhārhut is incomplete. For we still must imagine a larger complex agency organizing these specific donors/complex agents into a unitary whole: building the Sāñchi railing or producing the Bhārhut medallions must have involved commissioning artists and financial overseers, organizing participant donors and allotting their shares of money (or whatever), then keeping track of that allotment in order to have the inscriptions carved properly (again, in matching scripts that cannot have been willy-nilly graffiti). In the *Apadāna*, many such major additions to Buddhist monuments are made in this way: a single individual organizes a festival (*maha*) in order to have the thing constructed or the *pūjā* performed to it.[44] Each of the various spectacular additions to the great *stūpas* was probably produced as the result of such highly organized occasions in which the donors, for all their diversity (and differing personal motivations), came together and financed the project; festivals that occurred at least when the resources were first mobilized and when the specific project was declared complete. Illustrations of various sorts of royal festivals abound in the extant carvings, although they all have been considered representations of the same handful of historical stories: all royal processions are Ajattasattu's relic march, all royal tree worship is Aśoka's *bodhi pūjā*, etc. The truth may be far more straightforward than that: these are illustrations of the very festivals that have left as traces of their occurrence precisely the carvings, *stūpas*, and texts in question.[45]

This leads me to the second major point about the epigraphs and other archaeological remains that I want to make. Although the *stūpas* in their final form appear as a wild hodge podge of carvings, inscriptions, rails, umbrellas, and pillars, it is important that we think of the finished product as a series of layers that resulted from very specific, organized additions to whatever already existed at a specific point in time.[46] For example, it is well known that the Sāñchi rail (around the Mahācaitya) was built later than the *stūpa* itself, and that the famous carved gateways were added later than the rail. Architectural and art historical study, as well as palaeography, confirm this point. So the finished *stūpa* is the composite creation of successive complex agents who organized smaller units of collective agency at different points in time. Much work remains to be done, distinguishing and collating these "layers." But the work is vital, because in the process of distinguishing stages it is possible to be precise about dating and situating particular conceptions of, among other things, the Buddha biography.

Let me suggest how this is the case, even though I am not yet entirely satisfied with my own thoughts on the subject (mostly because there is an enormous amount of material that needs to be classified differently than it is currently classified). I have already mentioned that the *Apadāna* catalogues a wide range of ritual acts. It includes many that are mentioned in pre-Aśokan sources such as the *Mahāparinibbāna Sutta*: alms-giving, listening to the *Buddhavacana*, thinking about the Triple Gem, and constructing *stūpas* and worshiping them with garlands, wreaths, paint, and *añjalī*. But *Apadāna* adds to these a number of specific acts that are otherwise known only in the inscriptions: presenting lamp[-stands];[47] erecting stone pillars,[48] balustrades,[49], lion-thrones with footprint slabs,[50] ornamental umbrellas[51] and *dharma-cakras*;[52] participating in or organizing the construction of Buddhist rails;[53] and making reliquaries out of precious substances.[54] This catalog will be datable with a great deal of precision once the parallel development of the inscriptional technical discourse of pious acts has been charted out. The palaeographic stages show certain characteristics: the Mauryan inscriptions at Sāñchi and Amarāvatī know only of "pillar gift" or simply "gift"; subsequently new technical terms emerged: "cross-bar gift," "rail gift." With the passing of time more terms were added to this language: "lion-throne gift," "*dharma-cakra* gift," "lamp-stand gift," "coping stone gift," "carved slab gift," "entrance pillar gift."

My point in providing this detail is not to suggest that I have worked out the line of development of this language; I have not. In fact, the "line" will also have to include considerations of space, because certain terms in this lithic discourse occur first at different times in different places (e.g., a technical language of cave-gifts emerges first in the western cave temple sites; many *stūpa* ornamentation terms are unique to Andhra). My point is simply that the *Apadāna* is situated in the same discourse. It represents and participates in the development of the *stūpa* cult at a particular stage that can be discerned on the basis of "hard" evidence. For example, there are a number of specific donative gifts described in the *Apadāna* that appear as technical terms only in the inscriptions at Amarāvatī, whereas a number of the characteristic terms of the later (Ikshvāku) inscriptions at that site do not appear in *Apadāna*: this gives us some indication of both the place (Andhra Pradesh) and time (post-Maurya, pre-Ikshvāku) in which the *Apadāna* was current.

Similarly, it should be possible to locate the subtle developments of the cosmic Buddha biography from *Cariyāpiṭaka* to *Apadāna* within a nuanced understanding of the art historical stages discernable in the hodge-podge of carvings. For example, at Bhārhut many of the rail carvings, dated to about the middle of the second century B.C., contain identified scenes of *jātakas* that line up, in part, with *Cariyāpiṭaka*, but which seem to be, given their inclusion with different sorts of labelled scenes, incorporated within a this-life biography of Buddha as well as an explicit chart of previous Buddha-time. *Buddhavaṃsa*, then, may be roughly coeval with the Bhārhut railing. But there is still much to be done before any definite conclusions can be reached, since art historians will have to reevaluate their identifications of certain scenes in order to assess the degree to which they correspond to the texts that actually belong to the periods in question. Simple questions, like do we see the *Buddhavaṃsa* version of the Buddha's cosmic miracle illustrated in any of the carvings, have not even been asked. Again, my point is a general one: the texts and the carvings participate in the same story-telling tradition, the history of which will become clear only when they are examined together.

There is a third problem about the epigraphs that must be reckoned with, and that overlaps with the two points I have just made. Unlike the later Brahmī epigraphs that have been so masterfully analyzed by

Schopen,[55] the early Brahmī donative inscriptions that I have been discussing do not indicate a specific recipient. This goes deeper than an absence of that sectarian specification which began to characterize donative inscriptions only in about the first century A.D., under the Kushans and their Sarvāstivādin favorites. In the early Brahmī inscriptions we do not even have an indication of what it meant to give a gift, nor who was supposed to accrue the merit, nor how they were supposed to do so. The inscriptions are bare: generally just "the gift (*dānaṃ*) of (donor/s)."[56] How then do we go about reconstructing the epistemology according to which agents of various complexity considered it a good thing to join together in order to perform *stūpa* worship and other pious Buddhist acts known from the inscriptions of the day? What Buddhist ideology of gift-giving made giving Buddhist gifts rational? Considering the complex mobilization of resources and people that was required in order to effect any specific stage in the development of the great *stūpas*, it is reasonable to assume that there was such a shared understanding of the value of Buddhist piety, a shared understanding that united all these different agents (whatever their ulterior personal motivations) together in specific collective projects: giving Buddhist gifts.

My short answer to the problem of intent is that the *Apadāna* and related texts provide the ideological component or "insides" of human actions that left as their "outsides" wreaths of wilting flowers, remnants of oils and incense and food, and of course the actual pillars, cross-bars, etc., that still survive today. Among the many ways in which the language of the *Apadāna* parallels the epigraphs, it uses "*dānaṃ*" (gift) as a category unto itself, with all its subvarieties described and catalogued according to method and result in a self-referential discourse. In his or her *apadāna* each monk or nun states, paralleling the inscriptional remains, "I gave such-and-such gift (*dānaṃ*) during the time of such-and-such Buddha; I experienced no unpleasant states in subsequent transmigration; in the present I achieved arhantship: this is the fruit of that gift (*[type of] dānassa idaṃ phalaṃ*)." A donative inscription that simply states "the such-and-such *dānaṃ* of so-and-so" is not at all ambiguous if we remember that the ABCs were coeval with the giving and inscribing of the gifts. The *Apadāna* tells in full detail what a *dānaṃ* means, and why and how it is done. The only questions left open in its karmically black-and-white world[57] concern the variety of gift and the identity of donor (which is precisely the information recorded in the inscriptions). The very nature of the *Apadāna* rendered further elaboration on stone redundant. Such elaboration of purpose appeared in epigraphic records only later, after the *Apadāna* had been displaced by subsequent revisions of its "Great Story," starting with *Divyāvadāna*, that had different epistemological orientations.

So it is to the ABCs that we must look if we want to reconstruct the "insides" of the actions in question. I have already attempted to sketch out the general framework of meaning in which the ABCs set Buddhist action, the ideology of gift-giving reflected in and constituted by those Buddhist texts (i.e., the ABCs) that were being composed at the same time that the *stūpas* were being constructed and inscriptions inscribed. Positing this framework of meaning implies neither that the texts describe the actual practices nor that the actual practices were mere enactments of the stories in the texts. Instead, it implies that both overlapped at an "epistemic" or "archaeological" level of thought, to borrow Michel Foucault's useful terminology. The ABCs, unlike their inscriptional counterparts, provide insight into the philosophical sophistication of this thought,[58] which attempted to increase the value of the Buddha's legacy to humanity in light of new questions that emerged after Aśoka's imperial unification of the subcontinent constituted, for the first time, a totality of which the various Indian kingdoms and other social groupings became parts.[59] This universalization of the Path consisted of a series of biographical analyses of the religious act, first with reference only to the Buddha but finally with reference to other people who represent an enormous cross section of cosmic time and space, of cosmic society. *Buddhas* and *arhats* share a virtue that ordinary people do not: they know their previous lives. This well-established canonical detail had immense ramifications for post-Aśokan Buddhist practice, after it had been realized that those previous lives encode a program for action here-and-now. It is within this epistemology that we should imagine the acts that produced the *stūpas*.

In the next section I want to elaborate upon a few of the many ways in which the *Apadāna* narratives inform the nature of the actions represented by the surviving ruins. I will focus on three topics: the relationship between *stūpa* and biography, the symbolism of the *stūpa*, and the nature of the complex agency that produced the great *stūpas* of early post-Aśokan India.

Biography as Empire

The connection between biography and *stūpa* is more direct than I have yet allowed. As Paul Mus has shown us,[60] the *stūpa* is more than a representation of the cosmic Buddha biography: it *is* the cosmic Buddha biography. The *stūpa* of the Buddha is precisely what the Buddha biography has become in the time between the *Parinirvāṇa* and today. The relic it contains is the material body (*rūpakāya*) of the Buddha-in-*nirvāṇa* or some Buddhist saint-in-*nirvāṇa*.[61] The "stories" it illustrates are the teachings of Buddha, his body of Dharma (*dharmakāya*). According to Mus, at the *Parinirvāṇa* Buddha did not die in the way modern Westerners think of death; he was merely transformed. His legacy in the present, that is his ongoing biography within *saṃsāra*, is the combination of bodily and linguistic relics that the *stūpa* literally constitutes. The participants in the *stūpa* cult thus participate in an unbroken continuation of the pious activities that Buddhists did before Gotama was transformed in *Parinirvāṇa*: give food, garlands, flowers, scents, fences, stairways, walkways, houses, umbrellas, seats, clothes, flags, service, worship, praise, and memory to the Buddha himself, conceived as a participant in the present.

The ABCs confirm Mus' thesis entirely. Their language is rich with plays on the metaphors of Buddhism as the "inheritance" from the Buddha by his "children," of Buddha as the sacrificial altar and fires, and of other perspectives that Mus labored to suggest. Most important for our purposes, the *Apadāna* texts about *stūpa* (and Bodhi tree) worship echo unmistakably Mus' view that the worshiper regards the *stūpa* as though it were the Buddha[62] or as the Buddha himself,[63] who never died but was transformed into a *saṃsāric* collection of bones and books and an (unknowable) *nirvāṇic* state (all the ABC biographies, like those Mus actually studied, "end" with the Buddha alive and establishing his "estate").

Remarkably, Mus apparently came up with his analysis largely on the basis of intuition; it is notoriously difficult to develop (or even understand) his work because he seldom had actual textual passages to support his conclusions. Following Foucher, Mus discussed certain canonical suttas and then the usual range of later Pāli and Buddhist Sanskrit texts, but he did not discuss the ABCs. He was, as a result, forced (unnecessarily) into intellectual gymnastics in order to make the Buddhist texts reveal the ideology (that he had discerned through his creative reading of the *Brāhmanas* and *Upanishads*). For, it is only in the ABCs that this ideology is actually stated, described, and constituted. That is because the ABCs were composed in the critical period of transition between the canonical suttas and the Buddhist Sanskrit texts, and so they alone spell out in detail the process by which an ideology (of the cosmic Buddha/universal soteriology) that is absent (though perhaps foreshadowed) in the earlier suttas came to be simply presumed (and reworked) by the Buddhist Sanskrit authors. At the same time that the ABC authors were thus changing, embellishing, and praising the Buddha's *dharmakāya*, the participants in the *stūpa* cult were changing, embellishing, and praising his *rūpakāya*. These two groups overlapped; they participated in a single episteme: the *stūpa* is the union of the texts and the donative inscriptions, the union of ideology and practice.

Just as the *stūpa* does not *symbolize* the Buddha and his biography but actually *is* the Buddha and his biography, so too the *stūpa* is not the symbol of a universal society but the product and project of a universal society. *Apadāna* is the story of one enormous biographical web, in which Buddha and the saints in his dispensation knew each other and the same previous Buddhas, lived in the same ancient cities under the same ancient kings, and attended the same festivals or funerals or dharma-talks. Sometimes this is explicit: the Buddha's aunt reached *nirvāṇa* with 500 nuns who were her kinfolk and companions, *en masse*, throughout her previous lives.[64] Rāhula transmigrated with his sister;[65] many groups of monks transmigrated together;[66] the seven ancient daughters of Kikī King of Kāsi ended up sisters in the same convent;[67] marriages (including that between Buddha and Yaśodharā) are bonds for eternity.[68] The trope of the cotransmigration of social units (homologous to the complex agents in the inscriptions) is always implied, due to the basic epistemological position that the biographical web is still being spun by those who are part of it but have not yet escaped it. The *Apadāna* describes a series of Buddha eras in which large numbers of people, participating in the then-ongoing Buddha biography together, move on together through cosmic time until they are born together in the time of Gotama Buddha and achieve together the goal of his dispensation. The biography of the Buddha himself is indistinguishable from the biographies of all those who were involved in the complex agencies that provided the context for his (and their) actions throughout time. As the biography is ongoing, so too is the series of complex agencies that continues in this Buddha era to treasure a Buddha's legacy by caring for his earthly "bodies." His biography is their biography; *Apadāna* is part of the biography of a cosmic society still moving on together toward *nirvāṇa*: a universal society whose members are the participants, past and present, in the *stūpa* cult.

There are other ways, too, in which the ABCs drive home this point that the *stūpa* cult is the ongoing cosmic Buddha biography *qua* universal soteriology. In the *Apadāna* the participants in the *stūpa* cult are superhuman in addition to human: *devas, yakkhas, nāgas*, and other mythical beings are described as present at and active in the construction and festivals of worship of *stūpas*. This does more than provide insight into the presence of these beings at the *stūpas*, which was constituted by the *stūpa* sculptures and carvings (usually understood as "influences" on Buddhism of the fertility goddesses and animistic spirits that haunt the timelessly dreamy Indian mind). It allows us, more importantly, to understand that the universality represented in the *stūpa* cult is more than theoretical or symbolic: the entire universe really was centered around the *stūpa*, around the Buddha. The universally attended and extremely joyous festival in which the Buddha reveals the *Buddhavaṃsa* (a common trope in the self-understanding of later Mahāyāna sutras) is, in the *Apadāna* and the *stūpa* cult, homologous to the actual, then present-day, world. The actual festivals that effected the various stages in the development of the *stūpas* (and even the ideology of competitive one-upmanship is spelled out in *Apadāna*)[69] constituted the continuation of a Buddha biography that was simultaneously the continuation of a universal society, namely the congregation of all those donors (and the supernatural beings) under one complex agency that organizes and sponsors the festival.

Likewise, as I have already indicated in part, this extension of the Buddha biography across time (pre-Siddhartha lives and post-Gotama lives) was complemented by an extension of the Buddha biography across space. *Buddhavaṃsa* treats the "spreading out of the relics" (*dhātuvitthārikaṃ*)[70] of a Buddha as one among its many categories for telling Buddha biographies: just as it asks of each Buddha "how long did he remain an ascetic?" or "what was the name of his father?" so it asks, "were his relics 'spread out?' ". It turns out that the answer is "no" for sixteen Buddhas, "yes" for the remaining nine (including Gotama). The 'spreading out' of Gotama's relics—i.e., the distribution over space of his ongoing biography—is well known in Buddhological circles. *Mahāparinibbāna Sutta* contains a famous account of the distribution of relics after Gotama's funeral, which constitutes a geopolitical map of Magadha (northeastern India). *Buddhavaṃsa* not only categorically defines this "distribution" as part of the ongoing Buddha biography; it appropriates the actual verses out of *Mahāparinibbāna Sutta* and incorporates them within its own greatly expanded enumeration of the relics and their subsequent journeys.[71] In *Buddhavaṃsa* this is not just a map of Magadha; it is a geopolitical map of an India conceived on a scale that was possible only after the imperial unification of the subcontinent (under Aśoka).[72]

Again, this is not "popular legend" but extremely sophisticated thought about the then-real world. For the "cosmic" and "universal" society that I have been describing is, as I have already suggested, constituted by the people who actually participated in the *stūpa* cult (whether in the second century B.C. or one hundred thousand eons ago). The Buddha biography, extended in both time and space by the ABCs and the diffusion of *stūpas*, is the biography of a then-real, complex sociopolitical organization, namely the post-Aśokan Indian imperial formations of the Śungas and the Sātavāhanas. The inscriptions alone make it clear that the *stūpa* cult developed within the post-Aśokan imperial process.[73] And in light of the fact that the earliest "hard" evidence for the existence of any lithic record or the construction of any *stūpas* is Aśokan, that is imperial; in light of the improbability that anyone other than an emperor would have had the power to hold a festival and build a *stūpa* on the scale that we are talking about, and at major intersections of major land and water routes throughout the empire(s); in light of the certainty that subsequent additions to these *stūpas* by the later Sātavāhanas and Ikshvākus were decidedly imperial acts, it does not seem remarkable that the inscriptions should bear the names of emperors. It is the world-conquering Buddhist monarch, the *cakkavattin*, who is the agent organizing the pious work/festival that gathers together people from all those places (the extension of the Buddha biography in space) and all those walks of life (the extension of the Buddha biography in time) in order to constitute the continuing biography of the Buddha, cosmic society, and the empire: the *stūpas* are the constitutions of polities, the inscriptions the signatures of representative citizens, and the texts political philosophy.

As I have already mentioned, each *Apadāna* actor experiences in his or her cosmic biography a period of transition between the first performance of a Buddhist action—often a trivial gesture or fleeting recollection—and the final attainment of *nirvāṇa* in the time of a Buddha (Gotama). This period of transition lasts for countless eons, but it is entirely pleasant: only birth in heaven or on earth, and always in a state of luxury that vastly magnifies the original piety. These descriptions contain as a matter of course enumerations of the times that each monk or nun was a Wheel-Turning Monarch or his homolog the King of Gods (or their analogs, those kings' queens); the number of times that they attained "local kingship" within a larger empire is, when stated at all, sloughed off as "beyond reckoning."[74] The point is that the political and religious ideologies, which we tend to treat as distinct, are utterly entwined and presuppose each other: the *cakkavattin* is *cakkavattin* because he was once a pious Buddhist; *cakkavattins*, in order to demonstrate that they are *cakkavattins* (and because it is the very nature of *cakkavattins*) are pious Buddhists today.[75] The citizens of the empire, from "local kings" on down, participate in the ongoing biography (that the *cakkavattin* constitutes: the empire itself) because they are where they are today—human, after all—only having already participated in this biography during previous lives, and because the texts tell them how participation in it during the present life will assure future, greater blessings and eventual *nirvāṇa*.

Everyone benefits from the *cakkavattin's* festival, with the exception of those who do not, at least with an approving glance, participate. From the lowliest villager to the headman whose name goes on the pillar, from the offerer of a flower that he found on the highway[76] to the wealthy *seṭṭhi* or *vanija* who singularly makes a contribution equal to what others can give only if they rally together, all participants are assured a part in the Buddha biography, the cosmic story of their own salvation. All these people—even the workmen who clean the *stūpa* and the grounds,[77] the dyers,[78] the plasterers,[79] the musicians,[80] the onlooking children,[81] and the people there who speak words that praise the *Apadāna*[82]—can be certain that they will one day be local kings and world emperors themselves, will one day possess minds so enlightened that they will remember the moral acts of previous lives (including participation together in these very festivals) and will one day sing *apadānas* of their own beatitude in order to encourage others to perform these same actions.

Conclusion

The festivals for constructing, improving, and worshiping a *stūpa* (or a Bodhi tree, or a place sacralized by a Buddha's presence,[83] or the *sangha*) were the historical situations in which text, inscription, and carving came together. Festivals were the actions constitutive of the Buddha's then-present biography. Early post-Aśokan Indian Buddhist emperors, equating that biography with their empire(s),[84] constituted those empires by organizing such festivals: mobilizing people and resources in common projects that left as their effects the architecture and carvings, that claimed as their major (already complex) agents the donors, and that proceeded according to the ideological framework of the texts. I want to suggest that the texts were actually recited or performed during the festivals. There is plenty of reason to assume that they were composed for performance;[85] there is also every reason to think that they would be "festive additions" to such an occasion. The ABCs are all written in light and delightful Pāli verse, full of alliteration and rhyme, suspense and drama, pathos and humor.[86]

The purely entertainment value, however, is overshadowed by the relevance that these texts had for the festival as its ideological basis: it is the story that justifies the donor's participation in these particular forms of piety, that provides directions and specifications for that piety, that assures him or her of future bliss. It is the story that makes those present at the festival feel good about their participation.

In the end, feeling good—about one's actions, about the Buddha, about the empire—is what the texts, inscriptions, and carvings are all about. The texts and carvings produce aesthetic and religious pleasure at the same time that they narrate certain ideas about the nature of the world, the empire, and the Buddha; the happy willingness with which the donors participate is reflected in the act of carving their names in stone, for all to see at the festival. The *Buddhavaṃsa* account of the prototypical biography festival, in which the text itself is proclaimed amid throngs of human and supernatural beings, develops an almost untranslatable language of mental pleasure—laughing a huge laughter (*hasati mahāhasitaṃ),* horripilating with delight *(tuṭṭhahaṭṭha*), pleased with mental pleasure (*cittapasādena pasanna*), having a mind of delight (*tuṭṭhamānasa*), satisfied (*santusita*), overjoyed (*pamodita*), thrilled (*udaggacitta*), good-minded (*sumana*)—repeated over and over again. That is the state of all the people who participate in the paradigmatic biography festival, who listen to the *Buddhavaṃsa*. And they respond with song and dance and reflection and devotion. The happiness that makes the festival happen is excelled only by the happiness that it generates.

And it is precisely this mental act—being happy in a Buddhist context—that in the *Apadāna* defines the efficacy of ritual. It was "because of that deed well done *with intention and resolve*" (*tena kammena sukatena cetanāpaṇidhīhi ca*), or simply "because of that mental pleasure" (*tena citta-pasādena*) that monk after monk, nun after nun, and even the Buddha himself experienced lifetimes of pleasant existence, universal rulership, and material wealth, until finally they realized the ultimate happiness, the true perfection of mind, *nirvāṇa*. The festival, with its melodic chanting and pretty pictures, its crowds of people in the presence of big shots, the flowers and dancing, the lamps and the incense, constituted *that* happiness and was in turn constituted by it. That mental act was performed by the participants in the festival, who simultaneously acted as citizens in the empire and as characters in the ongoing Buddha biography.

Notes

1. In *The Biographical Process: Studies in the History and Psychology of Religion*, ed. Frank E. Reynolds and Donald Capps, (Mouton: The Hague, 1976), pp. 37–61, esp. p. 57.
2. Ibid., p. 42.
3. Ibid, p. 39.
4. Gregory Schopen, "Two Problems in the History of Indian Buddhism: The Layman/Monk Distinction and the Doctrines of the Transference of Merit," in Georg Buddruss et al., trans., *Studien Zur Indologie und Iranistik* 10 (Reinbeck: Dr. Inge Wezler Verlag für Orientalistische Fachpublikationen, 1985), pp. 9–47.
5. Gregory Schopen, "Mahāyāna in Indian Inscriptions," *Indo-Iranian Journal* 21 (1979), pp. 1–19; cf. "The Inscription on the Kushān Image of Amitābha and the Character of the Early Mahāyāna in India," *Journal of the International Association of Buddhist Studies* 10, no. 2 (1987), pp. 99–137.
6. Schopen occasionally treats the textual evidence as though it were largely irrelevant (e.g., Schopen, "Two Problems in the History of Indian Buddhism," pp. 9–23, esp. pp. 14, 22–23; cf. the treatment of textually based reconstructions of the "origin" of the Mahāyāna in "Mahāyāna and Indian Inscriptions"), although his work generally is directed at textualists, that is at evaluating the nature of texts on the basis of the inscriptions. Underrepresented in his work is the potential value texts have in confirming the points he makes about the epigraphic record (but cf. in this regard Schopen's use of *vamsa* texts for confirming epigraphic readings in "On the Buddha and His Bones: The Conception of a Relic in the

Inscriptions from Nāgārjunikoṇḍa," *Journal of the American Oriental Society* 108, no. 4 [October–December 1988], pp. 527–537). More important, Schopen has done little work from the other side: that is, allowing textual data to challenge and nuance the epigraphic conclusions just as the epigraphic conclusions challenge the texts.

7. My own perspective owes much of its substance to the combined work of my colleagues and teachers, especially Ronald Inden, in the ongoing Seminar on Text and Knowledge in South Asia at the University of Chicago. We have been developing and nuancing a "constitutivist" method, which in this context is a view that text and epigraph are mutually constituting discourses in time, constitutive of each other and also of the historical situation(s) in which they were produced. For examples of the new knowledge that such a reading of text-and-epigraph makes possible for all periods, see Inden's "Imperial Formation, Imperial Purāṇa," forthcoming in *Post-Orientalist Approaches to the Study of South Asian Texts*, ed. Inden, and my own contribution to that volume, "Buddhist History: The Sri Lankan Pāli Vaṃsas"; cf. Inden's *Imagining India* (Oxford: Basil Blackwell, 1990), especially chap. 6, "Reconstructions." The "constitutive" method builds on the work of modern critical thinkers including Michel Foucault, Antonio Gramsci, and Edward Said, upon the basis of the late R. G. Collingwood's systematic philosophy; for an introduction to Collingwood's philosophy, see his *An Autobiography* (Oxford: Clarendon, 1939) and *An Essay on Philosophical Method* (Oxford: Clarendon, 1933).
8. Gregory Schopen, "The Stūpa Cult and the Extant Pāli Vinaya," *Journal of the Pāli Text Society* 13 (1989), p. 96; cf. "Two Problems in the History of Indian Buddhism," p. 13.
9. Underlying this anachronistic scholarship is an assumption that the authors of the later texts merely repeated ancient oral traditions in which the stories already preexisted, full blown. But the evidence for that assumption is limited, in the early post-Aśokan period anyway, to the conclusions of scholars about what is represented in the carvings at Bhārhut and Sāñchi! This gets very slippery because most of the carvings from this period do not actually have labels at all, and reconstructing the stories they tell has largely been a matter for guesswork.
10. The fact may be that the carvings gave shape to the later texts that seem to correspond to them, rather than the other way around.
11. Mary E. Lilley, ed., *The Apadāna of the Khuddaka Nikāya* (London: Pāli Text Society, 1925, 1927), 2 vols. My citations are to Lilley's edition throughout, but there are much better editions available in Sinhala (I find the Hewawitarne Bequest edition reliable), Devanāgari, and Thai scripts. I cite Lilley's edition because I assume that despite its difficulties, it is more accessible to readers of English than (superior) editions in Asian scripts.
12. Definitive work on the dating of these texts remains to be done (my own work herein on the epigraphic evidence is meant as a contribution to this

project), but no scholar to my knowledge has suggested that they were composed before the time of Aśoka; the question is how long after Aśoka they were composed. A. K. Warder argues on the basis of meter that the texts belong to the second and first centuries B.C. (*Pāli Metre* [London: Pāli Text Society, 1967], pp. 303, 136; compare his statements in *Indian Buddhism* [Delhi: Motilal Banarsidass, 1970], p. 298), and I believe that this can be demonstrated on other grounds as well. In addition to my arguments in this essay about the overlap of these texts with the early Brahmī inscriptions that are dated to the same two centuries, the study of intertext further clarifies the point. *Apadāna* quotes *Cariyāpiṭaka* and *Buddhavaṃsa* in addition to many earlier texts (as discussed below); this gives some indication of how late it is. But *Apadāna* was known by the authors of early (Sarvāstivādin) Buddhist Sanskrit works, including *Divyāvadāna* (compare Lilley, *The Apadāna*, vol. 1, p. 6 v. 77 [*Buddāpadāna*] with E. B. Cowell and R. A. Neil, eds., *The Divyāvadāna: A Collection of Early Buddhist Legends* [Cambridge: Cambridge University Press, 1886], p. 469 [note the loss of the syntactical integrity of the Pāli when it is translated into Sanskrit]; ibid., p. 533 [*ājñātāni ca satyāni kritaṃ Buddhasya śāsanam*] is apparently a [poor] translation of the typical concluding statement of virtually every *apadāna* [*chaḍabhiññā sacchikatā kataṃ Buddhassa sāsanam*]; ibid., p. 195–196 [*prahāya mānushān kāyān divyān kāyān upāsate*] is similarly a Sanskriticization of a very familiar *apadāna* refrain) and *Anavataptagāthā* (see K. R. Norman, *Pāli Literature* [Wiesbaden: Otto Harrassowitz, 1983], p. 92); this gives some indication of how early it is. For an extended review of the evidence that the ABCs postdate the Buddha by "several centuries," see Oliver Abeynayake, *A Textual and Historical Analysis of the Khuddaka Nikāya* (Colombo: Tisara, 1984), pp. 164–182, 214–215. Heinz Bechert has tried to date the text considerably later than most scholars (as late as the third century A.D., even though he allows the possibility of second or first century B.C.—see his "Buddha-Feld und Verdienstübertragung: Mahāyāna-Ideen im Theravāda-Buddhismus Ceylons," *Bulletin de la Classe des Lettres et des Sciences Morales et Politiques* 5e. série, vol. 62 [Brussels: Palais des Académies, 1976], p. 48), but his argument is based on an understanding of both "Theravādin orthodoxy" and "Mahāyāna ideas" that is extremely problematic; see, for an initial critique, Schopen, "Two Problems," esp. pp. 46–47.

13. Lilley, vol. 1, *The Apadāna*, p. 37 v. 6 (Puṇṇa-Mantāniputta Thera), and vol. 2, p. 550 v. 90 (Khemā Therī).
14. Compare V. Fausboll, ed., *The Sutta-Nipāta* (SN) (London: Pāli Text Society, n.d. [1885]), pt. 1, pp. 6–12 (*Khaggavisāṇasuttaṃ*) with Lilley, *The Apadāna*, vol. 1, pp. 8–13 vv. 8–49 (*Paccekabuddhāpadāna*); the commentarial tradition on SN also attributes these verses to *Pacceka* Buddhas.
15. See H. Bechert, "Über das Apadānabuch," in E. Frauwallner, trans., *Wiener Zeitschrift für die Kunde Süd- und Ostasiens und Archiv für Indische Philosophie*, vol. 2 (Vienna: Verlag Brüder Hollinek, 1958), pp. 7–9.

16. The connection of these early saints' verses to the *Apadāna* is most intimate: many of the *apadāna*s take up and incorporate the same monk's or nun's verses in *Thera-Therīgāthā*, continuing the process, evident even in the latter texts, of adding biographical "rubrics" to the core verses. See Norman, *Pāli Literature,* pp. 89–90, who goes as far as saying that *Apadāna* is "almost an appendix to the Theragāthā and Therīgāthā" (p. 89). It might be better to think of *Apadāna* as "almost a commentary" on those texts. It, like another *Khuddaka-nikāya* text that is a "commentary" on *Sutta-nipāta* (*Niddesa*), represents a crucial stage in the development of commentarial thought within Theravādin history. In terms of *Apadāna,* the process is continued by Dhammapāla, who comments on the *Thera-Therīgāthā* by quoting the *apadāna* of each monk or nun after providing a prose account of it. It is thus the case that the biographical details in C. Rhys-Davids' famous translation of the *Thera-Therīgāthā* (*Psalms of the Sisters* and *Psalms of the Brethren*) owe their origin to the *Apadāna* stage in the commentarial process.
17. Rev. Richard Morris, ed., *The Buddhavaṃsa and the Cariyā-Piṭaka* (London: Pāli Text Society, 1882), p. 103 (*Itthaṃ sudaṃ . . . abhāsitthā ti*).
18. Compare ibid., p. 103 with Lilley *The Apadāna,* vol. 1, pp. 5–6 vv. 69–77 plus colophon.
19. Compare Morris, ibid., p. 3 v. 23 with Lilley, *The Apadāna,* vol. 1, p. 20 v. 79 (Sāriputta Thera), vol. 2, p. 364 v. 38 (Udena Thera), and p. 422 v. 9 (Nāṇatthavika Thera); vol. 2, p. 429 vv. 1–6 (Dhammaruci Thera) presupposes *Buddhavaṃsa,* employing its typical prediction (rather than the alternate form typical of other *apadāna*s) and making obvious reference to the *Buddhavaṃsa* account of Sumedha (compare Morris, *The Buddhavaṃsa and the Cariyā-Piṭaka,* p. 10 vv. 66ff); for examples of other *Buddhavaṃsa* verses quoted in *Apadāna* see Lilley, *The Apadāna,* vol. 2, p. 479 vv. 2–6 (Mahākoṭṭhika Thera) = p. 481 vv. 2–6; p. 484 vv. 2–6; p. 486 vv. 2–6 [etc.]. A listing of *Buddhavaṃsa pāda*s that appear in *Apadāna* would be even more extensive than a similar list of *Cariyāpiṭaka pāda*s in *Buddhavaṃsa.*
20. See Reynolds, "The Many Lives of Buddha," pp. 42–43 for a discussion of various perspectives in the scholarly tradition.
21. They are giving (*dāna*), moral discipline (*sīla*), turning away from the world (*nekkhamma*), wisdom (*paññā*), exertion (*viriyā*), patience (*khanti*), truthfulness (*sacca*), resolution (*adhiṭṭhāna*), love (*mettā*), and even-mindedness (*upekkhā*).
22. Even the one sutta that would seem to contradict this statement, *Mahāpadāna Sutta* of the *Dīghanikāya,* supports the contention I am making. It is true that it details the lives of previous *buddhas* and indicates that the Buddha made good *karma* then, which at least hints at the full-blown cosmic biography. And there is no doubt that the details of this sutta are a major basis for the *Buddhavaṃsa* (and consequently for the *Apadāna*) account, including the name, *Apadāna,* that defines the genre to

which all three ABCs self-consciously belong. But in *Mahāpadāna* the problematic frame is not universal soteriology; the question of the sutta is about whether Buddhas remember their own previous lives or learn about them from gods, not about the universality of Buddha's messages. Thus *Mahāpadāna Sutta* lacks the essential revelation that each *buddha* laid the foundation for all people, even those who did not achieve the goal there-and-then, to achieve it sometime. The stark contrast between *Mahāpadāna Sutta* and *Buddhavaṃsa* is best seen in a comparison of their respective tellings of the "Brahmā begs Buddha to preach" mytheme. In the former text this characterizes other *buddhas'* lives too (showing a stage in the development of the *Buddhavaṃsa*) but otherwise stays close to the original myth, in sharp distinction to *Buddhavaṃsa* itself, as described below.

23. Morris, *The Buddhavaṃsa and the Cariyā-Piṭaka*, pp. 102–103 vv. 8–14 (also quoted as the conclusion to *Buddhāpadāna*, Lilley, *The Apadāna*, vol. 1, pp. 5–6 vv. 69–75).
24. See T.W. Rhys-Davids and Hermann Oldenberg, trans., *Vinaya Texts* (Oxford: Clarendon Press, 1881), part 1, pp. 84–88 (*Sacred Books of the East*, vol. 13); V. Trenckner, ed., *The Majjhima-Nikāya* (London: Pāli Text Society, 1888), vol. 1, pp. 167–169 (*Ariyapariyesanasuttaṃ* [no. 26]).
25. Morris, *The Buddhavaṃsa and the Cariyā-Piṭaka*, p. 74: *Atītakappe caritaṃ ṭhapayitvā bhavābhave/imamhi kappe caritaṃ pavakkhissaṃ suṇohi me.*
26. Ibid., p. 67 v. 19: *ahaṃ etarahi sambuddho Metteyo cāpi hessati.*
27. Ibid., p. 67 v. 20: *Etesaṃ dhammarājūnaṃ aññesaṃ nekakoṭinaṃ/ācikkhitvāna taṃ maggaṃ nibbutā te sasāvakā ti.*
28. Specifically, the Buddha magically creates (*nimmināti*) with his mind a gem-studded palace and then imagines all the Buddhas and disciples of cosmic time together, in that palace. The palace itself bears a striking similarity to the *stūpa*, for in it the Buddha "provides" to the previous Buddhas precisely what people in this period provided to the Buddha (in his present "palace," the *stūpa* itself): wreaths, precious substances, incense, lamp-stands, banners, lion-thrones, musical instruments, celestial songs, rails with *toraṇa*s, etc. The situation created in the Buddha's mind is also homologous with the cosmic festival of the *Buddhavaṃsa*, and thus with the ancient festivals recorded in *Apadāna* as well as the then-modern festivals of the Śungas and Sātavāhanas in which, as I argue below, the texts were performed and the *stūpas* were built.
29. Lilley, *The Apadāna*, vol 1, p. 4 v. 50; cf. v. 48: *manasā dānaṃ*.
30. Ibid., vol. 1, p. 1 v. 1; cf. p. 7, p. 15, vol. 2, p. 512: *Atha buddhāpadānāni [etc.] suṇātha.*
31. E.g., ibid., vol. 1, p. 153 v. 4: *anupadinnā Buddhena sabbesaṃ bījasampadā* ("the fulfillment/growth of seeds [of karma] is assured by the Buddha for everyone").
32. We can include at least Lilley's numbers 3, 11, 15, 22, 38, 48, 61, 71, 116, 119, 141, 142, 143, 144, 145, 159, 193, 236, 239, 247, 253, 277, 291, 293, 331, 333, 373, 374, 394, 413, 426, 455, 456, 457, 458, 459, 483,

484, 495 and 538 (ibid.) of the *Therāpadāna* in a list of *apadānas* of monks whose root pious act was directly connected with the cult of *stūpas*/relics.

33. André Bareau, *Les Sectes Bouddhiques du Petit Véhicule* (Saigon: École française d'Extrême-Orient, 1955), p. 36 (et passim: see p. 36 n. 1); cf. Étienne Lamotte, *History of Indian Buddhism: From the Origins to the Śaka Era*, trans. Sara Webb-Boin (Louvain-la-neuve: Université Catholique de Louvain, Institut Orientaliste, 1988), pp. 523–526.

34. Schopen, "Two Problems."

35. Uma Chakravarti, *The Social Dimensions of Early Buddhism* (Delhi: Oxford University Press, 1988).

36. Collingwood's most extensive description of "complex agency," situated historically and defined philosophically, is his *The New Leviathan or Man, Society, Civilization and Barbarity* (New York: Thomas Crowell, 1971 [1942]). Collingwood begins with action motivated by the human passions, "personal motivations," but demonstrates that human agency always extends beyond the passions because people act simultaneously as members of social units from families right up to civilizations. All human action thus has collective, societal dimensions characterized by rational activity aimed at constructing, defining, maintaining, improving, and/or regulating the social formations of which individuals are constitutive. The passions may still play a role in action, but collective action—"complex agency"—implies and necessitates overlapping "collective motivations" in the form of an epistemology that is shared and thereby constituted as the arena in which consensus is produced. Because epistemology is, for Collingwood, created in time and space by the human thought that also produced the texts (or inscriptions or monuments) that survive today as evidence of it, rather than some essence (e.g., collective consciousness, cultural proclivity, sociopolitical "context") that exists outside of and is merely expressed by actual texts, its recovery is a strictly historical problem that requires an imaginative reconstruction, based upon a learned reading of the evidence itself, of the relationships between human thoughts and sociopolitical formations in any given historical period. "Collective motivations" (e.g., ideologies, soteriologies, Buddhologies) and collective agencies (kingdoms, caste groups, religious sects) are recovered in the single act of interpreting the primary evidence that was constituted by and constitutive of both theory and practice. Inden has made brilliant use of Collingwood's ideas about "complex agency" in his *Imagining India*, especially the idea of "caste as citizenship." Compare here Lamotte (*History*, p. 414), who recognizes (as have other scholars) the *fact* of complex agency (although not in those terms) but does not then explore the ramifications of such a view.

37. E.g., C. Sivaramamurti, *Amaravati Sculptures in the Madras Government Museum, Bulletin of the Madras Government Museum, New Series, General Section, vol. 4* (Madras: Tansi Press, 1977), "Inscriptions," pp. 271–304 nos. 17, 42, 48, 52, 75, 97, and 120 (members of immediate family); nos. 35,

41, 44, 124, and 126 (friends, family, and relatives); cf. H. Lüders, *A List of Brahmī Inscriptions (Epigraphia Indica* 10, pp. 1–179), nos. 1214, 1278.

38. E.g., Lüders, *List,* no. 1180 (guild of corn dealers: *daṃñikaseṇi*).

39. The best example is the famous set of inscriptions on the Bhaṭṭiprolu *stūpa*'s relic caskets: see G. Bühler, "The Bhattiprolu Inscriptions" (*EI*2, pp. 323–329). Here, the richness of "complex agency" in the construction of *stūpas* is apparent. A king called Kubera[ka] organized at least two committees (*goṭhi*) and a mercantile town (*negamā*), the members of which are listed at length on the actual caskets and which themselves already represent complex agencies, into a single complex agency that effected the enshrinement of the three caskets together in a single *stūpa*. Compare in this regard Lüders, *List*, no. 234 (Sāñchi; "Buddhist Committee" [*bodhagoṭhi*] from Dharmavardhana: ibid., no. 351), no 273 (Sāñchi, a *goṭhi* from Vidisā). Cf. further no. 782 (Bhārhut, a group of *dāyakas* from Purikā); no. 214 (Sāñchi; *upāsikas* from Navagrāma) and others.

40. Lüders, *List*, no. 195 (Sāñchi; the village of Vejaja), no. 401 (Sāñchi; village of Aśvarāvatī), no. 625 (Sāñchi; village of Chuṃvamoragiri (?)); cf. Sivaramamurti, *Amaravati Sculptures*, no. 22 ("of the Paḍipuḍia community").

41. Sivaramamurti, *Amaravati Sculptures*, nos. 12, 16 (?), 58 (*dhañakaṭakasa nigamasa*; cf. Lüders, *List*, no. 1261 (Amarāvatī, *bhadanigama*, no. 705 (Bhārhut, Karahakaṭa *nigama*).

42. E.g., ibid., no. 69 (a nun, herself a pupil of the monk who is overseeing the repairs at Amarāvatī, acting as the representative of her daughters), no. 80 (nun acting for her siblings); Lüders, *List*, no. 163 (Sāñchi, groups of nuns); at Bhaṭṭiprolu (Bühler, "Bhattiprolu Inscriptions" p. 328 no. 5) it would appear that Kuba's technical title was "Monk of/for the Committee" (*goṭhisamaṇo*).

43. A beautiful example of complex agency in the *Apadānic* understanding of *stūpa* construction is Lilley, *The Apadāna*, vol. 1, pp. 70–74 (Upavana Thera). Compare ibid., vol. 1, p. 33 v. 2 (Mahākassapa Thera; "calling together my relatives and friends [*ñātimitte*]"); and vol. 2, p. 425 (Dhātupūjaka Thera; "calling together my relatives"), p. 89 v. 2 (Ayāgadāyaka Thera; "having addressed the people in charge of repairs I gave the capital").

44. E.g., Lilley, *The Apadāna*, vol. 1, p. 59 (Pilindavaccha Thera; organizes an alms-giving to the *sangha* in conjunction with *thūpapūja*; ibid., p. 171 (Vedikāraka Thera; holds a rail-festival [v. 2: *vedikāya mahaṃ katvā*]); ibid., p. 172 (Saparivāriya Thera; participates in a group *pūja*); ibid., p. 172) (Ummāpupphiya Thera; participates in a "great *stūpa* festival" [v. 1: *mahāthūdpamaho*]); ibid., p. 249 (Dhammasaññaka Thera; participates in a "great Bodhi tree festival" [*mahābodhimaho*]); vol. 2, p. 391 (Ekasaṃkhiya Thera; participates in a *mahābodhimaho*; ibid., pp. 513–514 (Mekbaladāyikā Therī; gives a 'girdle' [at the festival] to finance a *stūpa* then another [at/for the festival] when it is finished).

45. Art historians have been very conscious of the fact that the ancient carvings that contain pictures of *stūpas* illustrate them as they appeared at the time of the illustration, and thus encode a history of the development of the form of the *stūpa*. It is thus remarkable that scenes portraying kings and queens have always been identified with scenes from some sort of collective historical memory (the texts that are supposed to embody these tales are, remember, considerably later than the actual carvings), rather than with the actual practices of the then-present monarchy; likewise festival scenes illustrate archetypal stories rather than the *stūpa* worship, *bodhi pūjā*, singing and dancing and above all happy times that probably built the rails or gateways on which the illustrations are actually displayed. Sometimes the same historical scene is said to appear several times in a single set of carvings! Moreover, even if these *are* historical scenes, it is important to ask why they should have been represented at all, hundreds of years after their purported occurrence. In the texts, different tellings of the tales often reflect the different historical circumstances in which they were composed, because the authors of those texts thought about their own pasts in light of a homology to the present. Thus even if it could be demonstrated that all the illustrations are of famous kings such as Aśoka over and over, they may simultaneously illustrate the less-famous kings who, being Aśoka's imperial successors, coordinated the construction of these edifices.

46. A splendid illustration of the ideology behind ever-improving upon the predecessor's *stūpa* construction, a characteristic example of Indian imperial one-upmanship, is Lilley, *The Apadāna*, vol. 1, pp. 70–74 (Upavana Thera). Subsequent emperors would appropriate (in various ways) their predecessor's monuments, religious practices, etc., just as they appropriated their empires.

47. Compare ibid., vol. 1, p. 4 v. 40 (*dīparukkhā*—et passim: "Rev. Lamp Giver" is a very popular name in the *Apadāna*) with Lüders, *List*, no. 929u (Sārnāth: *pradīpa*); Sivaramamurti, *Amaravati Sculptures*, no. 118 (*divakhabho*—a late inscription?)

48. The pillar-gift (*tha[m]bhadānaṃ*) is easily the most common and certainly one of the oldest technical terms in this lithic discourse. Cf. Lilley, *The Apadāna*, vol. 1, p. 172 (Thambhāropaka Thera; erects a pillar [*thambha*] at the Buddha's *cetiya* [here, as elsewhere in *Apadāna* and extremely common in the inscriptions, "*cetiya*" is clearly synonymous with "*thūpa*"]).

49. Cf. ibid., vol. 1, p. 213 (Alambanadāyaka Thera; gives a balustrade [*ālambana*] for a Buddha['s cetiya(?)]), with Lüders, *List*, no. 921a (Sārnāth).

50. E.g., Lilley, *The Apadāna*, vol. 1, p. 55 (Sīhāsanadāyaka Thera; gives a lion-throne with 'foot stool' after the Buddha had reached *nirvāṇa* [i.e., for him as a relic, in a *stūpa* (?)]); ibid., pp. 188–189 (Sīhāsanadāyaka Thera [2]; gave a *sīhāsana* after the Buddha had died). It is of course very common to see people worshiping an empty lion's throne, and/or a 'footstool' containing footprints of the Buddha, in the carvings of early post-Aśokan Buddhist India. Such carvings (also carvings of people

worshiping Bodhi trees [= Enlightenment], of people worshiping *dharmacakra* pillars [= First Sermon], and of people worshiping *stūpas* [= *Parinirvāṇa*]) are considered "aniconic" representations of the various stages in the Buddha biography. But this view is not sufficiently nuanced in the scholarly literature. All of these objects are known to have been just that—actual objects of worship at the *stūpas* where the illustrations were displayed—on the basis of archaeological, epigraphic, and textual (i.e., *Apadāna* evidence. The carvings thus contain straightforward illustrations of the actual practices that constituted and were constitutive of the *stūpa* cult. For epigraphic confirmation of this point, see e.g., Lüders, *List*, no. 1223 (Amarāvatī, *sihaṭhāna*; nos. 1217, 1219, 1225, 1286 (Amarāvatī, footprint slab/foot stool). However, there is truth in the aniconic theory to the extent that people did worship these objects as symbols or representations of the Buddha and/or the important events in his life. So we need not go as far as Susan and John Huntington (*The Art of Ancient India* [New York: Weatherhill, 1985]) in denying aniconism altogether. My own view, however, has an advantage over "symbolist" studies of ancient Buddhist aniconism inso far as it puts aniconic thought at the level of actual practice rather than leaving it an abstraction redundantly represented by the artists and the patrons of the *stūpas*. I am grateful to Michael Rabe and Robert Brown for clarifying to me the complexity of the issues surrounding the aniconic theory.

51. Compare Lilley, *The Apadāna*, vol. 1, p. 170 (Adhicchattiya Thera; had an umbrella with covering [*chattāhichattaṃ*] made for a Buddha's *stūpa* and ibid., pp. 244–245 (Chattadāyaka Thera; put a white umbrella on a stupa) with Sivaramamurti, *Amaravati Sculptures*, no. 92 (*cediyasa chata*, "an umbrella for the cetiya"). Actual remnants of stone *stūpa*-umbrellas have been discovered (e.g., M. M. Hamid, et al. *Catalogue of the Museum of Archaeology at Sanchi, Bhopal State [Archaeological Survey of India]* [Varanasi: Indological Book House, 1982 (1920)], nos. 72, 77, 78, 79, 80, etc.) and it is of course very common to see umbrellas (even umbrellas that are themselves covered, as in *Apadāna*) adorning the *stūpas* that are illustrated in the carvings. The presence of umbrellas, given their significance in Indian royal practice and ideology, provides a constant reminder that these *stūpas* were constructed within a political world.

52. Compare Lilley, *The Apadāna*, vol. 1, p. 90 (Dhammacakkika Thera; placed a well-constructed *dhammacakka* in front of a Buddha's lion-throne) with any number of contemporary carvings that illustrate the worship of such objects at *stūpas* and other Buddhist sites (and cf. note 50, above, about the problems of seeing these carvings as "aniconic representations" of a Buddha from the past rather than as illustrations of Buddhist practice in the then-present). Cf. also Sivaramamurti, *Amaravati Sculptures*, no. 51 (*dhamacakaṃ*); Lüders *List*, no. 866 (*bodhicakra*).

53. The importance of rails (*vedi, vedika, veika, vetika*) around the *stūpas* of this period hardly needs to be documented; the illustrations as well as the ruins

abound in them, and the term is an old and common one in the lithic discourse. The idea of putting up rails is also common in *Apadāna* (e.g., Lilley, *The Apadāna*, vol. 1, p. 171 [Vedikāraka Thera], and p. 172 [Saparivāriya Thera]). The equally common lithic term for cross-bar gift (*sūci dānaṃ*), however, appears to retain only its original meaning ("needle-gift") in *Apadāna*; that text uses the term "leg" (*jaṃghā*) to refer to the parts of a rail. This may further indicate the specific situation in which *Apadāna* had meaning, although I would have expected, given the antiquity of *sūci* as a lithic term for cross-bar, to find it so used in *Apadāna*. Perhaps we can detect here the interest of the *Apadāna* authors in clearly distinguishing the various subvarieties of *dānaṃ*: it does not allow for a confusion of "cross-bar" and "needle," as does the lithic record.

54. See Lilley, *The Apadāna*, vol. 1, pp. 70–74 (Upavana Thera). Such reliquaries—gold inside of silver inside of precious stone, etc.—have actually been discovered in the *stūpas* of Andhra Pradesh (see Alexander Cunningham, [*The Bhilsa Topes; or Buddhist Monument of Central India* [London: Smith, Elder and Co., 1854] and A.H. Longhurst, *The Buddhist Antiquities on Nāgārjunikoṇḍa Madras Presidency* [Delhi: Manager of Publications, 1938] [Memoirs of the Archaeological Survey of India, no. 54] on Nāgārjunikoṇḍa excavations.)

55. E.g., Schopen, "Mahāyāna in Indian Inscriptions", cf. his "Filial Piety and the Monk in the Practice of Indian Buddhism," *T'oung Pao* 70 (1984), pp. 110–126.

56. There is of course the embarrassing possibility, given the structure of the epigraphic Prakrits (i.e., the indistinguishability of the dative and genitive cases, sometimes even the ablative), that we should translate all these inscriptions "the (*dānaṃ*) *for* (recipient of the merit)." It is long-established practice not to view the inscriptions this way, but it makes a degree of sense for certain ones among them.

57. In other work I have been exploring the legacy of *Apadāna's* karmic absolutism. My article "The Buddha's Bad Karma: A Problem in the History of Theravāḍa Buddhism" (*Numen*, June 1990) explores the long debate in later Theravādin history over the *Apadāna* position that even Buddhas must suffer the effects of previous bad *karma*; "A Voice from the Silence: The Buddha's Mother's Story" (*History of Religions Journal*, May 1994) explores the "feminist" response to the *Apadānic* certainty that in the long process of transmigration men remain male and women remain female.

58. On the basis of purely epigraphic records, Schopen too has insisted that the development of the *stūpa* cult in this period involved the finest minds of the day, scholar-monks who, we cannot doubt, were of the same status as (or actually were) the composers of the Pāli *Abhidhamma* and the preservers of the texts of "early Buddhism" (see "Two Problems," esp. pp. 24–26).

59. For standard historical accounts of Aśoka Maurya—of which there are many—see e.g., V. A. Smith, *Asoka: The Buddhist Emperor of India*

(Oxford: Clarendon, 1909); A. L. Basham, *The Wonder That Was India* (New York: Grove Press, 1959 [1954]); B. M. Barua, *Asoka and His Inscriptions* (Calcutta: New Age, 1946); B. G. Gokhale, *Asoka Maurya* (New York: Twayne, 1966); and R. Thapar, *Aśoka and the Decline of the Mauryas* (Oxford: Oxford University Press, 1961). A handy translation of the epigraphic remains from Aśoka's reign is N. A. Nikam and Richard McKeon, eds. and trans., *The Edicts of Aśoka* (Chicago: University of Chicago Press, 1978 [1959]). On the importance of Aśoka in later Buddhist thought, see Frank Reynolds, "The Two Wheels of Dhamma: A Study of Early Buddhism," in *The Two Wheels of Dhamma: Essays on the Theravāda Tradition in India and Ceylon*, ed. Bardwell Smith (Chambersburg, Penn.: AAR, 1972), esp. pp. 23–30; cf. John Strong, *The Legend of King Aśoka* (Princeton: Princeton University Press, 1983).

60. Paul Mus, *Barabadur: Esquisse d'une histoire du Bouddhisme fondée sur la critique archéologique des textes* (Hanoi: Imp. d'Extrême Orient, 1935), preface.

61. Schopen has confirmed this point in a creative reading of the Nāgārjunikoṇḍa inscriptions, which, grammatically at least, equate the terms "relic" and "Buddha" ("On the Buddha and His Bones"). But Schopen, who does not seem to be aware of Mus' theory, reads into this fact a foreign dualistic incarnationalism: the Buddha is somehow a "living presence" *in* the relic (p. 537). As Mus has demonstrated, the "indigenous Indian logic" at work in the *stūpa* cult is more complex than this, and decidedly nondualistic. The relic is the material face of a Buddha whose teachings on *nirvāṇa* makes the (gnostic) description of his "livingness" highly problematic (even though this sort of positive "gnosticism" does eventually emerge in Sanskritic Buddhist thought). Instead, Mus says, it is precisely the message, constantly driven home, that the Buddha's graspable (*saṃsāric*) biography is today only the biography of bones (and texts = *dharmakāya*), which "projects" the devotee into the extradiscursive realm of the Buddha as he really is today, that is *nirvāṇa*. Still, Schopen's point is an important one, and the *Apadāna* confirms his reading, as do many other texts that Schopen talks about in this context (add to his [single] *Apadāna* reference the texts cited below, n. 62 and n. 63).

62. Lilley, *The Apadāna*, vol. 1, p. 108 v. 2 (Dhajadāyaka Thera; "As though face to face with the Buddha I worshipped the unexcelled Bodhi Tree" [*sammukhā viya sambuddhaṃ avandiṃ bodhiṃ uttamaṃ* = p. 149 v. 3 [Ekāsanīya Thera] = p. 290 v. 3 [Bodhivandaka Thera]); ibid., p. 111 v. 2, vol. 2, p. 388 v. 5, p. 439 v. 27 (worshiping *stūpas* "as though face to face with the Buddha").

63. Schopen's argument about the meaning of "relic" in the Nāgārjunikoṇḍa inscriptions is that the word for relic ("*dhātu*") stands in grammatical apposition to words for Buddha, hence relic = Buddha. By this logic, all except the last text among those cited in n. 62 shares the same epistemology: the Buddha *is* the Bodhi tree or *stūpa* that is being worshiped (*sambuddhaṃ . . . thūpaṃ*). This connection is explicit in Lilley,

The Apadāna, vol. 1, p. 224 (Dhātupūjaka Thera; *Tāhaṃ dhātuṃ gahetvāna . . . paricariṃ tiṭṭhaṃ taṃ va naruttamaṃ* [which can be read: "taking the relic . . . I looked after it (which was) the Best of Men (Buddha) remaining (in the world)" or "(which was) the firm/solid Best of Men (Buddha)"]). We also find "Supreme *Stūpa*" (*Cetiyaṃ Uttamaṃ*) as an epithet of the living Buddha at ibid., p. 255 v. 1.

64. Lilley, *The Apadāna*, vol. 2, pp. 529–543 (Mahāpajāpati Gotamī Therī).
65. Ibid., pp. 551–557 (Uppalavaṇṇā Therī).
66. E.g., ibid., p. 473 vv. 33–34 (Dabbamallaputta Thera).
67. E.g., ibid., p. 546 vv. 31–34 (Khemā Therī) et passim.
68. E.g., ibid., pp. 584–592 (Yaśodharā Therī); pp. 578–584 (Bhaddā-Kāpilāni Therī).
69. See for example ibid., vol. 1, pp. 70–74.
70. The term is used in a similar technical sense in *Apadāna*, see ibid., vol. 1, p. 172 v. 2 (Saparivāriya Thera; a "diffusion [*vitthārika, vittharita*] of stupas").
71. See Morris, *The Buddhavaṃsa and the Cariyā-Piṭaka*, pp. 68–69.
72. Its focus, however, remains northern, which confirms my own view that *Buddhavaṃsa* belongs to the period of the Bhārhut railing, i.e., the Śungas, whereas the *Apadāna* belongs to the period of special importance for Andhra, i.e., the early Sātavāhanas.
73. On the Śungas at Bhārhut, see Lüders, *List*, nos. 687 and 688; on the early Sātavāhanas at Sāñchi see ibid., no. 346. There are many more examples of explicit references to the emperor(s) who created the context(s) in which the construction of *stūpas* took place. Such lithic references to emperors as agents of Buddhist change actually increase in number after the beginning of the Christian era, when the emperors themselves were increasingly Śaiva or Vaiṣṇava in personal practice. But these inscriptions are well known, and this is not the place to review them.
74. E.g., Lilley, *The Apadāna*, vol. 2, p. 378 v. 7 (Mañcadāyaka Thera; "there was [as a result of my karma] much local rule, incalculable by counting" [*padesarajjaṃ vipulaṃ gaṇanāto asaṃkhiyaṃ*]). Compare ibid., vol. 1, no. 22 v. 43.
75. This "*Cakkavattin* King" ideology must not be treated as some transcendent essence nor as part of Aśoka's own explicit imperial ideology. The sources that describe such an ideology, and that treat Aśoka as having such an ideology, are considerably later than the Aśokan period. This ideology was first being constituted (in the textual and political traditions) only during the early post-Aśokan period, i.e., the time of the ABCs. The sources in which it, and Aśoka, loom so large, were produced in self-conscious revisions/reworkings of the ABC tradition, in Kashmir and Sri Lanka. The ideology as a "new" idea should thus be treated within the early post-Aśokan period; the ideology as a "given" should not be dated before these textual revisions in Kashmir and Sri Lanka.
76. An allusion to the lovely *apadāna* of Nāgasamāla Thera, Lilley, *The Apadāna*, vol. 1, p. 119.

77. E.g., ibid., vol. 1, p. 198 (Kaṇḍaphulliya Thera); pp. 269ff. (Pabhaṃkara Thera).
78. E.g., ibid., p. 220 (Vaṇṇakāraka Thera).
79. Ibid., p. 237 (Potthadāyaka Thera).
80. Ibid., p. 151 (Citakapūjaka Thera).
81. It is a common trope in *Apadāna* that children "tagging on with father" participate in some pious activity (to which father is going), which becomes the guarantee of their own salvation.
82. Lilley, *The Apadāna*, vol. 1, p. 241 (Apadāniya Thera; "I praised the *Apadāna* of Well-Gone-Ones, the Great Sages, and I worshipped their feet with my head, pleased by these hands [that had performed *añjalī*]. In the ninety-two eons since I praised the *Apadāna* I experienced no ill-state, that is the fruit of praising. I experienced the four analytical knowledges, the eight deliverences, the six super-knowledges; the Buddha's *sāsana* is achieved!").
83. E.g., ibid., p. 183 (Desapūjaka Thera).
84. It is of course possible that the emperors who organized the *stūpa* cult conceived of this Buddha biography only as *part* of their empires, and that their practices constituted other "Great Stories" (like the epics) as other "parts" of those empires, simultaneously. However, in the early Brahmī period, as far as I am aware, there is no direct inscriptional evidence to confirm such a view; there is only proof that the emperors were, in various ways, involved with Buddhist cultic activity. By the time of the later Sātavāhanas (first–second centuries A.D.; e.g., Gautamīputra Satakarni et al. at Nasik and Amarāvatī) and especially under the imperial Ikshvākus of Andhra, (second–third centuries A.D.), on the other hand, it had become standard practice for non-Buddhist emperors to command the development of Buddhist history by empowering queens/vassals/ministers to act as the (organizing) agents of change.
85. I have already mentioned that the texts are addressed to a plural "you," an audience, that is enjoined to "listen." There are also internal reasons for making his supposition: unmarked changes of voice that would be unintelligible without separate performers, indeed the very style in which the texts are written (colloquialism, additions of entertainment value, and the like.) This is not the place for an extended discussion of the performative dimensions of the ABCs, which I plan to address in a later work. For initial reflections on performative context and its centrality to the historical interpretation of *apadāna* texts, see my "A Voice from the Silence."
86. Given the dating, we see here the prototype for the Indian epics, *Rāmāyaṇa* and *Mahābharata*, which are written in Sanskrit verse exactly paralleling the style of the ABCs, which tell "Great Stories" that bear obvious similarity to those in the ABCs (cosmicized "maps" of both time and space; India as a single web of interconnection, frame, and *karma*; the centrality of kingship), and which, during the Gupta period, emerged as the kind of imperial discourse that the ABCs had been shortly after the time of Aśoka. If I am right about the "festive" context of the ABCs, a great deal of light is also shed upon the performance history of the epics.

Part 3

The Jātakas and Biographies of Kings

Among more than five hundred stories of the Buddha's former lives, known as the *jātaka* tales, several identify the future Buddha as a king. The history of Theravāda Buddhism in Southeast Asia, where such stories are widely known, provides ample examples of royal rulers who self-consciously sought to emulate in their own lives the ideal of future Buddhahood. Cultural representations of the future Buddha as king and of the king as a future Buddha are therefore common themes in the sacred biography of Buddhism in Southeast Asia.

McGill's essay presents a discussion of a set of paintings depicting the Buddha in his penultimate life as King Vessantara. Through stylistic and epigraphic analysis, McGill links these visual narratives painted on canvas to the production of a particular Thai artistic genre in the service of popular ritual performances and recitations of the same narrative, the *Vessantara Jātaka,* as a royal occasion for making merit in order to encounter the future Buddha, Maitreya. His exploration of "Painting the 'Great Life' " uniquely links the production of a particular art genre to ritual performances centered on a common biographical theme, namely the story of King Vessantara.

Hudak describes the development from prose to poetry of a classical example of Thai literature. The narrative structure of this *jātaka* story underwent changes by multiple authors and conflates in its intentionality the biographies of the future Buddha and of the Thai king Narai in the seventeenth century.

Johnson presents both indigenous Thai and Western perspectives on the biography of King Mongkut in nineteenth-century Thailand. In doing so, he engages critical perspectives on the processes by which this royal biography is negotiated and draws attention to the simultaneous modern and traditional aspects this king combined in his life history.

Plate I. Vessantara Gives Away the Elephant. (Phoenix Art Museum, Gift of Mr. and Mrs. Paul Bird, 62.54.1)

Plate 2. The Brahmans Ask for the Horses. (Phoenix Art Museum, Gift of Mr. and Mrs. Paul Bird, 62.54.2)

Plate 3. The Overindulgent Jujaka. (Phoenix Art Museum, Gift of Mr. and Mrs. Paul Bird, 62.54.3)

Plate 4. Vessantara and His Family Are Reunited. (Phoenix Art Museum, Gift of Mr. and Mrs. Paul Bird, 62.54.4)

Painting the "Great Life"

Forrest McGill

The "Great Life," or *Vessantara Jātaka*, and the other stories of the Buddha's last ten lives have for centuries been among the most important texts for Southeast Asian Buddhists. The stories provide not only the amusements of well-told tales, but also moral instruction, as their protagonists have come to be seen as exemplars of Buddhism's Ten Perfections of patience, wisdom, giving, and so on.[1]

Four paintings now in the Phoenix Art Museum illustrate four of the key episodes of the *Vessantara Jātaka* (plates 1–4). Almost uniquely among published paintings they bear donative inscriptions. These inscriptions name the persons who gave the paintings and their home village, identify the chapters of the text depicted, and suggest the donors' motives. Thus we are in the unusual position of having four sorts of text—the *jātaka* itself; the paintings; the inscriptions; and, as will be seen, a Thai scholar's description of a relevant ceremony—to help us begin to understand what the "Great Life" meant to people in a nineteenth-century central Thai village.

In the story, Prince Vessantara is motivated by boundless generosity. When eight brahmans from a drought-stricken neighbor kingdom ask him for his own kingdom's rain-bringing white elephant, he gives it. His people angrily send him into exile. Before leaving, however, Vessantara dispenses enormous riches in the "great seven-hundredfold donation." Later, on the way to the forest retreat, Vessantara, his wife Maddi, and their two children are asked first for their horses, then for their chariot, which of course Vessantara readily bestows. Eventually he gives away his children to the brahman Jujaka and is only prevented from giving away his wife by a gentle trick played by the god Indra. Meanwhile, the royal children are ransomed from Jujaka by their grandfather, and Jujaka, enjoying a new life of wealth and luxury, dies from overindulgence. Grandparents and grandchildren are reunited with Vessantara and Maddi, and all return to the capital, where Vessantara resumes his royal duties.[2]

Because the *Vessantara Jātaka* tells of the Buddha's immediately previous life, the last and most perfected of 500 or more,[3] it must be particularly worthy of respect and attention. In fact, the *jātaka* informs us that it was first related by the Buddha himself. Shortly after the First Sermon the Buddha returned to his father's capital; in his father's presence he performed a miracle to awe some proud relatives, and then he told the story of his last life.[4] The Buddha's recounting the Vessantara story to his father and other relatives was echoed in traditional Thai custom. When a young man entered the monastery and became a novice, his family would gather to hear him recite part of the Vessantara story. In an even closer imitation of the Buddha's life, this custom was followed in the palace too. In 1817, 1866, and 1891 ceremonies were held in which a royal prince in his novitiate recited parts of the Vessantara story before his relatives and the king.[5]

Elaborate ceremonies for recitation of a full text of the *Vessantara Jātaka*, called *thēt Mahāchāt*, or "recitation of the 'Great Life,' " were annual events in many Thai towns. An important reason for this was the widespread popular belief that listening to a complete recitation of the *Vessantara Jātaka* would help assure rebirth in human form in the far future when the bodhisattva Maitreya descends to earth for his last life, during which he will attain Buddhahood. Meeting Maitreya was a common goal among Theravāda Buddhists; why this was so, what role the *Vessantara Jātaka* had, and how the Phoenix paintings served in achieving the goal will become clear later.

Thai Versions of the *Vessantara Jātaka*

Thailand's earliest version of the *Vessantara Jātaka* of which some parts may survive is the *Mahāchāt Kham Luang*, or "Royal Version of the Great Life," said to have been composed in 1482 by King Bǫrommatrailōkkanāt of Ayutthaya.[6] Much of this version seems to have been lost and replaced during subsequent centuries, and the present compilation dates only from 1815.[7] Other versions, including another *Mahāchāt Kham Luang* composed by King Song Tham in 1627, have continued to appear.[8] Writing in 1892, G. E. Gerini noted that "quite a number of different versions are now in circulation, and new ones are being prepared from time to time."[9] The number of chapters, their names, and the number of Pāli stanzas they include are, however, standard.[10]

The Phoenix Paintings

Phoenix paintings—clearly a set—measure 1.06 meters by 0.883 meters, or about half again as long in both directions as an unfolded newspaper. They are painted in bright colors on cotton fabric and have suffered considerable paint loss, perhaps from having been repeatedly rolled or folded. Each has a border decorated, at the corners and midpoints, with flowers and tendrils. Along the bottom, a sort of cartouche encloses an inscription.

The Inscriptions

The inscriptions are sometimes hard to make out because of damage. Fortunately, except for a few words, they are identical, and so the gaps in one can be filled by reference to another. Some spellings are nonstandard.

A.	สีกาหรุ่ม	อยู่บ้านแหลมช่าง	หิมภาน	๑๓๘	พระคาถา
B.	สีการอก or วอก	อยู่บ้านแหลมชาง	ทานกันท์	๒. .	. . . . .
C.	สีกาฟุก	อยู่บ้านแหลมชาง	มหาราช	๖๘	พระคาถา
D.	สีกาฟราง สีกาฟุก	อยู่บ้านแหลมชาง	ช่อมคีย	๓๖	พระคาถา

A. ขอให้ข้าพเจ้าทันพระศี_าริยเมตไตรย

B. . . . . ไต . . . . .อญ

C. ขอให้ข้าพเจ้าทันพระศีอาริยเมตไตร_เจ้านั้นเท_ญ

D ข_ให้ข้าพเจ้าทันพระศีอาริยเมตไตรยเจ้านั้นเทอญ

A.

B.

C.

D. นิพานปจจยโยโหตุ

Pious laywoman	(A) Rum	of Ban Laem sponsors the	
	(B) Rọ̄k (or Wọ̄k)		
	(C) Puk		
	(D) Prāng Phuk		

(A) Himavanta [chapter] in	(A) 134 stanzas.	May I meet
(B) Dānakaṇḍa	(B) 2.	
(C) Mahārāja	(C) 69	
(D) Chakhattiya	(D) 36	

(A) ∅	Phra Sī Āriya Mēttrai	(A) ∅.
(B) Lord		(B) (hortative particle).
(C) Lord		(C) (hortative particle).
(D) Lord		(D) (hortative particle).

(D) May [this donation] be a cause of reaching *nirvāṇa.*

Notes on the Translations[11]

—*Sikā* presumbly derives from *upāsikā*, "female lay devotee." In Thailand *upāsikā* is attested at least as early as a fifteenth-century inscription from Sukhothai.[12]

—Ban Laem is a town on the Gulf of Thailand about 150 kilometers southwest of Bangkok and fifteen kilometers or so north of Phetburi.

—^{1}*jāṅ* is presumably ^{2}*srāṅ*. They are pronounced identically. ^{2}*srāṅ* usually means "to make," "to build," or "to have something made or built." It is commonly found in donative inscriptions and in other contexts describing donations. When we notice that one can ^{2}*srāṅ* a Buddha image, an institution, or even a religious text we begin to need translations like "to commission," "to establish and provide for the continuing support of," or "to pay for the preparation and publication of." Exactly what may be meant on these paintings when we are told that someone ^{2}*srāṅ* a chapter of the *Vessantara Jātaka* will be discussed later. It should be noted that one can ^{2}*srāṅ* merit, that is, build it up by performing good deeds.[13]

—The word *dăn*, translated as "meet," usually means "to be on time" or "to catch up with."

—"Phra Sī Āriya Mēttrai" is a common Thai term for Maitreya. It is usually shortened to "Phra Sī Ān" in speaking.

—The phrase translated as "may [this donation] be a cause of reaching *nirvāṇa*," which occurs only in the inscription on painting D, is in oddly spelled Pāli: *nibāna paccayayo hotu*. This Pāli phrase turns up very frequently in donative inscriptions from at least the mid sixteenth century onward.[14]

The Depictions[15]

PLATE 1. (PAINTING A). CHAPTER 2, HIMAVANTA: VESSANTARA GIVES AWAY THE ELEPHANT. Prince Vessantara, astride the neck of his famous white elephant, pours water from a bottle toward the upraised hands of the eight brahmans. By doing so, he solemnizes giving the elephant to them.

Four Western soldiers wearing tall hats and holding rifles with bayonets stand at attention nearby. Through a gateway on a long wall, a group of men can be seen. They watch not Vessantara's edifying exercise of charity but a risqué vignette of a man grabbing the arm of a fleeing woman.

PLATE 2. (PAINTING B). CHAPTER 3, DĀNAKAṆḌA: THE BRAHMANS ASK FOR THE HORSES. Riding an elaborate chariot, Vessantara and his family go off into exile. Vessantara looks back longingly toward his home, and several of his former subjects, kneeling on the ground, express in conventional gestures their sadness to see him go. In front of the chariot four brahmans prepare to ask Vessantara, who has not yet noticed them, for the horses.

At first glance the setting, in front of a long, oblique wall with a guardhouse at the farther end, seems to be the same as that in the previous painting, but in fact the gateway and distant buildings are different.

At the guardhouse a couple converse. Once again observers watch them, not the religious drama of Vessantara.

PLATE 3. (PAINTING C). CHAPTER 11, MAHĀRĀJA: THE OVERINDULGENT JUJAKA. The brahman Jujaka, having asked Vessantara for his children and then ransomed them to their grandfather, basks in newfound luxury. Reclining in his mansion, he chucks a maiden under the chin, while serving women proffer refreshments and fan him and Chinese men bring in a pig's head and a crock. In the background a man attended by an umbrella-bearer seems to admonish two men kneeling before him. Off to the side, a man and woman engage in amorous play.

PLATE 4. (PAINTING D). CHAPTER 12, CHAKHATTIYA: VESSANTARA AND HIS FAMILY ARE REUNITED. In the upper part of the painting, Vessantara's children and his parents come in a stately procession toward his cottage. Below, Vessantara and his father greet each other with tears of joy, as do Vessantara's wife and her children and mother-in-law. The two exiles wear the tiger skin garments of hermits, but a courtier carries in the crown Vessantara will soon reclaim.

The History of Representations of the *Vessantara Jātaka* in Thailand

Representations of the *Vessantara Jātaka* are found among several of the earliest Buddhist art traditions of India.[16] In Thailand they appear carved in low relief on sema stones from the northeast that have been assigned to the ninth to eleventh centuries.[17] The famous partial set of *jātaka* representations at Wat Sī Chum in Sukhothai, usually dated to the fourteenth century, does not include the Vessantara. Whether it was included among the *jātakas* painted in the crypt of Wat Rātchaburana in Ayutthaya (1424 C.E.) is not certain. King Bọrommatrailōkkanāt of Ayutthaya, whom we encountered earlier composing a version of the *Vessantara Jātaka*, ordered the casting of sculptures of the Bodhisattva in all 500 *jātakas* in 1458. Among the few dozen fragments of these figures that have survived, however, none is identifiable as Vessantara.[18] Sri Lankan ambassadors to Ayutthaya in 1750 mentioned seeing murals of the *Vessantara Jātaka* in a building at Wat Chaiwatthānāram (founded in 1630–1631), but the building has long since disappeared.[19]

From the seventeenth century onward, painted representations of the *Vessantara Jātaka* survive in increasing numbers in murals and manuscripts. Unfortunately, many of these, particularly the earlier ones, cannot be dated with any precision. The development of Thai painting has received little systematic study, and so, for instance, a famous Ayutthaya manuscript of the *Trai Phum*, in which scenes of the *Vessantara Jātaka* are depicted, has been variously attributed to the sixteenth, seventeenth, and eighteenth centuries.[20] Another *Trai Phum* manuscript depicting Vessantara scenes is inscribed with a date equivalent to 1776.[21]

The problems of dating murals are complex. We may occasionally know when a building was built, but we cannot be sure that its present murals were painted at the time of construction. Also many murals, and not just the oldest, have been damaged or erased by neglect. Many others have been subjected to extensive overpainting, so that what we see today may be a mélange of 1790 with 1890. Furthermore, comparison with dated painted manuscripts or dated gilt lacquer cabinets is complicated by the fact that we do not know how closely stylistic developments in various painted media followed each other.

A list of seventeenth- to nineteenth-century representations of the *Vessantara Jātaka* in murals and other formats is included in the appendix.

Where and When the Phoenix Paintings were Made

No one would argue with a nineteenth-century date for the Phoenix paintings. Comparing them with various Vessantara representations listed in the appendix and with other central Thai painting shows that they are not unusual in their composition, style, motifs, or ways of presenting the narrative; on the contrary, all of their characteristics can be related to those of better known nineteenth-century paintings.

But how much more precise can we be? At the beginning of the century, Thai painters had highly sophisticated and internally consistent traditional means of depicting their artistic vision. As the decades passed they were confronted more and more with the very different tradition of Chinese and especially Western pictorial representation.[22] In the second half of the century they and their audience, like artists and audiences everywhere, also had their vision increasingly affected by photography.

Using foreign motifs and features of foreign painting styles was of course not new. The paintings in the crypt of Wat Rātchaburana in Ayutthaya, dating from about 1424, include Chinese persons depicted in a rather Chinese style. From the seventeenth century onward, much surviving evidence shows a taste for the exotic and foreign, and representations of Persians, Indians, Chinese, and assorted Europeans are common.[23] Thus the mere presence of a foreign motif or personage tells us nothing about a painting's date. Certain motifs may, however, be helpful. For instance, oval windows (seen in buildings in paintings B and D) have been associated with the popularity of Chinese-style architecture in the second quarter of the nineteenth century.[24] Other architectural features such as the European-looking gateways of paintings C and D, with their inscriptions in an approximation of the Roman alphabet, might suggest a date toward the middle of the century, as Western influences were increasingly felt.[25] Western-style buildings had been constructed in central Thailand at least as early as the second half of the seventeenth century, however, so we must be cautious.

The Western military uniforms in all four paintings may also provide clues, though it will take a specialist to evaluate them. Suffice it to say that the hip-length tunics of the guards in painting C may indicate a date in or after the mid-1850s, when longer tunics tended to replace shorter ones.[26]

Because Thai artists had for centuries taken such delight in wild anachronisms, we should not be surprised to notice that in painting D the procession of Vessantara's parents and children to his forest retreat includes a soldier apparently wearing a topi and carrying a Union Jack. There had been significant British diplomatic missions to Bangkok in 1821–1822, 1825–1826, and 1850. It is tempting, though, to see this flag bearer and the other Western soldiers as a reflection—however distant—of the extremely important British mission of 1855, when Sir John Bowring arrived "with both impressive pomp and the threat of force behind him."[27]

In the course of the nineteenth century, Thai painters increasingly experimented with Western perspective, though mastering the intricacies of the one-point linear perspective system took decades. Eighteenth-century Thai painters had often not troubled much with illusions of depth, and when they did, they generally used an unsystematic (but visually pleasing) isometric perspective. In the Phoenix paintings, however, the artist attempts to show the thickness of walls and often darkens the sides of rectangular solids (like gateways) to emphasize their three-dimensionality. In the roof of one gateway, that in painting A, there is even a try at converging perspective. All of this is what we usually expect of painting in the mid-century. Later on the experiments in perspective become increasingly exaggerated until, in some works from the 1860s forward, buildings in paintings dive, thrust, and tilt.

Various artists adopted changes at various rates, obviously. In the *Vessantara Jātaka* and other murals of 1886 at Wat Phawannaphirattaram in Thonburi, for instance, there is no attempt to depict buildings in converging perspective.[28] Western people do not make much of an appearance, but Western clothing and architecture—with window blinds and smoking chimneys—do. What seems newest is the representation of landscape. The backgrounds open into airy vistas of receding hills and fluffy clouds. There are even efforts to use aerial perspective and to maintain a continuous ground plane from near foreground to horizon.

The Phoenix paintings are considerably earlier than these, surely. Thus if some of the military uniforms in the Phoenix paintings were perhaps not in use until the mid-1850s, and experimentation with Western perspective and other pictorial conventions was growing more enthusiastic soon after, then it might seem reasonable to date the Phoenix paintings to the years around 1860.

The uncertainties are many, however. It bears emphasizing that much of what has been written about the history of Thai painting is of questionable reliability. Issues such as when various foreign costumes appear or when and how Thai painters began to gain familiarity with and make use of Western perspective have not been carefully analyzed. Problems of repainting, overpainting, and copying have not been worked out. We have little idea how far apart conservative painters and the avant garde were at any moment, and we cannot confidently tell an experimental painting of 1830 from an old-fashioned one of 1880. There is also the related question of the pace of change outside Bangkok.[29] How and when did other regions respond to developments in painting in the capital?

The donors named in the Phoenix paintings were from Ban Laem near Phetburi. Were the paintings made in Ban Laem? Or in Phetburi itself, which had for centuries been an important artistic center? Or in Bangkok? There is no reason to think that paintings such as these could not have been painted in Bangkok and sold with blanks for donative inscriptions to be filled in later.[30] Do the Phoenix paintings show any regional characteristics? They do not seem to. But would we know a regional characteristic if we saw one? Let us be satisfied to label the paintings "Central Thailand, second half of the nineteenth century."

The Ceremony of Reciting the *Vessantara Jātaka* (Thēt Mahāchāt)

"We and our relatives, being filled with zeal, presented bricks (to build) a pedestal for a statue of the Buddha. . . . After this, a dedication ceremony was held . . . then there was a ceremony inside our house, and a ceremony for our children too. Then we listened to the Mahāchāt."[31] These statements from an early fifteenth-century inscription from Sukhothai suggest the long history of ceremonies including a recitation of the *Vessantara Jātaka.*

Performances of such ceremonies in more recent times have been mentioned earlier, and now it is time to consider them in more detail. A wonderful description was written a quarter of a century ago by the great scholar of traditional Thai culture, Phya Anuman Rajadhon, and quoting it at considerable length will be useful:

> Every year after the traditional three month term of religious Lent and retreat of Buddhist monks expires . . . many wats or monasteries have their own "Thet Maha Chat" festival. "Thet" means to preach . . . but in this instance to recite or give a recitative sermon of the Maha Chat. . . . The recitation may be performed during the . . . mid-year Autumnal Festival in early October, or on other special occasions such as the raising of funds for the monastery. . . . In the former days the recitation of the Maha Chat might be performed at a private residence in special case[s]. . . . Nowadays the performance, as far as I know, is confined to the preaching hall within the precincts of a wat. The recitation begins early in the morning and continues sometimes to late midnight. It is the traditional belief of the people that whosoever hears the Maha Chat, or the Great Life in its complete story, will gain great merit. . . .
>
> There are thirteen monks each of whom is trained for a particular kan [chapter]. . . . Each kan must have a sponsor-owner either individually or collectively in number. It is the duty of the owner of a kan to provide a gift for the presiding monk with money and things fit for merit offering. . . . They include monks' robes and essential requisites for monks, eatables and sweetmeats and a large quantity of fruits. . . . Any person, apart from the owner, may join in the merit-making by contributing money or anything else to the common offering for whichever kan he prefers. . . .
>
> Although the hearing of such sacred words recited may give rise to mystical feelings, the people do not understand them and their emotions are not satisfied. The people want something more. . . . [T]he reciter has to display his wit and additions of his own are thrown into the recitation which sometimes border on drollery and vulgarity. The orthodox people frown. . . .

Now suppose you accept the invitation to be one of the owners of the thirteen kans. . . . There will be bustle and merriment in the house on the eve of the recitation . . . the cooking of food and the preparing of sweetmeats both for merit-making and for feeding the people. For such an occasion, neighbors will come to help you. . . .

On the actual day . . . all the offerings are carried in a procession with music and other performances. . . . There will be crowds of people along the route to witness the procession. . . . If there are many wealthy owners of different kans . . . it will be a great day. For there will be competition among themselves as to whose offerings and procession are the best and most costly. . . .

The entrance into the wat on the day of the Maha Chat recitation is made as a sort of gate decorated with branches of trees. . . . Sometimes the path [to the preaching hall] is made in a sort of maze or labyrinth . . . called "Khao Wongkot," the name of the mountain where Prince [Vessantara] had his hermitage. . . . There hang in some preaching halls thirteen paintings depicting the life of Prince [Vessantara] as narrated in the thirteen kans. . . .

Arriving at the wat the procession passes . . . into the path leading to the preaching hall. If the path is made into a maze there will certainly be fun when [you] get into a blind passage and become confused. You may even have to pay a fee to the guide. . . . When the procession arrives at the preaching hall, and if the preceding kan . . . is still in progress . . . you will have to wait outside until the preceding kan comes to an end. Then you carry all your offerings to their proper place in the preaching hall. . . . There is bustle and ado . . . when the offerings of the preceding kan . . . are taken out and the offerings of the next kan are carried in. . . . [T]here are small coloured flags equal to the number of a thousand [stanzas]. The number of these thousand [stanzas] is distributed unevenly among the thirteen kans. Suppose your kan has, say 80 . . . stanzas then you have 80 flags sticking in rows on both sides of the place where the offerings are placed. Besides the small flags there are also small beeswax candles equal in number to that of the small flags. There are flowers for offering too. . . .

Apart from the usual offering there must also be offered a boiled pig's head complete with its four legs and tail, and a "Bai Sri Pak Cham," a sort of ritual-boiled rice in a big earthen bowl. Nobody can give me a reasonable explanation of this offering, except that it is merely a tradition and a custom. . . .

Now when the . . . recitation is to begin, candles and incense sticks . . . will be lit, and an act of worship is made to . . . the Buddha, his Law and his Body of the Clergy. . . . After such rite has been performed, the recitation may begin. . . .

> If the reciting monk is well-known for his wit and humor, the place is packed to the utmost. . . . The young men will ask for encores and more money contributions will willingly be made. . . . In former days such recitations with additions of drollery and humor in some cases overstepped the limits of modesty.[32]

The Phoenix Paintings in Context

Now it is possible to see the Phoenix paintings and their inscriptions in context and to understand them better. No doubt they were made, along with nine other paintings, to be donated for a Thet Mahāchāt ceremony and to record the sponsoring—what Phya Anuman calls the owning—of the recitation of particular chapters. Thus "Laywoman Rum of Ban Laem ²*srāṅ* the Himavanta chapter in 134 stanzas" means not only that she also ²*srāṅ* the painting of an episode from the Himavanta chapter, but that she also ²srāṅ the recitation of the chapter by providing the food offerings, monks' robes, music, little flags, candles, flowers, and so on. Because the number of flags and candles must match the number of stanzas in the chapter, the number is specified in the inscription.

Sets of paintings on cloth of Vessantara scenes for use during recitation ceremonies seem to have been common.[33] Eight paintings from one set and several single paintings that probably came from such sets have been published, and a number more mentioned.[34] Most of the published examples appear to have been cut down, and only one now has a border and inscription.[35]

The Phoenix paintings' vignettes of flirtatious couples, nosy neighbors, foreign soldiers, gossiping servants, a grand parade, and so on really need no explanation. Thai paintings are full of such lively distractions. We are of course reminded of the *Vessantara Jātaka* recitations though. Gerini in 1892 reported that:

> At no very distant time all the resources of declamation and, eventually, of mimicry were occasionally taken advantage of by unscrupulous members of the clergy to make the exhibition more attractive to the auditory; and all sorts of tricks calculated to excite laughter in the multitude were resorted to. The blaring of trumpets, the ringing of bells, the whistling of birds in the recesses of the Himavanta forest, the noises of a storm and the pealing of thunder were imitated almost to perfection and were given after each Pāli distich with a flourishing of many whimsical adjuncts, to relieve the monotony of the entertainment.[36]

Gerini then tells of King Mongkut (r. 1851–1868), a serious-minded Buddhist reformer, objecting to such buffoonery: "he denounced the abuse in a proclamation full of trenchant remarks; and since that time the exposition of the Maha Chat . . . has become more dignified."[37] (The new dignity did not last long, it would seem from Phya Anuman's description.) In any event, one wonders if the Phoenix paintings and others like them were not displayed during the recitation, and whether the recitation may not have referred to their humorous and colorful anecdotal details as well as to their main scenes.[38]

Now let us take up the pig's head. A boiled one, together with an earthen bowl of special rice—these, Phya Anuman says, must be included among the offerings at a *Vessantara Jātaka* recitation ceremony. In the Phoenix painting C, it will be remembered, a pig's head and a crock of something that could be rice are being presented by two Chinese men to the luxuriating Jujaka. The joke seems to be that the offerings the donors intend for the monks go, in the paintings, not to the worthy Vessantara, who in his austere celibate exile is like a monk, but to the coarse and ridiculous Jujaka.[39]

We scorn Jujaka, but what other feeling do we have toward him? When we set out to present our offerings at the temple and hear the Vessantara story, we must pass through a maze representing the slopes of Mount Vamka (Phya Anuman's "Khao Wongkot") where Vessantara and his wife went into exile and lived as hermits. We may get lost and have to ask for guidance just as they did. We like to feel identified with Vessantara, naturally, and in making our donations we try to emulate him. But someone else got lost on those slopes and had to ask for directions: Jujaka. In fact his searching for the way to Vessantara's retreat extends through three chapters of the *jātaka*. Can we avoid feeling identified with him too? He, of course, was motivated by greed, while we intend our motives to be pure. He sought to take, we to give. Besides, Jujaka got fabulously rich, spent his money foolishly, and died of dissipation. If we were rich, we'd be more careful.

The Donors' Motives

Basic questions raised at the beginning now return: What were the motives of the pious laywomen of Ban Laem? Why were they donating these paintings and sponsoring chapters in the ceremony of reciting the *Vessantara Jātaka*?

Their wish, all of them tell us, is to meet Maitreya: that is, to be reborn in human form when he descends to earth for his last life, during which he will attain Buddhahood and preach the doctrine. Two of them add a common formula that means, more or less, "May [this donation] be a cause of reaching *nirvāṇa*."

The wish to meet Maitreya is shared by most Theravāda Buddhists, and has been for centuries.[40] In an inscription of 1357, the king of Sukhothai, addressing "all good people," speaks of someone in general who "makes the wish that he will be reborn in heaven, (that he will stay there) until Śri Āriyamaitri comes down (to earth) to become a Buddha, and that he will be reborn on this earth at the same time."[41]

In every succeeding century, Thai inscriptions can be found expressing a donor's wish to meet Maitreya. That the wish is still alive today is evidenced by leaders of uprisings in the countryside claiming to be Maitreya—and drawing followers.[42]

Now, how does one earn the opportunity of meeting Maitreya? There are several related answers. According to the *Anāgatavaṃsa*, the Buddha, specifying who will meet Maitreya, says "Those who feel pleasure at meritorious deeds shall see him. Those who further the religion of The Buddha, . . . make offerings of cloth, canopies, garlands, incense, or lamps . . . shall see him. Those who listen to the Vessantara Birth-Story shall see him, likewise those who give to the congregation offerings of food, etc."[43] In one version of the Phra Malai legend, an edifying story popular and widely known among Southeast Asian Buddhists, Maitreya tells us himself that "those who wished to meet him should listen to the recitation of the entire *Vessantara Jātaka* in one day and one night; they should also bring offerings of one thousand [the total number of Pāli stanzas in the Vessantara text] each to the temple."[44]

How would listening to the *Vessantara Jātaka* help in earning the chance to meet Maitreya? For Southeast Asian Theravāda Buddhist layfolk, to progress requires accumulating merit.[45] The primary means of accumulating merit are giving and morality, and, for a variety of reasons, "giving is psychologically more satisfying than morality."[46] The story of Vessantara is the story of the Perfection of Giving. After listening to it, we know what we must do: emulate Vessantara and give.[47] (Vessantara's reward, of course, was achieving Buddhahood and *nirvāṇa* in his very next life; we are so vastly less perfect than he—not being ready yet to give away our loved ones, for instance—that we do not expect *those* rewards soon.)

We may also be emulating Maitreya. He and Vessantara are parallel in some ways, after all. Both occupy a next-to-last position. Also, Maitreya has exercised the Perfection of Giving. In the Phra Malai text mentioned earlier, both the god Indra and Maitreya himself tell of Maitreya's charities, Indra mentioning in particular Maitreya's accomplishment of the Five Great Donations, which include giving away wealth, children, and wife.[48]

The laywomen of Ban Laem expressed their wish to meet Maitreya, and have done what is required. They have listened (or, at the moment of the inscriptions, are about to listen) to the *Vessantara Jātaka*, and have tried to absorb its lessons. They have already practiced giving, by donating the paintings and sponsoring their parts of the recitation and attendant ceremonies and celebrations. They have acquired substantial merit.

Why, though, do they want to meet Maitreya? Because in his regime the world will become a utopia: poverty, infirmity, cruelty will disappear.[49] Also, meeting Maitreya helps toward the even longer-term goal of attaining *nirvāṇa*, the goal cited by laywomen Prāng and Phuk. Maitreya will achieve Enlightenment and become a Buddha, and then will preach. For them to hear the Doctrine preached not by a monk, no matter how holy, but by a being whose wisdom and power are incalculably greater—and to have the chance to practice the Doctrine under his tutelage—will surely hasten their progress toward *nirvāṇa*.[50]

But do we really believe that *nirvāṇa* was the goal of the laywomen of Ban Laem? It is none too clear what *nirvāṇa* is: some say extinction. Attaining it is at best very far off. Is it so desirable?

"The pursuit of self-persistence in pleasant future rebirths is a central motif in Burmese thought and motivation," Melford Spiro writes. "The Burmese, of course, are not the only *Theravāda* Buddhists for whom a pleasurable rebirth is preferable to nirvana. All our evidence indicates that this preference obtains throughout the *Theravāda* world."[51] Certainly in Thailand it seems clear that the usual goal of merit accumulation through giving is not so much *nirvāṇa* as "a happy and virturous state of mind" in this life, and felicity and comfort in the future.[52]

What then of the fact that two of the laywomen state in the donative inscription their aim of reaching *nirvāṇa*? Spiro continues, "Every Burman, then, has learned to use the rhetorical mode of nibbanic [nirvanic] Buddhism, and many Burmese have sufficiently internalized its goal [the attainment of *nirvāṇa*] to feel guilty about the non-nibbanic motivation for their Buddhist practice. Nonetheless, their nibbanic aspirations are expressions more of traditional rhetoric than of a personal wish."[53] On the other hand, no matter how conventional the rhetoric, the pious women's hope for *nirvāṇa* may have been heartfelt.

So, as they made their way through the maze toward the temple hall, did the laywomen of Ban Laem think of themselves as Vessantara going into exile but continuing his Perfection of Giving and aiming always for *nirvāṇa*? Or as Jujaka, with troubles at home, in need of cash, seeking Vessantara to ask for a gift, which he then turned into the pleasures and luxuries that surround him in painting C?

If they had had the inclination to say more about their wishes and motives, and had had the services of a court poet, I suspect the laywomen of Ban Laem would have left a message as mixed as this one from the queen mother of Sukhothai in 1399: "By the power of my merit [from donations], may I be reborn as a male in the future, may I listen to the excellent

Dhamma of the Buddha. . . . May no other be my equal in any existence, in almsgiving for instance, or in beauty, renown, longevity or riches! May no one deprive me of these things which I wish to give away, and may my possessions be useful to the poor. Having plunged into the cool ocean of almsgiving, which is deep and limitless, may I attain perfect Enlightenment like the lord of ascetics!"[54]

Notes

1. G. E. Gerini, *The Thet Maha Chat Ceremony* (1892; reprint, Bangkok: Sathirakoses-Nagapradipa Foundation, 1976), p. 18. As will be seen, a good deal of what follows comes from or was suggested by Gerini's book. For background on the last ten *jātakas* in Thailand, see Elizabeth Wray, Clare Rosenfield, and Dorothy Bailey, *Ten Lives of the Buddha: Siamese Temple Paintings and Jataka Tales* (New York and Tokyo: Weatherhill, 1972).
2. For a translation of the ancient Pāli version of the *Vessantara Jātaka*, see E. B. Cowell and W. H. D. Rouse, *The Jataka, or Stories of the Buddha's Former Births* (Cambridge: Cambridge University Press, 1907), vol. 6, pp. 246–305. A chapter-by-chapter summary of one Thai version can be found in Gerini, *Thet Maha Chat Ceremony*, pp. 28–31.
3. Different Theravāda traditions record 500, 547, or 550 *jātakas*; see Reynolds' article in this volume. Also Betty Gosling, "Once More, Inscription II: An Art Historian's View," *Journal of the Siam Society* 69 (1981), p. 18.
4. Cowell and Rouse, *The Jataka*, vol. 6, pp. 246–247; Edward J. Thomas, *The Life of Buddha as Legend and History* (London: Routledge and Kegan Paul, 1949), p. 99.
5. Gerini, *Thet Maha Chat Ceremony*, pp. 34–36.
6. Chronicles of Ayutthaya, Luang Prasoet version, s.a. 844.
7. Prince Damrong's introduction to the first printing of the *Mahā Chāt Kham Luang* (1917), reprinted in *Mahā Chāt Kham Luang* (Bangkok: Khlang Witthaya, 1973), p. 4.
8. Chronicles of Ayutthaya, Royal Autograph version, s.a. 989.
9. Gerini, *Thet Maha Chat Ceremony*, p. 25.
10. A chart of the names of the chapters, their meaning, and the number of verses in each is provided by Gerini (ibid., p. 27).
11. I am indebted to Sirikanya Schaeffer of the Library of Congress and Thomas Hudak of Arizona State University for help with the translations.
12. A. B. Griswold and Prasert na Nagara, "Epigraphic and Historical Studies No. 22: An Inscription from Văt Hin Ṯăṅ, Sukhodaya," *Journal of the Siam Society* 67, no. 1 (January 1979); pp. 68–73. For a nineteenth-century occurrence, see Michael Wright, "Towards a History of Siamese Gilt-Lacquer Painting," *Journal of the Siam Society* 67, no. 1 (January 1979); p. 29, and *Tū lāi thǭng/Thai Lacquer and Gilt Bookcases*, pt. 2, vol. 3 (Bangkok: National Library, 1988), p. 322.

13. George Bradley McFarland, *Thai-English Dictionary* (Palo Alto: Stanford University Press, 1944), p. 115, s.v. *kuson.*

14. For instance, Hans Penth, *Kham čhārṳk thī thān phra phuttharŭp nai nakhǭn Chiang Mai* (Bangkok: Office of the Prime Minister, 1976), nos. 20 (1535–1536 C.E.), 50 (1841 C.E.), 114 (1877 C.E.), 142 (1891 C.E.), and 166 (1900 C.E.); *Prachum silā čharṳk, phāk thī 4* (Bangkok: Office of the Prime Minister, 1970), pp. 65–67; A. B. Griswold, "Five Chieng Sen Bronzes of the Eighteenth Century," *Arts Asiatiques* 7, pp. 104, 106; *Tū lāi thǭng*, pp. 322 and 363.

15. For a helpful brief account of which *Vessantara Jātaka* episodes are frequently depicted in Thai painting and how, see Elizabeth Lyons, *The Thotsachat in Thai Painting* (Bangkok: Fine Arts Department, 1969), pp. 20–26.

16. Piriya Krairiksh, "Semas with Scenes from the Mahānipāta-jātakas in the National Museum at Khon Kaen," *Sinlapa lae bōrānnakhadī nai prathēt Thai/Art and Archeology in Thailand* (Bangkok: Fine Arts Department, 1974), pp. 56 n. 70 and 57 n. 72.

17. Ibid., p. 57.

18. For more on Bǫrommatrailōkkanāt's *jātaka* set and those at Wat Sī Chum and Wat Rātchaburana, see my "Jatakas, Universal Monarchs, and the Year 2000" (*Artibus Asiae* 53, nos. 3/4 [1993]), pp. 312–348 passim and nn. 22, 24, and 25.

19. P. E. Pieris, "An Account of King Kirti Sri's Embassy to Siam in 1672 Saka (1750 A.D.)," *Journal of the Royal Asiatic Society, Ceylon Branch* 18/54 (1903), p. 27; Forrest McGill, "The Art and Architecture of the Reign of King Prāsātthǭng of Ayutthayā (1629–1656)," Ph.D. diss., University of Michigan, 1977, pp. 127–128, 145.

20. *Vessantara Jātaka* scenes from this manuscript are illustrated in Jean Boisselier, *Thai Painting* (Tokyo: Kodansha, 1976), fig. 125; and Chomphunut Phongprayun, comp., *Čhittrakam fāphanang nai prathēt Thai* (Bangkok: Fine Arts Department, 1969), figs. 16 and 17.

21. Klaus Wenk, *Thailändische Miniaturmalereien* (Wiesbaden: Franz Steiner, 1965), pl. 19.

22. For an overview of the history of Bangkok-period painting and the interest in Chinese and Western pictorial traditions, see Boisselier, *Thai Painting*, pp. 94–124. Note, however, that a typo on p. 105 has moved John Crawford's diplomatic mission from 1822 to 1882.

23. For many delectable examples of Thai artists' representations of Westerners, see No Na Pak Nam, *Farang nai sinlapa Thai* (Bangkok: Muang Boran, 1986).

24. Michael Jacq-Hergoualc'h, *Une Vie du Buddha dan les peintures de la sālā de Wat Ruak Bangbamru à Thonburi (Thaïlande)* (Paris: Centre d'Études des Monuments du Monde Indien, 1984), p. 38.

25. A portion of another Western-style gateway with a similar inscription can be seen in a detail of a mural at Wat Suthat, Bangkok (*Čhittrakam*

Forrest

fāphanang krung Rattanakōsin/Rattanankosin Painting [Bangkok: Fine Arts Department], fig. 37). This mural is said to date from the second quarter of the nineteenth century.

26. *Encyclopedia Britannica* 1962, s.v. "uniforms." The development of British military uniforms in the nineteenth century is very complex, as a look at such works as Philip J. Haythornthwaite's *World Uniforms and Battles, 1815–1850* (New York: Hippocrene Books, 1977) or Robert Wilkinson-Latham's *Uniforms and Weapons of the Crimean War* (New York: Hippocrene Books, 1977) shows. Uniforms differed according to rank, time of year, degree of formality, service, regiment, and so on. I doubt that the depictions of uniforms in these paintings are detailed enough to allow very precise conclusions. Also, a mid-nineteenth-century mural of the *Vessantara Jātaka* at Wat Pradū Song Tham, Ayutthaya, shows Western soldiers guarding a gate, but they wear what appear to be late eighteenth-century uniforms and carry lances with ax heads. They remind us to consider carefully what the Thai artists had seen in real life, what they had seen in books, and what they invented (No Na Pak Nam and Sangaroon Kanokpongchai, *Wat Pradu Song Tham* [Bangkok: Muang Boran, 1985], p. 67).
27. David Wyatt, *Thailand: A Short History* (New Haven: Yale University Press, 1984), p. 183.
28. Preecha Kanchanakom et al., *Čhittrakam fāphanang Thonburī/Dhonburi Mural Painting* (Bangkok: Society for the Conservation of National Art Treasures and Environment, Electrical Generating Authority of Thailand, 1980), pp. 31–61.
29. Boisselier, *Thai Painting*, pp. 114–115.
30. One Thai *Vessantara Jātaka* painting with a blank cartouche is known. This painting, in the Bekker Collection in Washington, D.C., resembles the Phoenix paintings in format, although its style is provincial or naïve, and when and where it was made is unclear. The painting depicts Vessantara giving away the chariot horses. There are two cartouches in the border, one above the painting and one below. The upper cartouche is inscribed "Dānakaṇḍa chapter in 209 stanzas" as we would expect. The lower cartouche is blank—presumably awaiting a donative inscription. The larger question, of course, is whether donors paid an artist to paint a set of *Vessantara Jātaka* scenes (and so might have influenced exactly what was painted, or how), or bought ready-made paintings.

    The Bekker Collection includes a number of very interesting *Vessantara Jātaka* paintings. I thank Dr. Sarah Bekker for her kindness in allowing me to study and photograph them, and for discussing them with me.

    While the Ban Laem near Phetburi is the only town of that name large enough to be found on most maps, two other towns with the same name are listed in the 1966 *NIS Gazetteer: Thailand* (Prepared in the Office of Geography, Department of the Interior; Coordinated by the Central Intelligence Agency). One of these is said to be in Trang province in the far south. It is not easy to imagine the Phoenix paintings having been produced there, but it is not impossible that the laywomen lived there and bought paintings produced elsewhere. The other Ban Laem is in Chainat province in central Thailand, and it might be a more likely alternative to the Ban Laem near Phetburi. In addition, the gazetteer lists a number of other towns called Ban Laem plus another word or two, for instance Ban Laem Hin. My thanks to Ketanda Jaturongkachoke for suggesting the probability of there being several towns named Ban Laem.

31. Griswold and Prasert, "Inscription from Văt Hin Ṯăṅ," p. 72. Note that the date of the inscription is not absolutely certain. I have taken the liberty of changing Griswold and Prasert's transliteration "Mahājāti" to "Mahāchāt."

32. Phya Anuman Rajadhon, *Thet Maha Chat* (in English) (Bangkok: Fine Arts Department, 1969). See also Gerini, *Thet Maha Chat Ceremony*, p. 25. The 1976 edition of Gerini includes modern photos of a ceremony in progress.

33. Boisselier, *Thai Painting*, p. 36; Elizabeth Lyons, *The Thotsachat in Thai Painting* (Bangkok: Fine Arts Department, 1969), p. 20. For descriptions of ceremonies for the recitation of the *Vessantara Jātaka* in northern and northeastern Thailand, and the use of painted cloth banners with Vessantara scenes in the northeast, see Bonnie Brereton, "Some Comments on a Northern Thai Phra Malai Text Dated C.S. 878 (A.D. 1516)" forthcoming in the *Journal of the Siam Society*. I sincerely thank Ms. Brereton for sending me a copy of her very valuable paper. S. J. Tambiah also describes a ceremony of reciting the *Vessantara Jātaka* in northeastern Thailand in "The Ideology of Merit and the Social Correlates of Buddhism in a Thai Village," in *Dialectic in Practical Religion*, ed. E. R. Leach (Cambridge: Cambridge University Press, 1968), pp. 77–83.

34. The eight are in William Warren and Brian Blake, *The House on the Khlong: The Bangkok House and Asian Art Collection of James Thompson* (New York and Tokyo: Walker/Weatherhill, 1968), figs. 51–58. Two of these same paintings are in Boisselier, *Thai Painting*, figs. 28 and 153. For the single paintings, see appendix items q and r below; also Henry Ginsburg, *Thai Manuscript Painting* (Honolulu: University of Hawai'i Press, 1989), fig. 26; and Lyons, *Thotsachat*, p. 22.

35. Boisselier, *Thai Painting*, fig. 12. The brief inscription is too damaged to read clearly, but appears to say "Chakhattiya 36," that is, the name of the chapter and the number of its stanzas. In fact this painting depicts the same reunion scene from the Chakhattiya chapter as the Phoenix painting D. Their compositions are quite different, however. Note that in the painting in Boisselier's book, all the women are on the left and all the men on the right. Between them, and overlapped by the similar-but-opposite-facing figures of Vessantara and his wife Maddi, grow two trees, light and dark, with their trunks entwined. What is more, not just Vessantara and Maddi, but all the male and female characters are almost mirror images of each

other. Thus the painting would seem to be about the great similarities and subtle differences between men's and women's worlds, and about the series of male-female reunions at the end of the Vessantara story. We are shown female relatives greeting female relatives, and male greeting male, but the entwined trees indicate what will happen next. Not only will father-in-law and daughter-in-law and son and mother be reunited, but so in a sense will husband and wife. Though living together, they had chosen to sleep apart for the duration of their now-ended exile. Visual symbolism of this complexity has very seldom been observed in Thai painting.

36. Gerini, *Thet Maha Chat Ceremony*, p. 25.
37. Ibid. Gerini includes part of King Mongkut's proclamation in an appendix.
38. On the fascinating history of Buddhist picture recitation, see Victor H. Mair, *Painting and Performance: Chinese Picture Recitation and Its Indian Genesis* (Honolulu: University of Hawai'i Press, 1988). Note too that Phya Anuman, *Thet Maha Chat*, p. 15, mentions theatrical enactments of the Vessantara story. See also Gerini, *Thet Maha Chat Ceremony*, pp. 36, 53. Such enactments were common in Burma. See Shway Yoe, *The Burman: His Life and Notions* (1882; reprint, New York: W. W. Norton, 1963), p. 294.
39. Phya Anuman notes that such a boiled pig's head and earthen bowl of special rice are sometimes offered to "the guardian spirit of the place" (*Thet Maha Chat*, p. 18).
40. E. Sarkisyanz, *Buddhist Backgrounds of the Burmese Revolution* (The Hague: Martinus Nijhoff, 1965), p. 48; S. J. Tambiah, *Buddhism and the Spirit Cults in North-east Thailand* (London: Cambridge University Press, 1970), pp. 46–47.
41. A. B. Griswold and Prasert na Nagara, "The Epigraphy of Mahādharmarājā I of Sukhodaya," *Journal of the Siam Society* 61, no. 1 (1973), pp. 102–103.
42. Charles F. Keyes, "Millennialism, Theravada Buddhism, and Thai Society," *Journal of Asian Studies* 36, no. 2 (February 1977), pp. 289 and 290 n. 29.
43. The *Anāgatavaṃsa*, quoted in Henry Clark Warren, *Buddhism in Translations* (1896; reprint, New York: Atheneum, 1963), p. 486. On the *Anāgatavaṃsa*, see Padmanabh S. Jaini, "Stages in the Bodhisattva Career of the Tathagata Maitreya," in *Maitreya, The Future Buddha*, ed. Alan Sponberg and Helen Hardacre (Cambridge: Cambridge University Press, 1988), pp. 54, 59.
44. Brereton, "Phra Malai Text." As Brereton notes, "though the variant forms of the *Phra Malai Sutta* have different emphases, the essential teachings . . . are the same"; on versions of the text, see ibid., n. 5. See also Gerini, *Thet Maha Chat Ceremony*, p. 21; Eugène Denis, "L'Origine cingalaise du P'răḥ Malăy" in *Felicitation Volumes of Southeast-Asian Studies Presented to His Highness Prince Dhaninivat Kromamun Bidyalabh Bridhyakorn*

(Bangkok: Siam Society, 1965), vol. 2; pp. 329–338; and John P. Ferguson and Christina B. Johannsen, "Modern Buddhist Murals in Northern Thailand: A Study of Religious Symbols and Meaning," *American Ethnologist* 3, no. 4 (November 1976); pp. 652, 658–659.

45. On the role of Maitreya in encouraging merit-making, see Joseph M. Kitagawa, "The Many Faces of Maitreya: A Historian of Religions' Reflections," in *Maitreya*, ed. Sponberg and Hardacre, p. 15.

46. Melford E. Spiro, *Buddhism and Society: A Great Tradition and Its Burmese Vicissitudes* (New York: Harper and Row, 1970), pp 93, 104. Spiro's chapter 4, "Kammatic Buddhism: II, The Central Concept of Merit," is highly recommended. See also Tambiah, "Ideology of Merit," pp. 42, 51, 70.

47. Two Thai kings, Mahāčhakkraphat (1539–1569) and Prāsāt Thọ̄ng (1629–1656), imitated a specific charitable act of Vessantara's, the "great sevenhundredfold donation" (Cowell and Rouse, *Jataka*, pp. 256, 261; Gerini, *Thet Maha Chat Ceremony*, p. 33n. 8; McGill, "Prāsātthọ̄ng," pp. 55, 62).

Note that whereas Vessantara theoretically exemplifies selfless giving, in fact he gives in order to get. Asking his son to cooperate in being given away, he says "my beloved son, my perfect state fulfil/ . . . and follow out my will. Be thou my ship to ferry me safe o'er existence' sea/Beyond the worlds of birth and gods I'll cross and I'll be free." Then, as he completes the gift he declares "Dearer than my son a hundredfold, a thousandfold, a hundred thousandfold is omniscience!" Vessantara seeks a reward worth much more than he pays for it (Cowell and Rouse, *The Jataka*, vol. 6; pp. 282–283; see also Tambiah, "Ideology of Merit," p. 117).

48. Brereton, "Phra Malai Text"; Gerini, *Thet Maha Chat Ceremony*, p. 33 nn. 8, 12. On what is known, in Theravāda sources, about Maitreya's earlier career, see Jaini, "Bodhisattva Career," Vessantara's major donations are solemnized by his pouring water from a flask onto the hands of the recipients. Such water pouring was understood as the confirmation of a gift in ancient India and in traditional Thailand (Cowell and Rouse, *The Jataka*, vol. 6; pp. 283, 293; Gerini, *Thet Maha Chat Ceremony*, p. 33n. 12). Scenes of Vessanatara pouring water are so common in Bangkok-period painting that the flask (represented with or without a spout) almost becomes an attribute of Vessantara. A flask (again with or without a spout) is a common attribute held by Maitreya in painting and sculpture in Southeast Asia and elsewhere, and one wonders if it marked him, like Vessantara, as a paragon of giving. The handful of Bangkok-period representations of Maitreya I know of do not, however, show him holding a flask.

49. *Cakkavatti-Sīhanāda Suttana* in *Dialogues of the Buddha*, trans. T. W. and C. A. F. Rhys-Davids (London: Humphrey Milford, 1921), pp. 72–74; *Maitreya-vyākarana* in *Buddhist Scriptures*, trans. Edward Conze (Baltimore: Penguin, 1959), 238–242; Sarkisyanz, *Buddhist Backgrounds*, p. 48. On the *Maitreya-vyākarana*, see Jaini, "Bodhisattva Career," pp. 54–55.

50. Kitagawa notes "a cluster of existential questions and problems for those who sensed the misfortune of living during the time between two Buddhas. . . . [T]he anticipation of the coming of the future Buddha Maitreya gave them grounds for optimism and hope" (in "Many Faces of Maitreya," pp. 15–16. For another way that the arrival of Maitreya may lead to *nirvāṇa*, see Spiro, *Buddhism and Society*, p. 169. A note on the Maitreya cult as "an extremely important aspect of lay devotional Buddhism" in Tibet and the Tibetans' hope of meriting rebirth in Maitreya's regime is found in Susan L. Huntington and John C. Huntington, *Leaves from the Bodhi Tree: The Art of Pala India (8th–12th Centuries) and Its International Legacy* (Seattle and London: Dayton Art Institute in association with the University of Washington Press, 1990), pp. 390–391.
51. Spiro, *Buddhism and Society*, pp. 73, 77.
52. Tambiah, "Ideology of Merit," p. 49.
53. Spiro, *Buddhism and Society*, p. 78.
54. A. B. Griswold and Prasert na Nagara, "The Asokārāma Inscription of 1399 A.D.," *Journal of the Siam Society* 57, no. 1 (January 1969), pp. 55–56.

Appendix: Some Seventeenth- to Nineteenth-Century Representations of Scenes from the *Vessantara Jātaka*

a. Illustrated Trai Phum manuscript (possibly seventeenth century). Boisselier, *Thai Painting*, fig. 125; Chomphunut, *Čhittrakam fāphanang nai prathet Thai*, figs. 16 and 17.

b. Murals in the ordination hall of Wat Prāsāt, Nonthaburi (possibly seventeenth century). *Čhittrakam fāphanang sakun chāng Nonthaburī/Murals of Nondburi School* (Bangkok: Faculty of Painting and Sculpture, Silpakorn University, 1963), fig. 20; No Na Pak Nam, *Mural Paintings of the Middle and Late Ayudhya Periods: Nonthaburi School at Wat Chomphuweg and Wat Prasat* (Bangkok: Muang Boran, 1987). It is not clear which illustrations in the latter book, if any, show the *Vessantara Jātaka.*

c. Murals in the ordination hall of Wat Chộng Non Sī, near Bangkok (possibly late seventeenth century). *Wat Chong Nonsi* (Bangkok: Muang Boran, 1982), pp. 78–80. Boisselier accepts the late seventeenth-century date in *Thai Painting*, p. 237–238n. 24.

d. Stucco relief of scenes from the last ten *jātakas* flanking a standing Buddha at Wat Lai near Lopburi (seventeenth–eighteenth centuries). Wray, Rosenfield, and Bailey, *Ten Lives*, fig. 5 (the *Vessantara Jātaka* is second from the left in the middle band: Vessantara can be seen pouring water over Jujaka's hands to confirm the gift of the children). On the date of the Wat Lai stuccoes, see McGill, "Prāsātthộng," pp. 228–231.

e. Murals in the "Residence of Somdet Phra Phutthakhōsāčhān," Wat Phutthaisawan, Ayutthaya (possibly late seventeenth or early eighteenth century). Santi Leksukhum and Kamol Chayawatana, *Čhittrakam fāphanang samai Ayutthayā/Mural Paintings of the Ayudhya Period* (Bangkok: Thammasat University, 1981), fig. 93.

f. Murals in the ordination hall of Wat Mai Thāpphanimit, Thonburi (possibly mid-eighteenth century). No Na Pak Nam and Sangaroon Kanokpongchai, *Wat Maithepnimit* (Bangkok: Muang Boran, 1983), pp. 22–34.

g. Illustrated manuscripts in European and American public collections. Listed in appendix of Henry Ginsberg, *Thai Manuscript Painting* (Honolulu: University of Hawai'i Press, 1989). One *Vessantara Jātaka* scene from a manuscript probably dating to the mid-eighteenth century is reproduced as pl. 23.

h. Illustrated *Trai Phum* manuscript with a date equivalent to 1776. Wenk, *Miniaturmalereien*, pl. 19.

i. Gilt lacquer bookcase (K.Th.285), with a date equivalent to 1791. *Tū Lāi Thọ̄ng*, pt. 2. no. 3: 371–3.

j. Murals in the ordination hall of Wat Rātchasithārām, Thonburi (first half of the nineteenth century). M. L. Surasawasdi Sooksawasdi, *Wat Ratchasittharam* (Bangkok: Muang Boran, 1982), pp. 22, 49–62; Boisselier, *Thai Painting*, fig. 124; Wray, Rosenfield, and Bailey, *Ten Lives*, pls. 27–32.

k. Murals in the ordination hall of Wat Suwannārām, Thonburi (second quarter of the nineteenth century). *Wat Suwannaram* (Bangkok; Muang Boran, 1982), pp. 16, 62–81; Boisselier, *Thai Painting*, figs. 73, 126.

l. Paintings at Wat Yān Āng Thọ̄ng (Wat Čhulālōk) near Ayutthaya (probably second quarter of the nineteenth century). *Mahāchāt Kham Luang* (Bangkok: Khlang Witthaya, 1973), p. 6 and at beginnings of chapters. What material these are painted on is not clear.

m. Murals in the assembly hall of Wat Pradū Song Tham, Ayutthaya (dates uncertain; varying styles and degrees of restoration; *Vessantara Jātaka* scenes mainly mid-nineteenth century). No Na Pak Nam and Sangaroon Kanokpongchai, *Wat Pradū Song Tham* (Bangkok: Muang Boran, 1985), pp. 67–70, 73.

n. Murals in the ordination hall of Wat Yai Inthārām, Chonburi (mostly nineteenth century). Silpchai Chinprasert, *Wat Yai Intharam* (Bangkok: Muang Boran, 1982), pp. 63–68.

o. Murals in the ordination hall of Wat Matchimāwāt, Songkhla (mid-nineteenth century). *Čhittrakam krung Rattanakōsin/Rattanakosin Painting* (Bangkok: Fine Arts Department, 1982), figs. 79–81.

p. Murals in the ordination hall of Wat Nāi Rōng, Thonburi (mid-nineteenth century). Preecha Kanchanakom et al., *Čhittrakam fāphanang Thonburī/Dhonburi Mural Painting* (Bangkok: Society for the Conservation of National Art Treasures and Environment, Electricity Generating Authority of Thailand, 1980), pp. 28–30.

q. Paintings on cloth in the collections of the National Museums Division, Fine Arts Department (eighteenth–nineteenth century). Listed in *Phra bat lae samut phāp Thai* (Bangkok: Fine Arts Department, 1984), pp. 78–80 and second plate.

r. Paintings on cloth in the J. H. W. Thompson collection, Bangkok (late eighteenth–nineteenth century). William Warren and Brian Blake, *The House on the Khlong: The Bangkok Home and Ancient Art Collection of James Thompson* (New York and Tokyo: Walker/Weatherhill, 1968), figs. 46–48, 51–58. Several of these paintings are also reproduced in Boisselier, *Thai Painting*, figs. 12, 28, 118 and 123.

s. Murals in the ordination hall of Wat Thǭng Nopphakun, Bangkok area (third quarter of the nineteenth century). *Čhittrakam krung Rattanakōsin/Rattanakosin Painting* (Bangkok: Fine Arts Department, 1982); fig. 68.

t. Murals in the ordination hall of Wat Phāwannāphirattārām, Thonburi (1886). Preecha, *Dhonburi Mural Painting*, pp. 59–61.

From Prose to Poetry: The Literary Development of Samuttakote

Thomas John Hudak

While the Indic stories of the Buddha's former lives (*jātaka*) are some of the most important literary forms to have come out of India, the *Panyatsa-jātaka*, a group of tales that do not appear in the original Pāli canon, are an even more influential set of Buddhist birth-tales in Southeast Asia. Literary tradition holds that these fifty tales were composed in Pāli in Chiengmai by monks sometime between 1457 and 1657, although a more recent study places their composition as early as 1265 in Hariphunchay.[1] Regardless of their date of composition, these tales have been major sources of inspiration in Burma, Cambodia, Laos, and Thailand, where they frequently appear as folktales or as subjects of sermons in the vernacular language. In addition, these stories have been major sources for the classical literature in the area, particularly in Thailand. One source, for example, lists sixty-three versions of twenty-one of these fifty tales in Thai classical poetry.[2] As poetic versions, the tales have frequently been altered with a variety of different transformations that involve additions, deletions, and permutations.

This essay examines those changes that have occurred in the Thai version of the tale *Samuttakote* (Pāli: *Samuddaghosajataka*). The poetic version of the tale, known as *Samuttakote kham chan*, was originally begun by the important courtier Maharatchakhru under King Narai (1656–1688). When the poem was left unfinished, probably because of Maharatchakhru's death, Narai himself continued the composition. Again the poem was left incomplete, and it was not until the nineteenth century that the Supreme Patriarch, Prince Paramanuchit (1790–1853), a famed Indic classicist and poet, continued the story and completed it.

Structure: *Samuttakote* as a *Jātaka* Tale

The traditional Indic *jātaka* tales consist of seven parts that form a distinctive structural frame: (1) a number that corresponds to the number of verses found in the story; (2) a title; (3) a quotation, immediately after the title, that probably serves as a means of identification; (4) an introduction that puts the story in the context of the Buddha's life—where he was and the circumstances that produced the story; (5) the *jātaka* proper, which tells of an incident in the Buddha's previous life; (6) Pāli verses that represent the canonical *jātaka*; and (7) an identification section that lists the characters and their identities in the context of the Buddha's life.[3] The *Panyatsa-jātaka* tales, in general, follow the same format, although the number refers to the order of the tale in a particular collection. In the poetic version of *Samuttakote*, however, this structural frame has been significantly modified. While the title remains, the number, the quotation, the introduction, and the Pāli verses have all been eliminated. The poet Maharatchakhru made these first significant deletions. In place of those deleted items, he substituted a frame that described a variety of entertainments held in honor of King Narai, entertainments which most critics interpret as an actual shadow puppet performance although they are described vividly enough to be actual seventeenth-century entertainments. These entertainments include wrestling matches, sword fights, boat races, animal fights, and a shadow puppet show for which *Samuttakote* was supposedly written. Whether or not the final identification section that follows the *jātaka* would also have been deleted remains open to conjecture. However, in completing the poem, Prince Paramanuchit did add an identification section, which reinforced the fact that the story was indeed a *jātaka* tale.

Content: *Samuttakote* as a Tale

In brief, the *jātaka* version of the tale has the following plot. After Prince Samuttakote had married Princess Phinthumadi, he obtained a magic sword from a heavenly deity known as a *pitthayathorn*. Then he and his bride flew across the Himalayas. At Lake Chaddanta, the prince revealed his previous existence as the elephant king Chaddanta. Likewise, his bride remembered when she was born as an elephant named Subhadda and when she married him in that life. From Lake Chaddanta, the royal couple continued their journey to Suvannabhumi. After a time, they descended on an island where they fell asleep. At that point, a wicked *pitthayathorn* stole the magic sword and stranded them. Upon awakening and realizing their situation, the royal couple attempted to swim across the ocean with a plank but were separated when the plank broke.

When the princess safely reached another island, she sold her ring to obtain money to build a palace. Within that palace, she directed an artisan to create a mural depicting her life with Samuttakote. At the same time, the spirit Manimekhala, the guardian of the seas, was sent by Indra to save the prince and to transport him to the island. When the prince arrived at the palace, he recognized the story painted by his princess and the two were reunited.

In the poetic version, three major additions to the plot significantly expand the story. First, the prince embarks upon an elephant hunt that allows the poet to describe in detail the elaborate classification of elephants that was probably adhered to during the Ayutthaya period (1351–1767). Included in this section is a detailed description of the hunt and capture itself. The elephant hunt sets the stage for the second major addition to the plot, the love affair, and eventual marriage, between Samuttakote and Phinthumadi. In the *jātaka* version, from the beginning the prince has one wife, Phinthumadi, with whom he shares all the adventures. At the beginning of the poetic version, however, Samuttakote has a different wife, Surasuda, who wishes to accompany him on the hunt but is left at the palace. It is on the hunt that Samuttakote is magically taken to meet Phinthumadi in the middle of the night and then magically returned to his camp. This meeting provides the basis for the third major addition. After Samuttakote's return to the hunt, both the prince and princess begin an extended search to find one another. They meet at the contest for Phinthumadi's hand in marriage. There the suitors must attempt to bend an iron bow, with the successful applicant winning Phinthumadi in marriage. When Samuttakote successfully bends the bow, he is then challenged to a battle with the other suitors whom he quickly and completely vanquishes, after which the two are married. From this point, Surasuda disappears from the story, and the first part of the poem, composed by Maharatchakhru, ends. The second and third parts, composed by Narai and Paramanuchit respectively, make no significant additions to the plot and continue to follow the story as in the *jātaka*. Other changes are insignificant: minor characters are named and names are modified to reflect the constraints of the Thai language in poetic composition.

Poetry: *Samuttakote* as a Poem

The most obvious change from the prose to the poetic version is the rendering of the story into poetic stanzas. The poetic version is written in *kham chan*, a style of poetry popular during the Ayutthaya period and consisting of two types of meters: *kaap* meters originally borrowed from Cambodian and *chan* meters borrowed from Pāli and Sanskrit. Depending upon the content of the section of the tale, a specific type of verse was employed: *kaap chabang* for narration; *kaap yaanii* for descriptions of nature or beautiful items; *kaap surangkhanang* for describing emotions such as excitement or anger; *intharawichian chan* for elaborate descriptions of nature or beautiful items; *todok chan* for light entertainment and amusing situations; *wasantadilok chan* for describing the actions of royal personages; *malinii chan* for describing the ancient army; *satthunlawikkiilit chan* for short stanzas describing deities, praising royalty, or paying obeisance to the Buddha; and *sattharaa chan* for use in the same manner as *satthunlawikkiilit chan*. The addition of literary devices, which have come to characterize classical Thai poetry, accompanied the transformation of the prose version into the poetic one.

Descriptive passages are the first of these added devices.[4] Often thought to be simply a means for a poet to demonstrate his poetic versatility, these long detailed passages help to set a scene or elaborate a setting. The descriptions are so detailed that they frequently present an accurate representation of art and architecture or of the physical surroundings of an area at the time of the poem's composition. Descriptive passages generally consist of stanzas organized into topics and comments. A single four-lined stanza may consist of a topic in the first line followed by the comment in the remaining three; or two topics and two comments; or four comments. In some cases, the topic begins in one stanza and the comment extends into the following stanza. The content of the passage usually has an overall spatial or chronological arrangement.

Three descriptive passages stand out in the poetic version: the description of the cities of Romyaburi and Phromburi; the description of the ascetic's dwelling; and the lengthy description of the Himawan heavens. While these are specific examples, the passages represent general types of descriptive passages that occur throughout classical Thai poetry. The following stanzas provide the beginning description of the cities:

Toward the southern barrier
Lies a splendid city,
So people say,
Filled with strong, skilled soldiers.

There, a festival
Of great joy and amusement

In splendid Romyaburi
Whose fame spreads through the land.

Seven levels of oceans,
Eternal shining circles,
With crystal spray splashing,
Scattering all around,

Like the seven rivers,
Places as pure as benign hearts.
Chrysanthemums mix
With golden lotus blossoms.

Seven levels of unrivaled walls,
Lines of jeweled mountains,
Precipices winding round,
Girding the space within.

Towering arched gates
Decorated in glowing gold,
Elegant doors beneath,
Studded with flawless gems.

Grounds of jeweled coral,
Wondrous and pure:
Gazing up it seems
The sun has split the city.[5]

The description of the monk's kudi is even more elaborate:

They gazed at the kudi,
That wonderous hermitage
Studded with innumerable gems
All close to one another.

The extended portico was lower
And the upper room, a place for pleasantries.
The verandah was arranged
In the customary way.

Golden poles glittered with jewels
In circular arrays,
Like Brahma's golden palace,
Equal to Brahma's world.

Various carved designs
Created a close-knitted cover.

Precious stones blinked brilliantly
Along with the pure gold.

Embellishments of gems
Intertwined in vine-like designs
Equal to Visanakam's work,
Skilled and detailed workmanship.

Carved kinnorns sparkled,
Their arms embracing kinnarees,
Their form as lovely as
The heavenly kinnarees.

Delicately polished purlins
Shone with decorations,
Glorious gems that shimmered
As though they were stars.

The superior, lofty beams linked,
Precious jewels spread light,
And blazing gold shifted back and forth
On delicately carved mouldings.

The golden floor with pieces of cat's eye
Closely inlaid appeared smooth.
Crystal streams of gems shimmered
With the royal lotuses.

Groups of small sconces,
Naga shaped, lined the walls,
Golden walls that glinted
With glittering jewels.

Leonine designs
Covered the splendid windows,
Pearls and gems
Radiantly beautiful.

The forward pillars were carved as lotuses,
Lotus blooms inverted,
Lotuses blooming everywhere,
Flowers blooming everywhere.

Suriya's rays shined through,
Beautiful shining rays

That glimmered and gleamed in the air,
Tongues of fire pleasing the eye.

Serrated eaves in cat's eye
Caught the eye glinting.
Unobstructed views of jewels,
Sheets of cat's eye and gold.

Jeweled beams and joists
With carefully constructed surfaces;
Beams and purlins in gold
Lay linked close together.

Like flowers ready to bud,
Budding flower designs,
Buds of phuttan,
In numerous carved designs.

Jewels studded the inner walls;
Ruby lotuses shimmered
And when Suriya shone,
Fiery flames flared up.

A spire lofty and soaring
With glittering rays,
A finial magically made
Sat in the heavens.

Ordered tips at the top
Next to one another
Like mirrors decorating
The celestial palace in the sky.

Ramparts and walls
Encircled the shining kudi
With pure golden projections
Built to catch the eye.

Other descriptive passages are those that delineate the actions of the king or some other royal personage: royal baths, dressing rituals, departures and arrivals of the king, to name a few. While presenting an accurate picture of the royal routine, such passages also elaborate and embellish the august nature of the king and his position. The following passage describes the king's departure:

The king mounted his decorated chariot,
Elegant as Indra,
King of the thirty-three divas.

The stringed orchestra strummed,
The victory bell clanged.
The conch cried, the drums drummed.

The charioteer urged the horses,
The swift horses,
Speeding like magic steeds.

Sounds of chariots and elephants:
Horses neighed whirling about;
Soldiers cheered out;

Sounds of eight weapons, twisted together,
Sending out smoke
Blown in airborne circles;

Sounds of heavenly blessings
Vibrating in the air;
Sounds of cheers spreading;

Sounds of Sindhu horses, swaying carts;
Sounds of elephants trumpeting,
Echoing over the land.

Of all the actions associated with the king, his erotic adventures have become the most famous. In Thai, these passages have a separate categorization, *bot atsacan* (miraculous passages). In many instances, the descriptions are quite explicit. In other cases, the acts of love are described metaphorically with images of blooming flowers or thunder and lightning, as in the following example:

His regal face next to her fragrant face.
His royal stomach next to her curved stomach.
His breast next to her comely fruit.
On top, he squeezes the splendid flower.
His heart overflows with joy,
Her hands grasp his
And lead, offering no resistance.

Conversations between royal characters are also distinctive with each interchange beginning with a stylized form of address that alternates throughout the conversation:

"O my beloved, where will we go?
In which direction? I'm lost and confused.

I see trees standing all around,
A forest surrounding and I don't know the way."

"O my husband, if we go
Into the forest, I'm unsure.
Lofty mountains and hills surround
And obstruct. How'll we go on?"

"O my beloved who's tortured,
It's necessary that we go;
This isn't our place to remain;
It's not fitting."

"O my husband, we must walk
Along the hills and forests,
And in the forests undergo hardships
And troubles as we walk."

"O my beloved, last night was hard,
Difficult to walk about;
Our hearts must persevere;
Don't be discouraged, disheartened, dismayed."

Catalogues represent another poetic device that significantly expands a poem. In content, these stanzas contain lists of birds, fish, flowers, and trees that one of the characters is admiring and which suggest particular emotions and feelings. Thus, as Prince Samuttakote admires the birds and their mates, he is reminded of his wife and the joys of marriage. It is in these catalogues that the poet's versatility in playing with sound is displayed. In *Samuttakote kham chan*, the catalogues include items arranged together solely by semantic field such as all flowers with no particular order; items arranged together by some sound and semantic field—flowers with initial [p], for example; and items arranged by pun. With an arrangement by puns, the name of the item has a secondary meaning that comments on the viewer's feelings. In the following stanza, the words *tum* and *sook* are tree names as well as words for "the sound of beating" and "sorrow" respectively:

The tum tree reminds me of sounds of hands striking
The chest about to break;
The sook reminds me of endless sorrow,
Impossible to escape from.

The catalogue of beauty represents another variation of listing. In this case, the microscopic listing of the attributes of the speaker's lover generates a detailed picture that intensifies his melancholy, longing, and love:

I remember her face, an unsullied, spotless moon.
I remember her night-dark hair.
I remember her black sapphire eyes, blooming lotuses, purple-dark.
Her ears, golden lotus petals.
I remember that flower's lovely skin, delicate as blue climber blossoms.
On each side gracefully arched eyebrows like curved fingers: she with the eight signs of love.
I remember the fragrance of her cheeks, the perfumed essence of blossoms in full bloom.
Those beautiful cheeks, none to compare with that beauty.
I remember her nose, an incomparable curve,
I remember its full and splendid tapering.
I remember her beautiful lips, her faithful heart.
Her sweeping smile, gone, no longer here to praise.
She was like the goddess of love, a joyful beauty,
Equal to the sun and moon, rising and setting.
The fragrant perfumes, my heart enraptured, O jeweled flower,
No woman as faithful as you will ever come—my heart bears this burden.
I remember her angelic voice, the melodious sounds of the cooing bird—now distant from me.
Her throat, the throat of the deer; her chin, the chin of the lion.
Her beautiful moon-shaped breasts, like those of the goddess of love.
Her swaying arms, elegantly curved elephant trunks.
I remember her shape, a beautiful woman, delicate and smooth.
I remember her legs, her lotus-like feet, like those of the lovely nymphs, all spotless and pure.

Summaries represent a final general characteristic of the poetic version. Periodically throughout the poem, a summary or recapitulation is entered. Thus, when Prince Samuttakote recognizes the painted frieze representing his life, the whole tale is once again told. While not present in all classical poems, such summaries are fairly common in the poetic version of *Samuttakote kham chan.*

Aesthetics: *Samuttakote* as an Aesthetic Reflection

As noted earlier, the poem *Samuttakote* is traditionally divided into three parts, with each part attributed to a different poet. And while the authorship of these three sections has been questioned in recent years, this tripartite arrangement is useful for a discussion of the aesthetics of the poem. The first part of the poem, attributed to Maharatchakhru, begins with the traditional salutation to the Buddha, continues through the description of the seventeenth-century entertainments, the elephant hunt, Samuttakote's meeting with Phinthumadi, their separation, the battle of the suitors, and finally the marriage between Samuttakote and Phinthumadi. In many respects, this is probably the most famous part of the poem. Ignoring the arcane lexical items, this section is actually a rather straightforward narrative. The syntactic patterns are relatively easy, causing few problems in interpretation. External rhyme patterns are rigorously followed, and internal rhyme sequences add a pleasing rhythm, but they do not dominate to the point that the narrative is obscured. In the second part of the poem, most of this changes.

The second part of the poem, attributed to King Narai, can be divided into two main parts, the description of the hermit's kudi and the battle between the *pitthayathorns*. With the description of the kudi, the lexicon and syntax become noticeably more difficult. Even assuming that the lexicon would be familiar to a seventeenth-century audience, the parataxis and the variations in the syntactic patterns make interpretation much more difficult. Emphasis is now upon description rather than on narrative. Concommitant with this new emphasis is an increase in internal rhyme patterns, seemingly a new emphasis upon sound over content. The battle of the *pitthayathorns* reflects a return to the narrative, but even parts of this sequence seem to be much more concerned with sound.

The third part of the poem outlines Samuttakhote and Phinthumadi's travels in the heavens, their separation, and their eventual reuniting. The author of the third part, Prince Paramanuchit, was a noted Indic classicist and scholar, and this is reflected in the poem. Unlike the first and second part, the third is an emphasis on both sound and content. With content, the prince returns to the *jātaka* tale and closely follows it to its conclusion. This narrative, however, is presented in a highly complex and erudite style. Indic references and lexical items abound. Frequent syntactic variations and paratactic structures make interpretation difficult. At the same time, there is an increased emphasis upon internal rhyme patterns and punning. This third part brings the development of the aesthetics of sound and content to a conclusion, with the aesthetics of the literary work following a pattern from an emphasis upon narrative with embellishments to an emphasis upon embellishments and finally to a combination of the two.

Samuttakote as a Process of Assimilation

As part of the opening stanzas to *Samuttakote kham chan* Maharatchakru relates how King Narai ordered the composition of the poem:

This king recalled the fame
Of the Glorious Master
As King Samuttakote, the incomparable.

When having ruled the heavens,
He placed himself
Midst mortals on this earth,

Showed his skill with bow and arrow
Battling kings
On battlefields, yearning

To win a princess named
Phinthumadi,
Long thought pure and elegant.

The king ordered a composition,
Wondrous rhyme and craft,
A song praising the Master:

"Carve a shadow puppet of beauty,
Replete and complete,"
The royal order read,

"Let skilled artists
Perform this work,
Their duty to entertain."

By ordering such a composition, Narai not only had a new literary work created, but also provided the opportunity for making a major religio-political statement. As noted earlier, the first part of the poem departs from the traditional *jātaka* with an elaborate personalization of Samuttakote. Maharatchakhru has emphasized Samuttakote's skills as a hunter, as a lover, and as a warrior. At the same time, the kingship, its pageantry, and its august nature have all been highlighted. With these changes, Maharatchakhru has effectively made Samuttakote, not the Buddhist moral, the focus of the tale. Although the story can be read merely as an exciting adventure story, it seems likely that Maharatchakhru was more intent upon assimilating the king, Narai, with Samuttakote, the future Buddha. Because Narai was a great elephant hunter and a valiant warrior and because his court and reign were noted for their cosmopolitan nature and royal pageantry, critics view the depiction of Samuttakote's court as a reflection of Narai's. Such assimilations appear to be common in classical Thai literature. For example, the claim has been made that King Lu Thai composed the *Trai Phum* not only to make the principles and precepts of

Buddhism more accessible to the laity, but also to present a picture of the ideal Buddhist monarch, the role he himself would fill.[6] A similar argument has been made for King Boramatrailokkanat, who in 1482 ordered the translation from Pāli to Thai of the *Vessantara Jātaka*, which became the *Mahachat kham luang* in Thai. In this case, the king became identified with Prince Vessantara, suggesting that he too had the characteristics of the Wheel-Turning Monarch or even perhaps the enlightened Buddha.[7] In like manner, at least for the first part of the poetical version of *Samuttakote*, the implication seems clear that Narai too may be a Wheel-Turning Monarch and that his reign will attain great heights of religious and political power. With the death of Maharatchakhru, Narai took up the composition of the poem, although the emphasis now shifted to descriptions of heavenly deities and realms rather than to feats of the king. The emphasis also shifted to the plot of the *jātaka*. Narai composed only a short section before leaving it unfinished until it was completed by Prince Paramanuchit in the nineteenth century. The final section also emphasized the plot of the *jātaka*, more intent upon clarifying Buddhist precepts than with assimilating Narai with Samuttakote.

Conclusion

The transformation of the prose tale of Prince Samuttakote has resulted in an elaborate and elegant poem. Originally begun in the seventeenth century, the poem provides evidence for the metaphors and poetical devices that dominated early classical Thai poetry. In the last section of the poem, composed over 150 years later, these devices continue to dominate, having become more detailed and elaborate. More than just a tale in verse, the transformation has also created a new type of *jātaka*. Now it is a *jātaka* of two individuals, the king and the Buddha, rather than just one. Although the poem is read today primarily as a literary masterpiece, it seems clear that the original intent, at least for the portion composed by Maharatchakhru, was to present a religio-political statement about the potential of the king, his rule, and his court.

Notes

1. Niyada Sarikphut, "Panyatsachadok: prawat lae khwamsamkhan thii mii to wannakam rooykrong thay" [The fifty *jātakas*: history and importance in Thai literary composition], in *Aksornsatniphon 2: ruam botkhwam thang phasaa lae wannakhadii thay* [Arts theses 2: collected articles on language and literature], ed. Trisin Bunkhacorn, Chonda Riangraklikhit, and Pornthip Phukphasuk (Bangkok: Faculty of Arts, Chulalongkorn University, 1982), pp. 264–298.

2. Ibid.
3. John Garrett Jones, *Tales and Teachings of the Buddha: The Jātaka Stories in Relation to the Pāli Canon* (London: George Allen and Unwin, 1979).
4. Thomas John Hudak, "Organizational Principles in Thai *phannanaa* Passages," *Bulletin of the School of Oriental and African Studies* 51, part 1 (1988), pp. 95–117.
5. All examples are taken from the third printing of the 1979 edition of *Samuttakote kham chan*, published by the National Library, Bangkok. Translations are my own. A translation of the complete poem is found in *The Tale of Prince Samuttakote: A Buddhist Epic from Thailand*, translated, annotated, and introduced by Thomas John Hudak, Monographs in International Studies, Southeast Asia Series, no. 90 (Athens, Ohio: Ohio University Press, 1993).
6. S. J. Tambiah, "The Buddhist Cosmos: Paradise Lost, Gained and Transcended," *History of Religions* 24 (1984), pp. 73–81.
7. Sombat Chantornvong, "Religionist Literature in Thai Political Perspective: The Case of the Maha Chat Kamluang," in *Essays on Literature and Society in Southeast Asia*, ed. Tham Seong Chee (Singapore: Singapore University Press, 1981), pp. 187–205.

"Rationality" in the Biography of a Buddhist King: Mongkut, King of Siam (r. 1851–1868)

Paul Christopher Johnson

A close examination of the biographical representation of King Mongkut of Siam over the last century provides one way of beginning to fill in the gap between indigenous and Western ideas of sacred biography. Mongkut provides a unique figure in this regard because he himself balanced precariously between Siamese expectations of kingship and Western ideals of the scientific, diplomatic, and commercial leader. Mongkut was extraordinary in that he was able to fuse at least two notions of the political "ideal man": the Western ideal of "progress" with the Theravāda Buddhist values of lineage and merit. As a result, both Western biographers and Siamese subjects remember Mongkut as a king of the *dhamma* (*dhammaraja*), one who lived in adherence to compassionate truth. The question raised here concerns the cultural foundations of Mongkut's "rationality." This essay argues, against a long Western biographical tradition, that the "rationality" (in the sense of a worldview or strategy) of Mongkut's kingship cannot be understood simply according to Western notions of "rationality" (in the sense of a strategy or worldview whose primary values are logic, science, consistency, and coherence). This biographical tradition portrays Mongkut as the sure man of letters guiding the way from dark, Old Siam to New Siam by the light of the torch of knowledge. Typical of this genre, for example, are the words of Malcolm Smith, a physician of Mongkut's court: "But Mongkut was the real maker of modern Siam, the pioneer who blazed the trail, the one who broke away from the old traditions and set up new standards of living in their place."[1] Against the simplicity of this kind of portrait, I argue that the "rationality" of Mongkut was a unique and complex negotiation among many competing ideologies, of which the West's was only one.

If the particular "rationality" of Mongkut is the primary interest of this essay, it also questions the means by which an individual's life is transformed into a biographical image of religious and cultural significance. Usually this sort of project has been undertaken as a part of a Western historical-critical reconstruction of other cultures' sacred biographies. The task here is both alike and different from such efforts. It is alike in that it endeavors to uncover mechanisms of transformation of an individual life into a cultural symbol. But it is different in that its subject is not sacred biographies but rather Western, modern biographies published between Mongkut's death and the present. The biographical transformation at work here is in the service of what is taken as "objective" history, rather than in the service of a sacred tradition characterized by myth-history. This "objective" form of biographical representation, however, veers frequently into its *own* sort of myth-history, a positivist hagiography of progress, science, and "rationality."

That the Western idealization of "rationality" as the culmination of the development of religions needs to be suspected is by now, of course, old news. Beginning with the work of Lucien Lévy-Bruhl[2] and Bronislaw Malinowski,[3] scholars of religion have slowly but surely dismantled evolutionary schemes of the relations between magic, religion, and science. Some scholars, such as S. J. Tambiah,[4] have questioned the very idea that "rationality" can be understood as free-standing and distinct from religion and magic. But these theoretical shifts have been played out on the stage of "primitive cultures" and in general terms of societies or movements. *Individual* figures, such as Mongkut (Rama IV), king of Siam (r. 1851–1868), have been left in their nineteenth-century positivist costumes.

Mongkut's "costume" is in the fashion of a hero of reason. As said, most of the Western literature on Mongkut portrays him as leading the revolution in Siam from "empty ritual" to "pure religion" and a scientific worldview. Core to this representation of Mongkut is an assumption that his "rationality" reflects a general evolution from a "superstitious" to a modern, scientific worldview. But "rationality," the means of making comprehensible and meaningfully whole one's experience of reality, is not as simple as that. The conventional usage of "rationality," as scientific explanation, must be treated with suspicion. In this regard I follow the cue of Tambiah, who, for example, accounted for the coexistence of such divergent phenomena as amulet cults, traditional structures of merit and *karma*, and Western science by seeing them as different but linked levels of meaning: those of "causation" and those of "participation."[5] This effort deliberately combats the temptation of explaining such multiple phenomena via the distinction between "popular" or "folk" religion and "high" religion or as a chronological evolution from the sentiment of traditional religion toward science and modernity. This essay takes the position that a similar suspicion must be applied to the West's biographical representation of Mongkut's "rationality."

Inasfar as this essay explicitly addresses the particular worldview or strategy of Mongkut, it also implicitly addresses the strategy of the academy in general and of the vocations of scholar and biographer: the effort to explain phenomena as completely, consistently, and coherently as possible. To what extent are these explanations, sometimes in the form of biographies, shared between people and cultures? How are they negotiated between cultures? Through looking at Mongkut as he has been represented in Western literature over the last century and trying to better explain his life and "rationality," the "rationality" of the biographical process itself is also examined.

The format for the argument is as follows: (1) setting up the problem: a sketch of Mongkut's life and a paradigmatic tale; (2) the West's representation of Mongkut; (3) a different perspective: the acts of the king; and (4) rethinking the "rationality" of Mongkut.

Prior to taking up the issue of "rationality," however, it must be noted that the biographical rendering of Mongkut as a hero of reason has not been his only representation in the West. Rather, he has also been depicted in Western popular media from his time until the present as a "noble savage": charming but uncivilized, generous yet tyrannical, spiritual yet hopelessly immoral. The roots of this popular caricature are to be found in the autobiographical reminiscences of Anna Leonowens,[6] who for five years was the English governess in Mongkut's court. Her writings, while not completely untenable, bear the sensationalized stamp of many late nineteenth-century English travelogues.[7] These were later compiled in a single volume by Margaret Landon,[8] which eventually became the basis for the Broadway musical *The King and I*, starring Yul Brynner as Mongkut. Central to this manifestation were his childlike, capricious charm and his impressive, usually half-covered physique. A. B. Griswold, one of Mongkut's biographers, aptly summarized this image as "Rousseau's noble savage interpreted by Gilbert and Sullivan."[9] In a certain sense this popularized version of Mongkut hardly seems too harmful. After all, it never claims to be any more than "feel-good" entertainment. Still, it is often just such stylizations, absurd or not, that most shape popular culture, because of their unlimited access to the public and the sheer repetitive volume of their presentation.[10]

The opposite representation, namely that of Mongkut's "rationality," while restricted to primarily scholarly discourse, is more subtle and perhaps more insidious in that it *does* make an historical claim. We now turn to the topic of "rationality(ies)"—of Mongkut and of the West.

A Sketch of Mongkut's Life and a Paradigmatic Tale

Born in 1806, Mongkut enjoyed the childhood and education of an heir to the throne. At twenty years of age, he entered the monkhood for the customary short period of training prior to resuming his adult life. Just then, however, Rama II died suddenly. For various reasons, among them Mongkut's youth, the instability of the country, and probably a good deal of political maneuvering as well, Mongkut was passed over for the throne in favor of his older and more experienced half-brother, Nang Klao. Mongkut decided to stay in the *sangha*, where he remained for the next twenty-six years. During this time he mastered Pāli and studied meditation techniques. Becoming dissatisfied with the lack of consistency between the Pāli texts and the Vinaya's practice, Mongkut embarked on a search to establish the purest texts and practice. He did this by establishing a new version of the canon through Sinhalese and Mon texts. His reforms culminated in the founding of a new, powerful sect, later called the Thammayutika. Mongkut did not hesitate to invite discord into the *sangha* when he felt a textual issue or an issue of purity was involved: his habit of wearing his robe in the Mon style (over both shoulders) and his questioning of the validity of other monks' ordinations stand as two examples of his zeal.

In 1851, following the death of Rama III, Mongkut mounted the throne. There he distinguished himself over the next eighteen years as a shrewd political tactician, heroically steering a course between voracious French and British appetites, or as he wrote, between the crocodile and the whale.[11] Mongkut also cultivated an interest in science, especially astronomy, and was concerned to reconcile religion and science. Partly as a result of his interest in science, he dismissed the traditional cosmology of the *Traiphum*[12] as false superstition. He learned many languages, among them English and Latin, and he was active in creating new legislation and initiating a whole array of civic construction projects. In October 1868, he died under circumstances that will be recounted below.

Tambiah summarized the concrete achievements of Mongkut's reforms in religion as follows: he raised the level of religious education and Pāli studies through his position as administrator of ecclesiastical examinations; he founded a press for printing Pāli works and fostering their spread, use, and influence; he established a new, pure Pāli canon by procuring and studying Sinhalese and Mon collections of the *Tripitaka*, thus revitalizing textual criticism and the production of commentaries; he instituted a "puritanical intellectualism" resulting in a housecleaning of "impurities," including the rejection of the entire *Traiphum* cosmology as well as all "mythological" and "superstitious" texts; and he led a push toward rationalism and Western science, and recognized a need to reconcile the *dhamma* with this science.[13]

There is no doubt that Mongkut was fascinated with what was to him the new explanative power of Western science. The cultivation of this interest, coupled with factors of Siam's new international exposure and Mongkut's scripturalist reforming zeal, led to sweeping changes under his leadership. Still, it is difficult to maintain that Mongkut exercised a consistent Western "rationality" when his life is examined more closely. The accounts of the end of Mongkut's life, which was focused on the observation of a full solar eclipse, illustrate the problems with such a rendering. When told in its rich details, the story of the events surrounding the eclipse provides a useful resource for understanding Mongkut's "rationality" and attempting to identify its various components.

Mongkut and the Eclipse[14]

The king had personally calculated the coming of a total eclipse of the sun on August 18, 1868. He considered that Hua Wan, an isolated beach on the Gulf close to the Malayan border, would be optimal for viewing. His calculations were based on old astrological texts of the Siamese and Mon, as well as many old American and English texts. A contingent of French scientists validated the king's figures by requesting permission to observe the eclipse in Siam as well.

The king issued several proclamations, first to announce the event, then to criticize the astrologers who disputed his predictions, and finally to calm the people who feared the eclipse foretold disaster. The royal flotilla of ships sailed several days before the event to the lonely beach. Grand entertainment ensued, including various dance performances and plays, diplomatic exchanges, and gift-givings. Griswold mentions that meals were prepared by a French chef, served by an Italian maître d'hôtel, and accompanied by champagne on ice.[15] The court had never been so open; the women and children of the court mingled freely among the close to 1,000 people, 50 elephants, 50 telescopes, and various cattle and horses assembled on the remote spot. Religious services, Christian and Buddhist, were also conducted.

When the day arrived, a wet monsoon was blowing and clouds covered the sky. Everyone was worried. The prime minister covertly asked all those accustomed to prayer to petition the clearing of the skies, fearing the king's mood should foul weather prevail. At 10:16 A.M. the clouds cleared partially and the eclipse began. A fanfare of music was sounded and the king performed a bath of purification.[16] By 11:20 the sky had completely cleared, just in time for the sun's complete eclipse at 11:36. The people of the nearby village beat their drums and set off firecrackers to scare away the demon Pra Rahoo, who they believed had swallowed the sun. Mongkut wryly joked to his guests that the people were merely celebrating the king's correct calculation.[17] Later, the king was to discover that the accuracy of his predictions surpassed the French by two seconds. Bradley rather floridly captured the atmosphere of the event in his journal: "Oh, that was a scene well worth a journey of hundreds of miles to observe, the gradual withdrawal of the sun's light being wholly unlike every other gradual diminution, leaving the darkness to come upon us without the least twilight and the king of day reduced to the smallest segment of a circle and then in another instant entirely shut in a death grasp, as it were, was a scene utterly sublime. There was something fearful in the aspect of things as though something dreadful was going to take place."[18]

In fact something dreadful *was* going to take place. Returning to the palace, the king fell ill with a fever, contracted at the observation point. It was probably malaria, although a cholera epidemic also raged at that time. The king initially tried all manner of herbal remedies and medicines to ease the pain. Two Western doctors first visited on August 30, but were refused admission by the king. The same response was repeated on September 12. Finally, on the nineteenth, one of the doctors, Campbell, was allowed to see the king, but his treatment was ignored. Campbell maintained that had quinine been properly administered, the King would have survived.[19] During the last week the king refused any treatment whatsoever from Western doctors. Bradley entered in his journal that it appeared that the king was "his own physician in the main," and on September 30 that Mongkut refused to see a doctor at all. On October 1, the day of the full moon, the king died in the position of the Reclining Buddha. He said simply that this was the way to die. Like Gotama, he died on his birthday (according to the old calendar) after having left a last testament to the *sangha*: "I lift up my hands in veneration of the Illustrious One, Who has attained the Perfect Wisdom, even though He has long reached Nirvana. I lift up my heart in worship of the Law. I bow before the True Disciples of the Lord Buddha. I have reached my refuge in the Triple Gems."[20]

In this story, the contradictions surrounding the theme of Mongkut's "rationality" are not difficult to locate. On the one hand, there is abundant support for the representation of Mongkut's scientific skepticism. His ability to calculate the event and his interest in doing so were considered unique and truly astonishing by Western observers. His evident desire to demonstrate the validity of a scientific cosmology to his people by predicting a natural phenomenon, in the process discrediting the astrologers and the myth of Rahoo swallowing the sun, were further testimony to his Western-"rational" attitude toward natural phenomena. Moreover, the atmosphere of the event, especially as pertains to the freedom of the Court women, was deemed no less than "revolutionary" by Moffat.[21] The king's demeanor throughout this international scientific event was seen as tolerant and gracious.

On the other hand, the events of the story indicate aspects of Mongkut that do not square with the image of a Western, scientific "rationality." First, although Mongkut was in a battle of words with the court astrologers over the prediction and meaning of the eclipse, the fact remains that he relied on court astrologers, and that they were, by some reports, in constant demand by the king.[22] The court physician, Malcolm Smith, stated that the King frequently requested the services of "prognosticators" and "magicians."[23] *The Dynastic Chronicles* report many instances of the king's use of astrologers. For example, the king at one point decided to bury a new zodiac of the city in Bangkok at the most auspicious moment calculated by the astrologers.[24] Such an action was not initiated by Court Brahmans, or necessarily required by Mongkut solely for the fulfillment of his duties. At such times Mongkut's acts display an astrological interest inconsistent with the purely "rational" and scientific stance for which he is remembered in Western biographical literature. Furthermore, popular and "superstitious" Thai religious practices are recorded in Mongkut's life that seem to contradict his zealous advocacy for the "pure" and "rational" nature of Buddhism. Three examples may substantiate this point.

First, Constance Wilson cites an instance when Mongkut conducted services inviting the good spirits (*thewada*) to drive out evil spirits and to enter two buildings newly constructed in the palace compound.[25]

Next, when one of the king's wives' slaves ran away and was later found, she received a severe whipping during which she died. This attitude toward slaves was (and still is in many places) not uncommon; it is Mongkut's response to her death that is of interest here. In response, the king ordered propitiatory plays given at all palace gates to ensure the protection of the spirit of the Grand Palace.[26] To be sure, the king's action may have been merely to quiet the fears of the palace guards.

But a third example lends insight to the king's ambivalence about purely scientific explanation: At the *Phrápathomceedii* pagoda, a ball of light was sometimes seen glowing over the *stūpa*, "as if a piece of white cloth were draped over it." The king went to witness this strange occurrence: "The King was of course immensely delighted. He said that it was [as] if he had been tricked by a ghost, and he did not know what to say. He said it was probably a certain element in the bricks as it came into contact with rain water that gave out the light. The reason that the King said so was because he did not want those who were not Buddhists to defame his judgment. However, all the amount of gold he had on his royal person he poured out as a contribution to the religious cause."[27] The king took a delight in the supernatural even as his sense of science and logic disallowed its validity. This brief anecdote recorded in *The Dynastic Chronicles* is significant for other reasons as well, however. It indicates that the king's response to this extraordinary appearance was negotiated among at least three considerations: the opinion of non-Buddhist observers, the opinion of Buddhist observers, and of course his own experience of the event. This points to one explanation for Mongkut's complex and apparently inconsistent "rationality," namely that it can be accounted for by the mixed political demands of Thai kingship. At this point, however, I only want to emphasize the ambiguity and tension reflected in the triangle of Mongkut's emotional response (delight at the extraordinary), his explanation (natural causes), and his behavior (a large contribution regardless of the supernatural or natural basis of the apparition).

Returning to the story of the eclipse, the king took a bath of purification precisely when the eclipse began.[28] This seems a significant pause coming as it does in the thick of the excitement of the clearing sky and dimming light. It is significant because it conforms neither to a "pure" Buddhism stripped of all "meaningless" ritual nor to the scientific proceedings of the occasion. That is, if Mongkut's *only* concerns were with the purity of Buddhism and with conforming to European scientific procedures, he would not have paused to bathe. It does, however, make sense as a *political* act of impressing the legitimacy of his kingship on those present through performing this ancient and familiar ritual. The musical fanfare sounded to accompany the bath lends credence to this argument; clearly it was not solely for the benefit of the king's devotional experience. Political expediency and the traditional expectations of Siamese kingship were both influential in the "rationality" revealed in the king's ritual bath.

Thus far the place of astrology in Mongkut's court and the purification rite he performed at the auspicious moment have been noted. A third feature of the story that is an obstacle to any consistent application of the typing of Mongkut as rationalist in a Western sense is the way Mongkut emulated the Buddha as he approached death. As stated, he died like the Buddha: on his birthday, in a Reclining Buddha position, and having imitated Gotama's words in his farewell address to the *sangha*. Also, as

Mongkut approached death according to this "script," he refused treatment by Western doctors Campbell and Bradley, and ignored their advice when it was finally given. One wonders at this juncture about his trust in Western science. It appears that it had been superceded by a "rationality" different from science: one distinctly his own.

A close analysis of King Mongkut's death calls attention to problems and paradoxes of his particular "rationality." That there are such problems makes clear that no Western caricature of Mongkut as a pinnacle of reason is sufficient to explain his words and acts. Indeed, the reduction of his life to a single determining aspect, "rationality," is an apt example of what Marshall Sahlins calls the creation of an event: "The event is a *relation* between a happening and a structure (or structures): an encompassment of the phenomenon-in-itself as a meaningful value, from which follows its specific historical efficacy."[29] The "happening" in this case was the viewing of a solar eclipse in Siam. The "event" is what was perceived, recorded, and conveyed to others about "what happened" there on the beach. The "event" might be that Mongkut predicted the onset and duration of a solar eclipse with two seconds' greater accuracy than the entire French contingent. Or it might be that the king performed a sacred bath of purification just at the moment that Pra Rahoo swallowed the sun. It could even be simply that the foolish king on his vain quest led everyone into a malaria patch, the consequence of which was his death. The "event" recorded as history depends on the structure of interpretation. For Western observers, the viewing of the eclipse was part of the larger "event" of the scientific, modern revolution sweeping Siam under Mongkut's leadership.

Sahlins has offered a helpful means of addressing the "in-betweenness" of representation: between the phenomenon-in-itself and what is called history. The next section explores the Western hermeneutic process that transformed the life of Mongkut into a significant event in the history of the West's interaction with Asia. Much of what has been written has the appearance of mere caricature. Like the writings of Leonowens, though, all caricatures contain half-truths and partial explanations, both about the writers and the object of their study. It is important to review the Western literature on Mongkut, therefore, both to fill out the portrait of Mongkut and, most crucially, to reveal the strategy in the West's understanding of Mongkut's "rationality."

The West's Representation

The first issue involved in the West's representation is, Why Mongkut? Why has he become an event more important to the West than earlier Chakkri kings or Chulalongkorn who succeeded him? This is important because the construct of "rationality" implies alternative modes of experience that are considered *ir*rational. Therefore, the choice to represent—to create an event—already implies a valuing of the object: to represent is to define oneself, either in alliance with or in opposition to the person or time under scrutiny. In the case of Mongkut, there are several good explanations for his popularity as an object of history, each more or less related to the issue of the West's self-definition as "rational."

One reason for the transformation of Mongkut from individual into event in the West is that the period of his reign coincided with the European "discovery" of Buddhism.[30] Since Mongkut was arguably Theravāda's preeminent emissary to the West during this time, it is not surprising that the West should have been as fascinated with Mongkut as it was with Buddhism. Further, as Phillip Almond has shown, Buddhism was assimilated in Western imagination at this time (1850–1900) primarily in two ways: as Noble Other, thus a ready and worthy target for colonial and mission expansionist experiments, and second, as a positivist ally by virtue of its "elevated, pure, and humanizing character."[31] Interestingly, the "search for origins" craze of the period (the time of Max Müller) suited both visions. In the first sense, Buddhism was seen as originally having been a civilized, ethical religion, now long since degraded and in need of enlightenment from the West. In the second sense, conversely, Buddhism was seen as the most evolved, most elevated representation of mental and spiritual enlightenment.[32] Mongkut was associated with this newly discovered Buddhism because of the historical timing of his rule, and because of his aggressive pursuit of religious as well as commercial and scientific dialogue with the West. This external, macro-environment of the West's relationship to Siam and to Buddhism allowed room for Mongkut to become an event either as ally or adversary to the West's self-defined "rationality." That he became an ally ("The 'rationality' of King Mongkut is like ours") is due to his combination of extraordinary abilities, which enabled him to respond to his historical situation with creativity and authority. This we might call an internal reason for the choice to represent Mongkut. Both external and internal reasons combined to transform the "happening" of Mongkut's kingship into a historical, ideological event. This event of Mongkut's reign came to be regarded in the West as the key shift in Thai history from Old Siam to New Siam. The making of this event will become clearer through a survey of the Western literature on Mongkut.

Missionaries who were active in Siam during the reign of Mongkut provided much of the firsthand information for the biographical representations of Mongkut. Mongkut's closest missionary associates were Bradley, Pallegoix, and Caswell. The king made a startling impression on all three. His open and curious stance toward Christianity and his interest in religious dialogue were a sharp contrast to the recent miscues at the end of Rama III's reign. In 1849, under Rama III, eight Catholic priests were banished for refusing to comply with the king's decree to turn over livestock to the Crown. This decree was intended to create merit, by saving the lives of the animals, for the combating of a cholera epidemic. The following year, four Protestant teachers were arrested for printing books discrediting Buddhism, or possibly for teaching Pāli, a sacred language, to foreigners. Vella suggests that both incidents came as secondary results of Rama III's failing health and a pervasive antiforeign sentiment.[33] In any case, Mongkut's kingship was indeed a surprising and welcome change to the missionaries. If they were surprised at the tolerant position he assumed, however, they were even more surprised by his religious beliefs; or rather what they perceived as his lack of religiosity. As Bradley recounted in his journal on July 1, 1854: "He (Mongkut) had occasion to speak his mind about Mormonism, giving us to understand that he had no confidence in it. Indeed he seemed to desire to intimate that he had no confidence in any system of religion, not even Buddhism."[34] This entry grants a view of Mongkut the skeptic, a role he seemed to particularly enjoy playing toward his missionary friends. On September 6, 1856, Bradley remarked on the gentleman-like conduct toward the French consul, M. Aubaret, who was at the time compelling him to abandon his treaty with the Cambodian king and so recognize French sovereignty over Cambodia: "The patience and forbearance of his Majesty seemed to border on pusillanimity and the conduct of the two Frenchmen on madness."[35]

Jean-Baptiste Pallegoix, a Catholic missionary from 1838 and Mongkut's Latin tutor and first intimate European contact, was particularly impressed with the industrious "europeanizing" of Mongkut's early reign.[36] "Europeanizing" influence involved new construction of modern roads and canals, patronage of the arts, industry and business, and the furtherance of liberty and tolerance. Mongkut was admired for his participation in and furtherance of this "Europeanness."

Jesse Caswell, more so than others, was regarded by Mongkut as a trusted friend. Caswell taught him English, but more significantly the two engaged in frequent lengthy discussions about religion. Caswell recorded that the king never stopped asking questions until Caswell pried himself away. In his journal entry of January 2, 1846, Caswell revealed the following insight into Monkut's Thammayut circle:

> I am getting a clearer insight into the character of the peculiar views of the new party in the priesthood. There is a strong tendency among them to the rankest atheism, but at the same time, there seems to be something that is praiseworthy lying at the foundation of this party. Chau Fa (Mongkut) and his priests have several times of late inquired whether

> there are any enlightened scientific men in America who do not believe in the existence of a God, of angels or devils, or of a future state of rewards and punishments. When I reply that there are some such, they say, "There are such here," yet in such a way as that none could accuse them of indulging such a belief.[37]

Caswell, and the other missionaries as well, seemed to get the impression that Mongkut, while interested in religious matters, did not subscribe to the perspectives of Christian missionaries. Their interpretive structure, along with Mongkut's baiting comments during discussions, formed their understanding of Mongkut, recorded in their journals, as irreligious and atheistic. It was this theme and others related to it that later biographers, largely following missionaries' sources, eagerly reformulated.

A. B. Griswold, for instance, offered this stunningly modern description of Monkut's religious practice: "In due course he learned the answer to his questions: the Buddha taught meditation for the purpose of clarifying the mind, gaining a deeper insight into reality, and achieving complete detachment. To use a term that is more familiar to us, it was a kind of self-imposed psychoanalysis; but it was a great deal more besides—a means of rapidly arriving at conclusions and then testing them, going back step by step to make sure that the logical sequence was complete and coherent."[38] Griswold saw Mongkut's project as stripping away errors so as to leave the doctrine in its pure beauty, purged of all traces of Brahmanism. In this process, Mongkut is enlightened by the sure guide of man's reason. He was able to value Christian ethics, although not Christian belief, because it "appealed both to his reason and to his innate goodness."[39]

Similarly, Robert Lingat focused on Mongkut's rejection of all forms of popular religion.[40] Lingat specified Mongkut's condemnation of popular religious festivals and "empty" ceremonies as useless and even dangerous. In avoiding such frivolities, he saw Mongkut as directing Buddhism toward the beauty and efficiency of sheer ethics: "La même caractere rationaliste, pragmatiste de la reforme projetée et opérée par le prince Mongkut devait aussi faire pencher de plus en plus le bouddhisme vers la morale pure."[41]

Yoneo Ishii's version, which discussed the rejection of the *Traiphum* cosmological hierarchy, claimed that this rejection undermined the theoretical base for merit-making and rebirth in popular Buddhism. Ishii suggested that Mongkut instituted such reforms in order to defend Buddhism from pressures of Western civilization. Thus this stripping of "heterodox accretions" and "folk beliefs" became for him a cultural expression of a new protonationalism inaugurated to better accommodate the West.[42] Here Mongkut was seen as statesman, strategist, and thoroughly modern by attempting to forge a Buddhism in accord with Western ideas of nationhood.

In still another example, William Bradley described Mongkut as an intellectual hero of the true antimagical "rationalism" of pure Buddhist teaching.[43] For him Mongkut was primarily an apologist, a mercenary of truth gunning down intellectual threats for the protection of the pure doctrine.

Finally, Craig Reynolds read Mongkut's reforms in a much more careful and nuanced way. Nevertheless, he considered Mongkut's attacks on mythology, especially in the *Traiphum*, as a clear demarcation of a positivistic movement that has continued through to the present. What is more, he alleged that the dismissal of the *Traiphum* as excessively superstitious shattered the traditional Theravāda hierarchy of existence.[44] Tambiah specifically disputed this claim as oversimplified,[45] and Lucien Hanks showed how the traditional hierarchy is still operational, merely concealed in relations of power and merit-making.[46] The fact that Reynolds saw the demolition of the *Traiphum* as the start of a unilinear positivism is striking, and indicative of the very bias illustrated throughout the examples cited here. It is striking for several reasons: first, it isolates a single textual interpretation and takes it as normative for an entire culture and for the entire history of New Siam; second, it again casts Mongkut in the role of pioneer of rationality, the monolithic quality of which is disputed here; third, Reynolds implies that a scientific worldview began to displace the traditional, religious one with the court's rejection of the *Traiphum* cosmology. Such a theory too neatly explains a cultural shift without accounting for the variance within that culture, across, for example, class lines. Moreover, it assumes a change of worldview (a religious and cognitive shift) on the basis of what may have been largely an act of diplomatic savvy. E. P. Thompson, writing about the "decline" of magic in eighteenth century Europe, eloquently describes the profound problems with this unified idea of *a* culture and *a* cause:

> One may suggest, very tentatively, that the presupposition of a unilinear, progressive process of "decline" (of magic) may be unhelpful. The Fascism of this century reminds us that progressive enlightenment does not always move in one way. And while no analogy is intended from this, it may set us on our guard against the impression that eighteenth century intellectual development was necessarily unilinear (did magic "decline" or did it change its form?) or that changes in reputable literate belief necessarily communicated themselves to the poor and the illiterate by a process of seeping-down.[47]

Thompson warns against the dangers of assuming a unilinear development of "rationality," and that, more often than not, the old cosmology persists in a new form, especially at the level of popular practice.

In sum, it appears that these biographical accounts created an event out of Mongkut's dismissal of the *Traiphum* as mere superstition and empty ritual. By seeing this event as the origin of the New Siam, these efforts did not focus on the ways in which, even in the person of Mongkut himself, "Old" and "New" continued to comingle as claims to authority invoked for diverse purposes.

The picture of Mongkut distilled from these descriptions is of a ruler who was leading a movement from popular, superstitious religion to true, pure religion. The character of popular religion here was assumed to be magical, ritualistic, and ceremonial, whereas the character of pure religion was taken as moral, rational, logical, and merely one step shy of a scientific worldview. Last, this movement was seen as for the good of the state.

That these secondary descriptions of Mongkut are so consistent is not too surprising since most of the biographers' sources and presuppositions are similar. Moreover, they probably chose to represent Mongkut, to make him an event in Western history, for similar reasons. Some of the likelier ones were enumerated above. These authors do differ in the degree of investment they seem to have in recognizing in Mongkut a familiar "rationality." When Griswold, for example, renders Mongkut's meditation as "self-imposed psychoanalysis" and "logical sequencing," this seems a more ridiculous stretch than some of the others undertake. The caricature is not only Griswold's, however; taken in their totality, all of the accounts selectively impress certain features and begin to read like a description of Voltaire: Mongkut as the gentleman, the scientific dabbler, the cosmopolitan, the democrat, the liberal, the mischievous confounder of priests.

All caricatures are littered with half-truths. The secondary biographies bring important aspects of Mongkut to light, but they represent only selected aspects and a prescribed notion of "rationality." This representation of "rationality" limits a full understanding of Mongkut's religious expression. More importantly, the predictable stereotyping of Mongkut as "rational" like the West perpetuates a positivist view of Thai religious development from superstition to science, for which Mongkut plays the mascot.

Another View: The Acts of the King

Throughout this essay, allusions have been made to the difficulties with the ascription of a simplistic, Western-oriented "rationality" to Mongkut's life. In the story of the eclipse, for example, the problem of Mongkut's "rationality" was set up by contrasting his reforming and scientific zeal with his interest in astrology, his continuation of certain Brahmanic and/or popular ritual practices in his personal habits, and the form of his death. In this section, excerpts of the king's own letters and official reinstitutions of public rituals are enlisted to further explore the twists of his particular "rationality."

Several letters address the king's view of religion and how it was to be understood as consistent with a scientific, materialist worldview. To a Mr. and Mrs. Eddy of New York, Mongkut wrote, "Allow me to say truly without any near case of falsehood or anigma as the truth is most important subject of all religion in the world." Later in the same letter he added:

> But I cannot receive you such advice (to convert) as my faith is but that morality and virtues of action and mind which were subjects of all religions of whole world is to be proper course for obtain eternal happiness. . . .
>
> Here are many gentlemen who formerly believed in the cosmogony and cosmography according to Brahmanical works which the old ancient Buddhist authors of books have adopted to their system without hesitation. . . . Now the skillful gentlemen and wise men of our country generally believed all foresaid (European) sciences.[48]

In these statements, Mongkut makes clear his feelings that all religions are true insofar as their morality and virtues of action and mind are true. He also states his view, apparently one common among the educated elite of Siam at that time, that his understanding of the world is informed by the scientific, European principles of physical matter over and against the ancient Brahmanic cosmology. Yet this stance is in fact not at all clear in Mongkut's reign. On the contrary, the Brahmanically formulated cosmology is, as will be illustrated, sometimes quite prominent in his kingship. Then too, in two letters Mongkut wrote to Pope Pius IX, he gave indication that his (Mongkut's) idea of religion was not based only in morality and virtues of action and mind.

In the two letters, Mongkut opens with acknowledging the "Superagency of the Universe": "From Rama IV, king by the blessing of the Superagency of the Universe."[49] Whether this was a merely diplomatic accommodation to the pope or an actual metaphysic of Mongkut's thought is not clear and will be taken up again in the discussion on merit and *karma* below. For now it is enough to note that in Mongkut's disavowal of gods and simultaneous affirmation of the "Superagency of the Universe," he is setting up a "rationality" that works by analogy to laws of matter and yet is decisively nonmaterial.

Mongkut's insistence on merit and *karma* as fundamental properties of the world, analogous to physical properties but at the same time distinct from them, distanced his "rationality" from that of Western science. He considered it a consistent position that, since there are laws to govern the physical universe, there must also be laws to govern morality and to account for difference among beings. If the differences between persons are merely random, after all, how can this be scientific, since science meant the opposite of randomness? Science, to him, above all meant that which is systematic or available to explanation. The laws of the moral system are accounted for in the concepts of merit-making, *karma*, and the causal nexus of dependent origination. Mongkut saw these as in one sense akin to physical laws, but in another sense as completely beyond the ken of rational thought. "The Superagency of the World," as cited from his letter to Pius IX, can thus be interpreted as his effort to name this nonmaterial but utterly systematic metaphysical principle. *Karma* and merit were thus seen by those in Mongkut's circle as fundamental structures of existence and "rationality" itself. Therefore, although new Western science dismantled, for Mongkut's coterie at least, the ancient cosmology, this science was not considered as relevant to the Buddhist ethical system or to *karma*.[50] Again, this reflects a distinct "rationality" vis-à-vis Western "rationality," the inequality of which is problematic for the representation of Mongkut as "rational enlightener."

If the letters of the king begin to answer some of the questions about Mongkut's particular "rationality," his creation and reinstitution of certain public rituals suggests other potential solutions to the puzzle. Already mentioned above is the instance of Mongkut's ritual bathing at the precise moment of the onset of the eclipse, and that this seems surprising given his zealous pursuit of a pure Buddhism purged of all superstitious Brahmanic myths and rituals. Some scholars have proposed that Brahmanic rituals and the cosmology of the *Traiphum* did not disappear under Mongkut at all, but rather were modified and transformed.[51] Indeed, it appears that Mongkut reinstituted ancient rituals as well as inaugurated new ones. For instance, Mongkut reconstituted the festival of Siva's Night (*Sivaratri*), which had not been performed since the fall of Ayudhya in 1767.[52] A more well known example of a Brahmanic resurrection is that of Mongkut personally playing Siva on Mount Kailasa during his son Chulalongkorn's tonsure ceremony, a role not performed by a king since the Sukhothai period (thirteenth–fifteenth centuries).[53] Instead, the king had always appointed a prince to act as substitute. That Mongkut should have chosen to play Siva for Chulalongkorn's tonsuring is a remarkable reinstitution of an ancient Siamese tradition steeped in Brahmanic mythology: the reception by Siva of Ganesha, now annointed with new, royal status. It is especially surprising since, as H. G. Wales sees it, the tonsure ceremony had for centuries been a rival initiation to the Buddhist novice ordination (*samanera*). In this case, then, it would seem that Mongkut actively supported a Brahmanic ritual tradition even to the possible detriment to the Buddhist novice ordination.

The logical argument for such changes would seem to be related to the kingship and Mongkut's desire to establish clear political authority. But Mongkut did not need to consolidate his authority in Siam with such a ritual validation, nor did Chulalongkorn (Rama V). Both enjoyed unrivaled popularity and authority. For whose benefit, then, did Mongkut make such a bold change from court tradition of the prior several centuries? For the West, perhaps. As much as Mongkut was curious about Western science and technology, he was equally concerned to maintain and defend Siamese tradition, "pure" Buddhism being only a part of this amalgam, against Western encroachment, both cultural and territorial. At least some of Mongkut's reinstitutions of Brahmanic rites can be understood as reassertions of Siamese tradition in response to modernization. The political expediency of establishing and legitimating authority over and against the West, "the crocodile and the whale,"[54] fits another piece of the puzzle of Mongkut's "rationality" into place.

Rethinking the "Rationality" of Mongkut

This essay began with the suggestion that theories of religion sometimes fail to account for religious individuals. It ends with two models that are both broad enough to encompass the range of Mongkut's "rationality" and have no need to essentialize Mongkut, since they presume religion to be transformational rather than evolutionary, and multidimensional rather than unilineal. Finally, I attempt to move beyond these two models to new ground in the biographical representation of Mongkut.

In *World Conqueror and World Renouncer*, Tambiah articulated a similarity at the phenomenological level between scripturalism (a "rational" religious practice) and other sorts of ritualistic activity.[55] Tambiah noted that scripturalism, the search for pristine, pure, and original texts and practices, can itself take the form of ritualistic activity. But since there is no actual chronological or geographical point of origin, and so nowhere to "arrive" in such a quest, then scripturalism, a part of Mongkut's "rationality," can be viewed as a ritual behavior performed for the achievement of a subjective state. In the Theravāda context, the subjective state would be an experience of purity and merit. This perspective seems to imply the fundamental nature of ritual: ritual could be any number of behaviors performed to achieve a subjective state of purity and merit. As such, ritual never dies but merely changes form. One might take as an example the Swinging Festival in Thailand: According to Wales, this was originally "magic," a ritual to coerce Surya, the Hindu sun-god, into fulfilling the function of bringing forth the crops through the principle of imitation. Later the ritual came to be seen as amusement for Siva who, during his ten-day visit, was entertained by watching the swinging. Under Mongkut, the Swinging Festival was given new form when two accretions were added: The king participated by coming to watch, and food offerings were placed before the

Emerald Buddha. In these transformations, no simple, unilinear development toward "rationality" can be discerned. Nor could one claim that the first manifestation was "superstitious" and the last, under Mongkut, was "rational." Rather, each transformation had multiple levels of meaning. In regard to Mongkut, then, his "rationality" of scripturalism ought not be considered antithetical to Brahmanic ritual, astrological beliefs, or "popular" Thai religious practices. All of these acts were behaviors manipulated for the achievement of a desired subjective experience. The very idea of "rationality" as distinct from ritual or "magic" is to be suspected here.

This argument resolves the contradictions in Mongkut's "rationality" by deconstructing "rationality" as a comparative category whatsoever.

But while the point is well taken that "rationality" may include varying domains of meaning, the term cannot be dismissed as merely an academic, artificial, or arbitrary designation. The concept of "rationality" was a significant one, not only in the rhetoric of the Western missionaries to Siam, but was also used by Mongkut in dialogues about religion.[56] "Rationality" denoted to many Thais, as it did to their Western contemporaries, a set of values relating to logic, consistency, and coherence. Thus the problem of Mongkut's "rationality" cannot be dissolved merely by deconstructing the term.

Christine Gray offered an alternative strategy for dealing with the apparent paradoxes in Mongkut's life in her idea of a "superior rationality."[57] Gray's "The Politics of the Middle Way" shows how Mongkut's life followed the same dialectical structure as Gotama's, a series of oppositions following a paradigm of (1) learning: "the transmission of knowledge and/or skills"; (2) mastery: "the development of these skills (and with this development, the creation of hierarchical relations among characters)"; and (3) renunciation: "a renunciation of a given set of exchange relations" (which) "then signals the beginning of a new developmental cycle."[58] Power is gained, Gray claims, in the renunciation yet concomitant synthesis of the knowledge mastered. From the higher position, the virtuoso is then free to use at will any of the transcended stages. So, for example, Mongkut studied first Vinaya and then sutta texts, and then resolved their "opposition" into a higher synthesis by becoming both an eminent textual scholar and a reformer of the Vinaya. Ultimately, Gray claims, Mongkut tried to resolve the categories superstition and science into a superior "rationality" of his own: "Through a series of arguments he opposed East to West, superstitious to scientific, exploitative to non-exploitative, implicitly pointing out how the Thammayut incorporated the best qualities of each, and transcended both on the grounds of a superior rationality."[59] From the position of the virtuoso's superior "rationality," one based on the middle way between Siamese tradition, the Pāli canon, and Western science, Mongkut was free to use ideas from each without contradiction.

However, Gray considered "rationality" only in the context of Mongkut's dialogues with Jesse Caswell, the American missionary. By arguing that Mongkut coopted the idea of "rationality" into the "superior rationality" of the Thammayut sect, based on its "unsuperstitious" and "non-exploitative" character, she reified a monolithic notion of "rationality" that is presumed to come from the West. At times Gray even veered toward the kind of hagiographies of science disputed here. By describing Mongkut as the "virtuoso" whose "superior rationality" is based on the virtues of being nonsuperstitious and nonoppressive (perhaps the two principal banners of the Western Enlightenment), she failed to emphasize the unique, creative, and distinctly Thai nature of Mongkut's "rationality" outlined here.

I would like to propose that "rationality" is neither a mere construct that can be utterly dismantled nor a single, reified entity that can be coopted across cultures. Rather, "rationality" is both a concept and a construct and therefore balances precariously between shared and negotiated qualities. "Rationality" must be shared to be meaningful at all. Furthermore, it must have a shared character that is commensurate across cultures. Such a definition of "rational" may have three shared aspects: (1) logic: "rational" thought tries to make sense of things; (2) consistency: "rational" thought tries to make sense of things in such a way as to be replicable; it makes things meaningful over time; and (3) coherence: "rational" thought makes things meaningful, over time, as they relate to each other. It is this shared quality that allows us to ask about the particular shape of Mongkut's "rationality," because it presupposes his words and actions make sense to him and to his context, and that there is at least limited access to this sense for us by virtue of a shared conceptual ability.

On the other hand, "rationality" has a negotiated aspect that is based on the particular exigencies of one's experience in the world. Tambiah cites Jon Elster on this point: "Why should individual want satisfaction be the criterion of justice and social choice when individual wants themselves may be shaped by a process that preempts the choice?" Elster, reflects Tambiah, is asking "why he should take account of individual preferences as the building block of rationality, if actors in fact tend to adjust, adapt, and over time, change their aspirations and preferences according to the possibilities and circumstances that they face."[60] Hence Tambiah paraphrases Elster. "Rationalization" is an adaptive mechanism that shapes the perception of a situation rather than its evaluation.[61] This describes well what I am calling the negotiated aspect of "rationality," which adapts to situational needs and may be in tension with the shared meaning.

The "rationality" of Mongkut reflects such a tension between shared and negotiated meanings. On the one hand, as Gray made plain, he appealed to a shared meaning and assimilated the Western meaning into what he thought of as the "superior rationality" of the Thammayut sect. This aspect has been amply represented and indeed, I have claimed, made into an event by Western observers and secondary biographers. The negotiated aspect of his "rationality," however, does not submit as tamely to late nineteenth-century Western evolutionary paradigms of religious and scientific development. That Mongkut reinstituted and celebrated, with great pomp, rituals that he at other times disdained as "empty" and "superstitious" seems confusing. That he mingled belief in *karma,* reincarnation, and a "Superagency of the Universe" with a materialist view of the physical universe appears contradictory. That he modeled his death on a hierarchy of values in which continued physical survival is not the ultimate value seems a contrast to his passion for the discovery and elimination of physical causes of illness, although it makes perfect sense in terms of Buddhist "rational" thought. In fact, all of these examples are paradoxical only when logic, consistency, and coherence are seen as the private domain of the Western, scientific worldview. Mongkut's "rationality" was negotiated between various interests, of which Western science was only one. It also included his kingship,[62] his fear of colonial encroachment, and his sojourn and refuge in the Triple Gems: as novice, then as monk and abbot, and finally as king of the *dhamma.*

Biographers also both share and negotiate "rationality." In significant ways the exploration of Mongkut's "rationality" has been revealing of the biographical process in general. Biographers share a search for explanations that prove cogent over time and that cohere with what they know or assume to be true in their own and in neighboring disciplines. Yet alongside this shared meaning, there lies also the "rationality" that is negotiated and created according to the particularity of each historical period. The "rationality" of Mongkut depicted across the biographies of the last century, evidently considered sufficient in their time, now seem painfully inadequate and outdated, their biases transparent. Just as Mongkut's "rationality" only makes sense when seen as negotiated among the varying and sometimes competing interests of his time and place, so the "rationality" of biography can only be deciphered when firmly located in the time, place, and interests of its production: the means by which it turns "happening" into "event" and the ends for which it does so.

Notes

1. Malcolm Smith, *A Physician at the Court of Siam* (London: Country Life Ltd., 1947), p. 34.
2. Lucien Lévy-Bruhl, *How Natives Think* (French edition, 1920), trans. Lilian Clare (New York: Washington Square Press, 1966), as well as other works that followed.

3. Bronislaw Malinowski, *Coral Gardens and Their Magic*, 2 vols. (New York: American Book Co., 1935); and more explicitly in *Magic, Science, and Religion and Other Essays* (Glencoe, Ill.: The Free Press, 1948).
4. Stanley J. Tambiah, *Magic, Science, Religion, and the Scope of Rationality* (Cambridge: Cambridge University Press, 1990).
5. Ibid., pp. 105–110.
6. Anna Leonowens, *Siamese Harem Life* (1873; London: A. Barker, 1952).
7. For instance, many scholars have objected to her contention that Mongkut had prisoners buried alive at the palace gates in order that their restless spirits would defend the palace against evil spirits. The practice had long before fallen into disuse at the Siamese Court.
8. Margaret Landon, *Anna and the King of Siam* (New York: John Day Co., 1944).
9. A. B. Griswold, *King Mongkut of Siam* (New York: The Asia Society, 1961), p. 56.
10. Roland Barthes calls this mechanism the creation of "myth," which is seen to be the collective representation of mass media; see Roland Barthes, *Image, Music, Text* (New York: The Noonday Press, 1977), p. 165.
11. "Since we are now being constantly abused by the French because we do not allow ourselves to be placed under their domination like Cambodians, it is for us to decide what we are going to do; whether to swim upriver to make friends with the crocodile or to swim out to sea and hang on to the whale" (from a letter printed in King Mongkut, *The King of Siam Speaks*, letters compiled by Seni Pramoj and Kukrit Pramoj (Bangkok: Central Library, Chulalongkorn University, 1958), pp. 191–192.
12. Frank E. Reynolds and Mani B. Reynolds, trans., *Three Worlds According to King Ruang: A Thai Buddhist Cosmology* (Berkeley: Center for South and Southeast Asian Studies, University of California, 1982).
13. Stanley J. Tambiah, *World Conqueror and World Renouncer* (Cambridge: Cambridge University Press, 1976), pp. 211–214.
14. I have taken this story from consistent accounts in the following sources (where there is divergence among them, specific citations are given): George Bladen Bacon, *Siam: The Land of the White Elephant As It Was and Is* (1873; New York: Charles Scribner's Sons, 1893), pp. 118–120; Rev. Dan Beach Bradley, *Abstract of the Journal of Reverend Dan Beach Bradley, M. D.*, ed. Rev. George Haws Feltus (Cleveland: Pilgrim Church, 1936), entry of August 18, 1868; Griswold, *King Mongkut of Siam*, pp. 50–53; Abbot Low Moffat, *Mongkut, the King of Siam* (Ithaca: Cornell University Press, 1961), pp. 169–181; Smith, *Physician at the Court of Siam*, pp. 45–50; Cawphrajna Thiphakorawong, *The Dynastic Chronicles: Bangkok Era, The Fourth Reign, B.E. 2394–2411*, trans. Chadin Flood (Tokyo: The Centre for East Asian Cultural Studies, Tokyo Press, 1965), pp. 532–558. Griswold, Moffat, and Bacon cite as a common source an "eyewitness" account written by an officer in Governor Ord's entourage at the eclipse. According to Griswold, it was recorded for publication in *The Bangkok*

Calendar (1870). I have not been able to locate the original printing of this account. See also Henry Alabaster, *The Wheel of the Law: Buddhism* (1871; Varanasi: Indological Book House, 1972).

15. Griswold, *King Mongkut of Siam*, p. 51.
16. Thiphakorawong, *The Dynastic Chronicles*, p. 538.
17. Alabaster, *The Wheel of the Law*, p. 10.
18. Bradley, *Journal*, entry of August 18, 1868. See also Smith, *Physician at the Court of Siam*, p. 36.
19. Smith, *Physician at the Court of Siam*, p. 49.
20. Mongkut, *The King of Siam Speaks*, p. 245.
21. Moffat, *Mongkut, the King of Siam*, p. 171.
22. This is particularly conspicuous in the writings of Smith and Leonowens. As stated, Leonowens' work needs to be handled cautiously.
23. Smith, *Physician at the Court of Siam*, p. 36.
24. Thiphakorawong, *The Dynastic Chronicles*, p. 95.
25. Constance Wilson, "State and Society in the Reign of Mongkut, 1851–1868: Thailand on the Eve of Modernization" (Ph.D. diss., Cornell University, 1970), p. 421.
26. Thiphakorawong, *The Dynastic Chronicles*, pp. 374–375.
27. Ibid., pp. 515–516.
28. Ibid., p. 538.
29. Marshall Sahlins, *Islands of History* (Chicago: University of Chicago Press, 1985), p. xiv, emphasis in the original.
30. See Phillip Almond, *The British Discovery of Buddhism* (Cambridge: Cambridge University Press, 1988).
31. Ibid., see esp. p. 94 on Buddhism and Comtism. Quoted words are Max Müller's, said not without irony, according to Almond (p. 3).
32. There are many examples of Buddhism's influence on philosophical developments during the nineteenth century. To cite only two, Almond has given attention to Buddhism's role in Comtism (ibid., p. 94), and Guy Richard Welbon has tried to chart Buddhism's role in the thought of Schopenhauer, Wagner, and Nietzsche (*The Buddhist Nirvana and Its Western Interpreters* [Chicago: University of Chicago Press, 1968], pp. 154–194).
33. Walter F. Vella, *Siam under Rama III* (Locust Valley, N. Y.: J. J. Augustin, 1957), p. 36.
34. Bradley, *Journal*, entry of July 1, 1854.
35. Ibid., entry of September 6, 1856. Note the English-French animosity in the tone.
36. "Dès son avénement au trône, Sa Majesté s'est occupée de faire exercer ses troupes à l'européenne, de creuser des canaux, faires des routes . . . favoriser les artes, l'industrie et le commerce; elle a établi une imprimerie royale; elle accorde la liberté de l'enseignement religieux aux diverses nations qui composent la population du royaume" (Jean-Baptiste Pallegoix, *Description du Royaume Tai ou Siam* [Paris: La Mission de Siam, 1854], p. 101).

37. William L. Bradley, "Prince Mongkut and Jesse Caswell," *Journal of the Siam Society* 54 (1966), p. 39.
38. Griswold, *King Mongkut of Siam*, p. 14.
39. Ibid., p. 25. In contrast to Mongkut's goodness and reason, Griswold saw the rest of Siam as full of pearl-divers, fierce bandits, sea-gypsies, primitives like shy animals, remote matriarchal communities with grim-faced women and harems of men, and pygmies that the Malays hunt for sport (p. 31).
40. "Les divertissements populaires, les mascarades, les mimique bouffones qui accompagnaient la cérémonie de l'ordination ou le sermon de la Mahajati sont condamnés comme inutiles, sinon dangereuses" (Robert Lingat, "La Vie Religieuse du Roi Mongkut," *Journal of the Siam Society* 20 [1926], p. 128).
41. Ibid., p. 138.
42. Yoneo Ishii, *Sangha, State and Society: Thai Buddhism in History*, trans. Peter Hawkes (Honolulu: University of Hawai'i Press, 1986), pp. 149, 159.
43. Bradley, "Prince Mongkut and Jesse Caswell," p. 31.
44. Craig J. Reynolds, "The Buddhist Monkhood in 19th Century Thailand" (Ph.D. diss., Cornell University, 1973), p. 136.
45. Stanley J. Tambiah, "The Buddhist Cosmos: Paradise Lost, Gained and Transcended," *History of Religions* 24 (1984), p. 80.
46. L. M. Hanks, "Merit and Power in the Thai Social Order," *American Anthropologist* 64 (1962), pp. 1247–1260.
47. E. P. Thompson, "Anthropology and the Discipline of Historical Context," *Midland History* 1 (1972), p. 34.
48. Mongkut, *The King of Siam Speaks*, letter of July 14, 1848.
49. Ibid., letters from 1852 and 1864.
50. Tambiah, "The Buddhist Cosmos," pp. 73–84.
51. For instance, see John W. Butt, "Thai Kingship and Religious Reform (18th–19th C.)," in *Religion and Legitimation of Power in Thailand, Laos and Burma*, ed. Bardwell Smith (Chambersburg: Anima Books, 1978), pp. 34–52.
52. H. G. Quaritch Wales, *Siamese State Ceremonies: Their History and Function* (London: Bernard Quaritch, Ltd., 1931), p. 296.
53. Ibid., p. 135. This was a purification rite in which water is dripped over a Siva linga and into a *yoni* (symbolic of Uma, Siva's cosmic energy) and then into pots. In the morning the Brahmans shared a meal, bathed in the river, and then anointed their heads with the water collected from the linga in order to wash away sins.
54. See note 11.
55. Tambiah, *World Conqueror and World Renouncer*, p. 211.
56. Christine Gray, "The Politics of the Middle Way: A Study of King Mongkut's Monastic Career (1824–1851)" (Master's thesis, University of Chicago, 1977), p. 74–77.
57. Ibid., p. 77.
58. Ibid., p. 31.

59. Ibid., p. 77.
60. Tambiah, *Magic, Science, Religion, and the Scope of Rationality*, pp. 119–120, quoting Jon Elster, *Sour Grapes: Studies in the Subversion of Rationality* (Cambridge: Cambridge University Press, 1983).
61. Tambiah, *Magic, Science, Religion, and the Scope of Rationality*, p. 120.
62. Obviously the kingship is in itself an immensely complex topic in Thai history. Mongkut's self-understanding as king in relation to traditional Thai kingship is a massive theme at which this essay only hints.

Part 4

The Biographical Genre in Local Buddhist Cults and Practice

The essays in this section explore, from an anthropological perspective, the articulation of sacred biography in Thai and Burmese cultural practice.

Schober presents mythic, textual, and ritual perspectives on Mahāmuni, an image believed to have been created as the Buddha's Living Twin and representative in his absence. The essay explores the ways in which ritual service to this image is used to create the Buddha's presence and shows how the image is used in the negotiation of royal and individual patronage, social status within communities, and nationalistic identification within both traditional and contemporary cosmologies.

Taylor's essay focuses on the simultaneous textualization and contextualization in an ascetic tradition that began in northeastern Thailand. He describes the process by which a local, oral hagiography at the Thai periphery is transformed to create a cult of relics patronized by Thai elites at the center of the nation.

Houtman examines the biography of a modern Burmese lay meditation teacher from the perspective of indigenous literary conventions in order to legitimate its place within the hagiographic traditions. His discussion of the biography of this particular lay meditation teacher further engages critical perspectives on the categories by which Buddhist sacred biography is constructed.

In the Presence of the Buddha: Ritual Veneration of the Burmese Mahāmuni Image

Juliane Schober

In his discussions of cosmogony and the regeneration of time, Mircea Eliade[1] has called attention to the pervasive tendency across religious traditions to define the present in terms of a pristine past. Eliade's observation has been borne out in studies of Theravāda Buddhism, many of which have focused, in some measure, on the tendency in this tradition to interpret the present in terms of ideal constructs of a "pristine" past. For example, much attention—among scholars and within the tradition itself—has been paid to the continual purification of the teachings (*dhamma*) and monkhood (*sangha*), two of the Three Refuges or *tiratana* in the Buddhist confession of faith, in order to recreate them in their pristine forms.

Contextualizing the present in the terms of an idealized past is a strategy also encountered in the sacred biographies of religious founders and saints whose lives become models for religious practice.[2] This essay examines the ritual veneration of the first Refuge, the Buddha, as an alternative religious strategy for constructing or recreating a pristine past and field of merit for the Buddhist community. In particular, it analyzes the image of Mahāmuni in Burma as an icon and ritual expression of the Buddha's continuing biography. The popular veneration of this image illuminates the ways in which sacred icons[3] are used to create a presence of the Buddha in rituals and myths, linking his sacred biography to the local contexts of contemporary Burmese Buddhists.

The Mahāmuni image has been among the most venerated images in Burma for centuries and, according to myth, was cast during the Buddha's last life. It was enlivened—or consecrated—by the Buddha himself in order to create a "living twin" who would counsel kings and, in his absence, preach sermons to the community. In Burmese Buddhist ritual and belief, the Mahāmuni image functions, in Tambiah's terms,[4] as an indexical symbol that encompasses multiple religious modes, including rituals of veneration, myths of creation and lineage, and narrative analogies to miraculous episodes during the Buddha's last life recounted in Theravāda texts. Symbolic and evocative references among these religious modes invoke multiple interpretations of the Buddha's biography. The image extends the life of the Buddha to the local cosmologies of Burmese Buddhists who participate in the ritual construction of his continuing biography. The merit the community gains for its ritual observances manifests itself in diverse local contexts.

The myth of Mahāmuni legitimizes both the creation and veneration of the image and perpetuates sacred biographies of both the Buddha and the image in local contexts. Its narrative places events purported to have occurred during the Buddha's life into local geographic contexts and incorporates miraculous occurrences in the biography of the Buddha that are similarly recounted in the *Dhammapada* Commentary, a Theravāda text known throughout Burma and Southeast Asia. The rich and complex mythology associated with this image includes episodes that parallel other stories about the Buddha and evoke specific textual passages, such as the Twin Miracle,[5] to authenticate its content. In the *Dhammapada* account, these episodes are used to universalize the Buddha's presence throughout the cosmos. The rituals and myths of Mahāmuni thus accomplish two aims simultaneously: they place local contexts and actors within a universal Buddhist cosmology, and they locate a continuing biography of the Buddha in the Buddhist polities of Arakan and Upper Burma. Theravāda polities characteristically extended the biographical mode of recreating the Buddha's presence and associated it with the power of kings and other patrons of this image. The veneration of this Buddha image is thus informed by local conceptions of religious patronage in sociopolitical domains.

At various points in its legendary past in Arakan, the image was said to have been an object of competition among royal patrons in Southeast Asia. The Burmese king Anawratha (r. 1044–1077) is said to have failed in his attempt to move the image to his capital, Pagan. Centuries later, King Bodawpaya's (r. 1782–1819) military envoy, however, succeeded in capturing it as a prized trophy of war and transported it to Upper Burma, where he enshrined it there in a religious complex now called the Mahamuni Pagoda and located on the outskirts of his capital, Amarapura. Today the pagoda precinct forms a part of the city of Mandalay, the subsequent capital of the later Konbaun dynasty under Mindon (r. 1853–1878) and his son, Thibaw (r. 1878–1885). The transregional and cross-ethnic veneration of the Mahāmuni image continued after the demise of the Burmese royal court and the British annexation of Upper Burma in 1885. The image and its cult retained their attraction for Mandalayans and other pilgrims, in spite of the absence of Buddhist kingship.

The Mahāmuni image and its popular veneration, history, and legends exemplify similar processes and biographies of Buddhist icons. Parallel cults of image veneration exist in Thailand, Sri Lanka, and elsewhere in the Theravāda world.[6] Comparable examples are found in the Emerald and *Siṇhala* Buddha images in Thailand, which are believed to have been cast with the aid of divine inspiration in the likeness of the Buddha and to be infused with his relics.[7] Generally, such images are thought to be linked to the Buddha's biography in that they are cast in his likeness and, as in the case of the Mahāmuni, "enlivened" or consecrated by him so that they may act as his rightful representative in his absence. Such sacred icons also engender their own continuing biographies associated with miraculous powers and events in local contexts and specific historical circumstances. Their popular veneration and biographical stories build on the biography of the Buddha and extend it to local contexts, myths, and societies. As analogous local or even national cults, they share salient characteristics that authenticate actors and their motivations, develop rituals of veneration, and construct local histories and biographies.

A common denominator of these cults of veneration and biography lies in their creation of the "likeness" or resemblance to the living Buddha. Frank Reynolds and Charles Hallisey note that popular "practice often ascribes a living presence to the statue, whether by placing a relic within it or by a ritual of consecration that infuses it with 'life.' "[8]

In addition to functioning as an extension of the Buddha's biography, such images often become popular pilgrimage sites and, particularly in the case of images that are readily portable, travel themselves in peripatetic fashion as they come under the patronage of competing kings and polities.[9] Concerning early, autonomous biographies of the Buddha, Reynolds and Hallisey remark that they often "incorporate stories that had developed at the pilgrimage sites associated with the Buddha's birth and great renunciation, his Enlightenment, and first sermon."[10] The conception of images in the likeness of the Buddha as a locus of power thus is integrally linked to their function as pilgrimage sites in various sociohistoric contexts. The myths associated with them characteristically incorporate and extend to these local contexts biographical episodes in the lives of the Buddha in order to authenticate their popularity as objects of worship and veneration. The Mahāmuni image and its cult typify this pattern of pilgrimage to the theaters of the Buddha's biography and the site remains today a popular pilgrimage destination in Burma. The complex continues to attract large numbers of ethnically diverse, local, and transregional pilgrims who seek to infuse their lives with the sacred power of the image, thus incorporating the ongoing biography of the Buddha[11] into their existence. Competing modern ideologies not withstanding, many Buddhists in Burma continue to revere the image and thus retain certain aspects of a premodern Burmese cosmology within a universal Buddhist framework.

At least three components combine to form such supraregional cults of veneration. First, the presence of the Buddha is constituted by conjoining both his physical form (*rūpakāya*) and the efficacy of the *dhammakāya*, the spiritual body of the Buddha and his teachings in rituals that center on consecrated images. This may involve the power of sacred words recited before the image, affirmations and actions performed in its presence, and the consecration ritual itself.[12] A second component concerns myths of the image's origination and provenance and builds on salient episodes in the narratives of the textual tradition. Such legends intertwine biographical themes recounted in the texts of the tradition with local contexts in order to legitimize the motivations of specific actors and the karmic consequences of their deeds. A third commonality concerns the patronage an image enjoys. There is a prevalent attention in myths and other texts to the social and religious hierarchy of patrons who appropriate or sponsor the Buddha in his physical form (*rūpakāya*). Their deeds—either to obtain the image in the first instance or to provide for its subsequent veneration—renders the ritual observances a continuing source of merit for others. These cults of veneration are ritual means for invoking the Buddha's presence so that religious acts may be performed before him as a demonstration of service to him and as an act of incalculable merit. The biography of the Buddha thus is intertwined with the biography of the image and extends into the social and historical contexts of contemporary, local actors who perform ritual acts of merit in the Buddha's presence in order to participate in an ongoing cosmogonic regeneration of his biography.

Ritual Veneration of Mahāmuni at Dawn[13]

The Great Lord (*hpaya: gyi:*)[14] or Mahāmuni, as the image, its pagoda, and surrounding area are colloquially called, is central to contemporary religious life in Mandalay. The complex, whose original colonnades and central shrine fell victim to fire in 1879 and again in 1884,[15] is surrounded by a large grassy area and a number of monasteries, the most significant among them being the Mahāmuni monastery, a Thudhamma[16] teaching monastery housing nearly four hundred monks. Shops located in the neighborhood and inside the colonnades leading up to the main shrine specialize in selling religious items such as images, rosaries, candles, flower, incense, as well as sandals, robes, and religious texts. A number of tea shops and restaurants surround the complex and cater to the pilgrims visiting the pagoda in the early mornings.

Inside this pavilion, the Mahāmuni image is housed in a narrow chamber[17] that barely accommodates its large and disproportionate dimensions. The image is made of brass and placed on a block more than six feet high. It measures 12 ft. 7 in. in height, 9 ft. 6 in. around the waist, and about 6 ft. from shoulder to shoulder.[18] Its name, Mahāmuni, is one of the epithets of the Buddha[19] and the image depicts him at the point of enlightenment in a *bhūmisparsha mudrā*,[20] a ritual gesture of the right hand touching the earth to witness his past deeds. It is a crowned image, seated on a throne, and clad in royal style with Brahmanic cords and regalia crossing its chest.[21] The legs of the image are crossed and its feet turned inward. Its left hand appears disproportionately large and distorted. It rests in the lap with the palm facing up. Its right hand is smaller, well formed, and appears incongruous with the rest of the image's base and torso. Over the centuries, thick layers of gold leaf have been affixed to it and cover its base, torso, arms, and shoulders. The right hand, head, crown, and other iconographic attributes of royalty are free of gold leaf and thus give the impression of having been added or replaced in the late nineteenth century.[22] As a result, the image lacks aesthetic coherence as its appearance is plump and its proportions are distorted.

Each morning at the break of dawn (Burmese *ayone*; P. *arūna*), the face of the Mahāmuni image is washed in an elaborate ritual sequence.[23] Particularly on sabbath and full moon days, the Face Washing attracts a large crowd of people who assemble around two o'clock in the morning, waiting for the pagoda gates to be unlocked. Some vendors open their shops early and flower sellers walk through the crowd peddling jasmine strings to those waiting. Almost everyone has brought containers filled with cooked rice, curries, cakes, sweets, water, flowers, or candles and some even carry traditional offering baskets.[24] When the gates open about an hour later, the crowd proceeds to the main pavilion that houses the image. At this pagoda, only men are allowed to approach the image and enter its fenced-off antechamber. Some men sit by themselves near the front of the assembled congregation, although many heads of households come in the company of their entire family and seat themselves toward the middle or rear of the pavilion. However, women are among the most fervent devotees of this cult.[25] They participate in this ritual seated in the back rows of the pavilion. Many middle-aged and elderly women come to observe the Face Washing and make offerings by themselves or in the company of their children. Seated in the square opening before the crowned image, they bow to the Buddha three times and recite the Triple Gem Prayer[26] and the precepts, while others amble about chatting and waiting for the ritual veneration to commence.

At four o'clock, the pagoda drums are struck three times to mark the official beginning of the ritual at dawn. A senior monk from the adjacent Mahāmuni monastery enters the chamber housing the image. Behind him follow two or three laymen in white clothes, which signify dedication and service to religion. Their attire includes a formal hat that was once the prerogative of men of high status. The men prepare paraphernalia for cleansing the image's face, which includes expensive luxury items: a large pile of new towels, soap, a giant toothbrush, kerchiefs, and fans. Standing at the base of the image, they hand to the officiating monk various paraphernalia he requires in the course of the ritual and fan the image throughout the cleansing. Only the monk may scale the lap of the image so that he can reach its huge, square face. While preparations continue, another lay assistant in the outer square of the fenced-off antechamber leads the congregation in prayer and in the recitation of the *Mettā Sutta*.[27]

The hour-long cleansing of Mahāmuni's face begins as the monk carefully and with devotion performs his daily service to the image. He wipes the face with a towel, giving special attention to the eyes.[28] Then he applies a white, soap-like ointment to the face, rubs it with a fresh towel, wipes it off with yet another towel, and then repeats the entire process. Next, his lay attendants hand him a very large toothbrush, which he moves back and forth across the lips of the image, mimicking a motion of brushing its teeth. Again, the face is wiped with a seemingly endless supply of fresh towels. A paste of ground sandalwood is then applied to the face and wiped off again. Next, the monk scents the image profusely with spray bottles of perfume. On sabbath days, the monk also drapes an orange stole over the shoulder of the image to signify observance of the precepts. Finally, he fans the image with a small palm-leaf fan typically used by monks, while his helpers below him use larger fans bearing the insignia of high civil status. During the ritual, those who have brought food and other offerings place them neatly on a tray that they hold above their heads while reciting prayers. The food, candles, flowers, and water are thus offered to the image. When the monk has completed the devotional washing, the congregation calls on the Earth Goddess to witness the merit they made by attending this ritual service and making offerings. The audience vows to share this merit with all sentient beings.

They bow and recite three times the well-known formulaic incantation: "May we share equally in the merit made here." Thereafter, the congregation disperses. Some of the men rush to enter the antechamber, requesting the lay attendants to affix gold leaf to the image on their behalf. Some obtain in return one of the towels used in the Face Washing. Still others deposit money into one of the many collection boxes placed in the outer square.[29] The content of each box is dedicated to a designated purpose in the maintenance of the image and its pagoda grounds. As the ritual concludes, the sounds of early morning bustle fill the area around *hpaya: gyi:* as shops open, cars and buses fill the streets, and neighborhood residents begin another day.

When asked why they attend this ritual when perhaps an offering to an household image or to one in their local neighborhood prayer hall might bring similar merit, Burmese refer to the Mahāmuni myth to explain the extraordinary powers attributed to this image. Others explain its significance in reference to a family tradition of making offerings to this particular image or the fact that it was venerated by Burmese kings. Particularly on the full moon days that punctuate the annual ritual calendar and entail symbolic referents to events in the last life of the Buddha, Burmese may seek in this way an "audience" in the presence of this image. Others may simply seek out this image on festival days because, to them, its veneration confers social prestige and status.

Mahāmuni's Past

Much of what is known of the Mahāmuni image exemplifies Theravāda conceptions about sacred icons and kingship, but offers only sparse historical facts. The image was originally enshrined in Arakan, a region in Lower Burma that is now predominantly Muslim. According to Arakanese sources,[30] the Mahāmuni image was created as the palladium of an Arakanese king, Candrasuriya, who is said to have lived at the time of Gotama Buddha.[31] Forchhammer[32] notes the lack of historical sources about the image and its shrine until the late eighth century C.E., when inscriptions at the site indicate that the shrine was rebuilt twice. The inscriptions at the shrine in Arakan also credit kings from Prome, Pagan, Pegu, the Shan hills, and other regions with its periodic restoration of the natural or inflicted decay that the complex had suffered at various points in its history. Others are said to have waged war against the Arakanese with the aim of gaining possession of this image and transporting it to their own homelands. Whatever the motives for the journeys undertaken by many royal patrons, Forchhammer[33] claims that the original Mahāmuni Shrine in Arakan had been a well-known pilgrimage site for centuries, housing what he believed to be the oldest cast image in the region.

In 1784 the Burmese king Bodawpaya conquered Arakan as the first stage in the expansion of an empire he created in the course of his reign. He ordered the Mahāmuni image to be taken from its original shrine and moved to a new one he had built for this purpose a few miles north of his capital Amarapura in Upper Burma.[34] Burmese sources describe his feat as a glorious accomplishment, while the Arakanese lament it as shameful and demeaning.

> The acquisition of the Mahāmuni Image was looked upon as a wonderful triumph which would bring to the dynasty and to the country unfailing good luck.[35]

> Until the removal of the Caṇḍasāra image the Mahāmuni pagoda was the most sacred shrine in Indo-China; the entire religious history of Buddhistic Arakan centers around this "younger Brother" of Gotama; the loss of this relic sank deeper into the hearts of the people than the loss of their liberty and the extinction of their royal house.[36]

The conflict over the image still informs popular perceptions among different ethnic groups in Burma. It is not surprising that there should be rivaling stories[37] about its transport from Arakan to upper Burma. Some versions claim that the Burmese army failed to transport the colossal image and that the original sank in the river, while a replica was enshrined in Upper Burma. Others claim that the image was too large to be transported in one piece and that it had to be dismembered and subsequently restored, thus implying its sacrilegious treatment at the hands of the Burmese. Still other sources[38] give detailed explanations of the difficult route that enabled its successful transport.

Intent on acquiring other sacred objects during his subsequent battles and engaged in financially exhaustive construction of religious monuments elsewhere, Bodawpaya did not treat the Mahāmuni image as the chief palladium of his reign. Nevertheless, the image received the royal veneration due to its significance and fame. Symes, one of the few contemporary voices, reports that Bodawpaya arranged for him and his company a sightseeing trip to the Mahāmuni shrine:[39] "One hundred and twenty-five Arakanese prisoners and their families were dedicated as slaves[40] to serve the shrine, while everyday offerings from the palace were borne there in state." Other sources also report that the image regularly received offerings from the palace presented according to royal etiquette. Harvey[41] reports that "Bodawpaya and the court went out to meet (the Mahāmuni image upon its arrival)" and goes on to say that "(n)owhere, even at the Shwedagon or Shwesettaw, is the devotional atmosphere more intense."[42] Shway Yoe[43] similarly writes:

The shrine in which it stands is one of the most splendid in the country. The image itself is covered by a great, seven-roofed *pya-that*[44] with goodly pillars, the ceiling gorgeous with mosaics. Long colonnades, supported on 252 massive pillars, all richly gilt and carved, with frescoed roofs and sides, lead up to it, and daily from the royal palace used to come sumptuous offerings in stately procession, marshalled by one of the ministers and shaded by the white umbrella, the emblem of sovereignty and the prerogative of the Arbiter of Existence. . . . In a long gallery, there is an enormous number of inscriptions, gathered from all parts of the country, many on gilt slabs of marble, a still greater number on sandstone. All day long circles of constantly renewed worshippers chant aloud the praises of the Buddha, and the air is heavy with the effluvia of candles and the odours from thousands of smoldering incense-sticks. Within the precincts of the pagoda is a large tank, tenanted by sacred turtles, who wax huge on the rice and cakes thrown them by the multitudes of pilgrims.

Popular veneration of the Mahāmuni image continued throughout the remainder of the Konbaung dynasty and the British colonial era to the present. The continuing popularity of affixing gold leaf to the image is indicated by Than Tun[45] who reports that nearly two hundred pounds of gold were removed from it in 1884, when it was restored from fire damage 100 years after its transport to Upper Burma. These descriptions of popular veneration and of stately and royal offerings indicate historical continuity of the Mahāmuni cult. The popular belief in the extraordinary efficacy of this image rests on the myth of how the image came to be created and of its consecration by the Buddha himself.

The Myth of the Mahāmuni Image

The myth[46] claims that the casting and consecration of the Mahāmuni image occurred as a result of the desire of the Arakanese king Candrasuriya to pay homage to the Buddha. Perceiving by his divine powers the king's wish to make offerings to him, the Buddha resolved to visit the king so as not to expose him and his retinue to dangerous travel. Accompanied by Ānanda and 500 saints (*arhat*), the Buddha flew through the air and alighted on the Selagiri Hill in Arakan. There he recounted to Ānanda and the saints his visits to nearby mountains during previous lives and uttered prophecies about future religious monuments at these sites that would contain his relics. To witness his words, Mount Meru trembled and the oceans boiled. King Candrasuriya was alarmed by these signs and asked his astrologers about the cause of this unusual occupancy. He was told about the Buddha's arrival and proceeded in grand state and with his entire retinue to the place where the Buddha had alighted to pay homage to him. He approached the Buddha, offering flowers, perfumes, garlands, and parched rice. The Buddha instructed him in the precepts and ten rules of royal conduct. Candrasuriya became enraptured with joy and invited the Buddha to visit his capital. During the seven days of his stay, the Buddha converted the king and his subjects. When he prepared for his departure, the king lamented that he and his court would no longer be able to pay homage to the Buddha and asked for an image in his likeness. Reflecting on the greatness of the kingdom and the king's need to gain inspiration, the Buddha consented to the king's request. Candrasuriya collected gems, gold, and other treasures for the casting, while the Buddha sojourned with music, song, and dance for another seven days in a pleasant pavilion that Sakka and his assistant Vissakamma[47] magically created for him. Sakka and Vissakamma cast his image and created an exact replica of his physical appearance. Then, the Buddha breathed upon the image to impart life in it and "the image was transformed into a life-like one, so life-like indeed that to the eyes of men, nats, Sakra, and Brahma, there appeared to be two Pras."[48] King Candrasuriya and his subjects made offerings to the Buddha, and overjoyed, the king embraced his feet and became again lost in rapture. The king then placed the image on a bejewelled throne under an turret, built monasteries surrounding it, and entrusted the monks with its care. When the Buddha gazed upon the image, it rose as if possessed of life, greeting his elder brother. The Buddha extended his right arm, waved his hand, and said:[49]

> Younger brother, do not stand up. I shall enter Nirvāna in my eightieth year; but you, endowed with the supernatural power of a Buddha, shall exist for 5,000 years, which I have prescribed to be the limit of my religion; you shall be the means of working out the salvation of men and nats." After delivering this prophecy the Blessed One continued: "In one of my former existences I was a king on the island of Cheduba. I broke the thigh-bone of the gardener and sliced off a piece of flesh from the back of a young prince; you (addressing the image) are my representative on earth and you shall suffer the results (*Kammavipāka*) of these two deeds.

The Buddha then preached a sermon and named the image Caṇḍasāra.[50] The king offered the remaining gems to the monks, who refused to accept them and thus buried the gems beneath the image's throne. The Buddha uttered another prophecy about the future prosperity of the Arakanese kingdom and the generosity of its inhabitants toward monks. He then alighted to rejoin Ānanda, to whom he recounted the story of his many former lives as a king in this region and predicted again the presence of his relic enshrined in this area in the future. Meanwhile, Candrasuriya paid homage to the Mahāmuni image, Caṇḍasāra, who acted as the Buddha's representative on earth and as an adviser to the king. The Arakanese text goes on to enumerate nine miracles that the image caused to take place[51] while enshrined in its original temple. Accordingly, the holy water used in its absolutions would never overflow from its receptacle, and the water in the tank where the head of the image was washed was of the same pure quality all year. Its six-colored rays shone brightly in the evening and when the faithful worshiped it, but faded in the presence of heretics. The shrine's precinct was so spacious that it could always accommodate more worshipers, and the stone quarter guardians kept away those who approached the image with evil intention of plunder. The foliage of surrounding trees always turned toward the image, and birds did not fly above it.

Burmese often explain that the image used to speak, act as an advisor to kings, and preach sermons, but it fell silent with the progressive decline of the Buddhist dispensation and the defilement in the world. Both Burmese and Arakanese interpret the turbulent history of the image and the decay and injuries it sustained as reflecting the Buddha's prediction that the image would suffer the consequences of his demeritorious deeds in former lives.

In Theravāda terms, the discourses the Buddha delivers upon his arrival in Arakan and again just prior to his departure map a sacred geography of Arakan and link each site mentioned with the biographies of his previous lives and with the continuing presence of his relics in the future. Central themes in the core episodes of the Mahāmuni myth are also encountered in one of the most significant passages of the *Dhammapada Commentary*, namely the story of the Twin Miracle, which recounts how the Buddha, during his last life, miraculously created several living doubles of himself and pervaded the whole universe with his presence. The Twin Miracle in the *Dhammapada Commentary* is a textual model for the creation and popular veneration of "living doubles," which clearly inspired local proliferations of mythic traditions like that of the Mahāmuni image.

The Miracle of the Buddha's Duplication as a Textual Model for Mahāmuni

Various passages in the *jātakas*[52] and the *Milindapañha*[53] refer to the Twin Miracle as the creation of double appearances. A detailed version of this episode is found in the *Dhammapada Commentary*,[54] a text that is widely known in Burma.[55] Themes central to this account and repeated three times in the narrative are the creation of the "living twin," the miracles of the six-colored rays, and the karmic benefits of his feats and discourses to the audience. They are also emphasized in similar ways in the myth about the creation of the Mahāmuni image.

In the *Dhammapada Commentary*, the narrative begins by setting out the general conditions for the proper performance of miracles and then moves on to a description of the events that led the Buddha to perform those most awesome miracles that may be performed only by a Buddha. Ostensively, the Buddha is moved to carry out these miracles because pernicious rumors by heretics challenge his power. Yet, as each Buddha performs the same sequence of acts in that very location, these miracles illustrate the universal presence of the Buddha and his dispensation throughout the cosmos. Most immediately relevant for our discussion of the Mahāmuni myth is the creation of a living double with whom the Buddha interacts and converses on points of doctrine for the benefit of the large assembled audience. In the course of the story, the Buddha performs the Twin Miracle three times, once prior to his ascent to Tāvatiṃsa heaven, during his lent retreat there, and upon his descent back to the human realm. Up to this point, the story of the Twin Miracle focuses on how the Buddha creates his living doubles in separate realms of existence, namely the human realm and in Tāvatiṃsa heaven. But the broader significance of creating living doubles is revealed when viewed in the context of the culminating episode of the Twin Miracle story. Just prior to the moment of his return to the human realm, the Buddha demonstrates his power through a still grander miracle: he illuminates all realms of existence in the universe, making his presence manifest at once to all sentient beings in all realms of the entire cosmos. In this culminating feat, he creates his presence simultaneously throughout all realms of existence in the universe, defining an infinite realm of his dispensation where his presence pervades an all encompassing, universal Buddha field.

In the story, the Buddha prohibits monks from the display of supernatural powers, but does not see himself bound by this precept. Thus, during his ascent to Tāvatiṃsa, he causes fire, water, and six-colored rays to spew forth from his body simultaneously and creates a jeweled walk in the sky on which he and his "living double" amble back and forth. Many of his listeners gain a clear understanding of the *dhamma* on account of his miraculous acts and discourse. The account of the Twin Miracle continues with the Buddha's ascent to Tāvatiṃsa heaven where he spends the rainy retreat preaching the Abhidhamma to his mother. While his audience on earth bemoans his absence and empty throne, the Buddha's discourse in Tāvatiṃsa heaven enlightens not only his mother, but also many others in her company. During his sojourn in the Tāvatiṃsa realm, the Buddha creates another living double who continues his sermons when the Buddha desires to rest or leaves the realm to go on alms rounds in the Himalayas. "And thus, for the space of three months without interruption, he recited the Abhidhamma Piṭaka. Now when it was time for him to go on his round for alms, he would create a double and say to him, 'Preach the Law until I return.' Then he would go to the Himalayas, . . . he would bring his alms . . . and eat his meal."[56]

Sāriputta, his disciple whose practice is a model of wisdom, follows the Buddha each day to Tusita heaven where he waits upon the teacher, listens to his sermons, and returns with the memory of extraordinary sermons. According to the Theravāda tradition, this was how human beings came to know the words of the Buddha contained in the Abhidhamma. After the three months of the lent—when his audiences on earth still anxiously anticipate his return—the Buddha descends again to the human realm. During his descent, he repeats again the same miracle performed during his ascent, the creation of a double and its associated miracles of water and fire, six-colored rays, and the jeweled walk. He then illuminates the entire cosmos so all sentient beings may perceive him and his universal radiance at once. Thus, the text explains, the many who had faith in the Twin Miracle derived multiple spiritual gain from it.

The Twin Miracle and the Mahāmuni myth[57] share a number of similarities, including narrative themes. Both stories emphasizes the performance of miracles and the creation of the Buddha's living doubles to further the propagation of his dispensation (*sāsana*). In each story, many of those who witness his miracles and listen to his discourse gain insight and understanding of his dispensation. In both narratives, the Buddha interacts and converses with his twin on religious topics. Both the Twin Double and the Mahāmuni Caṇḍasāra act in the Buddha's absence as his legitimate, living extensions in the propagation of the *dhamma*. Some of the same characters occur in both stories. For instance, in the Mahāmuni story, Sakka prepares a throne or pavilion where the Buddha rests prior to creating his double. In the Twin Miracle, Sakka similarly tends to the Buddha's throne just prior to his ascent to his mother's abode.

Both stories are biographical to the extent to which they describe the presence of the Buddha in the world and the creation and veneration of his "living double." Both stories share a common biographical time frame in that the events are purported to have taken place during his final life. And in both stories, the creation of the Buddha's living doubles is interspersed with episodes about his former lives. Reynolds and Hallisey note a pervasive pattern in Buddhist biographical texts "of using biography to provide narrative context that authenticates the teachings."[58] Whereas *jātaka* tales typically are framed by stories of the present that set the stage for the Buddha to recount his former lives,[59] in the Mahāmuni myth this narrative structure is reversed as the myth recounts events in the Buddha's final life that are framed by stories of his former lives. In this way, the narrative focus of the myth is shifted to the Buddha's visit to Arakan, and the events purported there are legitimized in reference to stories the Buddha tells about his visits to this region in previous life times or the enshrinement of his relics in the future. The Mahāmuni myth is framed by discourses that the Buddha gives to Ānanda and an accompanying entourage who, upon hearing him speak, are said to progress toward enlightenment. Similar statements are found, among other places, in the concluding commentaries in *jātakas*[60] in which the Buddha identifies himself and other actors in the story to indicate the karmic consequences of the events recounted.

Beyond these similarities in texts, another parallel to the Twin Miracle story emerges from the ritual recitation of the final volume of the Abhidhamma during the annual pagoda festival at the Mahāmuni Shrine in Mandalay. It is the recitation of the *Book of Conditional Relations* (*Paṭṭhāna*), a highly abstract, philosophical text thought to contain the *dhamma* in its purest form. According to the Twin Miracle, this text was among the discourses the Buddha delivered to his mother in Tāvatiṃsa heaven. Burmese, like other Theravādins, also believe that it will be the first to disappear when the Buddha's dispensation declines.

The *Paṭṭhāna* is recited during the Mahāmuni Pagoda Festival held annually at the end of the Buddhist lent. The festival itself commemorates the pagoda's history and provides an occasion for popular entertainment and festivities. Many pagodas[61] in Burma are the focus of such annual celebrations of local histories. Their continuing significance is affirmed in the present through merit-making, offerings to monks, and sermons. Such occasions also offer the added attraction of popular entertainment, music, theatrical performances, and opportunities to socialize with one's family, neighbors, and visiting friends.

The Mahāmuni Pagoda Festival is a popular celebration that attracts thousands of Buddhist pilgrims to the temple and to the city of Mandalay. In addition to large-scale communal donations to the monkhood, sermons preached by distinguished monks, and the daily Face Washing Ceremony, the Mahāmuni Pagoda Festival includes a complete recitation of the *Paṭṭhāna* text that extends over several days and is broadcast in Pāli over loudspeakers. Every few hours, small groups of two or three monks take turns in chanting and reading the text from printed editions. The benefits of its ritual recitation are believed to be great even though most people living in the adjacent neighborhood do not spend much time listening to it and are only superficially familiar with its content. Nor do most understand the language of recitation, Pāli. Yet many Burmese say that the lives of residents and the dispensation itself will be protected as far as the sound of the recitation can be heard. Similar ritual recitations take place at other pagoda festivals, but Burmese explicitly state that the recitation at the Mahāmuni is performed as a ritual analogy to the Buddha's exposition of the same text to his mother in Tāvatiṃsa heaven. They further note that the two recitations of the last volume of the Abhidhamma coincide in the annual ritual calendar and mark the end of lent. One of the pagoda trustees explained: "In the past, the image used to speak, but it fell silent. Now we recite the Paṭṭhāna text to gain the protection of the Buddha's dispensation." His statement voices a salient Burmese interpretation among Burmese Buddhists and underscores the perceived preeminence of the Mahāmuni image within a conceptual hierarchy of Buddha images. Those of my Burmese neighbors who claimed social status—on account of their descent from Burmese royalty or simply on account of their present economic circumstances—would seek out the Mahāmuni image on major religious holidays because they felt that the image's "past" proved its extraordinary efficacy in comparison to other Buddha images.

Veneration of the Buddha in Text and Ethnography

Until recently, Theravāda textual scholarship explored only reluctantly cultic veneration of the Buddha. Several reasons may account for this. For one, traditional Pāli scholarship sought to distance "true" Theravāda texts from the cultic veneration of the Buddha in the form of relics or images. An example of that approach can be found in I. B. Horner's introduction to the *Milindapañha*, where she raises issues concerning the veneration of the Buddha through relics and images and writes, "(T)he Buddha had wished to continue to be represented merely by symbols so as to discourage the growth of a Buddha-cult once images of himself, however much stylised, were made. Why then were they allowed?"[62]

This kind of bias against cultic veneration may have been strengthened coincidentally by the character and historical development of the Pāli textual tradition itself. While canonical texts like the *Mahāparinibbāna Sutta* discuss at length reverence to be paid to the Buddha's relics, images as a manifestation of the Buddha's living presence developed centuries after his *parinibbāna* and are not mentioned in Pāli canonical texts, perhaps due to the intentions of the redactors.[63] While veneration of the Buddha's image is mentioned only rarely in the commentarial literature, it figures prominently in local texts, such as chronicles (*vaṃsa*) composed in Sri Lanka and in the Burmese *Sāsanavaṃsa*.[64] In a Burmese retelling of events that followed immediately after the Buddha's *parinibbāna* found in Bigandet,[65] the first miracle caused by the Buddha's relics occurs soon after his *parinibbāna* when Mahākassapa pays homage to his deceased but not yet cremated body. The Buddha's remains miraculously shine through the funerary shrouds and create a levitated apparition of his physical body. The veneration of the Buddha during his last life is also elaborated at several junctures in the Pāli texts. The *jātakas*[66] relate how the Buddha not only encouraged, but expected royal supporters to pay homage to him. Other episodes in the *jātakas* illustrate how offerings of food or other alms to a future Buddha bring merit to the donor and detail great karmic consequences for such acts of generosity. In contrast, in the *Milindapañha*,[67] the Buddha is said to have discouraged Ānanda from worshiping his physical body (*rūpakāya*) because that practice would not further the work of his disciples.

More recent scholarship moved away from the presumption of a "pure" and internally consistent body of Theravāda texts divorced from historical and cultural contexts of compilation and transmission. With regard to the veneration of relics, Schopen[68] points to the incongruity between extant Pāli Vinaya texts and the monastic practice of *stūpa* veneration documented in early Indian inscriptions. He argues that the silence on this issue in the Pāli Vinaya—which are presumed to be among the earliest Buddhist writings extant today—may be the result of relatively recent text revisions. In the course of discussing the context of compilation of the Pāli canon and its historical development, Collins similarly remarks that "(A)lthough a number of uncertainties beset our understanding of the earlier history of images and image veneration in Buddhism, there is no doubt that they have come to play an important role in mediating the Buddha's 'presence.' "[69]

The relative sparsity of references to image veneration in the Pāli canonical and commentarial literature is mitigated, in part, by epigraphic and architectural evidence from medieval Indian monasteries, beginning with the fourth/fifth centuries, which Schopen has recently considered.[70] He argues that, beginning with the fifth century, Perfumed Chambers (*gandhakuṭī*) housing images of the Buddha became central aspects in the emerging rearrangement of monastic architecture. These " 'private chambers' [reserved for the Buddha] were formally recognized as distinct organizational components of their monasteries and had specifically titled monks or groups of monks attached to them."[71] He further states that "the Buddha was thought to have been a current resident and an abiding presence in medieval Buddhist monasteries . . . the Blessed One himself was thought to be *in* the Perfumed Chamber."[72] Schopen cites archaeological evidence from the ninth/tenth centuries to show that images "housed in the Medieval monastic *gandhakuṭī* were cognitively classified with the living Buddha . . . [and] thought to *live* in these establishments." Upon their inevitable decay, they were treated ritually like the remains of deceased

Buddhas and enshrined in *stūpas*, thus underscoring the equivalence of "image" and "actual person."[73]

Strong has already shown[74] that forms of veneration of the Buddha represented by images or by empty thrones are found in texts and practice across the Buddhist tradition. In his essay on the Perfumed Chamber (*gandhakuṭī*), he shows that the cultic practice of offering flowers, candles, and perfumes to the Buddha and the personal devotion expressed in this way are "deeds of devotion which more immediately transform the very milieu in which they are made."[75]

A wealth of ethnographic examples can be adduced to document veneration of the Buddha's image as a common mode of religious practice throughout the Theravāda world. In Burma, consecrated Buddha images, such as relics and other sacred icons, are objects of religious veneration. There is a significant range of interpretations Burmese entertain on how the icon manifests the presence of the Buddha. Perhaps the greatest degree of consensus emerges in the ritual veneration of Buddha images, because in the context of that ritual observance, all Burmese Buddhists tend to act as though the Buddha was present, even though they may not accept that premise explicitly.

A consecrated image is found in nearly every Burmese Buddhist household where offerings of food, water, candles, and fragrant flowers are placed before it and religious affirmations and vows are made in its presence.[76] Paying homage "as though the Buddha was alive" is a common exegesis for this type of veneration, even for those Burmese who believe that an image serves primarily as a cognitive reminder of the Buddha's spiritual discipline and exemplary mastery of the Path. Others view consecrated images as powerful because, to them, they constitute literally the presence of the Buddha's power in the context of their own lives. The salience of popular conceptions about the veneration of images and relics as extensions of the Buddha's physical body is illustrated by its widespread practice. To Theravādins, taking an oath before a Buddha image is a sacred act that attests to the truth of this affirmation. Many Burmese consider it equivalent to making the affirmation in the presence of and witnessed by the Buddha.[77] When such vows are broken, potentially disastrous consequences and great demerit are thought to ensue.

Most household images have been consecrated in living memory at least once, if not several times. Consecration ensures that the powers of the Buddha emanate throughout the house and surrounding compound and protect its residents from ill fortune of many kinds. Once consecration has been properly performed and the *dhammakāya* invoked, all images embody the powers of the Buddha. The consecration ritual,[78] entails the enlivening of the image as monks recite the *Dhammacakkappavattana Sutta*, the first sermon the Buddha recited upon his enlightenment, which set the Wheel of Law in motion. The power of the monks' utterances,[79] so carefully pronounced to stay true to what is believed to be the original Pāli, rests on the fact that both content and form of their recitation is part of the *dhammakāya*, the spiritual body of the Buddha,[80] which thus is imparted into his image, *rūpakāya*. Once consecrated, the image is believed to contain the powers of the Buddha and hence becomes part of both the spiritual and physical extensions of his dispensation.

The power of consecrated images may be jeopardized by imperfections in ritual performance, sacred speech, or prior defilements of the monks who invoked the *dhammakāya* during the consecration ritual. Once consecrated and empowered, an image must be treated with careful attention to proper conduct in its presence. Improper conduct, and particularly sexual behavior, should not take place in the image's presence. Similarly, one's feet should never be pointed toward the image. Many Burmese sleep with their heads oriented toward the image and some, mindful of potential offenses, install curtains around the image to remove the context of ordinary life from its sight.

The ritual reverence commonly paid to Buddha images and other forms of the Buddha's presence underscores the pervasiveness of beliefs about the Buddha's presence in the world. Accepting that premise, further explanation is needed to determine why Burmese perceive some images to be more efficacious than others and to define the principles underlying the conceptual hierarchy of images Burmese entertain, but articulate often only vaguely. The extraordinary efficacy attributed to some images—but not to most ordinary images in households or neighborhood prayer halls—seemingly contradicts the general belief that all consecrated images embody equally his *rūpakāya* and are "enlivened" by his *dhammakāya*. In principle, there should be no differentiation concerning the efficacy attributed to consecrated Buddha images. Yet, like most Theravādins, Burmese recognize a conceptual hierarchy of more and less powerful images even though they sometimes find it difficult to explain this differentiation on grounds of principle. This apparent contradiction is often "resolved" by a myths of origination and "lineage" that combine to create a biography of the image itself. Such biographies of images are further authenticated by the deeds of merit of those who brought it under their patronage. A differentiation in the efficacy attributed to images may thus be a reflection of the relative store of merit of lay donors who sponsor their creation, subsequent consecration, or veneration. Particularly when housed in places that are publicly accessible, such images become sources of merit for a potentially unlimited number of other karmically conditioned lives. Hence the most honored title a Burmese lay sponsor may earn is that of a donor of an image, *hpaya:*

taga, a honorific held in greater esteem than the sponsorship of an ordination. It indicates the primary obligation of the Theravāda laity to provide for all physical dimensions of the dispensation: the construction of temples and monasteries, the material requirements for the monkhood, and so on. Being the donor of a consecrated Buddha image is therefore the most prestigious sponsorship of religion. It extends lay patronage and protection over a social domain of the Buddha's dispensation (*sāsana*) and attests to the lay patron's previous and future merit, his spiritual abilities, and social power.

Postscript: Mahāmuni's Modern Reification

The ethnography on which this essay has been based thus far drew on fieldwork conducted in 1981–1982. A recent return to Mandalay in the spring of 1994 illuminated the arguments developed here in unforeseen ways. In the course of extensive, government-sponsored religious construction throughout Burma, several buildings have been added recently to the Mahāmuni complex in Mandalay. Most significant for the purposes of this essay are two museums, one dedicated to the myth of Mahāmuni and the other to the Buddha's biography and his continued presence both at the site of this shrine and simultaneously throughout the universe. As both structures are intended to popularize and interpret for pilgrims a particular understanding of the known text about the complex and its image, some brief descriptions are in order.

The new building dedicated to the mythohistory of the creation of the Mahāmuni image, Anawratha's failed attempt to bring the image to Pagan, its transport to Upper Burma, and grand investiture by King Bodawpaya in its present location displays approximately thirty huge panels of oil paintings along a circular walk that follows the episodes of the myth. Each panel of canvas measures approximately 6–7 meters in length and 3 meters in height and is accompanied by a caption describing the scene portrayed in both Burmese and English. The representational style of these paintings is epic, not only in its proportions, but also in the mood and tenor this grand national myth seeks to evoke. At the cost of historicity, the display emphasizes precisely those scenes likely to instill or resonate religio-nationalist emotions among the viewing pilgrims. For instance, the ship that Bodawpaya's son and military commander used for transporting the image upriver is shown to be a huge galleon vessel with many sails reminiscent of the sort of fleet ship explorers like Christopher Columbus might have commanded on their seafaring voyages. The caption beneath explains that the image is brought "back" to Burma, without, however, providing a referent for this retroflexive syntactic construction. The next panel shows the ship anchoring at the Irrawaddy river bank and the king, Bodawpaya, marching out into the waters to pull the ropes guiding the ship to the pier. The display ends with the enshrinement of the image by the Amarapura court. For the pilgrims who visit the museum, both the medium of representation and its style strike awe-inspiring chords. Most of them have never seen before paintings of this size or style, let alone ones depicting emotive themes of a text with which they have familiarity prior to visiting the sacred precinct of Mahāmuni. Many leave visibly impressed and inspired by the religious and nationalistic meanings conveyed.

The message that the pilgrim is now in the presence of Mahāmuni is enforced by a second new complex dedicated to the biography of the Buddha and the spread of his teachings. One enters this building through a set of stairs leading to a balcony on the second story. Its entrance is flanked on either side with a painting fashioned after a photograph of King Mindon and others of *jātaka* stories. Most significant are the four depictions of the Buddha's place of birth and the sites of his enlightenment, first sermon, and passing into *parinibbāna*. The passage then leads into a quadrangular balcony that exhibits along the walls pictures of Buddhist pilgrimage sites in India, Nepal, Tibet, Sri Lanka, Thailand, Cambodia, Vietnam, China, Korea, Japan, and Borobudur in Indonesia. These are followed by replicas of Buddha images from various Burmese dynastic periods, including Pagan, Pegu, Ava, Sagain, and Mandalay, and others representing artistic styles of Buddha icons from Thailand, Sri Lanka, India, and other Buddhist countries.

The most spectacular display, however, is revealed in the view from the balcony down to the ground floor, where a sculpted cosmography of the Buddhist world unfolds. This center of the exhibit is constructed simultaneously in modern, geographic and traditional, cosmological terms and presents a Burmese sculptural interpretation of the Buddha's illumination of the universe as recounted in the *Dhammapada*. The huge cosmographic map in sculpted relief on the ground floor below shows all major sites of Buddhist pilgrimage, including Buddhagaya in India, Kandy in Sri Lanka, Wat Phra Kaeo in Thailand, Angkor Wat in Cambodia, Borobudur in Indonesia, and many others in Nepal, Tibet, China, Korea, and Japan. At the center of this cartographic relief lies Myanmar, the modern Burmese nation whose landscape is cluttered with markers indicating the location of national shrines like the Shwedagon Pagoda and other charismatic pilgrimage sites in the peripheral regions of the Burmese heartland. At the cosmographic center of Myanmar lies, naturally, the site of the Mahāmuni Pagoda in Mandalay. From this axis mundi, the viewer's eye rises up to a jeweled stairway poised in midair against a glimmering blue universe. Atop this stairway rises the Buddha, illuminating the universe below him and also above, where Brahma, Indra, and other celestial beings stand reverently to witness the miracle of his presence. The Buddha's luminous radiance is conveyed by colorful rows of electric and neon lights that border the staircase and link the site of Mahāmuni with the highest reaches of the universe. The entire cosmographic display rests on Mount Meru and is surrounded by the seven *cakkravala* and seas beyond the Southern Island.

The symbolic messages of the entire museum dedicated to the life of the Buddha and the spread of his message thus center on the conflation of two popularly known texts in visual form, namely the Mahāmuni myth and the passage of the Twin Miracle created by the Buddha upon his return to earth after preaching the Abhidhamma to his mother in Tusita heaven. The cosmogeographic model of the Buddhist world thus culminates in the illumination of the Buddha throughout the universe with the Mahāmuni Pagoda as its axis mundi. The visual impact of the scene is highly evocative and inspiring, combining in its arrangements features of modern geography, national boundaries, pilgrimage sites, and the spread of Buddhism encompassed by a traditional Buddhist cosmology that centers on the site of the Mahāmuni image at the moment when the Buddha performed his most spectacular miracle, the creation of his living twin.

The messages conveyed by these two museums are hardly modified by curatorship or museological concerns for preservation and display. Instead, the many pilgrims who behold these displays faithfully find their expectations matched, if not heightened, by the ethos and beliefs these exhibits articulate. These recent additions to the Mahāmuni complex offer yet another example of a continuing interpretive process of prior texts and further seek to document, in mytho-religious, biographical, and cosmological terms, the place of Mahāmuni, the Buddha's living twin in the modern Burmese world.

Conclusion

The Mahāmuni complex—that is, the image, rituals of veneration, myths, and their narrative allusions to the broader Theravāda textual tradition—functions, in various combinations, as a set of indexical symbols in multiple cultural and religious contexts. Together they evoke the construction, in practice and exegesis, of an ongoing biography of the Buddha in a specific locality, Mandalay. Such interpretation firmly links a remote Southeast Asian periphery to an universal Buddhist cosmography and cosmology. By venerating the Mahāmuni image, Burmese Theravādins incorporate into their lives the living presence of the Buddha in his ritual form. The icon, its rituals, and myths thus become extensions of an open-ended Buddha biography in which Burmese Buddhists continue to participate.

The belief in the efficacy of ritual service and offerings before this image is legitimated in complementary and mutually reinforcing ways that incorporate sociohistorical contexts and religious conceptions within a broader Buddhist framework. The image's veneration by mythic and historic kings provides a link to a pristine past that originated with the Buddha's visit to the local cosmography of Arakan. The ritual also amplifies the field of merit of worshipers who pay their service and obeisance to the Buddha at the Mahāmuni Temple, which further enhances the belief in its extraordinary efficacy. At a social and political level, the Mahāmuni cult locates within a single field of merit all those social and political groups who claim, in some form, its appropriation to their own lives. The veneration of the Mahāmuni image has therefore been the focus of merit-making rituals of various ethnic groups who claimed patronage over it.[81] Its patronage by Burmese kings and the present government not only implied an analogy to its mythological patron, the Arakanese king Candrasuriya, but also serves as a symbol of control over social groups. This fact explains why competition and patronage by polities over possession of this image—and others like it—was, on occasion, intensely contested. In as much as the story of the Twin Miracle is a model for universalizing the dispensation of the Buddha and his "living doubles" in certain cosmic realms, the Mahāmuni image and cult represent a particular, local extension of the Buddha's dispensation among the Burmese. They provide a rationale and motivation for the Theravādin participation in the Buddha's ongoing biography in religious, social, cultural, and historical arenas.

Acknowledgments

Earlier versions of this essay were presented at the Burma Studies Colloquium at Northern Illinois University and at the annual meetings of the American Academy of Religion in San Francisco during the fall of 1992. Richard O'Connor, Stephen Collins, F. K. Lehman, Victor Lieberman, Frank Reynolds, Gregory Schopen, Michael Aung Thwin, and Mark Woodward read earlier drafts. I would like to acknowledge their comments and suggestions, which improved the arguments presented here. All mistakes and omissions are my own.

The Smithsonian Institution, the Wenner-Gren Foundation, the Woodrow Wilson Foundation, the Social Science Research Council, and the faculty grant-in-aid at Arizona State University supported various stages of research and writing on the Mahāmuni complex. I am grateful for the support they provided.

Notes

1. See Mircea Eliade's *The Myth of the Eternal Return or, Cosmos and History*, Bollingen Series no. 46 (Princeton, N.J.: Princeton University Press, 1954, 1974), pp. 49 ff.

2. This topic is also explored in the contributions to this volume by Houtman, Taylor, and McGill. A broader discussion is found in *The Biographical Process: Studies in the History and Psychology of Religion*, edited by Frank E. Reynolds and Donald Capps (The Hague: Mouton, 1976), particularly in the Introduction by the editors and in Reynolds' "The Many Lives of Buddha: A Study of Sacred Biography and Theravāda Tradition." Concerning hagiography in the modern Thai context, see Stanley J. Tambiah's *The Buddhist Saints of the Forest and the Cult of Amulets*, Cambridge Studies in Social Anthropology Cambridge: Cambridge University Press, 1984).
3. Unless otherwise specified, I used the term *icon* to refer to representations of the Buddha either in the form of relics, images, or other artistic modes rather than in its Peircian sense.
4. Tambiah uses the concept of indexical symbols or "shifter" extensively in *The Buddhist Saints of the Forest.* He points to the dual role of indexical symbols that conveys both semantic meanings and pragmatic conventions and argues persuasively that indexical symbols provide an analytical entrée into "the study of text and context, semantics and pragmatics, meaning that refers back to classical constructs and forward to uses in the present" (p. 4).
5. Although an etymological violation, I retain in this discussion the meaning of "Twin Miracle" as referring to the miracle of the Buddha's duplication. Following Alfred Foucher (The Great Miracle at Śrāvastī, in *The Beginnings of Buddhist Art*, L. A. Thomas and F.W. Thomas [trans.], [1914: reprint, Varanasi, 1972], pp. 147-284), Robert Brown (The Śrāvastī Miracles in the Art of India and Dvāravatī, *Archives of Asian Art*, vol. 38, 1984, p. 85) writes that Foucher "decisively argued that the twin miracle is the display of fire and water from the Buddha's body, while also pointing out that as early as 1880 scholars confused it with a miracle described in several Pāli texts, the duplication of the Buddha." Brown also notes that both miracles, i.e. the mixing of fire and water (*yamakapāṭihāriya*) and the creation of a double, occurred in conjunction and suggests that "there could have been confusion among ancient readers of these texts as well." (Ibid.)

   The passage telling the story of the Buddha creating his own double is found, amongst other places, in book 14, story 2 of E.W. Burlingame's translation of the Dhammapada Commentary, entitled, *Buddhist Legends*, 3 vols., Harvard Oriental Series, vol. 30, Pāli Text Society, 1990.
6. Several examples of major cults in the Theravāda world can be cited that center on the veneration of Buddha images or relics. For example: A. M. Hocart's *The Temple of the Tooth in Kandy*, Memoirs of the Archaeological Survey of Ceylon, vol. 4 (London: Luzac and Company for the Government of Ceylon, 1931), provides a descriptive account of the Sri Lankan relic shrine. Kevin Trainor, in his "When Is a Theft Not a Theft? Relic Theft and the Cult of the Buddha's Relics in Sri Lanka" (*Numen*, vol. 39, fasc. 1, pp. 1–26), looks at the fundamental tension the relic cult

poses for the tradition between the desire to possess relics and the doctrine of nonattachment in Buddhist practice. He juxtaposes canonical sources such as the *Mahāparinibbāna Sutta* and the Pāli literature of chronicles (*vaṃsa*) which recount, in mythohistorical fashion, the lineage of local kingdoms and the provenance of relics or images or their movement from one location to another to lend authenticity to new sacred centers of power.

The Thai Emerald Buddha and the myths and rituals associated with it have been discussed by Frank E. Reynolds in his "The Holy Emerald Jewel: Some Aspects of Buddhist Symbolism and Political Legitimation in Thailand and Laos," in *Religion and Legitimation of Power in Thailand, Laos, and Burma*, ed. Blackwell Smith (Chambersburg: Anima Books, 1978), pp. 175–193).

Another famous image, the *Siṇhala* Buddha, is the subject of a chapter on the "likeness" of this image to the original Buddha in Stanley Tambiah's *The Buddhist Saints of the Forest*, pp. 230–242.

7. It is worth noting that the origination myths of both the *Siṇhala* Buddha and the Mahāmuni image share many narrative resemblances. However, as we will see below, the Mahāmuni myth is much more explicit about the Buddha's direct involvement in creating a living double, whereas the myth of the casting of the *Siṇhala* Buddha draws on the miraculous appearance of his relics, which become fused with the image itself.
8. See their article entitled "Buddha" in the *Encyclopedia of Religion*, ed. Mircea Eliade (New York: Macmillan, 1987), vol. 2, p. 327.
9. For example, the Mahāmuni image traveled from Arakan to Upper Burma when it fell under Burmese patronage. Stanley J. Tambiah documents (*The Buddhist Saints of the Forest*, pp. 230–242) the extended travels of the *Siṇhala* image between competing Thai polities, redefining with each move the center of power within these local cosmologies.
10. Reynolds and Hallisey, "Buddha," p. 324.
11. Burmese practices of ritual devotion and personal service to the Buddha are the subject of a forthcoming paper of mine on Burmese devotional lay societies and its relation to the ideal of personal devotion personified by Ānanda. See also John Strong's article on "The Transforming Gift: An Analysis of Devotional Acts of Offering in the Buddhist Avadāna Literature," *History of Religions* 16 (1977), pp. 390–406.
12. See also Tambiah's discussion on image consecration (*The Buddhist Saints of the Forest*, pp. 195–292); Richard Gombrich's "The Consecration of a Buddhist Image," in *Journal of Asian Studies* 26, (1966) pp. 23–36; and Tambiah's article on "The Magical Power of Words," in *Culture, Thought, and Social Action: An Anthropological Perspective* (Cambridge, Mass.: Harvard University Press, 1985), pp. 17–59; and my "Paths to Enlightenment: Theravāda Buddhism in Upper Burma" (Ph.D. thesis, University of Illinois at Urbana, 1989), for a discussion of vows taken before images. For a more general discussion of the role of sacred words, see William Graham's *Beyond the Written Word* (Cambridge: Cambridge University Press, 1987).

13. A similar description of this ritual is found in my "Paths to Enlightenment," where it is discussed as a source of communal merit.
14. A note on the name of the image and its complex is appropriate here. The translation of the colloquial Burmese name (*hpaya: gyi:*, Great Lord) and of the more formal Pāli name, Mahāmuni (Great Sage) denote an appellation of the Buddha. The Burmese term *hpaya:*, or Lord, is also used to refer to the Buddha, to address monks, or in the past, to address nobility or royalty.
15. See Than Tun's *The Royal Orders of Burma A.D. 1598–1885* (Kyoto: Center for Southeast Asian Studies, Kyoto University, 1989), vol. 9, pp. xxvii and xxxiv.
16. The Thudhamma lineage is the largest monastic lineage in Burma.
17. The architecture of this chamber clearly evokes imagery of the Mahāmuni image as placed within a Perfumed Chamber, the Buddha's place of residence in medieval Indian monasteries and other sacred loci across the Buddhist tradition. This issue is taken up again below.
18. These dimensions are taken from Taw Sein Ko's *Archaeological Notes on Mandalay* (Rangoon: Superintendent, Government Printing Press, 1915), p. 18.
19. See Malalasekara's *Dictionary of Pāli Proper Names* (London: Pāli Text Society, 1974), vol. 1, p. 808.
20. The Jambupati style is a common style of crowned images in Burma. The *mudrā* depicted here is well-known among Burmese and described, among other places, in Paul Ambrose Bigandet's *The Life, or Legend, of Gaudama, the Buddha of the Burmese* (London: Trübner, 1880), vol. 1, p. 91, where the Buddha calls on the goddess of the earth to testify to his generosity as King Vessantara. The passage is similarly described in the *Nidānakathā*, the Ceylonese introduction to the *Buddhist Birth Stories*, translated by T.W. Rhys-Davids (London: Trübner and Co., Ludgate Hill, 3rd ed., 1880), vol. 1, p. 101.
21. J. George Scott (in J. George Scott and J.P. Hardiman, *Gazetteer of Upper Burma and the Shan States*, part 1, vol. 2 [Rangoon: Superintendent, Government Printing, 1900], p. 134) describes this ornamentation as one of the official status distinctions assigned to nobility at the Burmese court. He adds that the king wore twenty-four of these strands, the crown prince eighteen, and so on, in descending order. The number of strands also indicated immunity from corresponding types of criminal offenses.
22. Detailed, critical art histories on the iconography and dates of the image have not been compiled. Hence its stylistic features are difficult to date precisely. Its throne, crown, and royal insignia are in the style of the Burmese Konbaung dynasty. It is possible that the face, crown, right hand, and insignia of the image underwent restoration in 1879 and 1884, when fires destroyed the temple. Dating the image is also impeded by the thick and distorting layers of gold leaf that cover its base, torso, and shoulders.

23. Ritual veneration of images similar to the daily Face Washing at the Mahāmuni Temple are also the focus of cultic devotion elsewhere in the Theravāda world, such as veneration of the Tooth relic in Kandy, Sri Lanka, and the Emerald Buddha in Thailand.

24. This arrangement displayed on many Burmese altars is called a *gado.pwe:*, which translates as "asking pardon for wrong doings committed." Characteristically, it contains a green coconut with a braided stem and a bunch of bananas. It is traditionally presented to the Buddha and others of high status.

25. The reason for this fact lies in the special supplications women often seek when making offerings to this image. As some of these women have told me, through this offerings they seek to gain the protection of the image—or of the Buddha—to aid their physical and spiritual ailments, including infertility, and the health of their children. Ill people, particularly children, are made to eat the food offered to the image and thus imbibe its power.

26. The text of this prayer is found in Pe Maung Tin's *Buddhist Devotion and Meditation: An Objective Description and Study* (London: S.P.C.K., 1964).

27. The name of this sutta means "loving kindness." It is translated by R.C. Childers in his "Khuddakapāṭha," *Journal of the Royal Asiatic Society* (1870), p. 309ff. See also Melford Spiro's discussion of this sutta in his *Buddhism and Society: A Great Tradition and Its Burmese Vicissitudes* (New York: Harper, 1980), pp. 269–270.

28. The opening of the image's eyes plays a symbolic role not only in rituals concerned with the pure beginning of a new day, but also marks the "coming of life" of an image during consecration.

29. Gregory Schopen has recently argued that the Buddha was considered an owner of property in the organizational context of medieval Indian monasteries where donations made to him were to be used for the upkeep and rituals of the Perfumed Chamber (see his article on this subject in the *Journal of Indian Philosophy* 18 [1990], pp. 181–217). I return to these and related issues below.

30. Emil Forchhammer in his *Report on the Antiquities of Arakan* (Rangoon: Superintendent, Government Printing, 1892), pp. 2–14, and San Tha Aung's *The Buddhist Art of Ancient Arakan* (Rangoon, 1979), p. 113, recount essentially identical versions of the Mahāmuni myth. Both versions appear to be based on the *Mahāmuni Thamein:*, a history of the Mahāmuni Temple in Arakan for which no date is given, and on an Arakanese palm leaf manuscript entitled *Sappadānapakarana* and dating to the sixteenth century.

31. In his *History of Burma* ([London: Frank Cass, 1967], pp. 303 and 369), G. E. Harvey places Candrasuriya's reign during the second half of the second century C.E. However, this chronology is mostly derived from local texts and largely mythological in character.

32. See Forchhammer, *Report on the Antiquities of Arakan*, p. 5.

33. Ibid., p. 6.

34. This site north of Amarapura is the same site that now houses the Arakanese image in Mandalay. Bodawpaya's original choice was to build a shrine in a remote area at some distance from his capital. The location of the newly constructed Mahāmuni Shrine became integrated into populated areas only after Mindon moved this palace in 1858 to what is now Mandalay. Today it is incorporated in a central part of Mandalay.
35. W.S. Desai, *A Pageant of Burmese History* (India: Orient Longmans, 1961), p. 99.
36. Forchhammer, *Report on the Antiquities of Arakan*, p. 7.
37. The dispute over the mode of transport has direct implications concerning the authenticity of the image now housed in Mandalay or the sacrilegious dismembering it may have undergone in the process. The issue remains a matter of debate and speculation reflected in the writings of earlier historians such as Harvey, *History of Burma*; Scott, *Gazetteer of Upper Burma and the Shan States*; and Desai, *A Pageant of Burmese History*. Contemporary discussions of this issue among Burmese and Western historians continue to be inconclusive.
38. See Arthur P. Phayre's *History of Burma* (London: Susil Gupta, 1883; reprint 1967), p. 215; and Harvey, *History of Burma*, p. 303.
39. See p. 214, n. 81, by D.G.E. Hall who edited Michael Symes' *Journal of His Second Embassy to the Court of Ava in 1802* (London: Allen and Unwin, 1955).
40. Both Harvey, *History of Burma* p. 156; and Shway Yoe in *The Burman, His Life and Notions* (New York: W. W. Norton, 1882; reprint 1963), p. 170, report that the number of pagoda slaves was regularly increased.
41. See Harvey, *History of Burma*, p. 156.
42. Both of these sacred shrines are popularly venerated. The former is located in Rangoon and believed to house the Buddha's hair relic, while the latter, located in Mingun, Upper Burma, houses a footprint of the Buddha.
43. See Shway Yoe, *The Burman, His Life and Notions*, p. 170.
44. With this Burmese term, Shway Yoe refers to a spire that is a traditional feature of Burmese religious architecture.
45. Tun, *The Royal Orders of Burma*, vol. 9, p. xxxiv.
46. The myth recounted here follows Forchhammer's (*Report on the Antiquities of Arakan* p. 2ff.) rendering of it found in the Arakanese manuscript *Sappadānapakarana*, also mentioned in San Tha Aung's monograph (*The Buddhist Art of Ancient Arakan*). In the course of ethnographic fieldwork, I collected a number of versions identical with the one recounted here and in Schober, "Paths to Enlightenment."
47. Vissakamma is known as Sakka's superb craftsman and architect, who has built hermitages for the future Buddha during previous lives. He also plays a similar role in the creation of Thai and Sinhalese images cast in the Buddha's likeness.

48. Forchhammer, *Report on the Antiquities of Arakan*, p. 4. The term *pra-s* is a nonstandard spelling of *hpaya:*, the Burmese word for "lord," which designates both religious and worldly rulers such as Buddhas and kings.

49. Forchhammer (ibid., pp. 4, 5) adds that this prophecy is believed to have been realized as the image was damaged extensively on several occasions. The passage also offers an explication as to why ill fortune happens even to the Buddha.

50. The name *Caṇḍasāra* translates as "the part (of the whole) that is uncontrolled or passionate," meaning that the image was indeed a part of the Buddha's physical existence, albeit the part that had to suffer the karmic consequences of the Buddha's passionate deeds in former lives, as noted below.

51. The miracles are enumerated in Forchhammer, *Report on the Antiquities of Arakan*, p. 5.

52. See the introductions to *Sarabhamiga Jātaka*, no. 483, and *Vessantara Jātaka*, no. 547, in *The Jātaka or Stories of the Buddha's Former Births*, ed. by E. B. Cowell (London: Luzac and Company for the Pāli Text Society, 1957).

53. See references to the Twin Miracle in stanza 349–321; to the Buddha's preaching of the Abhidhamma in 350–353; and to the descent to earth of Buddha and attendant deities in 350–354 of I. B. Horner's translation, entitled *Milinda's Questions* (London: Luzac and Company, 1969).

54. See book 14, story 2 in E. W. Burlingame's *Buddhist Legends*. Burlingame (p. 57ff.) dates the *Dhammapada Commentary* to 450 A.D., arguing that it postdates the composition of the *jātakas*. Although Buddhaghosa is often associated with this texts as its translator from ancient Sinhalese back into Pāli, John Ross Carter and Mahinda Palihawadana concur in the introduction of their translation of the *Dhammapada* [Oxford: Oxford University Press, 1987], p. 4) that the identity of the translator of the commentary on the *Dhammapada* remains a mystery. The text is not strictly a commentary on the *Dhammapada*, but rather expands the *Dhammapada* and becomes itself a "huge collection of legends and folk-tales" (Burlingame, part 1, p. 26). In Burlingame's view, the author or redactor modeled the *Dhammapada Commentary* after the *jātakas*, as evidenced by similarities in the narrative structures.

55. Burmese referred to this text repeatedly in interviews. Its salience in Burma and elsewhere in the Theravāda world is attested by various translations of the Pāli version into local languages, including Burmese. In translating this text, Burlingame also relied on a Burmese rendition of this text.

56. See Burlingame, *Buddhist Legends*, part 3, p. 51.

57. Other textual examples, such as the *Mahāparinibbāna Sutta*, speak to this theme as well.

58. See Reynolds and Hallisey, "Buddha," vol. 2, p. 325.

59. See also Reynolds' and Hudak's essays in this volume for discussions on the structural forms of biographical narratives in the *jātaka* tradition.

60. See, for instance, the concluding comments of the last ten birth-stories, where the Buddha identifies himself and others in that particular life.

61. Spiro includes a discussion of pagoda festivals in his *Buddhism and Society*; pp. 229–231; and Schober "Paths to Enlightenment," pp. 159–177.

62. Cited from Horner's introduction to the translation of the *Milinda's Questions*, p. xxxi; see also pp. xxvii, xxxi, and xxxii and stanzas 172ff. Concerning the cultic veneration of *arhats* and miracles associated with places containing relics (see Mil. 309), she concludes that "(w)onders of this particular nature are unknown to the Pāli Canon, I believe" (p. xxxii).

63. See Steven Collins' excellent treatment of the historical developments in the canonization of the Pāli canon and its political and symbolic implications in his "On the Very Idea of the Pāli Canon," *Journal of the Pāli Text Society* 15 (1990), pp. 89–126. There, he analyzes the role of the Mahāvihāra lineage in Sri Lanka in formulating a written Pāli canon in a context marked by tensions between the politics of royal patronage and religious differentiation from competing monastic lineages and their interpretations of doctrine. The transmission of some form of this redaction of the Pāli canon to Southeast Asia, where it underwent further transformations, is well established.

64. For a discussion on the role of images in the commentarial literature, see Walpola Rahula's *History of Buddhism in Ceylon* (Colombo: M. D. Gunasena, pp. 121ff.), and also Steven Collins' references to image houses mentioned in the commentarial literature in his "Nirvāṇa, Time and Narrative," *History of Religions* (1992), pp. 215–246, esp. n. 47). The veneration of relics in Sri Lankan chronicles has been analyzed by Kevin Trainor in an article published in *Numen* cited above and in his "The Relics of the Buddha: A Study of the Cult of Relic Veneration in the Theravāda Buddhist Tradition of Sri Lanka" (Ph.D. diss., Columbia University, 1990).

65. See P. Bigandet's *The Life, or Legend, of Gaudama, the Buddha of the Burmese* (London: Trübner, 1880), vol. 2, pp. 88ff., where Mahākassapa experiences this miracle of the Buddha's *rūpakāya*.

66. In the introduction to the *Vessantara Jātaka* (Cowell, *The Jātaka or Stories of the Buddha's Former Births*, vol. 6, no. 547, pp. 246ff.), the Buddha creates an apparition of himself to convince his relatives, members of the Sakyā clan, who were reticent to pay homage to him. Amazed at his miracles, they paid homage to the Buddha, who proceeds to tell them the story of Vessantara.

67. See I. B. Horner's translation (*Milinda's Questions*, vol. 1, pp. 249–254, stanzas 177–179) on the veneration of relics. Milinda raised with Nāgasena the seeming paradox of the Buddha's injunction against Ānanda's worship of his relics and his encouragement for gods and mankind to venerate his relics. Nāgasena explains that the injunction against worshiping his body was intended to encourage monks to work toward those goals that

represent work commensurate with the abilities of a monk. In Nāgasena's view, that excludes worship of the living Buddha's body, but entails veneration to his relics.

68. See Gregory Schopen's article "Stūpa Cult and the Extant Pāli Vinaya," *Journal of the Pāli Text Society* 13, pp. 83–100.
69. Collins, "Nirvāṇa, Time and Narrative," pp. 236–237.
70. See Gregory Schopen, "The Buddha as Owner of Property and Permanent Resident in Medieval Indian Monasteries," *Journal of Indian Philosophy* 18 (1990), pp. 181–217.
71. Ibid., p. 193, text in brackets added.
72. Ibid., p. 196.
73. I am paraphrasing here Schopen's more detailed argument, ibid., p. 203.
74. See John Strong, "*Gandhakuṭī*: The Perfumed Chamber of the Buddha," *History of Religions* 16 (1977), pp. 390–406, where he traces the veneration of the Buddha in his Perfumed Chamber through both Pāli and Mahāyāna sources, including Pure Land.
75. Ibid., p. 406.
76. See Schober, "Paths to Enlightenment," for an analysis of offerings to Buddha images in the Burmese context. For a more broadly conceived, but analogous examination of offerings presented, see again Strong's "The Transforming Gift," pp. 221–237.
77. See Schober, "Paths to Enlightenment."
78. For a comparison of the consecration of Buddha images in the Theravāda world, see Richard Gombrich's "The Consecration of a Buddhist Image" for a Sinhalese example; Schober, "Paths to Enlightenment" (pp. 36ff.) for Burma; and Donald Swearer's "Hypostasizing the Buddha: Image Consecration in Northern Thailand," a paper presented at the annual meeting of the American Academy of Religion, San Francisco, 1992.
79. For an analysis of the ritual power of monastic chanting, see Tambiah's "The Magical Power of Words."
80. For a discussion on the Buddha's bodies, see Frank E. Reynolds, "The Several Bodies of Buddha, Reflections on a Neglected Aspect of Theravāda Buddhism," *History of Religions* 16 (1977), pp. 374–389; and also Paul Mus' discussion of *dhammakāya* and *rūpakāya* as Theravāda conceptions in his "Le Buddha Paré," *Bulletin de l'École française d'Extrême-Orient* 28 (1928), pp. 153–278.
81. The image continues to be sought out by ethnic minorities that reside at considerable distance from Mandalay. For instance, I observed an extended Shan family who went on a pilgrimage to the Mahāmuni image in Mandalay in order to initiate there several young boys into novicehood. I learned that this was an annual event in which Shans from all parts of Burma participated. Their explanation for arranging for the ritual performance there, rather than in their home town, rested on their claims of descent from Shan royalty and the belief that it behooved royalty to conduct initiation rituals only in this manner.

The Textualization of a Monastic Tradition: Forest Monks, Lineage, and the Biographical Process in Thailand

James L. Taylor

This essay examines the prolific life accounts of the ethnic Lao Buddhist "saints" (*arhat*) in Thailand since the beginning of the 1970s. Significant biographies in this tradition centered around the lineage of a widely acclaimed religious virtuoso of modern times, Ajaan[1] Man Phuurithatto (1870–1949).[2] Many of Man's early wandering ascetic disciples spent most of their lives on the fringe of the nation-state, and they eventually became famous after they settled and were integrated into the tightly regulated religious establishment.

In the course of anthropological fieldwork, informants in isolated northeastern Thai villages would relate tales of wandering eremites who founded monasteries in nearby forests that are no longer extant. It is not only the charisma of the spiritual leader that is recognised and becomes routinized[3] or domesticated, but also direct pupillages claiming the founding master, or his first disciples, as monastic teachers. These lineage monks are featured in biographies, commemorative texts, and monastery histories as founders and agents of monastic reform. They were forest-dwellers, popularly considered as saints (*arhat*). Their monasteries became the focus of relic cults and their mass popularity in the late 1960s engendered in the following decade a new genre of hagiographical writing in Thailand.

Local Legends and Biographical Modes in the Theravāda Tradition

In general, autobiographies and biographies can shed light on the underlying social and cultural historical processes. This can also be claimed for the life accounts of Ajaan Man and his forest monk disciples. In particular, I consider Ajaan Man's biography a landmark or *leitmotiv* in modern Buddhist hagiography that gave renewed respectability to mystical practices and beliefs in Theravāda Buddhism in Thailand.

Prior to Ajaan Man, popular religious texts fell into two categories: the erudite commentaries on standard Pāli texts and fantastic thaumaturgical tales of mystical experiences. Man's biography encompassed both of these dimensions and spawned a new class of popular religious literature, such as the many magazines on mystic monks and practice. Subsequently, supernatural phenomena gained renewed respectability and was given credence by converted, literate skeptics in the metropolis. The life stories of meditating monks became the fashionable subject of many professional writers in a new literary genre. Even if fantastic meditation experiences, encounters with wild animals, and discourse with celestial beings did not actually occur, writers used their imagination to produce the many popular so-called venerable father (*Luang Phor*) publications mentioned above.

Man's main biographers, Ariyakhunaathaan, Wiriyang,[4] and Mahaa Bua, were his disciples. They were largely responsible for developing Man's national reputation. These monk-biographers had been close to their master at various junctures in his life and enjoyed privileged access to his introverted, personalized modes of teaching and living. Since Man's early biography appeared in 1971, biographical texts on the master's first disciples also proliferated in the following years, many of them published in limited editions of cremation volumes. This is not unusual as a great deal of extant and nonextant Thai historical literature appears in limited editions and is published and distributed on the occasion of a famous person's cremation.[5]

These biographies share common biographical patterns, such as early visionary experiences in meditation or symbolic revelations in dreams that vindicate legitimacy in the master's line. Man reputedly received his *dhamma* instruction directly from the Buddha's first disciples, as in the instance when these saints shared with him their knowledge on "walking meditation" during a meditation-vision (*samaathi-nimit*).[6]

These life accounts typically commence as oral legend in the local idiom like tales of incredible, mystical feats, encounters with potentially dangerous spirits, wild animals, roving bands of forest monks encamped in cemeteries away from human habitation, surviving malarial fevers, or extensive fasting in the forest. Such tales are told about wandering forest monks initially by the master's own disciples and in isolated village communities. Eventually, they take on homiletic guises and are transposed into written biographies that are nurtured in the capital with a great degree of definity about the subject's extraordinary accomplishments. From humble origins, local oral accounts become national hagiographies that are reworked and, in many cases, rewritten in the central Thai idiom.

For the anthropologist, autobiographical accounts are only beginning to be appreciated as a counterpoint to ethnography and as a means of merging real life experiences with the writer's own vision.[7] They have, as one writer said, a "commitment to the actual."[8] In a wider sense, they expose the underlying structure of tradition, or provide insight into an experiential enactment "predicated on a moral vision, on a vibrant relation between a sense of self and a community."[9] Langness[10] earlier bemoaned the fact that "life histories" had not been considered sufficiently by anthropologists and that immense possibilities for gaining insight into the individual actor and his community remained latent and unexploited.

In the case of the northeastern forest monks, written life accounts show the interplay between an individual and the micro social dimensions of his monastic community, on the one hand, and the wider social milieu of state elites, urban-dwelling monks, villagers, and local patrons on the other. Biographies also reveal something about the narrator, or interlocutor, the "saint" as subject, and about the place the writer claims for himself in the enactment of textualized tradition.

Life accounts[11] of forest monks permeate a sense of connectedness with an indeterminate, allegorized, and pristine past. Associations between the segmental monastic community that transmits the tradition through identified pupillages and modern forest monks are enhanced in local oral tradition until finally textualized. Forest monks, who are conceived to be soteriologically and doctrinally normative, live and are expected to live in conformity with classical hagiographical themes and, thus, become the very stuff of local legend.[12] In effect, a self-conscious patterning or replication of normative themes from the Buddha's life, is expressed in popular tales.[13] This trend represents a homespun, but veracious universal product in which the *jātakas* take on contextualized form. This well-known process of localizing a textual tradition is encountered in the Lao version of the Ramayana, where classical Indic heroes are adapted to conditions in and around the Maekhong region,[14] and in the popular Thai-ized *Ramakien*. Paul Mus[15] noted a similar parochial adaptation in Cham literature.

In regard to the principal biography on Man, well-known Thai texts such as the *Pathamasambodhikatha* written by the prince-monk Paramaanuchit-chinorot (1790–1853)[16] and the later *Phutthaprawat* (P.: *Buddhapavatti*), written by another prince-monk Wachirayaan (1859–1921)[17] may have been conscious or unconscious sources of inspiration for the narrator, named Ajaan Mahaa Bua Yaanasampanno. Both texts are used in the national ecclesiastical *dhamma* courses (*nak tham*) with which Mahaa Bua would have been familiar, having spent the first seven years of his monastic career as a scholar (*pariyat*) monk. The former work is a series of sermons intended for ritual recitation at events such as the *Wisaakha Buuchaa*, which are held all night in commemoration of the Buddha's birth, enlightenment, and decease. It represents a Thai version of the standard biography of the Buddha, which is based on canonical and Sinhalese commentarial works and written in ornate prose style.[18] Paramaanuchit-chinorot also wrote the *Sunthornkosaa* based on an old Ayutthayaa version. Wachirayaan's *Phutthaprawat* is written in brief, critical prose instead of colorful homilies, and from the perspective of nineteenth-century rationalism. It compares different life accounts, evaluates their reliability, and refutes any references to the supernatural. Wachirayaan is also the author of a straightforward biography of one of the Buddha's disciples (*arhat*).

Mahaa Bua, without citing specific Buddhist texts, offers a partial answer to likely sources of his inspiration in the introduction to Man's biography. There he states that "the method of presentation . . . follows that of the ancient compilers [*keji-aajaan*] who recorded the hagiographies of some of the Noble Disciples in various texts."[19] In several recorded sermons, Mahaa Bua claimed that the inspiration in his departure to the forest to practice came from reading biographies of the Buddha and his early disciples, from his empathy for the hardships encountered by the *arhats*, and from his desire to reach the same spiritual level. In other words, we learn that the "text informed experience"[20] and provided a motivation for religious practice in the context of everyday life. By writing the biography of his teacher, Mahaa Bua wanted to provide others with an inspiration similar to his own that developed from reading textual accounts of the Buddha and his *arhat* disciples. The structure of Mahaa Bua's version of Man's biography is patterned after the Buddha's renunciation and quest for salvation. It also reflects the narrator's purpose to stress the inspirational, especially in showing that, context aside, Man's life followed a path universal Buddhist saints had traversed in previous lives. Essentially, forest monks insist that

ractice and pattern of personal salvation quest preceded the hagiographi-
l writing. Mahaa Bua stresses this point in his own sermons; the "ways of
ie heart" form the basis for the *dhamma* and parables in the texts, not the
ther way around.

Classical events may not be replicated identically in changing historic
ontexts, for, as Keyes[21] commented, even consciously faithful imitations of
ie pristine model cannot be the same. The biographer then has to show
iat, external conditions aside, the "underlying structure of life is that
und in the path of the Buddha."[22] Regardless of diachronic vistas, the
nderlying biographical pattern remains basically unchanged.[23]

In examining Man's biography, Tambiah[24] referred to a theoretical
ndexical symbol" to make sense of its "duplex" feature. This dual feature
dicates, on the one hand, the semantic level or underlying meanings of
ilturally conditioned assumptions and conventional understandings and,
n the other hand, in a pragmatic sense, "the social and interpersonal con-
xt of action, the line-up of the participants, and the processes by which
ey establish or infer meanings."[25]

Tambiah's use of "indexical symbol" thus allows us to understand
mbolic and structural meanings as well as what he calls "indexical exis-
ntial, and pragmatic meanings" that, together, constitute a totality of
eaning.[26] Man's life story then becomes "symbolically and semantically
lated to the classical conventional hagiographies of the Buddha and
emplary Buddhist saints." Yet, as Tambiah continues, the "composition
f the text] is indexically and pragmatically related to the purpose and
jectives of the disciple-author [Ajaan Mahaa Bua Yaanasampanno, Wat
a Baan Taat, Udornthaanii Province, Northeast Thailand], the context
which he composed it, and its distribution to and reception by the pub-
."[27] However, the underlying motives of the disciple-author, apart
om lineage affiliations, are not made explicit. Kris[28] states that in the
insmission of the "model" biography, its reception depends largely on
cial and political circumstances, which blur the boundary between the
dividual and tradition. This perspective may account for the popularity
this hagiographical genre and of charismatic forest monks and urban
iddhist cults in the early 1970s, which was a period of internal and
ternal political crisis.[29]

A significant departure in Man's biography from its literary predeces-
rs must be noted here. While the latter generally conclude with the dis-
bution of the Buddha's relics, Man's life account ends with a final
mpelling homily. Thus his biography was not constructed solely to
gender respect and reveration for Man—which, clearly, it did. In addi-
n, it also offers discursive pedagogic and performative insights that
courage the reader to apply *dhamma* to meditation practice (*patibatthham*).

Man and His Biographer: The Legitimation of Text and Lineage

Mahaa Bua is today regarded as the patriarch of the forest tradition—strict, direct, and occasionally unpredictable teacher who continues maintain control over his monastic disciples. After years of trying to inte view the now aging teacher, I was only permitted to exchange a few word Mahaa Bua, like many forest-dwellers, is emblematic of the classic renu ciant, lives a largely reclusive life-style, and remains disinclined to comme much, unless on matters of *dhamma*. My dilemma as an anthropologist w the foreboding sense of intrusion and likely social disequilibrium caused my temporary presence. I had to find a balance between being unobtrusiv and sensitive, yet with critical discernment necessary for the fieldwork. I way of compromise, I spent considerable time with Mahaa Bua's senior di ciples, past and present.

Despite his poor health, Mahaa Bua's reflexes, responses, and acute perceptive faculties are those of a man less than half his age. His attainmen are beyond doubt by those close to him. Although a guarded discretion maintained among Mahaa Bua's close disciples, it is believed that became a saint (*arhat*) nine years after he commenced his practice and si teen years after his monastic ordination.

Since Man's biography first appeared in 1971[30] Mahaa Bua has situat himself as the focus of national attention and simultaneously as the centr figure in the northeastern forest tradition. His sermons legitimate his pos tion of claiming textual authority through interwoven discourse, includi apologues and interspersed verbatim with the master's voice, so that one never really sure whether it is Mahaa Bua or the interlocutor (Ma homilizing. This intertextured synergic characteristic is, in fact, a comm feature of biographies written by disciples of the master. In Man's biogr phy, obvious allusions are made to the writer having a close affinity with h teacher since their first meeting, when Mahaa Bua felt "a great feeling trust and admiration."[31] From Mahaa Bua's perspective, he had encou tered a unique monk who was intent on following the normative doctri path of orthopraxy, and thus sought to revive pristine "saintly" ideals.

An early visionary experience makes explicit to the reader his priv leged relationship with the master, although in fact this appears to be tr only of the later years, that is, from 1940 onwards. In his biography Man, Mahaa Bua relates a vision in which he wandered through a den forest and came across a fallen clump of bamboo obstructing his passage. H managed to crawl through a small opening by taking off his outer robe a pulling it, his bowl and meditation umbrella (*klot*) behind him. He th came out into an open space facing the ocean. He noticed an island in t ar distance and decided to take a boat out to it. When he arrived, he ncountered Man, sitting pounding betel nut. Man inquired how he had nanaged to get through the thicket, as the trail was very arduous and no ne besides himself had dared come that way. Mahaa Bua was then handed he pestle and continued to pound betel nut for his master until Mahaa Bua woke. After this dream, Mahaa Bua went to his teacher for explanation. He was told that it showed his determination to persevere in the practice, and that although the path is difficult, he should not succumb to the tasks ahead.

Persistence and endurance are integral themes in the discourse of contemporary forest monks. Man's *arhat* disciple Ajaan Khao Anaalayo is reported to have once said: "If we practice *Dhamma* consistently and relentlessly, the fruit of the *arahan* [arhat] path must follow."[32] Man further told Mahaa Bua that the beginning is usually more arduous than the final stage of the path, but with persistence, he would eventually arrive on the island, which was an allusion to *nibbāna*.[33] Forest monks often metaphorically refer to a schematization of four normative paths (*mak*; P. *magga*), four "fruitions" (*phon*; P. *phala*), and the ultimate enlightenment.

In Mahaa Bua's version of Man's biography, the master predicted that he would have only two "faithful" followers capable of attaining sainthood. Mahaa Bua reputedly said that, looking around, he did not see likely candidates. Yet some informants suggested that Mahaa Bua's dream indicated that he is one of the two selected exemplary disciples. Nevertheless, popular *arhat* acclaim has been widely accorded many of Man's early disciples, most of whom are now deceased. Moreover, those Thai-Lao forest monks about whom there are no extant texts are now all but forgotten. Another account mentioned that prior to his death Man nominated four monks to succeed him and related the names to a senior, scholar monk and friend from northeast Thailand, Phra Thammajedii "Mahaa Juum" from Wat Phothisomphon in Udornthaanii province. The four monks are said to be Ajaans Khao, Fan, Bua, and Mahaa Bua. Only the latter is still alive and his leadership position largely taken for granted.

Mahaa Bua, to whom his by now numerous dispersed disciples refer as "Than Ajaan Yai," the senior teacher, is an important figure in the perpetuation of Man's forest tradition. Had it not been for his conscious, unremitting intent to keep the memory and teachings of Man alive through ritual enactment and repetitive discourse, little of the master would be remembered today. In fact, Mahaa Bua's own disciples recite tales of Man from their teacher's sermons or from the biography of Man written by Mahaa Bua. Tales about the master tend to be reworked from the same material, passed around in discourse, and used for instructional purposes, although each episode displays its own individual traits.

Written life accounts as "narrative art" entail a transformation from ora to written text, which constitutes a complex and "charged" process of cod- ification. Clifford writes that "one source of the peculiar authority . . . find both rescue and irretrievable loss—a kind of death in life—in the makin of texts from events and dialogues. Words and deeds are transient (anc authentic), writing endures (as supplementarity and artifice). The text embalms the event as it extends its 'meaning'."[34]

This is exemplified in my own field experience with forest monks, when during the interviews I assumed that some of my informants were offering information on Man's life from firsthand knowledge. After some time, I found that many stories were founded in the "authority" of Mahaa Bua's widely read biography.[35] The text had itself taken on independent life. While there are exceptions, this process suggests that with the passage of time and the passing away of informants able to relate cognizant oral accounts from firsthand experience, the creative movement of material from oral performance to descriptive text disappears. Instead, as Clifford said, a new kind of creativity emerges in which "cultural data" progresses from "text to text" and "inscription becomes transcription."[36]

Mahaa Bua's primary aim in textualizing Man's life and the ascetic tradition he revivified in the stream of the early twentieth-century Thammayut[37] reforms was his stated desire to keep alive the legacy of Man and his forest way of life. In the preface to the text, Mahaa Bua states that he relied on information from diverse sources in addition to his own memory and that, therefore, details may be imperfect. But Mahaa Bua felt the urgency to proceed with his biographical writing and thought that, in time, significant details "fade from the memories of his [Man's] contemporary disciples."[38] Mahaa Bua's sense of urgency is expressed in his statement that had he not written this account, future generations would be deprived of the benefits of learning from Man's exceptional experience and practice. Kris[39] argues that life accounts are an effective means for transmitting the life pattern of an "exemplar type" to successive generations. Man's life practice has become a compelling example that shapes the self-conceptions and lives of his disciples. According to Mahaa Bua's disciples, the teacher, concious of his central role, fears that the forest tradition may not survive his own decease. It is also plausible that one of Mahaa Bua's close disciples may then write an account of his teacher, and so maintain the biographical process.

At another discursive level, the frequent references to the pristine normative tradition in Mahaa Bua's biography of Man links the master to an exclusive mythic lineage of saints (*arhat*) that commenced during the Buddha's lifetime. The elaboration and parochialization of pristine mythic paradigms in the biographical accounts has two functions. First, it enables the person recounting the story, in this case the author, to provide mythic sanction to the text and to his own personal creativity. Second, the local reader is reassured "that the religious truths recounted had become manifest among themselves, and not in faraway places."[40]

This cultural grafting of local onto universal tradition legitimates the lineage that links Indic, Sinhalese, and Thai traditions into a "seamless cloth" from the time of the Buddha to the present day.[41] Another example of this process is recounted in the biography of yet another of Man's acclaimed *arhat* disciples, Ajaan Khao Aanaalayo, who died in 1983. According to this account, the monk was visited by Mahaa Kassapa Thera, a disciple of the Buddha who excelled in forest practice. It is revealing that Mahaa Bua also authored Khao's biography at the request of the cremation committee, which comprised senior reformist Thammayut administrative monks and some of Man's disciples.[42]

Mahaa Kassapa represents the ideal practice of forest monks in the Theravāda tradition. He was reputed to be the only monk to be so privileged as to exchange with the Buddha his rag-robes, which are the mark of a forest-dweller. This act of exchange constitutes the Buddha's endorsement of forest-dwelling meditative life and legitimized Mahaa Kassapa's ascetic practices (*dhutanga*) as a normative part of the teachings (*dhamma*). In fact, he assumed leadership of the *sangha* after the Buddha's decease.[43] The Buddha once questioned Mahaa Kassapa about his reasons for living a reclusive eremitic life. Mahaa Kassapa replied that it was for his own well-being and that of future generations "which when learning about such a life, would emulate it."[44] The Buddha was said to be pleased with this response and, at a time when the *sangha* was becoming increasingly settled, gave approval to continue living in seclusion.[45]

Man would have been familiar with this tale. He, too, is believed to have been a disciple of the Buddha in a former life. Some informants said that although Man could not attain sainthood at that time, he made a prophetic wish to return when religion was in decline. Thus, they said, Man knew the pristine, monastic code of conduct (*vinaya*) and the forest practices espoused by the Buddha. This shows how the historical particularities of the *Dhamma-Vinaya* as a product of the nineteenth-century Siamese reforms and of the universal tradition became intertwined.

Mahaa Bua has written many published texts, including sermons interposed with personal experiences as apologue, or tales from the master's life that are now distinctive of Mahaa Bua's personal style. In this way, the narrator's name itself assumes a classificatory function[46] that helps to mobilize and control discourse for specific purposes.[47] Mahaa Bua's statements on Man's life and teachings are discourse markers transfused into the text that the reader perceives as statements of fact or truth. In writing about his teacher, Mahaa Bua places himself firmly in the narrative and becomes an inseparable part of the whole. Thus author and work become mutually defining. Moreover, by documenting the little-known life of his teacher, Mahaa Bua has situated himself as the rightful heir to his teacher's lineage, which was left ramified and dislocated after Man's decease.

Biographers are privileged in having direct access to their subjects and other primary sources of information. Mahaa Bua has implied that his privileged access to the master, during the last nine years of Man's life, uniquely qualified him to write Man's life story. This close spiritual association between Man and Mahaa Bua is reflected in the cosmological layout of the forest hermitage (*samnak*) where Man spent the last five years of his life. This hermitage was located on the outskirts of Baan Norng Pheur, a village in an isolated part of the Phuuphaan mountain range in Sakon Nakhorn province. Typical of all forest monasteries, the layout consists basically of individual meditation huts (*kuti*) dispersed in the forest. This pattern has not changed over the past forty years. Mahaa Bua's *kuti* was located closest to Man's former dwelling. Radiating in *mandala* fashion outwards from the master's hut, which was the sacred center of the monastery, are now largely abandoned, dilapidated dwellings that once were occupied by monks of lesser discursive importance, the novices and, at the impure outer periphery, those of the female ascetics section (*khana mae chii*).

Significant shared features emerge from contrasting Man's biography with Sinhalese compositions such as the nineteenth-century Sinhalese forest-dweller Paññananda that Carrithers analyzes in some detail.[48] Paññananda, active from 1850 until his death in 1887, was described by Malalgoda[49] as a source of inspiration for many forest monks. Today, both Man and Paññananda are seen as typifying the canonical norm of ascetic practice. Keyes[50] observes that the importance of Mahaa Bua's biography of Man is the demonstration that Man was without doubt a saint (*arhat*) and that "his life contains a supreme example which can be emulated by others, including the biographer himself."

The life stories of Man and Paññananda are full of homiletic references to other Buddhist legends, and they set precedents in both Theravāda countries for later biographies of eremitic recluse monks. Beneath the embroidered narratives of Man and Paññananda, we see two determined world renouncers intent on living in conformity with doctrinal tradition. Both accounts contain a similar rejection of domesticated religion and its accretions. Also, both accounts are set against a backdrop of national monastic reforms. Both monks became embodiments of universal tradition, while retaining particularized cultural forms. Each engendered his own distinctive lineage of disciples who, in turn, influenced national religion.

One of the implicit, discursive aims of hagiographies written by disciples about their master is to establish a succession order or lineage within the conventional authority structure of the monastic order (*bhikkhu sangha*). A means of achieving this is by showing that the author-disciple had a close and immutable relationship with his master and, in a sense, access to privileged knowledge. Stories about their shared encounters with wild animals, the underworld, or heavenly beings reinforce the close, dyadic relationship between the teacher and his disciple during the course of their ascetic wandering. Both teacher and disciple experience similar visions and the latter's are cast clearly in the mold of the former.

Recurrent Features and the Biographical Process in Man's Lineage

In the course of research, I examined oral histories, biographies by often unknown authors whom in many cases I presume to be senior disciples of the master, monastery histories that offer accounts of the founding forest monk, and autobiographies. All of these sources pertain to the lives of Thailand's northeastern forest monks in the lineage of Phra Ajaan Man, which is ethnically Lao. Where possible, these texts were cross-checked with oral accounts from forest-dwelling monks and elderly lay informants to identify consistency and divergence. However, this process of verification was complicated by the fact that some informants tended to seek confirmation in the textual accounts. In general, oral accounts take on creative accretions and diverge from the textual accounts. In the process of comparing oral and written accounts, these discrepencies—where identified in the transmission—had to be considered in the total formulation of the biographical tradition of forest monks.

In the written and oral life accounts, certain distinctive biographical patterns and consistent, analogous themes emerged: (1) The subject expressed dissatisfaction with monastic life in the pervasive Mahaanikaai, the largest of the two Thai orders that comprise all monks who are not ordained in the smaller reformist Thammayut sect, or with scholastic (*pariyat*) pursuits through the Thammayut Nikaai; (2) The narrator usually had an impressionable meeting with wandering pupils of the meditation master Ajaan Man, or with the master himself, who stayed temporarily near the narrator's residence; this was often followed by ascetic wandering under the guidance of either Man or his senior pupils; (3) With some exceptions, the narrator was reordained in the Thammayut sect some two or three years after the initial meeting so that he could participate in the now important formal acts or ceremonies of the *sangha* performed by high-ranking northeastern monks (P. *Sanghakamma*); (4) The narrator experienced an early vision, sign, or mental image (P. *nimitta*) during meditation, or dream symbolism, confirming his orthopraxy as espoused by the master; (5) The next themes tend to be tales of incredible feats, supernatural experiences, and thaumaturgy that leave no doubt in the reader's mind about the spiritual potentialities in the normative path; this often entails subjugation of the representations of universal negative forces (P. *Māra*) and the powerful spirit world through "righteous" practice of normative religion, that is, of the "Triple Gem"; (6) The subsequent theme recounts the interaction with isolated villagers and missionization of the *dhamma* and the meditative vocation (*wipatsanaathura*) preached by the teacher, Man; and (7) Finally, the narrator settles and is integrated into institutionalized monasticism, either near his home village or elsewhere at the invitation of local villagers and influential land owners.

The reader of Mahaa Bua's principal biography on Man would note these themes, as in the many subsequent life accounts of northeastern forest monks. The initial process of recording Man's life and teachings was through Mahaa Bua's sermons. Mahaa Bua's own disciples or lay followers recorded his orations on tapes, which he later edited and eventually wrote down. Drafts would find their way to Bangkok through urban supporters and were published by a company owned by long-standing lay supporters of northeastern forest monks. However, prior to the publication of Mahua Bua's widely publicized biography of Man, an earlier, less widely distributed version appeared as part of Man's cremation publication in 1950.[51]

This first biography on Man was compiled by a prolific scholar monk and meditator, Phra Ariyakhunaathaan Seng Pusso, at the request of the cremation committee, which included some of his senior disciples. Seng was born in Khorn Kaen province, northeast Thailand, in 1908 into a poor farming family. He was ordained at the age of fourteen as a novice at Wat Paa Sutthaawaat near the northeastern town of Sakon Nakhorn, and then stayed for some time at Wat Samphanthawong in Bangkok. There he commenced his studies and, at twenty-one years of age, took his higher monastic ordination under the royal monk Somdet Phra Wachirayaanawong—the Eighth Supreme Patriarch of the Thai Sangha in the present Ratanakosin period. Seng held a number of administrative positions in the northeast and then became deputy abbot of the royal Wat Phrasiimahaathaat in Bangkok. He resigned his position there to practice *dhamma* in the northeastern mountains, where he became known as "hermit (*ruesii*) Santajit." He disrobed toward the end of his life due to health problems.

Seng's material on Man came mainly from a lesser-known forest monk, Thongkham Yaanaphaso. Thongkham was sixty-eight years of age at the time of my interview in 1988 and had been Man's disciple for the last six years of the master's life. He subsequently disrobed in 1964.

Thongkham was then twenty-eight years old and one of several junior monks who cared for the ailing teacher until his death at Wat Paa Sutthaawaat. Thongkham had collected various utterances and other teachings (*Thammathesanaa*) by Man. His original compilation was cross-checked with Ajaan Thet Thetsarangsii, who is one of Man's senior disciples and who reputedly stayed close to the itinerant master during Man's eleven years in Chiang Mai. Other details were taken from Seng's own memory of his meetings with Man in the northeast. In recent times, there has been some controversy among Man's inner group of disciples concerning this biographical compilation. Its title *Muttothai* (P. *Muttodaya*) refers to a comment supposedly attributed to an influential northeastern scholar monk, who was a contemporary admirer of Man, *Jao Khun* Ubaalii. His comment implied that Man had "released his heart" during his teaching and conveyed to his listeners "the birth place of liberation" (*daenkoet haeng khwaamludphon*).

While sources on Man's monastic life are prolific, nothing of substance has been recorded of his sermons. This may appear unusual for a monk acclaimed unequivocally as a national saint (*arhat*). As Man taught one-to-one or in small groups, each talk was tempered to the intuitive understanding of the listener. His teachings were thus highly personalized and must be seen in context. As Thanissaro Bhikkhu mentioned in his translation of *Muttothai*,[52] Man's teachings were always face-to-face in the "form of people: the students whose lives were profoundly shaped by the experience of living and practicing meditation under his guidance."

Because of Man's personalized teaching mode, his disciples felt that it was inappropriate to transcribe his sermons and that perhaps his sermons should remain an oral tradition to which they, his disciples, will be the spiritual heirs. This insistence on the oral transmission of his teachings may be seen as a discursive shift from a sanctified domain to the mundanity of the written word, which, in the textualizing process, would lose its inherent luminosity. There are historical antecedents in the meditation tradition for this antitextual stance.[53]

Muttothai is written in three parts and based on Man's talks in Laotian. This text was later rewritten—and probably reworked—in Central Thai (*Thai Klaang*) by Pusso Seng. The first part consists of early sermons. The second part contains later sermons written down by two disciples, Thongkham and the late Ajaan Wan Uttamo of Sakon Nakhorn province. The third part consists of short composite talks (*botpraphan*), examples, and *dhamma* sermons (*botthammabanyaai*). These later talks were supposedly written down by Man himself while spending lent at Wat Sapathum in Bangkok at the request of the abbot, Phra Panyaaphisaanthen Nuu, a northeastern friend and monastic senior of Man. Thongkham states that the impetus for publishing this compilation came about when Seng stayed with Thongkham at Wat Paa Norng Pheur, where Man, too, spent the last few years of his life. Seng noticed the unedited manuscript lying in a corner and asked Thongkham for permission to take it with him.

This work reflects the understanding of a scholar well versed in the Pāli Canon. The sermons center on pithy Pāli utterances and quotations from the suttas. If it is not Man's product, it may well be that the writer or writers projected into the discourse their own reflexive insights. At the very least, it indicates that Man's understanding of the canon may have been better than hitherto assumed, as Man spent nearly all of his monastic life wandering in the forests without advanced formal religious education. Providing an answer to this paradox, a former disciple of Man explained that Man's canonical knowledge was intuitively acquired as a result of his meditation experiences and that, as a disciple of the Buddha in a former life, Man had direct access to the founder's oral teachings and ritual mnemonics. Whatever the arguments, the *Muttothai*, along with a lesser known small document, the *Khanthawimutti-samangkhiithamma* (the dhamma of liberation from the "khandha"), are the only extant texts on Man's teachings.[54]

Forest monks in Man's lineage regard Mahaa Bua as the authority on contentious matters like the *Muttothai* and his biography of the master as the most authoritative text.[55] However, a public controversy developed among the religious establishment shortly after Mahaa Bua's biography of Man was published. In this incident, the former Prime Minister Kheukrit Pramoj criticized Mahaa Bua's account in his widely read weekly magazine, *Sayaamrat*. He accused Mahaa Bua of sensationalizing the *dhamma* and interspersing his account with tales of early saints, which, easily abused and misunderstood, can readily degenerate into "mere entertainment." The particular point of contention was Man's visionary experiences (*nimit*) in which he conversed with some of these early saints—including Mahaa Kassapa—a mystifying and incomprehensible event to Western-educated rationalist thinkers such as Kheukrit.

In fact, a similar discourse was related in Mahaa Bua's subsequent book[56] on the now famed Ajaan Khao Anaalayo, where he mentioned that Khao also communicated with celestial beings (*thewaa*), spirits (*phii*), and two early saints (*arhats*), Phra Phaakula and Mahaa Kassapa Thera. Khao reputedly attained sainthood at a specific time and place in Man's lifetime and is said to hold *dhamma* discussion with Man that left no doubt about the spiritual attainment of both monks. Events such as these are plausible to the writer and his inner circle, but may not be seen so by a wider urban Western-educated readership. Derrida[57] stated that, "the meanings and intention of the author may not coincide with that of the reader" and that much depends on the circumstances and context in which the text is read.

One of Mahaa Bua's royal supporters, *Mom Luang* Jitti Nopphawong, replied to Kheukrit's critique by saying that those who do not practice lack insight and that dialogic mystical events mentioned in the account would be difficult to comprehend from a worldly perspective.[58] Mahaa Bua subsequently received many letters from curious, educated, urban readers asking for confirmation of the incredible mystical incidents attributed to Man. Mahaa Bua has said that the events mentioned in the biography are merely a few of such happenings and capabilities of Man, which he (Mahaa Bua) withheld from relating publicly. Nevertheless, resulting from this controversy, interest was stirred up among the middle classes and elites in the metropolis. The former social grouping is comprised largely of professionals and technocrats; the latter include royalty as well as high-ranking civil servants and major business leaders; in many cases both were linked by "kinship, common interests and life-style."[59]

Several informants commented that Mahaa Bua became cautious after publishing Man's biography, such as the attention it received and the all-pervasive presence of insatiable urban "saint hunters" (*naklaa arhat*) in the northeastern forests.

Mahaa Bua's work was discreetly criticized by other former monastic disciples of Man, such as the now deceased Ajaan Thet Thetsarangsii of Wat Hin Maak Peng in Norngkhaai province, who was his formal monastic senior. Thet commented that the account showed only the fierce side of Man's personality, which reflected the author's own trenchant and ferocious personality. Among other disciples of the master, Ajaan Chorp Thaanasamo of Wat Paa Khokmon in Loei Province is said to have taken displeasure in being mentioned in this biography and in the resultant surge of attention and interest by popular mystical publications. In this manner, the social field of the forest monk in the northeastern frontier provinces took on a greater dimension, in contrast to its relatively discrete, bounded origins.

In Mahaa Bua's writing, Chorp is portrayed as the ideal forest monk, as a lone wanderer for much of his early monastic life, and is noted for his extended retreat in the forest and his adventures with tigers. Thet[60] commented that Chorp was strict in his austerity (P. *dhutanga*) practices and a "rare, encouraging example to others." Chorp was partially paralyzed for many years and cared for prior to his demise by supporters among the urban elite. In fact, many of Man's disciples, since the publication of his biography by Mahaa Bua, found themselves at the center of intense urban interest. However, this trend had already begun in the early 1960s.

Middle-class and elite readership, however, had already encountered the northeastern forest tradition prior to Man's biography through Jitti's popular and now defunct weekly *Siisapdaa*. In this magazine, Man's life and teachings were first serialized from Mahaa Bua's manuscript, which were followed by sequels.[61] This work makes explicit and implicit mention of some of Man's principal, first-generation disciples.

Conclusion

Despite his simple parochial rural origins, Ajaan Man has become a hagio-legend of national proportions. His lineage today is the focus of elite patronage and control. This is largely due to the construction and distribution in the metropolis of life accounts on Man and his early disciples during the 1970s.

Many Thai-Lao villagers would not doubt the "saintly" attributes of Man, as Kheukrit and others did, as they themselves first nurtured these tales from their own understanding rooted in their local cosmology and worldviews. The oral tales, verified by close monastic disciples, were passed through social and kinship networks and from village to village where Man and his wandering disciples encamped individually or in small settlements in the forests. In time, the many personal tales and accounts were transformed into written hagiographies published in the capital over the past two decades, a long way from their rural, peripheral beginnings. Although marginal to the formal monastic establishment and to the routinized monastic hierarchy, forest monks, nevertheless, are the mystical core of orthodox Thai religion. In Thailand, the transformative and integrative process of hagiography turned local legendary recluses into institutionalized[62] national figures.

Notes

1. *Ajaan* is the Thai equivalent term for the Sanskrit/Pāli *Ācariya*, in this context meaning a monastic teacher.
2. On this monk see C. F. Keyes, "Death of Two Buddhist Saints in Thailand," *Journal of the American Academy of Religion, Thematic Studies* 48, nos. 3 and 4 (1982), pp. 149–180; J. Placzek, "The Thai Forest Tradition," in *Southeast Asia: Women, Changing Social Structure and Cultural Continuity*, ed. G. B. Hainsworth (Ottawa: University of Ottawa Press, 1981); S. J. Tambiah, *The Buddhist Saints of the Forest and the Cult of Amulets* (Cambridge: Cambridge Studies in Social Anthropology, 1984), and "The Buddhist Arahant: Classical Paradigm and Modern Thai Manifestations," in *Saints and Virtues*, ed. J. S. Hawley (Berkeley: University of California Press, 1987); J. L. Taylor, "From Wandering to

Monastic Domestication: The Relationship between the Establishment of the Thammayut Nikaai in the Northeast Region and Ascetic Monks in the Lineage of Phra Ajaan Man Phuurithatto," *Journal of the Siam Society* 76 (1988), pp. 64–88, and *Forest Monks and the Nation-State: An Anthropological and Historical Study in Northeastern Thailand* (Singapore: Institute of Southeast Asian Studies, 1993).

3. This argument is based on Max Weber's discussion on the "routinization" of charismatic authority; see A. M. Henderson and Talcott Parsons, trans., *Max Weber: The Theory Of Social And Economic Organisation* (Glencoe, Ill.: The Free Press, 1947), pp. 363–373; and S. N. Eisenstadt, ed., *Max Weber On Charisma And Institution Building* (Chicago: University of Chicago Press, 1968), pp. 54–61. See also Tambiah's critique, *The Buddhist Saints of the Forest*, chap. 21.

4. A later disciple of Man named Wiriyang also wrote a biography on his master, which appeared in 1980, although regarded generally as less credible than Mahaa Bua's text. See Phra Ajaan Wiriyang (Phra Yaanawiriyaajaan), *Chiiwaprawat Than Phra Aajaan Man Phuurithatto (Chababsombuun)* (The complete biography of Phra Ajaan Man Phuurithatto) (Bangkok: privately published, 2523 [1980]).

5. See, for instance, Grant A. Olson, "Thai Cremation Volumes: A Brief History of a Unique Genre of Literature," *Asian Folklore Studies*, vol 51, 1992, pp. 279–294; and "Thailand's Funeral Books," *Asiaweek*, June 8, 1986, pp 57–58.

6. Mahaa Bua Yaanasampanno, Phra Ajaan, *Patipathaa Khorng Phrathudongkammathaan saai Than Phra Aajaan Man Phuurithatto* (The practice of the wandering meditation monks in the lineage of Phra Ajaan Man Phuurithatto) (Bangkok: Por Samphanphaanit, 2529 [1986]), p. 31.

7. J. Clifford and G. E. Marcus, eds., *Writing Culture: The Poetics and Politics of Ethnography* (Berkeley: University of California Press, 1986).

8. Fischer, "Ethnicity and the Post-Modern Arts of Memory," Clifford and Marcus, *Writing Cultures*, p. 198.

9. Rampersad, quoted in Clifford and Marcus, *Writing Cultures*, p. 197.

10. L. Langness, *The Life History in Anthropological Science* (New York: Holt, Rinehart and Winston, 1965).

11. Keyes, "Death of Two Buddhist Saints," said that written biographies of well-known monks were produced after the beginning of the twentieth century when a "radical change" affected Thai literature through Western influences in printing methods. Protestant missionaries were the pioneers in this field: see Charnvit Kasetsiri, "Thai Historiography from Ancient Times to the Modern Period," *Perceptions of the Past in Southeast Asia*, ed. A. Reid and D. Marr (AASA Southeast Asia Publications Series, Singapore: Heinemann, 1979), p. 160; B. J. Terwiel, *A History of Modern Thailand* (University of Queensland Press, 1983), p. 134; Tambiah, *The Buddhist Saints of the Forest*, p. 112; see esp. K. E. Wells, *History of Protestant Missionary Work in Thailand 1828–1958* (Bangkok: Church of

Christ in Thailand, 1958), pp. 5, 10. As Charnvit (ibid., p. 151) remarked, even before mass-produced accounts, oral tales of famous monks existed and were the stuff from which later written biographies drew their inspiration.

12. M. Carrithers, *The Forest Monks of Sri Lanka* (Delhi: Oxford University Press, 1983), p. 88.
13. This has been referred to as "tertiary narrative reproduction" (see Carrithers, *Forest Monks of Sri Lanka*, p. 79); "enacted biography" (Ernst Kris in *The Biographical Process: Studies in the History and Psychology of Religion*, ed. Frank E. Reynolds and Donald Capps (The Hague: Mouton, 1976), p. 18); or as an "amalgam of classical precedents and parochial elaboration" (Tambiah, *The Buddhist Saints of the Forest*, p. 131).
14. See Dhani Nivat, "The Rama Jataka: A Lao Version of the Story of Rama," *Journal of the Siam Society* 36, no. 1 (1946), pp. 1–22.
15. Cited in ibid., p. 21.
16. Paramaanuchit-chinorot was King Mongkut's (Rama IV) uncle, a well-known writer and the Seventh Ratanakosin Supreme Patriarch of the Siamese Sangha from 1851 until his death at the age of sixty-four in 1853; see A. Wichian and S. Sunthorn, comps., *Prawat Samanasak lae Phat-yot* (History of Clerical Ranks and Fans) (Bangkok: Rongphim sii-anan, 2528 [1985]), pp. 46–47.
17. Wachirayaan was the single most important figure in the reformation of the modern Siamese Buddhist order. He was King Mongkut's son and the brother of King Chulalongkorn (Rama V). Wachirayaan had written many books, including a life of the Buddha, Buddhist Proverbs, a standard work on monastic discipline, and a written system of ecclesiastical examinations in use today. He was the Tenth Ratanakosin Supreme Patriarch of the Siamese Sangha from 1910 until his death at the age of sixty-two in 1921; see C. Reynolds, ed., *The Life of Prince-Patriarch Vajiranana* (Ohio University Press, 1979).
18. See Frank Reynolds, "The Many Lives of Buddha," in *The Biographical Process*, ed. Reynolds and Capps, p. 53; and personal communication with Thanissaro Bhikkhu, Wat Thammasathit, Rayong, 1989.
19. Mahaa Bua, Siri Buddhasukh, trans., in *The Venerable Phra Acharn Mun Bhuridatta: Meditation Master* (1976; Bangkok: Funny Publishing Ltd. Partnership, 1982). I use my own reference to the original Thai text for the term *keji-aajaan*.
20. Brian Stock, *The Implications of Literacy* (Princeton, N.J.: Princeton University Press, 1983).
21. Keyes, "Death of Two Buddhist Saints."
22. Ibid., p. 152.
23. Kris, in *The Biographical Process*, p. 19.
24. Tambiah, *The Buddhist Saints of the Forest*.
25. Ibid., p. 4.
26. Ibid., pp. 5, 132.

27. Ibid., p. 132.
28. Kris, in *The Biographical Process*.
29. Tambiah, *The Buddhist Saint of the Forest*, pp. 344–345.
30. Mahaa Bua Yaanasampanno, *Prawat Than Phra Aajaan Man Phurithatta Thera* (Biography of Than Phra Ajaan Man Phurithatta Thera) (1971; Bangkok: Por Samphanphaanit Ltd. Part., 2529 [1986]).
31. Mahaa Bua, *The Venerable Phra*, p. 72.
32. Mahaa Bua Yaanasampanno, Phra Ajaan, *Straight from the Heart*, trans. Bhikkhu Thanissaro (Bangkok: Por Samphanphaanit Ltd. Part., 2530 [1987]), p. 40.
33. Mahaa Bua, *Straight from the Heart*, pp. 114–116.
34. J. Clifford, "On Ethnographic Allegory," in Clifford and Marcus, *Writing Cultures*, pp. 115–116.
35. For a similar discussion in a different context, see George E. Marcus and Michael M. J. Fischer, *Anthropology as Cultural Critique: An Experimental Moment in the Human Sciences* (Chicago: University of Chicago Press, 1986), pp. 36–37.
36. In Clifford and Marcus, *Writing Culture*, p. 116.
37. The Pāli term for this sect is *Dhammayuttika-nikaya*, the Dhammayut Order.
38. Mahaa Bua, Sivi Buddhasukh, trans., "Writer's note," in *The Venerable Phra Acharn Mun* (n.p.).
39. Kris, in *The Biographical Process*. pp. 19, 29.
40. Tambiah, *The Buddhist Saints of the Forest*, p. 129.
41. C. Reynolds, "Religious Historical Writing and the Legitimation of the First Bangkok Period," in *Perceptions of the Past*, ed. Reid and Marr, p. 103.
42. Mahaa Bua, *Patipathaa Khorng*, pp. 89–97.
43. H. Hecker, *Lives of the Disciples: Maha Kassapa; Father of the Sangha*, Wheel Publication no. 345, (Kandy: B.P.S. 1987), p. 32.
44. Hecker, *Lives of the Disciples*, p. 17.
45. See *Samyutta Nikaya*, 16, 5 (in Hecker, *Lives of the Disciples*, p. 17).
46. M. Foucault, "What Is an Author?" in *Textual Strategies: Perspectives in Post-Structuralist Criticism*, ed. Josue V. Harari (Ithaca: Cornell University Press, 1979), p. 147.
47. M. Foucault, *The Archaeology of Knowledge*, trans. A. M. Sheridan Smith (London: Tavistock Publications, 1972).
48. See Carrithers, *The Forest Monks*, esp. chap. 4.
49. Kitsiri Malalgoda, *Buddhism in Sinhalese Society 1750–1900* (Berkeley: O.U.P., 1976), p. 168.
50. Keyes, "Death of Two Buddhist Saints," p. 159.
51. A second limited edition was republished by the Electricity Generating Authority of Thailand's active Buddhist Association—under its then president, Kesem Jaatikawanit, in 1984.
52. This was entitled "A Heart Released: The Teachings of Phra Ajaan Mun Bhuridatto," unpublished, trans. Thanissaro Bhikkhu (1988). The text in

the Thai original is *Muttothai: owaat khorng Phra Aajaan Man Phuurithattathera* (Bangkok: Por samphanphaanit, 2530 [1987]).

53. This antitextual stance is in large part due to the understanding by the ascetic meditator that the doctrinal truths can only be comprehended noetically and intuitively. Thus the use of the text has only a limited function as a teaching aide and emphasis instead being placed on the personalized transmission of higher knowledge as technique (yet in the Theravāda tradition contextually situated in terms of reaffirmation with doctrinal sources).

    It should be noted that this antitextual stance is institutionally embedded in the traditional division between scriptural learning (*pariyatti*) and praxis (*patipatti*) as historical process since at least the early Christian era in Sri Lanka (the so-called Commentarial period); see for instance Richard Gombrich, *Theravada Buddhism: A Social History from Ancient Benares to Modern Colombo* (London: Routledge and Kegan Paul, 1988), pp. 152–153.

54. The *Khanthawimutti-Samangkhiithamma* was supposedly written by Man around 1915 while the master was residing at Wat Pathumwan in Bangkok during one of his rare early visits to the capital. It was rediscovered at Man's relic museum at Wat Paa Sutthaawaat in Sakon Nakhorn province and translated into English in 1995 under the direction of Ajaan Thui Chantha Karo, a second-generation disciple of Ajaan Man. The "khanda" (Thai: Khantha) refer to the five aggregates of conditioned existence.

55. See Phra Ajaan Wiriyang's version of Man's biography, *Chiiwaprawat Than.* of conditional existence.

56. Mahaa Bua, *Patipathaa Khorng.*

57. See J. Cullen, "Jacques Derrida," in *Structuralism and Since: From Levi-Strauss to Derrida*, ed. J. Sturrock (Oxford: Oxford University Press, 1979).

58. This seemed to have all the makings of a division between, on the one hand, urban elite meditators and traditionalism and, on the other, rationalist intellectuals and modernism.

59. R. Korff, "Urban or Agrarian? The Modern Thai State," *Sojourn* 4, no. 1 (1989), pp. 48–49.

60. Phra Ajaan Thate (Thet Thetsarangsii) Desaransi, *My Life*, trans. Siri Buddhasukh (Bangkok: Bangkok Printing Press 2521 [1978]), p. 171. See also a more recent English translation by Bhikkha Ariyesako, *The Autobiography of a Forest Monk* (Bangkok: Amarin Printing and Publishing, 1993).

61. Mahaa Bua, *Patipathaa Khorng.*

62. I use the word *institutionalized* in the sense of a processual transformation in which individuated relatively "free floating" charisma becomes regulated and domesticated through absorption into the bureaucratic control of the state. This word is closely connected with Weber's notion of *routinization* (mentioned at the beginning of this paper, see note 3) in

reference to the transformation of charismatic leadership based on personal attributes into traditionalized, institutional routine structures. Essentially I am arguing that the biographical process in Thailand facilitated the institutionalization and domestication of wandering forest monks.

The Biography of Modern Burmese Buddhist Meditation Master U Ba Khin: Life before the Cradle and past the Grave

Gustaaf Houtman

With the rise of individualism during the early eighteenth century, writers became more interested in the uniqueness of persons and biography came to signify the story of the life of an individual human being.[1] Biography has a long history going back at least as far as the Egyptian tomb stones and early oral history. Yet biography also has a short history in that it has been subject to relatively recent trends. Kindall found that the word biography was first employed in the seventeenth century to mean a literary tradition used "to create a separate identity for this type of writing."[2] Today "biography" is a dedicated Western literary genre with strict rules of classification. In the *Encyclopaedia Britannica* biographical literature is defined as seeking "to recreate in words the life of a human being, that of the writer himself or of another person, drawing upon the resources, memory and all available evidences—written, oral, pictorial."[3] Derived from Greek *bio-* (life) plus *graphy* (writing), the term suggests three distinct orders of meaning, extending from "life-course of a living (usu. human) being," "written life of a person," to "a branch of literature dealing with persons' lives."[4]

Yet not everyone understands "biography" in quite such a restricted sense. Sometimes the term is used to mean something much wider in scope, namely the record of the life of any life process, ranging from the life of an insect to a geological process, or even of an organization.[5] *At-htok-pat-tí*,[6] the Burmese term for biography, has such "dispersed" quality as it goes beyond events pertaining to a human life and may include events pertaining to any object, whether animate or inanimate: for example, it may concern variously an animal, a spirit, an institution, a mountain, a dictionary, or a human being.[7] Indeed, the concept for "biography" may have many other uses in the vernacular apart from a literary "genre": in everyday Burmese the term is used to mean variously "facts," "events," "a statement of fact," and "narration of events." The Burmese concept therefore carves out a larger and less circumscribed field of meaning than our literary sense of "biography" allows for, and includes additionally what we might call variously "story," "history," or "fable."

Often several different, sometimes contradictory notions of biography compete side by side within the same culture. For example, influenced by secular education and socialist thought, contemporary Burmese authors are apt to interpret biography in terms of the much narrower range of meanings provided by its Western secular-literary equivalent concept. This has been fostered by the centralized Burmese government with a strong tendency toward censorship over the last few decades.[8]

With this essay I have two aims. The first is to present the biography of a meditation teacher and accountant-general of Burma, U Ba Khin (1899–1971). This biography must be understood in the context of the increased popularity of Buddhist meditational practice since British colonial rule began in Burma in the early nineteenth century. It was King Mindon (r. 1853–1878) who first incorporated insight contemplation into royal discipline in the 1840s–1850s. However, it was at that time very much an aristocratic technique intended for the royal court and the monks, and the first-known *wí-pat-tha-na* (P. *vipassanā*) insight contemplation center for the masses was not dedicated until 1911 in Myó Hlá, where the Mìn-gùn Hsa-ya-daw taught. Since then, some one-thousand meditation centers have emerged all over Burma, but also many abroad, which advocate a Buddhism of personal practice.[9] These centers, which range from converted monasteries and factories to centers newly built for the purpose, are a major national service industry. U Ba Khin, the subject of this biography, is an unordained individual who played his part in this movement. In the run-up to 1948 National Independence and the reorganization of the colonial civil service, he rediscovers meditation as the core message of Buddhism and seeks to have his office, the Burmese civil service, and the foreigner take an interest in it.

The second aim of this essay is to look (from a Western secular-literary angle) at the "fuzziness" of traditional Burmese Buddhist biography with respect to the distinction between history and biography. The biographer of U Ba Khin sought to "historicize" his teacher so much that only 27 out of 614 pages are devoted to the subject's life, the rest being devoted to the lineage of pupils. Although this would hardly qualify as a biography from the Western secular-literary point of view, such designation is quite acceptable from a Burmese Buddhist-literary perspective. After all, the biographer writes the U Ba Khin biography in celebration of its subject's realization of insubstantiality and no-self. This, it is argued here, cannot be readily reconciled with a narrow conception of the "individual" who is presumed to have the consistency of a self, and the two understandings are bound to come into conflict. After declaring the complicated interlinking between vernacular biography and vernacular history, I shall conclude by arguing that at least some authors of Burmese vernacular Buddhist biography (including the author of the U Ba Khin biography) aspire for their biography to be a history in which the subject is not readily confined in time and place.

The U Ba Khin Biography

The biography of U Ba Khin considered here is entitled *Burma's Honourable Special Teacher U Ba Khin (His Biography and Missionary Works).*[10] One of few renowned unordained insight teachers, his religious aspirations blossomed late in life, and his fame as an important civil servant preceded him. The biography portrays a dual career: a secular career leading up from the post of clerk at the Office of the Accountant-General in November 1917 to the post of accountant-general of Burma at national independence in 1948; and a religious career, leading from a budding interest in insight on January 8, 1937 to becoming a teacher in the *a-na-pa-ná* tradition of the Le-di Hsa-ya-daw[11] during his visit to the Wei-bu Hsa-ya-daw[12] in July 1941, and finally, opening up his own insight center on November 9, 1952—the International Meditation Centre. The author of the preface suggests that the purpose of the biography is to portray U Ba Khin (hereafter BK) as a Buddhist.

> This book is not a preaching (*da-má*) work in the sense of a collection of discourses. But this is a biography (*at-htok-pat-tí*) in the sense of a collection of events and experiences of a person who was successful in practice according to the discourse exercises, and in teaching his pupils. The Great Teacher Ba Khin must be considered a master of perfection (*pa-ra-mi shin*) who succeeded in the propagation of Buddhism (*tha-tha-na*) in an unusual way. Without having preached around the world, his

pupils nevertheless enjoy his teachings everywhere. Meditation centres have appeared in many countries in Asia and Europe—England, America, Canada, New Zealand, Australia.[13]

Published in 1980, nine years after BK's death, it is based on interviews, reminiscences of BK's biographer, letters and publications from pupils (mainly foreigners), and publications and broadcasts on Buddhism by BK himself. The relationship between Ko Lei, the author, and his subject has been described in some detail elsewhere.[14] Suffice to note here that the author is a retired vice chancellor of Mandalay University and BK's pupil. Ko Lei started the biography in 1963, but BK did not want to have it published until after his death, which explains its late publication date.[15] Ko Lei includes in the book much information about himself and his relationship to BK, including a summary in the introduction, and the entire chapter 6 ("The Great Teacher and I").[16] In brief, they first met through work in 1934, when the author was unaware of BK's religious aspirations. He became BK's pupil only after being reintroduced to him by foreigners impressed with his teachings.[17] At one point Ko Lei even describes BK as resembling his own father (demised in 1946) in stature, appearance, manner of walking, and manner of talking.[18]

U Ba Khin

BK's life is described in the second chapter under the heading, "From Accountant-General to Great Teacher."[19] BK was a true Rangoonite. The son of U Pàw, a broker,[20] and Daw Sàw Mei, he was born in 1898 in a Rangoon neighborhood.

Under the subheading "From study to work," it is described how his education began with traditional monastic training in a local monastery until the age of eight (1907), after which he went to a Methodist school, where he stayed until the seventh standard (1907–1914). "Ever since young, he was of exceptional intelligence, and without fail first in every class."[21] At the end of the seventh standard he was awarded a government scholarship and went to St. Paul's, Rangoon, a college of excellent reputation. He was always at the top of the class and was awarded a scholarship at completion, but did not continue his studies. With both parents deceased by then, he had no one to encourage him. He decided to go his own way.

His first job was to work at *The Sun (Thu-rí-yá)* newspaper, one of the first Burmese-language nationalist newspapers set up by some of the founders of the YMBA movement. By November 1917 he had become a low-grade clerk at the Office of the Accountant-General, and in November 1926, having passed the Indian Government Accountancy exams, he was promoted to assistant office supervisor. These offices were known as the "Indian Offices" because they employed no Burmese. Only three Burmese people worked there at the time and most other employees had left their positions in this office due to oppression by the Indians. This trend continued despite the efforts of the Accountant-General to turn the "Indian Office" into a "Burmese Office" by hiring six highly educated Burmese among whom was also the author of BK's biography. Only BK stayed on. He was held up by some as an example of how a Burmese could get on after passing the exams. Without a university education, BK had been promoted from an ordinary clerk to a deputy supervisor over nine years. He showed courage and a strong commitment to studying for the accountancy exams. He had such good memory that he could recite the accountancy books from back to front. In 1937, when Burma was to have a separate Accountancy Department from India, BK became a special supervisor at the Office of the Auditor General. On February 28, 1941, he was promoted to accountant officer of the Railways' Board.

The section on "The Great author Khin Shwei Chó," describes how BK authored novels of which, however, he was not proud.

Under the subheading "The seeker of truth," BK is described in his quest for Buddhist truth. Although already studying the *a-bí-da-ma* in Bassein in 1931,[22] and helping to organize a visit by the Mò-hnyìn Hsa-ya-daw to Rangoon in 1934, it was not until his forties, from 1937 or 1938 onwards, that Ba Khin took a serious interest in Buddhism. As Ko Lei put it, "at that time The Great Teacher changed from his pursuit of ordinary literature to literature on the Buddha's preachings."[23] He was particularly interested in the works of famous Le-di Hsa-ya-daw. He became a member of various Buddhist associations such as the Dawn Merit Association (*a-yon a-thìn*) and the Religious Duty Recitation Society (*wut yut a-thìn*), and a member of an *a-bí-da-ma* discussion group[24] at Su-le Pagoda. "In this manner, The Great Teacher already carried out his various duties in the Three Jewels to the Buddha and the Order as a fully aware and devout Buddhist (*bok-dá-ba-tha ta-ú*)."[25] Even when traveling, he faithfully observed religious obligations.

BK started his mental culture without prior design. On a duty day in late December 1936, he accompanied a relative to the house of U Ei Maung, a Burmese school teacher and pupil of Hsa-ya Thet-Gyì, who soon taught him the rudimentaries of mental culture. BK began practicing "concentration" meditation (*tha-ma-htá*) on January 1, 1937.[26] BK discovered that his concentration was so good that he could play with imaginary light before his mind's eye in any way he wanted to. He practiced *a-na-pa-ná* at home by himself. The same signs occurred, and he resolved to go to Da-lá-byaw-bwe-gyì Village to learn the method from Hsa-ya Thet-gyì himself. He obtained a leave of absence from his office,[27] but he did not meditate seriously until January 8, 1937, when he practiced for seven days. When made to recite a Pāli verse, BK immediately felt impermanence throughout his body and he contemplated throughout the night with these feelings. The next morning Thet-gyì came to enquire about the experiences, which he did every morning and every evening. He was pleased with BK's progress and told him to sit in mental culture for seven days, and to wear a white cloth[28] around his shoulders. Before BK left, Thet-gyì showed him the monastery and pagodas of the area. It was very windy, and Thet-gyì turned to BK, asking him, "You who knows the teachings (*ta-yà*), do you have the courage to withstand the wind of the Law (*ta-yà*)." He told BK to continue his practice at home. From 1937 onwards BK visited Thet-gyì every year to learn the method. Thet-gyì also went occasionally to Rangoon to receive his students' homage and give instructions in BK's house.

Under the subheading "From Rangoon to Wei-bu Hill," it is described how BK's earliest encouragement for teaching mental culture came from a famous member of the monastic order. In 1941 BK became a Railways' Department accounts officer. On July 2 BK went to work at Myit-thà station by train. Upon his return the train halted at Kyauk-hse station for a considerable time. In front of the station he could see the inviting Shwei-tha-lyaùng Hill, which he climbed without delay, together with the assistant station master, to worship. Upon looking north he saw a small monastery at the foot of a mountain. The deputy station master told him that the venerated Wei-bu Hsa-ya-daw[29] resided there who was thought by many in the area to be enlightened (*ya-hàn-da*). BK immediately wanted to go there, but the deputy station master remarked that Wei-bu was unlikely to receive them at that time of the day. After lunch at the station, BK went into his railway carriage and, taking the doctrine (*ta-yà*) as the object of his consciousness, sent loving-kindness to the Wei-bu Hsa-ya-daw and petitioned the Hsa-ya-daw in his mind to let them come and pay their respects.

At about 3 P.M. they made their way by horse cart to this monastery, passing by the Kò-na-win Pagoda on the way. They met two nuns, who suggested that they should visit the Wei-bu abbot either during morning breakfast or for evening preaching. BK said that either time would be suitable, as long as they might bow their heads in reverence. Then he sat down and, at the place where he had taken his slippers off, he bowed his head aiming in the direction of the monk and thought, "Having come from Rangoon I have come to worship you Hsa-ya-daw." At exactly that time the door of the monastery opened and the Hsa-ya-daw's face showed. He asked "By what need do you worship layman?." BK answered, "Because I have the wish to achieve the path and fruition of enlightenment (*mek-hpo neik-ban*), oh lord." The Hsa-ya-daw then inquired, "Right . . . if you want to go to enlightenment (*neik-ban*), how do you propose to go?." BK replied, "With *wí-pat-tha-na* knowledge I shall go, oh lord. Now I am also putting insight (*wí-pat-tha-na ta-yà*) as object of consciousness, oh lord." "Very well . . . *tha-dú, tha-dú*, how did you get this teaching (*ta-yà*)?" the monk asked. BK recounted how he had practiced under his benefactor Hsa-ya Thet-gyì for the first seven days, and how he always practiced mental culture on the train while traveling. "In that case you layman must have perfection (*pa-ra-mí*). I thought one had to go into the forest for it and that it was such exhausting work," the teacher responded. They spoke like this for about an hour. BK left and went back the next day to offer the Hsa-ya-daw a vegetarian meal. People were surprised to see the Wei-bu converse so much as he was not usually talkative. In the end the Wei-bu Hsa-ya-daw instructed: "The teaching (*ta-yà*) you layman have received, you are likely to have to share with others. You do not know when you will see again the layman in your company now. Pass the teaching on to him while you are still meeting up. Give him a method. Give him the teaching (*ta-yà*) as a layman after having changed to wearing a white cloth."[30] Back at the Kyaukhse station, BK taught the deputy station master in a railway carriage according to the Wei-bu's instructions; this was his first pupil in mental culture. Thus, without relinquishing his responsibilities of government, he had not only started practicing but also teaching mental culture.

Under the subheading "Accountant-General and Great Guru[31] U Ba Khin," it is described how he achieved the pinnacle of his two careers. During the war, BK's responsibilities in government increased as English and Indians were leaving the accountancy department.[32] He also taught various government ministers mental culture, including Myan-má A-lìn Ù Tin, Prime Minister U Nu, and Minister of Education U Hlá Mìn. They all could only reach the level of breathing as the object of meditation (*a-na-pa-ná ka-mạ-htàn*). BK arranged for these ministers to practice with his teacher Hsa-ya Thet-gyì, but government responsibilities prevented them from traveling. It thus fell upon BK to assist them with their difficulties in practice. Hsa-ya Thet-gyì had impressed upon the ministers that BK was like a doctor taking care of the sick. They should listen to the teaching (*ta-yà*) given by BK, and his morality, concentration, and wisdom should be accepted. The English returned after the war, and BK was promoted on May 16, 1945 to the rank of deputy accountant-general.

Bits of information about BK's health problems, his death, and the institutionalization of his work pertaining to mental culture are found throughout the remaining chapters. While practicing at the A-le-tàw-yá monastery, BK developed trouble with one of his eyes, which ultimately required an operation. He was not allowed to see in daylight and had to stay in the dark. Meanwhile Hsa-ya Thet-gyì fell ill too, and he came to Rangoon for treatment. They were not far away from each other, but as they were both patients they could not meet up. On the night of his death, December 14, 1945, Thet-gyì gave BK in his dream the instruction to preach the First Sermon (*Ḍa-ma-set-kya*).[33] Thet-gyì was put in a cave north of the Shwei-da-gon, now called Martyr's Hill.[34] When BK's eye disorder recurred and he was off work for a month the following year, he healed himself through his practice of mental culture: "Great Teacher resolved to follow a prolonged fasting. After having practiced *wí-pat-tha-na* he observed the *ta-yà* so as to see the impermanence in parts of the face. For nutrition he took only three mouthfuls of rice with oil and salt . . . after about one week he was free from disease, and it never came back."[35]

On Independence Day, January 4, 1948, BK became the first accountant-general of independent Burma with a salary of 1,600 kyats. Since starting in November 1917 as the lowest clerk with only a 40-kyat salary, he had by then transformed the office from an Indian into a Burmese one. BK also achieved a geometrical progression in religious works and reached the pinnacles of his dual career as a teacher of mental culture and as an accountant, at roughly the same time. He began to teach at his office. Upstairs in his office he arranged a small room with a Buddha shrine, then taught his employees insight (*tha-ma-htá wí-pat-tha-na*).[36]

In 1951 the institutionalization of his methods truly began. On July 18, 1951, BK set up the Accountant-General Vipassana Research Association.[37] The foundation of this society was morality. The society was devoted to progressive scientific research beginning with work on concentration, and only continuing with insight work once concentration was matured, testing whether it was in conformity with *Wí-thok-di mek*, and whether it was possible to achieve a break-through in respect to the thirty-seven Factors of Enlightenment (*bàw-dí-pek-hkí-yá ta-yà*). From this inquiry it appeared that the path to true "practice" (*pa-dí-pat-tí*), at the basis of which are morality, concentration, and knowledge, required only a few days practice with those methods. Practicing like this, they could achieve insight, but at the same time, they found the development of special knowledge[38] to wash away the defilements and craving for origination.

Some Indians were still in the office, and BK not only taught Burmese Buddhists but also these Indian Hindus who had an intuitive access to concentration meditation. After they practiced meditation with breathing as its object (*a-na-pa-ná*), they saw a light omen and were grateful to BK, who had become their "Gu-ru." Mr. Venkataraman, one of the Indian employees, even became a master of perfection (*pa-ra-mí*) and went beyond meditation on breathing (*a-na-pa-ná*) to find the true understanding that is insight. This was confirmed by the Ma-sò-yein Hsa-ya-daw. Not only BK's staff, but also their families attended BK's teachings (*ta-yà*) so that more space was needed on the top floor of the office to accommodate them all.

BK called a meeting on January 11, 1952, to set up a committee of ten persons to raise funds to buy the grounds for an insight center. His pupils came and had a look at it: the Indian Venkataraman sat down on the ground and having taken the teaching (*ta-yà*) as his object of concentration, the four guardian *nats* of the teachings (*tha-tha-na*) arrived and encouraged him to take it quickly as it was true vantage ground.[39] BK and his pupils decided where to place the pagoda and bought the land in May 1952. The Accountant-General Vipassana Association[40] was set up on April 24, 1952, and teaching began at the center in a temporary hut on May 1. On May 8, construction of the Da-má-yaung-chi Pagoda began, which was completed by November 9, 1952, when its umbrella was hoisted. The International Meditation Centre (IMC)[41] had come into being. It was the time of preparation for the Sixth Synod (*Than-ga-yá-na*), and there were many foreigners in Burma who sought to know about insight.

From 1952 on, BK felt his main task was to teach foreigners. Though retired by June 1953, BK still worked hard to fulfill his many national responsibilities.[42] At the same time, he himself practiced daily, taught, and preached. During 1955 the number of foreigners at the IMC increased.

When the revolutionary government came to power in 1962, BK played an important role in nationalizing Burma's industry and demonetizing the 50- and 100-kyat notes. He served on various committees, including the Investigative Committee on Religion set up by the 1962 Revolutionary Council, of which BK eventually became treasurer. By October 1962, BK resigned from this committee and, by October 1964, retired from almost all government work due to further health problems and his desire to devote all of his time to teaching mental culture. BK moved to the International Meditation Centre. His request to obtain government permission to visit Sri Lanka was denied in March 1966 on policy grounds. BK's dreams to missionize abroad in person were not to be realized. The news that he could not go abroad was brought by the permanent secretary to the Home Ministry himself. "For normal people this refusal to allow him to go abroad would have been terrible, but BK could bear it."[43]

By April 1969, it became clear that even if the government were to change its position, BK would no longer be able to go abroad: he was seventy-one years old and frail. He decided to send a letter to a number of foreign students he identified as Masters of Perfection (*pa-ra-mi shin*), informing them that he had been refused permission to go abroad. He also indicated that he had successfully experimented with remote control and could guide them from a distance, much like transmitting radio waves. He ended with a request to them to come to Burma to be trained as teachers.

His choice of whom to train was made carefully, as they had to be free from physical and mental disease. BK eventually instructed them by mail, as permission to travel to Burma was denied.

In 1969 BK underwent three kidney operations and received a blood transfusion. BK died on January 19, 1971, due to kidney malfunction and internal hemorrhage. BK's ashes and bones were scattered in the Irrawaddy River after cremation on January 21. Candles were lit at night and the pupils practiced. On January 21, 1971, an offering was made to seventy-three monks, and BK's remaining bones were cleaned in coconut milk. BK had taught 3,500 yogis, including about 300 foreign visitors and distinguished Burmese government officials, among them ex-president Sàw Shwei Thaik and former Prime Minister U Nu.

Although the text makes no direct statement about his achieving enlightenment,[44] his saintliness is implicit: "The brilliance of the benefits of the merits of the morality, charity and mental culture which Hsa-ya-gyì performed in this life will be very great. Among these merits, is the gift of the *da-má* which is the most noble, and there is no mistaking that his benefits will include that he will have reached the top."[45] Also,

> It is no surprise that Hsa-ya-gyì could not support the blood given by the doctors. Hsa-ya-gyì was someone who, with the strength of *da-má dat*, helped to destroy greed, ignorance, and anger, and ameritorious elements called "defilements" (*kí-lei-tha*). He was a person who understood that only knowledge of the nature of impermanence can overcome these defilements. He was a man who took great care not to let these demeritorious defilements find a way into his work and environment. He wanted the Da-má-yaung-gyi Pagoda as a pure retreat and only accepted money from pupils who had practised under him. He was careful to deny donations from strangers who, wanting to make merit, came to donate food and things, as these may be impure. Being someone who upheld this principle, how could he accept the introduction of blood into his body that was derived from people who had not practised the *ta-yà* with him and did not know the state of his physical particles; surely, it was only to be ejected.[46]

The Biography Analyzed

Here I wish to look at how the Ba Hkin volume could be considered a biography in the Burmese vernacular sense even though only a small section of the text is devoted to recounting his life.[47] A chronological account of his life is given only in chapter 2 (22 pp.), the briefest of chapters, and appendixes (6 pp.), which list details such as the posts he held, his publications, his salary, and even the number of his identity card. Some small episodes on his life are also recounted in other sections, but proportionately very little deals with BK as a person, and most deals with BK as an institution: about his foreign pupils, his insight center and its pagoda, the nationally famous monks in attendance at events he organized, and so forth.

Sacred Biography versus Hagiography

Reynolds distinguished between "sacred biography" and "hagiography."[48] The first refers to "those accounts written by followers or devotees of a founder or religious savior" and "primarily intend to depict a distinctively new religious image or ideal." The latter "chronicle lives of lesser religious figures" and "present their subject as one who has realized, perhaps in a distinctive way, an image, ideal, or attainment already recognized by his religious community." The BK volume is, strictly speaking, a hagiography, given that it portrays how BK implemented the Buddha's teachings as he inherited them. Yet it is also a sacred biography, given that BK modified the methodology he inherited to suit unordained people, and that he founded his own institutions and lineage while pursuing his secular career at the same time.

There are four ways in which the biographer establishes BK as a saintly person. First, Reynolds[49] suggested that one mark of a hagiography is that "slight attention is given to chronological rendering of the life" because there is an overarching need to "emphasize the virtues or attainments manifested in the subject's life." This, indeed, is the case here. This biography illustrates the continuity of Ba Khin's spiritual lineage more than it recounts the chronological story of his personal life. Its order is not without a sense of unfolding chronologically from the beginning of BK's life, in chapter 2, to the commemoration ten years after his death in chapter 10. However, the episodes are chronologically disjointed so as to allow the passages on BK's predominantly foreign pupils to convey indirectly the unfolding of his life. The result is a pupil-centered hagiography in which inflated episodes of the lives of BK's pupils structure the plot and give meaning to BK's life. In other words, it is an account of an individual's life dispersed into the context of a lineage history.

Second, if I consider biographers having the choice, to "humanize" or to "spiritualize" a subject, by "including episodes which reflect his common humanity" or "by expunging references to his human weakness, mental lapses, signs of occasional cruelty, and so on," this biography has clearly spiritualized its subject.[50] BK's emotions and inner contradictions are not considered, and the master is portrayed in conventional terms of exaltation typical of any biography on Buddhist subjects: he has the attributes of Buddhist saints, namely of "perfection" (*pa-ra-mi*);[51] "morality" (*thi-lá*), "concentration" (*tha-ma-dí*), and "insight" (*pyin-nya*).[52] He radiates "loving kindness" to his pupils.[53] He is characterized as a "benefactor" (*kyeì-zù-shin*).[54] He also practiced some degree of dietary asceticism by abstaining from "four-legged" meats, and eating only fish and fowl. On the front cover BK is also depicted with a halo[55] around his head. The success he enjoyed in his career as a civil servant closely shadowed his career as an insight teacher, almost as if it were a measurable indication of his perfections (*pa-ra-mí*) and superhuman status.

Third, perhaps converse to the above, the author has suppressed relationships and episodes in the subject's life insofar as these could possibly shed doubt on his sanctity. This leads to a life story skewed away from the formative family relationships and toward the spiritual lineage. This biography is almost entirely limited to the latter half of BK's life, after he learned mental culture from 1937 onwards. Completely lacking is the description of BK as a family man: nothing is conveyed about his family life, his wife, and his children. The name of his wife is mentioned only in passing in the episode of his death.[56] I was told by informants that he had three children, a son and two daughters. But I do not know much about his natal family or about his interactions in a family context. The first nineteen years of his life are dismissed in less than half a page.

Fourth, the biographer sought to impress upon the readership the importance and reality of this sanctimonious image. The scholarly style in which the BK biography is written—with full appendixes, letters, and bibliography—may be interpreted as part of the hagiographical principle. Ko Lei struggles to include as many facts as possible in the text's 614 pages. The division into chapters with numbered subheadings, the many appendixes, and an extensive bibliography are evidence both of the author's conviction that BK was a man of significance, and of the author's academic background. It is this urge to record all of BK's achievements exhaustively and in a scholarly manner that appears to be responsible for the length and complexity. This style may befit an educated author, but the scholarly approach is also intended to validate the life of an apparently secular layman. This strategy is reminiscent of nineteenth-century biography as described by Nadel, who states that "The acceptance of the multi-volume life in the nineteenth century, inflated by lengthy excerpts from letters, reflects the importance of documents to validate a life, a defense as well as a justification of the biographical form."[57] Though in my summary of his life I have concentrated mainly on those episodes important to our understanding of BK's life, nearly two-thirds of the biography focuses on correspondence with foreigners and their lives.

Through these four hagiographical devices a carefully constructed picture emerges of an influential man characterized by sanctity and superhuman achievement. Or, as Reynolds might put it, a biographical image appears that "takes precedence over a simple chronicling of biographical facts."[58]

Historicized Biography

However, a fifth device is equally crucial to this biography, if not more so. This is the tendency to historicize BK and to extend his influence far and wide. The author viewed BK's work as a "milestone in history" and BK was depicted in a way that goes beyond his personal time and space.

Most insight teachers are monks. Monk insight teachers commonly have two spiritual lineages. The first, known as the scriptural learning lineage (*pa-rí-yat-tí -a-sin-a-hset*), traces the teachers through whom monastic ordination and scriptural learning were derived. The second lineage, known as the practice lineage (*pa-dí-pat-tí a-sin-a-hset*), traces the lineage of teachers from whom mental culture was derived. The scriptural learning lineage does not include the unordained, and BK had only a practice lineage linked to the unordained Hsa-ya Thet-gyì as teacher. Although the latter instructed him to teach, a lay teacher could not give BK, also a layman, the credibility of a monk with his scriptural learning lineage through ordination.

This problem of spiritual continuity was resolved in two ways. First, it is described how BK had a sacred *stūpa* built, the power of which he could tap and use to send waves to distant places beyond the geographical boundaries he was never allowed to cross. This *stūpa* was consecrated in his insight center compound with the aid of beings in the Brahma realm who themselves perpetuated the Buddha's teachings and who allowed him to tap cosmic energy (*dat*), which he emanated to his pupils abroad at set times when he was incapable of being in their presence.

Second, the author established BK's spiritual credentials by focusing on the master-pupil relationship so crucial to this biography. Hsa-ya Thet-gyì had been told to teach by his monastic teacher, the famous monk Le-di Hsa-ya-daw. BK needed also a famous monk to legitimize his teaching so as to place him within a continuous tradition going back to the time of the Buddha. He sought the sanction from the famous monk insight teacher Wei-bu Hsa-ya-daw to teach and also be ordained under him. This compensates at least to some degree for BK's unordained status and lack of a scriptural learning monastic lineage.

This emphasis on BK's teachings as derived from the ancient Buddhist teachings through evidence of historical continuity is, of course, a feature of Buddhist biography at large. Teachings have to be authenticated, the inheritance of duties and commands have to be substantiated; a hagiography serves to establish legitimacy after death. The Buddha derived legitimacy by making merit through paying homage to previous Buddhas. One may recall here the episode where, in his life as the hermit Thú-mei-da, he lay across a ditch to allow the Di-pin-ká-ra Buddha to walk across and subsequently made the vow to become a Buddha himself one day.[59] It ends with an account of his pupils, the Buddhist Councils, the distribution of his relics and teachings, and the legacy he left behind up until contemporary times. And so also the BK biography, like biographies of other teachers, carefully documents the lineages through which its subject received his methods, and how he transmitted these to his own pupils, some of whom are generally acknowledged teachers in the Burmese tradition of practice. The legitimacy of these lineages also encompasses those who learn mental culture with BK. BK was therefore historicized through the master-pupil relationship by his biographer, who projected back into history a place of significance for his subject, and extended BK's influence through intergenerational transmission beyond the present, pointing at the future.

So far I have noted that there is an important historical dimension to this biography. Central to it is the individual's achieving sanctity not just by his own efforts at mental culture, but by tapping into ancient knowledge as transmitted through ordination, lineage, scriptural learning, and supernatural preservation of knowledge in the higher heavens. This attempt to prove the historic affiliation of BK's knowledge takes the biography away from the much more narrow focus on BK as an individual.

But there is yet another way in which the biographer portrayed BK as a "historic institution," which brings this volume closer to Reynolds' sense of a sacred biography of the founder of a movement. The biographer saw BK as a founder of an important new movement, the history of which needed to be written. The history of the insight traditions as these have been documented in Burma hitherto, are shallow, dating from the end of the nineteenth century at best.

A common view by students of Buddhist practice is that its history until the end of the nineteenth century is one of "sleeping texts"—texts that were meaningless because they were not put into practice—on the one hand, and conversely of "silent Buddhas"—experienced contemplators who did not bother to teach their practice to others—on the other.[60] Only in the course of this century did Buddhist texts come alive by having been put in practice. Experienced yogi, rather than disappearing without a trace after quietly achieving enlightenment in the forest, had now actually come out to teach others. The biographer judged Buddhist history in a similar vein when he wrote that the conventional history of Buddhism was a history of scriptural learning, where Buddhist "practice" (*pa-dí-pat-ti*) and its fruits "remain hidden."[61] He portrayed BK as a pioneer who broke silence by teaching mental culture to the unordained. In turn, the biographer himself, by writing the biography of BK, aimed to textualize contemporary practice for posterity, thereby providing the Burmese tradition of practice with a historical continuity that it would not otherwise have. This emphasis on documenting lineage history in the BK biography, therefore, must be understood in this context of urgently compensating for a dearth of historical information about the tradition of practice.

Burmese "Biography"

So far I have sought to explain the emphasis on history in this volume in terms of both a more universally shared "hagiographical" theme of establishing continuity with the past and determining rules of succession, and the "sacred biographical" theme of establishing the uniqueness of a subject's role in the twentieth-century movement from text to practice. Furthermore, Ko Lei was conscious of the importance of his biography as documenting this historical transition from text to practice.

At this point I want to raise two questions. First, how "dispersed" can a biography become before it ceases to be a biography? If, for whatever reason, a biographer emphasizes mainly the subject's historical-institutional dimensions and devotes little space to the subject's life between cradle and grave, can it still be termed a biography? In order to comprehend this I must convey something about Burmese ideas about biography.

Various early Burmese genres incorporate biographical information.[62] The earliest stone inscriptions (*kyauk-sa*) included information about Ma-ha-ek-gá Pan-dí-ta (1174 A.D.) and King Da-má-zei-dí (1479 A.D.). With the expansion of literature in the course of the fourteenth and fifteenth centuries, much biographical information came to be conveyed in stylized literary genres, mostly composed in verse (*ga-bya*), often by monks and courtiers specifically for the ear of royalty. This included the historical records (*màw-gun*), which took notable events in the king's life as their theme. Eulogies (*eì-gyìn*) are verse biographies commonly composed about members of royalty on the occasion of important life-cycle ceremonies in the form of an address to a royal child, which told the child of the great achievements of his or her royal ancestors, tracing the line back to ancient progenitors of the family. Historical accounts of a campaign (*a-yeì-daw-bon*) pivot around the exploits of a member of royalty. From the sixteenth century onwards, biographical episodes of monks and kings in interaction with each other were recorded in the royal chronicles (*ya-za win*).

The introduction of the printing press in the nineteenth century marks a significant increase in the sheer quantity of biographies in circulation. It also marked a completely new era in Burmese biography, of which contemporary Burmese teacher biographies are an example. They were the result of a movement in twentieth-century literature: from verse to prose, and from Pāli or Pāli-Burmese *neik-tha-yá* (P. *nissāya*) to the vernacular. Also, until the 20th century the laity and the commoner were rarely subject to biographical description, but they gradually became worthy biographical subjects. Since almost all early biography dealt either with kings or monks, the volume considered here is representative of the trend toward biographies of unordained nonroyal persons.

Somewhere along this historical time scale the term *at-htok-pat-tí* came to be understood in a somewhat exclusive way. Some have argued that this term took over in popular reference from the more ancient scriptural term *a-pá-dan* (P. *apádāna*).[63] But the term was already in use during the life of the famous monk author Thi-lá-wun-thá (1453–1518), who used it in the title of his biography of the Buddha (*Bok-dok-pat-tí*). And yet, despite this evidence, some critics have suggested that there has never been any form of *at-htok-pat-tí* in Burma until very recently in the latter part of the colonial period: "Biographies [*at-htok-pat-tí*] have been almost completely absent in early Burmese literary history. As for part-biographical works such as the ruling by Hkon-daw Maung Kyá-bàn, the *A-yu-daw Min-ga-la* petition . . . these were not complete biographies. Biographies came with modern Burmese literature among such works as *Pi-mò-nìn i Pi-mò-nìn*, which records experiences in Oxford University"[64] This notion that the Burmese did not have "biography" until they visited Oxford, despite all the evidence cited already to the contrary, needs closer examination.

Today the term *at-htok-pat-tí* serves as the Burmese generic term for biography. It is a Pāli compound loan word, made up of *at-htá* (sense, meaning, import, a principle, fundamental idea) and *ok-pat-tí* (occurrence).[65] In the Pāli texts it meant "occasions, esp. an occurrence giving occasion to a *dhamma-desanā*," meaning that some event required didactic elaboration in terms of the *dhamma* as derived from a context larger than apparent to those who were witness to it.

At-htok-pat-tí has a wide range of meanings. First, it recounts the story not so much of a biological individual, as of a person in terms of their life (or multiple lives), which are not strictly circumscribed. Life is not only a matter between the cradle and the grave, but it covers the story of an individual's many births in different guises—spirit, animal, or human. This does not necessarily mean that a person's life will *always* be recounted in terms of many different lives, but biographers have creative license to write about relationships as if they were bound to have evolved as the effect of actions in past lives in terms of Buddhist principles. Contemporary Burmese censorship laws prevent too imaginative a claim. In particular the popular biographies of concentration meditators, *weik-zas, bo-daws*, and *gan-da-ri* practitioners have been banned from publication and are confiscated from the bookstalls. Such "occult" biographies include for example Paw Ù (1952) and Sein Gán (n.d.) on the life of Bò Bò Aung,[66] and Maung Gyì (1952) on the life of Aung Mìn Gaung.[67] These extend the lives of individuals beyond the normal human life span and allude to the maturation of powers of their subjects over many lives as the result of concentration meditation and occult practices. But even in the mainstream Buddhist tradition of insight contemplation (*wí-pat-tha-na*), there are allusions to previous lives. For example, the author of the Ma-ha-si Hsa-ya-daw, a famous teacher, suggested that the meeting with his benefactor was bound to happen as in a past life they were associated and they had the same lay name.[68] Literary critics may dismiss this as merely a literary device. However, this dispersal of life by projection of it into history beyond the individual's life span also, I would argue, affects notions of "history," "tradition," and "lineage," and can potentially turn a hagiography into a form of religious history based on the exploits of more than a single individual.

Second, the use of the Burmese term *at-htok-pat-tí* in everyday vernacular (i.e., not as a literary genre) pertains to "events" in the widest sense without strict delineation as to the exact nature of the subject to whom these pertain, including those referring to objects and institutions. Taking "life" in its widest meaning of cause-and-effect, it is used to indicate variously "facts," "events," "a statement of fact," and "narration of events."[69] Thus I can refer to the *at-htok-pat-tí* of a dictionary or an institution as well as of a human being. In other words, where I discriminate between "fact," "event," "history," "story," or "fable" in English, in the Burmese vernacular this may all be loosely referred to by the term *at-htok-pat-tí*. In this way it is, for example, difficult to determine the life of an occult wizard (*weik-za*) known as Aung Mìn Gaung, which is billed as both a "royal history" (*ya-za-win*) and a "biography" (*at-htok-pat-tí*): does this latter use of the term mean "biography" or simply "events" (Paw Ù 1952)? Given that Aung Mìn Gaung was presumed to have extended his life through the process of an ordeal (*htwet-yak pauk thì*), it is quite plausible that life should be billed as both biography *and* history. This common emphasis in biography of yogi on transcendence of the here and now shows that the BK biography is but one example of the situation where any rigid distinction between vernacular biography and vernacular history melts away. This vernacular sense of *at-htok-pat-tí* as the story that goes beyond the individual in the here and now is thus bound to come into conflict with the more narrow Western secular-literary criteria of biography, the purpose of which is exactly to confine the person to time and place and to divulge his or her true self.

There are, however, other important ways in which Burmese "vernacular" differs from "secular-literary" sense of biography. First, where secular-literary criteria are typically author-centered, vernacular criteria are typically subject-centered. Observers of biographical literature have sometimes sought to make a distinction between early and contemporary Western biography. Beckson and Ganz (1990) suggest that modern biography, as a carefully researched and relatively dispassionate type of literature, is comparatively recent.[70] With the Renaissance and Reformation, they argued, there grew an emphasis on the individual, when the modern biography evolved (e.g., Boswell's work on Dr. Johnson). With the Romantics and later Freudian influence, the inner life of the subject was emphasized, as in André Maurois' work. However, more than an increased emphasis on the individual as the subject of the biography, I might in fact conclude that this development represents an increased emphasis on scrutinizing the biographer's ability to write about the subject.

This shift in emphasis toward the author, which Foucault dubbed the "author" function, would appear to have marked a change in Western biography. For example, Cockshut observed that Boswell used the term "biography" to cover both autobiography and biography, after which he suggests that: "We may suppose that this was because more interest was felt in the actual record of a life and in the facts shown than in the point of view from which it was written. When the question of point of view becomes crucial for the reader, then only comes the awareness of autobiography as a separate form."[71] In other words, here the distinction between biography and autobiography was less the result of an increased interest in the individual subject than in the author who wrote it. It recognizes biography as a creative effort by a qualified author. At this point, I suggest that the skill of the author to get under the skin of the subject in a truthful manner becomes more important than the inevitable story of the archetypal saint as a historical motif. In this way, contemporary Western secular-literary classification as introduced after Boswell's work at the end of the eighteenth century, namely which distinguishes between *bio*graphy (the author writes about someone else) and *auto*biography (the author writes about him/herself), is not crucially important in traditional Buddhist biography, where the historical imagery of the subject reigns, not the author's skills at evoking this, and where the distinction between different classes of biographical subject (e.g. "human," "monk," or other) is more important.

Second, Western secular-literary classification emphasizes facts[72] and sets great store by demarcating historically verifiable from fictional events, as in the distinction between "fictional" (historically not verifiable) and "historical" (historically verifiable) biography. This particular distinction is not really an issue in Burmese traditional biography, which is probably why the Burmese government decided to take such a strong line against traditional biography, which could ascribe all kinds of miraculous supernatural powers to the subject, and hence potentially destabilize the political order by the uncontrolled appropriation of charisma by biographers to their subjects. Burmese criteria are more concerned with the evocation of awe for the subject of the biography than whether such claims are historically accurate or not.

The differences between secular-literary and Burmese vernacular approaches are reflected in the respective classification of biographies themselves. If, as suggested, Western secular-literary classification is based on the author and author's style of writing, as in ordinary (the author writes about someone else), auto- (the author writes about him/herself), fictional (historically not verifiable), or historical biography (historically verifiable), vernacular biographies are "personalized" biographies, classified on the basis of the subject they consider, as in: for Buddhas (*Bok-dok-pat-tí*); for monks (*Than-gok-pat-tí* or *Htei-rok-pat-tí*); for novices (*Thá-ma-nok-pat-tí*); for "humans" (*lu*) simply by prefixing the name (e.g., *Za-nok-pat-tí*); and for particular named individuals (e.g., *Ma-ha Bok-da-gàw-thok-pat-tí* or *Shin Rá-htá-tha-rok-pat-tí*).[73]

Based on unspoken conventions and emulation of previous authors, the criteria of vernacular biography are subconscious, implicit, and unanalyzed; this is different from Western scholarly secular-literary criteria, which are highly explicit, analyzed, and sharpened by a long intellectual debate about the value of biography in history versus its literary merit.

Plummer suggests that during the Victorian era there was a shift in emphasis which "marked a lesser concern with the praise of great men to a stronger concern with accurate research: the modern biographer has a wealth of facts at hand that have to be sifted out, made into theory, carefully checked."[74] Also, the biographical subject here is no longer an illustration of historical sanctity, but a creation of the individual author that can be only as truthful as the author's methodology and circumstances allow. The biographer at this point is more a researcher and a creative literary writer than a person who has to write because he or she is overcome by the superior and appealing purity of the subject.

But it would be wrong to suggest that all senses of Burmese biography operate in the vernacular sense sketched so far. Alongside the vernacular classification just described, there is a tradition of biography that operates with a much narrower and concise concept similar to the secular-literary concept as described above. In Burma also, the Western secular-literary emphasis on author and historical verifiability has become, in some way or another, a central force in the classification and understanding of biography, thus shifting away from the traditional focus on the subject's significance. Elsewhere I have shown how Burmese Buddhist biography today is placed uncomfortably alongside "modern" Burmese biography as defined at a conference on biography organized by the Burmese government.[75] This forum adopted the usual Western secular-literary classification, by now influential internationally, and regarded virtually all previously produced Burmese biography as an anomaly because it is unchanging, legendary, and not true to reality, where all "bad is drowned and only the good tends to be recounted."

Biographized "History"

In the discussion so far I have noted that *at-htok-pat-tí*, the Burmese term for biography, is in its vernacular sense a remarkably flexible term that can be made to mean the story of almost anything, including animate and inanimate subjects, and that could also mean the history of a lineage. Furthermore, a flexible notion of life encompassing the idea of rebirth extends an individual's life into the past and allows a biography to be potentially more historical than I could imagine in terms of the secular-literary understandings of this genre. Where I talk of influence and emulation of historical personages, the Burmese biographical subject is potentially multiple historical personages.

Conversely, however, it should be noted that the Burmese have for a long time conceived of their history within a biographical framework. Reynolds drew attention to this phenomenon,[76] which was further elaborated by Tambiah.[77] Tambiah developed the notion of "periodization" in the context of his analysis of biographies of Thai teachers. He distinguishes between two notions of biography in the Buddhist tradition, namely *avadāna*, the earliest scriptural instance for a biographical episode, as it "seems to have referred to a great action having decisive consequences" used to "highlight a point of discipline or a moral precept." This he contrasts the concept with *vaṃsa*, a much later development that "implied some kind of succession of kings or teachers." In the latter the Buddha biography itself became the kernel of elaborated histories. In the Sinhalese *Mahāvaṃsa* and the Thai *Jinakalamali*, the Buddha biography forms "a necessary prelude to their (Sinhalese and Thai) religio-political tales"—i.e., both to the monastic religio-history as well as the secular chronicle.[78]

In Burma, there is a very similar relationship between biography and history. History was for a long time the history of the Buddhist teachers and their teachings (*tha-tha-na win*), and the rulers and their dynasties (*ya-za win*). The Buddha's biography invariably prefaces both of these, and his relics and footsteps link various geographical regions into a single history. Indeed, the Buddha's biography may be seen to envelop Burmese history, for his manifestations have not come to an end. His *da-tú neik-ban*, the final reassembly of his relics, will initiate the decline and eventual disappearance of religion 2,500 years from now, which will mark the end of history for this world-system. Hence, as pointed out by Tambiah, the Buddha's biographies not only show, but participate in "a remarkable view of the 'historical' unfolding of Buddhism."[79]

The Buddha is not only placed at the apex of Burmese vernacular history, but Burmese conceive him as perhaps the most significant source from whom they not only derive their spirituality, but also their language and physique. This view Burmese have of continuity with both the "spiritual" lineage back to the Buddha through the tradition of ordination and the "physical" lineage through the lineage of kings is also reflected in the way the Burmese language is thought to have originated with the language of the Buddhist scriptures ("the original language," *mu-lá ba-tha*) so that there is a tendency for the etymology of the Burmese vernacular terms and for the grammar of the vernacular to be sought in Pāli. Western historians and linguists have ridiculed this view as uninformed and inaccurate. For example, Burmese vernacular history has been derided by colonial historians such as Harvey, who found that "perhaps as much as half the narrative told as historical down to the thirteenth century is folk-lore."[80] History, colonial historians proposed, should be consistent with Western linguistic, geographic, but in particular racial classifications. As Harvey put it, "the Burmans are a Mongolian race, yet their traditions, instead of harking back to China, refer to India . . . the surviving traditions of the Burman are Indian because their own Mongolian traditions died out."[81] In similar vein, Luce wrote that "the Abhiraja/Dharaja legends showing the continuity in the Buddha's Indian lineage with those of Burmese royalty were presumably invented to give Burmans a noble derivation from the Sakiyan line of Buddha Gotama himself. But one only has to put a Burman between a North Indian and a Chinese, to see at a glance where his racial connections lie."[82]

Where colonial historians conceived of history in terms of "racial" and "linguistic" continuity of a people, Burmese vernacular historians were more concerned with the "spiritual" continuity from the time of the Buddha from which all history was conceived to come forth, irrespective of race or language. The Buddha's personal visits (often marked by footprints) and his relics determined the periphery of his immediate geography, by virtue of which all shared a common history. But this vernacular scheme of history, where Burmese considered themselves as having a closer historical relationship with people in India, was contradicted by the view emerging during the colonial era, which proposed that they were racially and linguistically "mongoloid" with more affinity to the Tibetans and, more distantly, the Chinese, than with the Indian subcontinent.[83] In relation to this it is interesting to note that insight contemplation, by its emphasis on impermanence, change, and non-self, releases individuals from their immediate past and allows the integration of Buddhism with this much changed contemporary society as it was inherited from the colonial experience. Historical accounts of practice are unlike the older vernacular histories, for they do not commence their history with the life of the Buddha, but limit themselves only to the history of practice in Burma. In this respect perhaps, these new genres of literature have recognized a geographical "break" in accordance with contemporary "secular" ideas about their origination.

So traditional Thai and Burmese history could be seen as "biographized" because they recount history in terms of developments in the life of the Buddha and his relics.[84] But the BK biography considered here is, though related, slightly different. The BK biography is "historicized biography," namely a biography of lineage rather than just of an individual's life.

How Historical Can Biography Be?

Given the dispersed, largely historical nature of BK's life as it comes across from his biography, and given the important role of biography in vernacular history, I may ask what this means in the light of our own conceptions of the relationship between history and biography as genres. Are there any limits to biography? At what point does a biography become, for example, a "history"?

As noted above, the conference on Burmese biography adopted the author-centered classification of biography and dismissed most pre-twentieth-century Burmese biography as an improper form of biography. If this genre, of which the BK biography is part, is not "biography," is it a form of "history"? Some historians, such as Collingwood, class biography as not only "non-historical," but "anti-historical."[85] When I ask why, I find that Collingwood points at the biological limitations on the life of a human being, the framework of which allows the tides of thought to "flow crosswise, regardless of its structure, like sea-water through a stranded wreck." Collingwood here makes two assumptions.[86] First, he views biography as limited by the cradle and the grave, so that he cannot conceive of alternative constructions of life in other cultures, e.g., comprising rebirth or documenting the authenticity of an individual within a tradition. Second, his exclusive view on history as "what historians think it is" does not leave much room for alternative vernacular history of any sort. Although he recognizes historical value in religious documents and biography, as these are not based on the premise of history as a science and do not involve the qualified interpretation of evidence, these can not be called "history."

In a sense, then, if I am to accept the criteria advanced in the arguments of both the government conference on biography and of Collingwood, the

BK biography is neither biography nor history. But neither the government conference nor Collingwood were prepared to advance biography as constructions by the biographer's and historian's respective sociocultural backgrounds. Closer to the social sciences I find historians and literary critics prepared to modify this "hierarchical" notion. Here the author's function is extended to the author's social environment. The social sciences have thereby come to exert an important influence on history, and a gradual shift has taken place where, for example, the relativity of science is recognized as the product of an author at a particular time with a particular socioeconomic or other background,[87] which allowed the development of new branches of history such as oral history.[88] Nevertheless, here I have merely extended the same secular-literary qualification of biography, which is that this recognizes both biography and history to be not only "created" by authors, but also in a wider sense by the author's sociocultural environment and personality. These therefore attribute agency for the life story to the author more than, as in the vernacular biography, to the immutable story sanctity which the author merely has the privilege of "facilitating." The reader's preoccupation has changed from a "literal" interest in the text as simply true in a divine sort of way, to a "literary" interest as a text that has been "humanly" created at a particular time in a particular place.[89]

Vernacular biography and history are both literal (not literary) subject-centered (not author-centered) genres in which a subject moves somewhere in between the interstices of life episode, life, lineage, and history. "Biography," in this way, could refer to "history", and, conversely, "history" could refer to "biography."

Vernacular biography therefore merges into vernacular history without a clear boundary in between. I have shown how vernacular history is sometimes prefixed and enveloped by the biography of the Buddha. However, I have not yet noted that the biography of the Buddha is the only biography of an individual to merit the designation "history" (*win*) in Burmese. For example, as used by Da-má-reik-hkí-tá (1980) the term *bok-da win* refers to the biography of the Buddha with no other episodes beyond information directly relevant to his life. Out of 101 pages, only the first deals with his vow to become a Buddha during his life as the hermit Thú-mei-da and the last page deals with his relics in the Rangoon Shwedagon Pagoda: the rest deals with his life directly. Yet the term *bok-da win* can also refer to the lineage of the twenty-four Buddhas, in which case the prefix Buddha should be read in the plural. Furthermore, when the term *dispensation* is added, as in *bok-dá tha-tha-na win*, I may find a combination of a biography of the Buddha and the history of the religion until the present. For example, in Za-na-ká (1951) two pages are devoted to the Buddha's previous life as Thú-mei-da who gives away his wealth and, as a hermit, prostrates himself in front of the then Buddha, forty-nine pages to Gotama's birth and his life, seven pages to the distribution of his relics and the councils after his demise, and a final six pages to Buddhism in Burma. But there is no doubt that, when used in the sense of Da-má-reik-hkí-tá, (1980) the term *bok-da win*, which strictly speaking means "history of the Buddha," is the biography of Gotama Buddha only (without the story of other Buddhas) and without the additional history. Use of the term *win* in the sense of "biography" is not acceptable reference to the biography of anyone else but the Buddha.

I suggest, therefore, that the Buddha biography is conceived as both a history and a biography. If this is to be interpreted as a role model for Burmese biographies, I may ask whether there are aspirations here to be a "history" too. Indeed, there is some evidence to suggest that this is the case. The one evolves almost surreptitiously from the other. Burmese Buddhist literature recognizes two different types of biographical description. The first, with the suffix *htok-pat-tí*, implies the story of the individual whose name precedes the suffix, as in *Ma-ha-si htei-rok-pat-tí*, the biography of the venerable Mahasi. Here the story is recounted with the person as a focus, though it may, as with BK, quite readily depart into the historical realms away from the person as an individual and just seek to understand the origination of his spirituality deep into the past, and/or his historical influence on others.

The second type of description, with the suffix *win*, implies a succession of biographies related by lineage to a main personage. Derived from *wun-thá* (P. *vaṃsa*), i.e., "race," "lineage," "tradition," "dynasty," "spiritual lineage," or "history of persons or places," the term *win* itself has come to mean history. I have also noted that *Bok-dá-win* is sometimes exceptionally used to refer to a single biography,[90] and may be used (apart from meaning "biography" in the case of the Buddha) to refer to the lineage of the twenty-four Buddhas who preceded Gotama Buddha and not just to his life as Gotama, connected to one another by vows to become Buddhas taken in the presence of previous Buddhas. Here it is used in the sense of a compilation of biographies within a lineage. In this way, the biographies included in the *tha-tha-na win* reflect an ordered historical succession of persons related by pupilage to a single teacher.[91]

There is evidence that sometimes the "history" (*win*) is composed before the "biography" (*at-htok-pat-tí*) of its founder is issued as a separate document. In this way, the biography of the Mahasi, the chief monk of one of the biggest insight associations in Burma, was first published in 1974 in the context of the ambitious *History of Practice* (*pa-dí-pat-tí tha-tha-na win*), which strung together his biography with 186 brief biographies of his pupils who were teaching at insight centers all over the country.[92] His biography was published only much later in 1982, separately as a biography in the first sense, namely as a *htei-rok-pat-tí* (in much the same format).[93]

While Mahasi's biography was initially published as a prelude to many subsequent biographies, as the lineage's standard only to be published later as a separate biography, the BK tradition, in contrast, lacks any consistent record of a preceding separate "lineage." There is only one document by Ko Lei, which happens to be a "biography" but must at the same time address the historical dimensions of the BK heritage.

I do not here wish to suggest that vernacular biography (*at-htok-pat-tí*) always evolves from a prior vernacular history (*win*). It is, for example, quite possible for biographies to precede the development of a vernacular history. Indeed, Hteì Hlaing (1981) and Wí-thok-dí (1976)[94] chronicled the tradition of practice in Burma by summarizing from preexisting biographies of monks and lay people renowned for their practice. What I do suggest, however, is that vernacular biography stresses the historical dimensions of its subject and that it is in the nature of the Buddhist tradition to emphasize historical continuity of the subject as early as possible, without which a biography can not be a credible proposition. The BK biography, by having no preceding "history" (*win*) published, serves not only as a biography in the narrow sense of recording someone's life, but as a biography in the wide-ranging Burmese sense of *at-htok-pat-tí*, meaning a description of the continuity of his teachings with the past, and of his heritage amongst his pupils. In other words, it is biography as well as history in the vernacular sense.[95]

Conclusion

Kindall argued that "biography as an independent art form, with its concentration upon the individual life and its curiosity about the individual personality, is essentially the creation of Western man." He furthermore suggests that in Asia, and in particular in China and Japan, biography developed as a by-product of historical writing, so that "biographical literature does not show the development, nor assume the importance, of Western life writing."[96]

When we look at Burma, Kindall's statement would, at first sight, appear to be valid. It is undoubtedly true, as I have noted in the case of the BK biography, that there is an emphasis on history in this biography. It is also true that the distinction between biography and history is not self-evident. But once the vernacular categories are considered in some detail, I find that what Burmese might refer to as "biography" I would often prefer to call "lineage history." Conversely, what Burmese call "history" could readily be interpreted as a form of biography.

As the BK biography shows, the relationship between history and biography can evidently be conceived in various ways. Biographies of insight teachers document continuity and seek to legitimize the new lineage these teachers engender. In building upon Reynolds (1976) and Tambiah (1984), I suggest that, once the interest in a person's life persists, this life becomes rewritten as the focal point of a lineage strung together in the form of multiple linked biographies called *tha-tha-na win*, which may (and it is probably the author's intention that they should) become national histories. The BK and Mahasi biographies illustrate intersections along these trajectories of *at-htok-pat-tí*, where individual persons are teased out of their "individuality" in the here and now to transcend the contemporary world and to become a force in history. A successful biography here is one that can convince the readership of the claim to a long historical period of influence on the subject, and by the subject on others. To this extent, then, vernacular biography both encompasses and is encompassed by vernacular history, and a strict typological distinction between the two is false. These are not discrete, bounded genres, but "dispersed" genres always in the process of evolving from one into the other.

It would therefore appear that Kindall's two premises should be qualified as follows. First, it is not that Burmese biographical writing is a by-product of historical writing; instead, it represents an appeal for legitimacy of its subject which, by virtue of the nature of Buddhism, must be rooted in a historical discourse about lineage and spiritual continuity. Second, it is not that biographical writing is any less important in Burmese literature as compared to Western literature; instead, it is that they both involve an entirely different genre based on different conceptions of life and history. The Burmese concept incorporates animate as well as inanimate subjects and, by virtue of perceiving life as dispersed across different species and lives, takes potentially a broader "historical" time scale in view.

These arguments are, of course, largely moderated by secular education introduced in the course of this century, when the genres of "biography" and "history" came to be redefined in Burma much along the lines supported by the Western syllabus introduced into the schools and universities. Nevertheless, the way Buddhist teachers such as BK are historicized in their biographies is bound up with the historical nature of Burmese Buddhism. In fact, the tendency to accentuate the subject as a historical dispersed individual is still evident in the Burmese classification of "Buddhist." Different vernacular terms have come to be used to designate different classes of Buddhist, depending on how pure and how historically close the person is to the Buddha's teachings in terms of ordination and mental culture. Buddhists are designated either as "inside Buddhism" (*bok-dá tha-tha-na win*) or "inside Buddhendom" (*bok-dá ba-tha win*).[97] The first is closest to the original historical source in ordination, interpretation, and practice. The last is more distant, having been inherited through convention, birth, and parental education. The point to note here is that the term *win* has a double meaning. First, it means sometimes "history," when a historical sequence of events is recounted with reference to either the Buddha's teachings (*tha-tha-na win*) or several generations of rulers (*ya-za win*). Second, the term *win* is used sometimes to refer to a "core" Buddhist by ordination or action (e.g., mental culture), as in *tha-tha-na win*. If the first takes *win* in the sense of Pāli *vaṃsa*, which implies a succession of generations and the source of this, the second refers to an individual member "within" this history (as in "Party member," *pa-ti win*). The tendency toward historicizing BK is therefore not just another device of the biographer, but it is generic to the definition of "Buddhist," so much so that, for an individual to be a true Buddhist, they have to be designated as an incumbent in a historical tradition. This reinforces the view that I have already developed here, which is reflected in the Burmese genres of "biography" and "history," namely that there is an overall emphasis on situating the Buddhist subject in a long history, in historicizing the Buddhist.

Reynolds showed in his analysis of the Buddha biography how a gradual process of incorporating new elements over time culminated eventually in full-life stories of the Buddha. There is one important point easily overlooked in the overwhelming detail of this process. The Buddha's last life as Gotama seems to have received less attention in the early biographical material extant than did the accounts of previous Buddhas in the lineage of Buddhas and Gotama's previous lives. Perhaps, as in the BK biography, the presumption that realization of no-self has been attained in mental culture can only lead to biographies that step beyond the limits of individuality set by the secular-literary criteria discussed in this essay.

Acknowledgments

I would like to thank a number of people for their help and stimulating discussion (but I am not implying that they necessarily agree with this essay): U Hla Pe, Richard Burghart, Michael Carrithers, Charles Hallisey, Mark Hobart, John Knight, Khin Nyo, Lans Cousins, and Dominique Remars. I am grateful to the Leach-RAI Fellowship for assistance in completing this essay.

Notes

1. Though biography, in the general sense of "human document," goes back to the most ancient of times, most who look at the history of biography

have pointed at the seventeenth and eighteenth centuries as a watershed. Ken Plummer, *Documents of Life: An Introduction to the Problems and Literature of a Humanistic Method* (London and Boston: George Allen and Unwin, 1983), p. 8, suggests that, although autobiography goes back to Egyptian tomb inscriptions and oral history, the sense of individualism that arose in the eighteenth century provided a new sense of biography much in the way Lionel Trilling (*Sincerity and Authenticity* [Oxford: Oxford University Press, 1972], p. 42) said that "at a certain point in history men became individuals." At this point in time people "start to develop fully a sense of themselves as objects of introspection, of interest, of value, when the individual begins to brood and reflect over his or her inner nature; a time when the individual starts to retreat from the public life into the realms of privacy—the inner thought, the private home, the real self." Boswell's *Life of Samuel Johnson* (1791) in particular stands out as the most eloquent example of biography. R. Gittings (*The Nature of Biography* [London: Heinemann, 1978], p. 35) suggested that biography failed to develop as a distinctive form until the Victorian era, with the writings of Carlyle, Mrs. Gaskell, and Lytton Strachey.

2. Paul M. Kindall, "Biography" (*Encyclopaedia Britannica*, 15th ed., Macropaedia, vol. 2, 1980), p. 1011.
3. Ibid.
4. *The Concise Oxford English Dictionary* (Oxford: Clarendon Press, 1982).
5. W. R. Siebenschuh, "Biography" (*American Academic Encyclopedia*, Compuserve, 4/28/91).
6. The romanization of Burmese adopted here is the conventional transcription with accented tones as developed in John Okell, *A Guide to the Romanization of Burmese* (James G. Forlong Fund, vol. 27 [London: Royal Asiatic Society, 1971], pp. 66–67).
7. The Burmese term has been used in relation to a hill, as in "The biography of Pok-pa hill" (*Pok-pà-taung i at-htok-pat-tí*) by Tha Tin, Hseì-hsa-ya-gyì and Ù Bá Sein (n.p., n.d.).
8. G. Houtman, "Traditions of Buddhist Practice in Burma" (Ph.D. diss., University of London, 1990), pp. 326–37.
9. The implications of the vernacular terminology for "Buddhism" and "Buddhist" from the perspective of this new-Buddhist movement have been analyzed in G. Houtman, "How a Foreigner invented Buddhendom in Burmese: from *tha-tha-na* to *bok-dá ba-tha*" (*Journal of the Anthropological Society at Oxford*, vol. 21/2, 1991).
10. Ko Lei, Ù (see also under pen-name Zei-ya Maung), *Myan-má-gon-zaung-pok-ko-htù Hsa-ya-gyì Ù Bá Hkin at-htok-pat-tí hnín tha-tha-na-pyú lok-ngàn-myà* [Burma's special person glorious Hsa-ya-gyì Ù Bá Hkin, his biography and missionary works] (Rangoon: Ngwei-sa-yìn mìn-gyì-yōn Wí-pat-tha-na A-hpwé, 1980), cited hereafter as KL.
11. The Le-di Hsa-ya-daw (1846–1923) was a famous monk-scholar who, although he did not set up dedicated meditation centers, was extremely

influential in the meditation traditions of Burma. He taught many monks and some lay people who went on to found meditation centers throughout the country.

12. The Wei-bu Hsa-ya-daw (1896–1977) was a famous meditation teacher.
13. KL (1980, p. i).
14. See Houtman (1990, 204–205).
15. KL, pp. 9, 66, 160.
16. Ibid., pp. 245–321.
17. Ibid., pp. 261–266.
18. Ibid., p. 294.
19. Ibid., pp. 66–88.
20. We do not know what kind of broker his father was.
21. KL, p. 67.
22. Ibid., p. 591.
23. Ibid., p. 76.
24. *A-bí da-ma pyán pwà yeì A-thìn.*
25. KL (1980, p. 76).
26. Ibid., p. 591.
27. It should be noted that BK's leave for meditation was taken three months before the accountancy office was to be separated from India, which may not have been a coincidence.
28. *Ta-bet-hpyu*, for which another word is *law-bet*. Commonly put on during Buddhist duty day.
29. In Burma, abbots are popularly known by the name of the region in which they reside. Hence, the Wei-bu Hsa-ya-daw derives his name from a nearby mountain spur.
30. "A white cloth" is *peik-hpyu lè-pì*; KL (1980, p. 83).
31. The designation of U Ba Khin as a "guru" in Burmese is interesting, as it is not a Burmese term and not normally used to address a teacher. However, as explained in this essay, U Ba Khin worked in an "Indian" office that he eventually transformed into a "Burmese" one. But he was a teacher to some Indians, and many foreigners who came to Burma were more comfortable with the Indian designations than with the Burmese "Hsa-ya-gyì."
32. During the period of Japanese occupation (1942–1945), BK was director of the Accountants and Auditors Department (KL 1980, p. 592).
33. Ibid., p. 592.
34. The name of the hill was *A-za-ni Kòn.*
35. KL (1980, p. 359).
36. This association, known as Bok-dá-tha-tha-ná a-kyò-hsaung A-thìn, was founded on November 10, 1950; it counted 497 members, of which 24 were officials (KL 1980, p. 592).
37. Ngwei-sa-yìn-mìn-gyì-yòn Wí-pat-tha-na-dat-pyin-ya A-hpwé.
38. *Weik-za-dat a-htù.*
39. KL (1980, p. 99).

40. Ngwei-sa-yìn mìn-gyì-yòn Wí-pat-tha-na A-hpwé.
41. A-pyi-byi-hsaing-ya Pa-dí-pat-tí-lok-ngàn Hta-ná (KL 1980, p. 100).
42. He was still head of the Department of Merchandise and Crops, head of the Traffic Auditors, and head of the Accountancy School.
43. KL (1980, p. 405).
44. The term *pa-rí-neik-ban san thi* is not used for death.
45. KL (1980, p. 440).
46. Ibid., p. 437.
47. Other episodes on BK's life include: a subsection on "the looking for a place and the building" (KL 1980, pp. 98–100); an episode in the chapter on the relationship between the biographer and BK (chap. 6); on the deteriorating health, death, and subsequent commemoration of BK (chaps. 8,9); and on the contents of his preaching (chap. 11). Elsewhere I identified three pervasive themes both in this and in the biography of the Ma-ha-si Hsa-ya-daw: namely, the distinction between different forms of Buddhist action, in particular between scriptural learning (*pa-rí-yat-tí*) and practice (*pa-dí-pat-tí*); the foreigner and the notion of "globality"; and the master-pupil relationship and the notion of "lineage" (Houtman 1990, p. 214–233).
48. Frank Reynolds, introduction to "The Many Lives of Buddha: A Study of Sacred Biography and Theravada Tradition," in *The Biographical Process: Studies in the History of the Psychology of Religion*, ed. F. E. Reynolds and D. Capps (The Hague: Mouton, 1976).
49. Ibid., p. 5.
50. Ibid.
51. E.g., KL (1980, pp. i, iii, 83, 375).
52. Ibid., pp. 373, 393, 440.
53. Ibid., pp. 42, 278.
54. Ibid., p. 462.
55. A Burmese friend interpreted this halo as a "clever" presentation, because—with U Ba Khin sitting outside—it could also be interpreted as the full moon appearing behind him.
56. KL (1980, p. 439).
57. Ira Bruce Nadel, *Biography: Fiction, Fact and Form* (London: Macmillan Press, 1984), p. 6.
58. Reynolds (1976, p. 4).
59. The story of Thú-mei-da and Di-pin-ka-rá forms the first couple of illustrations in a book about the Buddha's life by Da-má-reik-hkí-tá, *Bok-da-win-yok-pon* [Illustrated life of the Buddha] (Rangoon: Sa-be-ù, 1980), pp. 5–6, and in a book by Bí-wun-tha Za-na-ká, *Yok-son bok-dá-tha-tha-na win* [An illustrated history of Buddhism] (Rangoon: YMBA, 1951). In both of these the Gotama Buddha-to-be lies across a ditch with flowers held up high in offering to the previous Buddha, who walks over him. Both have the distribution of the relics and the way Rangoon Shwedagon commemorates these, but only the latter has the story of the Councils.

60. These interpretations come from two works on the practice tradition: Da-má-sa-rí-ya Ù Hteì Hlaing, *Myan-ma Naing-ngan pa-dí-pat-tí tha-tha-na-win: ya-hàn-da hnín pok-ko htū myà* [History of the Burmese practice tradition: enlightened and special persons] Rangoon: Bok-da A-than Sa-bei, 1981) p. 12; and Thi-la-nan-da (1979, p. i). See Houtman (1990, p. 76–96).

61. KL (1980, pp. ix–x).

62. I am indebted for my understanding of early Burmese biographical literature in particular to Prof. Em. Hla Pe, "Burmese Literature" (typescript submitted to *Letteratura d'Oriente*, n.d.) and Ù Hlá Kyaing, *Myan-ma at-htok-pat-tí tha-maìng* [The history of Burmese biography] in *At-htok-pat-tí sa-bei-hnì-hnàw hpa-hle-bwè sa-dàn* [Proceedings of the conference on biography] (Rangoon: Sa-bei Beik-man, 1971), pp. 1–39.

63. Hlá Tha-mein, *Myan-ma Naing-gan gan-da-win pok-ko-gyaw-myà at-htok-pat-tí* [Collected biographies of famous authors from Burma] (Rangoon: Han-tha-wá-di, 1961), p. *nyá* and Nei-yìn Ù Kàw-wí-dá, *Mō-hnyìn Ma-ha-htei-ra-pa-dan* [Biography of the Mò-hnyin Hsa-ya-daw], 1st ed. (Rangoon: Nei-yìn Ù Kà-wí-dá, 1971), p. xiv. This is the main biography of a meditation teacher pupil of the Le-di Hsa-ya-daw, which includes an astrological chart on pp. 15–16.

64. *At-htok-pat-tí, Myan-má swe-zon kyàn* [MSK] [Burmese encyclopaedia], vol. 15/1976, compiled by Myan-ma Naing-gan Ba-tha-byan Sa-bei A-thìn (Rangoon: Sa-bei Beik-man Pon-hneik-daik), pp. 353–354.

65. Pāli *atthupatti*, "sense, meaning, explanation, interpretation" (T. W. Rhys-Davids and William Stede, *Pali Text Society's Pali-English Dictionary* (London: Pāli Text Society, 1921–1925, reprint, 1979. Rhys-Davids & Stede suggested P. *attha* means "interest, advantage, gain; (moral) good, blessing, welfare; profit, prosperity, well-being," which is also used to refer to interpretation according to the "letter" (P. *attha*) as opposed to the "spirit" (*dhamma*) of a particular passage. Htùn Myín in *Pa-lí thet wàw-ha-rá a-bí-dàn* [A dictionary of Pāli loanwords] (Rangoon[?]: Tek-ga-tho-myà sa-ok-pyú-sú htok-wei-yeì kaw-mi-ti, sa-zin 31, 1968), pp. 460, 461, translates *at-htá* as meaning *a-kyaśng a-ya*, for which J. A. Stewart and C. W. Dunn in *A Burmese–English Dictionary* (London: Luzac and Co (pts. I–II), SOAS (pts. III–VI), 1940–1981) give "the facts." Htùn Myín (1986) translates *at-htok-pat-tí* as *hpyit-zin*, meaning "occurrence," "event," or "happening." Biographies are sometimes not referred to in the title as either *htei-rok-pat-tí* or *at-htok-pat-tí*, but simply as "his life" (*thú ba-wá*), as is the case for example with Hteì Hlaing, Da-ma-sa-rí-yá Ù (*A-na-gan Hsa-ya Thet-gyì thú ba-wá, thú-ta-yà hnín thú kyeí-zù* [*He who has introduced Burma to the world—A-na-gan Hsa-ya Thet-gyì, his life, his teachings, and his grace*] Rangoon: Nì-thit Sa-ok-daik, 1978).

66. Ù Paw Ù, *Pok-pà-taung-ka-lat weik-za-do Aung Mìn Gaung í htwet-yak-pauk ya-za-win at-htok-pat-tí* (Rangoon: Mí-bá Myit-ta Pon-hneik-daik, 1952); Pa-hta-má-gyaw Ù Sein Gán, *Bò Bò Aung at-htok-pat-tí hnín kò-gwe-nì* (Rangoon: Myan-má-yok-shin-sa Pon-hneik-daik, n.d.).

67. Ù Maung Gyì, *Weik-za-do Aung Mìn Gaung i htwet-yak-pauk ya-za-win at-htok-pat-tí* (Rangoon: Mí-bá-myit-ta Pon-hneik-daik, 1952).
68. Thi-la-nan-da (1979, p. 8).
69. Examples of the term *at-htok-pat-tí* are as follows: "as for the history of a country, these are the records of a country's *at-htok-pat-tí* or past happenings" (*Nain-ngan-tha-maíng hso-thi-hma naing-ngan i at-htok-pat-ti" (wa) sheì-haśng-hnaśng hpyit-dó-go yeì-hmat-htà-thí hmat-tàn-bin hpyit thi, MSK* vol 6, p. 110); "the *at-htok-pat-tí* and circumstances of printing the dictionary" (*A-bí-dan yaik-hneik-gyìn at-htok-pat-tí*), which refers to the Pāli Dictionary on which the Le-di Hsa-ya-daw had been commissioned to work by Western Pāli scholars (Le-di Ù, Wun-ní-tá *Le-di Hsa-ya-daw Ma-ha-htei-myat-gyì i ma-ha-htei-rok-pat-tí-gá-hta* [The biography of the Le-di Hsa-ya-daw], [Rangoon: Han-tha-wá-di, 1956], p. 191); or in the title "The history of *events* relating to the BTNA organization of the Union of Burma" (*Pyei-daung-zú Myan-ma-naing-ngan-daw Bok-dá Tha-tha-na Nok-ga-há A-hpwé at-htok-pat-tí tha-maìng*). It is used as "fact" in: "considering the *facts* that the eyes are staring and do not wink, he must be the god Sakka." It is used in the sense of "statement of facts" in "they told (the King) where his (Mahosadha's) parents dwelt and *all about them* and his age."
70. Karl Beckson and Arthur Ganz, *Literary Terms: A Dictionary*, 3rd ed. (London: Andre Deutsch, 1990).
71. Michel Foucault, "What Is an Author," in *Language, Counter-Memory, and Practice: Selected Essays and Interviews*, ed. Donald F. Bouchard (Oxford: Basil Blackwell, 1977), pp. 113–138. A. O. J. Cockshut, *The Art of Autobiography in Nineteenth and Twentieth Century England* (New Haven: Yale University Press, 1984), p. 13.
72. Nadel (1984, p. 5) emphasizes this when he says, "The importance of fact in biography corresponds with the seventeenth-century rise of science, the eighteenth-century emergence of empiricism, the nineteenth-century dominance by history and the modern emphasis on individual experience rather than a collective tradition. . . . Facts, evidence, establish the authenticity of a life, as realism—aligned with objectivity—replaces romance."
73. See Houtman (1990, pp. 326–327).
74. Plummer (1983, p. 10).
75. Houtman (1990, p. 326–337).
76. Reynolds (1976, p. 55).
77. Stanley Jeyaraja Tambiah, *The Buddhist Saints of the Forest and the Cult of Amulets* (Cambridge: Cambridge University Press, 1984), pp. 16–19.
78. Ibid., pp. 119–121.
79. Ibid., p. 19.
80. G. E. Harvey, *History of Burma: From the Earliest Times to 10 March 1824, the Beginning of the English Conquest* (London: Longmans, 1925), p. xvii.
81. Ibid., p. 5.

82. G. H. Luce, "Old Kyauske and the Coming of the Burmans," *Journal of Burma Research Society*, vol. 63 (1959), p. 000.

83. For the debate about the merits of colonial versus Burmese vernacular history, see Htin Aung, *Burmese History Before 1287: A Defense of the Chronicles* (Oxford: The Asoka Society, 1970).

84. This so-called "biographical view of history" is not unique to Burmese or Thai history. The practice by Western writers of dating events from the time of Christ's birth is thought to have originated with the Chronographia (Chronicle) of Eusebius at its earliest, a Latin adaptation by St. Jerome, and the influential Bede's (672–735) "Ecclesiastical History of the English People." With these genres, local history came to be dated from and inextricably bound up with the life of Christ.

85. R. G. Collingwood, *The Idea of History* (Oxford: Oxford University Press, 1983), p. 394.

86. Ibid., pp. 10–11, 302.

87. E.g., E. H. Carr, *What Is History*?, 2nd ed. (London: Penguin Books, 1990), p. 165.

88. Paul Thompson, *The Voice of the Past: Oral History*, 2nd ed. (Oxford: Oxford University Press, 1988).

89. See also A. J. Minnis, *Medieval Theory of Authorship: Scholastic Literary Attitudes in the Later Middle Ages*, 2nd ed. (Aldershot: Wildwood House, 1988), p. 5, who describes how between the twelfth and the thirteenth centuries commentators of the Bible began to view texts as creations not of the divine author, but of human authors, so that the interest changed from a "literal" to a "literary" interest.

90. The term *win* could refer, as noted above, to history in a much wider sense when prefixed with other terms. Most of the information about Burmese history is derived from the *win*. Nine traditional categories mentioned include: (1) the lineage of the Buddhas (*bok-dá win*); (2) the lineage of the Buddha's relatives (*ma-ha win*); (3) the lineage of kings (*ya-za win*); (4) future events (*a-na-gá-tá win*); (5) the lineage of the relics of the Buddha, silent Buddhas, and *ya-hàn-da* (*da-hta da-tú-win*); (6) the history of Sri Lanka (*di-pá-win*); (7) the history of stupas and pagodas (*htu-pá win*); (8) the history of Bodhi trees (*bàw-dí win*); and (9) the history of Buddhism (*tha-tha-na win*) (See A-shin Bí-wun-thá Ma-htei-myat Aw-ba-tha *Thú-dei-tha-ná tha-yok-pyá a-bí-dan* [A reference dictionary] (Rangoon: Thú-dam-má-wa- di Sa-pon-hneik-taik, 1975). We may add here *gan-da win*, the history of the Pāli Canon, and the recent "history of practice" (*pa-dí-pat-tí win*).

Yet the contemporary generic term for history is no longer *win*, but *tha-maìng*, a term which has undergone a shift in meaning during the colonial era. If as late as 1906 the term *history* was still translated into Burmese by using *win*, this soon changed. Tin Ohn, in "Modern Historical Writing in Burmese" (*Historians of Southeast Asia*, ed. D. G. Hall [London 1961], p. 93), noting the important changes in Burma during the 1920s, including the introduction of secular schools, English as a language of instruction, and new-style Burmese syllabi for schools, observed that the Burmese sense of history had also changed. These changes involved recasting the term *tha-maìng* to signify history of all sorts, including secular history; it came to mean "history" or "chronicle" (Hok Sein 1981), and "the knowledge and systematic study of past events pertaining to, e.g., nations, creeds, institutions and peoples" (*Myan-ma A-hpwé A-bí-dan*). From the end of the 1920s, Tin Ohn noted, there was a "growing acceptance of the meaning of the word history in its wider sense," so that it "has acquired a new connotation, namely, a history that covers political as well as economic, social, and cultural life of the people."

It should not be mistaken that the term *tha-maìng* acquired this meaning quite late. Harvey (1925, p. xviii) still characterized *tha-maìng* as "local histories . . . frequently late, . . . written by individuals, they have not the range and accuracy of the great official compilations," and Pe Maung Tin (1960, p. xxi) glossed these as "mainly devoted to objects which testify to the establishment of the religion," and, though sometimes also used for other objects such as monasteries and towns, this is "generally associated with the prose-history of a pagoda." The *Burmese Encyclopaedia* (*MSK*, vol. 13, p. 33) gives the following: "The term *tha-maìng* means records in either prose or rhyme of special places such as pagoda, cave, monastery, pagoda stairs, pagoda porch, refuge for worship of the Buddha, epistle, and special people."

91. The Ma-ha-si Hsa-ya-daw was chief monk of the BTNA (Bok-dá Tha-tha-na Nok-ga-há A-hpwé-gyok), which was originally set up by influential ministers of the 1948–1962 democratic government and in 1996 had over 300 meditation centers in Burma and abroad.

92. Ma-ha-si Tha-tha-ná Yeik-tha, *Ma-ha-si pa-dí-pat-tí tha-tha-na win* [The tradition of practice of the Ma-ha-si Hsa-ya-daw] (Rangoon: Tha-tha-ná Yeik-tha, 1974 (BurE 1336)), p. 756. As it said in the preface to this "history": "We have had to publish the *History of Ma-ha-si practice* (*Ma-ha-si pa-dí-pat-tí tha-tha-na win*) only: in order that there be no possibility of hiding from Buddhists the Ma-ha-si's vigor in energetically achieving the brilliance of practice-oriented Buddhism (*pa-dí-pat-tí tha-tha-na*) to reach beyond Burma—such as Asia, America, and Europe, and inasmuch as it is the responsibility of present Buddhists to advance Buddhism (*ta-yà*) for the benefit of those who come later; and in order to establish and prolong practice Buddhism." (Thi-la-nan-da, A-shin Bí-wun-thá, *Ma-ha-si Hsa-ya-daw-hpa-yà-gyì i htei-rok-pat-tí* [The biography of the Ma-ha-si Hsa-ya-daw], part 1 [Rangoon: Tha-tha-ná Yeik-tha, 1979], p. vi).

93. The transition from history to biography is also evident elsewhere. Modern Burmese biography has its "roots" in the religious (*tha-tha-na win*) and secular chronicles (*ya-za win*), from which during the twentieth century the biographies of famous monks and kings came to be composed retrospectively. The biographies of U Thi-lá and the Htut-hkaung Hsa-ya-daw, famous for their practice, appeared many decades after their lives

ended, only after adherents of practice, becoming self-conscious of history and lineage of practice, pulled these subjects from their embeddedness in the chronicles.

94. Wí-thok-dí, Tha-tha-ná Ù (also known as Bo Theìn Hswei), *Sśn-lśn ya-pyeí-meín-gśn da-má àw-wa-dá-myà* [A century of the teachings of the Sùn-lùn Hsa-ya-daw] (Rangoon: A-myō-thà sa-ok-daik, 1976).

95. Hagiography thereby continuously recycles through unique constructions of continuity between life episodes into lives, between lives into lineages, and between lineages into a country's history, and the other way around. To the extent that history is about constructing sensible strands of continuity between biographical episodes, by means of which it extends the lives of teachers into their pupils and of kings into their subjects' lives, hagiography is at the root of history. To the extent that contemporary hagiography is retrospectively composed from royal and monastic lineage histories, history is at the root of hagiography.

96. Kindall (1980, p. 1013).

97. Houtman (1991).

Index

Bruner, J., 40–41
Brynner, Yul, 234
Buddha: ancestors of, 31; biography of, 1, 17–18, 332–333; birth of, 25, 32; contact with, 73; death of, 20, 28, 82, 141–142; doubles of, 10, 48, 269–273, 279–280, 282; enlightenment of, 25–28, 32, 35; family of, 113–128; final life of, 6–7, 271–272; future, 2, 8, 167, 193; genealogy of, 28; historical, 15, 20, 28, 40, 59, 163; as human, 3; lives of, 2–3, 238–239; living, 10, 12, 282; longevity of, 137–140; paintings of, 193, 195–217; past lives of, 3–4, 7, 9–10, 20–21, 25, 30, 32, 40, 64, 162, 165–167, 172, 183, 196, 272, 332–333, 336; physical body of, 27–28, 51, 100, 158, 174–175, 262, 274–275; presence of, 10, 12, 18; present life of, 165–166, 172, 175; spatial biography of, 177–178; speaking, 94; spiritual body of, 276; in Western scholarship, 40; wisdom, 36. *See also* Gotama
buddha darśana, 73
Buddha era, 167
Buddha field, 270
Buddhagaya, 278
Buddhaghosa, 7, 30–31, 43, 47–49, 61, 80, 286
Buddhahood, retained by Bodhisattva, 40
Buddha images, 71–74, 78–79, 81–82, 92, 94, 96, 101, 198; consecrated, 275–277; hierarchy of, 276; movement of, 281–282; and nationalism, 277–278; and power, 261–262, 265, 276; as sources of merit, 276; unfinished, 79, 83, 104; veneration of, 274–276
buddha-jñāna, 73
Buddhāpadāna, 168
Buddhāpadāni[ya], 165
buddhas, 140–141, 143, 174; differences between, 57; final existence of, 57; future, 45, 50, 52–55, 134; as humans, 59; longevity of, 133–135; multiplicity of, 49–53; *Pacceka*, 47, 54, 57, 168; previous, 25, 29–30, 45, 50, 52–53; as saints, 133–135; seven, 24–26, 36, 63; silent, 323, 342; twenty-four, 24, 26–27, 29–30, 32, 332–333
buddha-śabda, 73
Buddhavacana, 171
Buddhavaṃsa, 8, 11, 26–30, 32–33, 37–38, 40, 45–46, 49–55, 57, 63, 160, 162, 180, 182–184, 191–192; Mahāyāna perspective in, 37; Therāvada perspective in, 37
Buddhendom, 335
Buddhism: biography in, ix–x, 1–15; Burmese, 10–11, 208, 259–288, 310–344, 335–336; as creation of Victorians, 58; diversity of, 1–2; elite, 8, 158–159; as founded religion, 50; history of, 342; Indian, 7, 129, 137, 144, 150; influence on philosophy of, 253; lay, 144; local, 10–11, 257, 280, 290–293; modern, 11, 289–309; monastic, 144; original, 36; at Pagan, 87; pleasure in, 179–180; popular, 8, 15, 144, 158–159, 243, 262, 267, 272; practice in, 343; purity of, 36, 239; Siamese, 306; Sinhalese, 87; Southeast Asian, 195; Thai, 9, 11, 208; Western, 42, 241
Buddhist Councils, 323
Buddhist creed, 99, 108–109
Buddhologists, Western, 41, 113
Buddhology: and biography, 41–43; challenges to, 161; Theravāda, 27
Burlingame, E., 49, 286
Burma, 86–93, 102, 218, 257; *jātakas* in, 22; Lower, 265; modern, 277–280; stūpas in, 102; Upper, 260–261, 266–267, 277, 282, 285; Western influence on, 342–343

caityas, 71, 75
cakkavatins, 178, 191
Cakkavati-Sihanada Sutta, 52
cakkravala, 279
cakravartins, 118, 126
Cambodia, 218, 242, 252, 278
Caṇḍasāra, 266, 268–269, 271, 285
Candra, 126
Candrasuriya, King, 265, 267–269, 280, 284

Maitreya, 215; national, 261; of Rāhula, 150–151; relic, 8, 11, 99, 290; of saints, 142; salvation, 42; *stūpa*, 8, 99, 158, 172, 175–177, 188–189, 190, 192; Thai, 2; Theravāda, 281, 283; Upagupta, 136, 143; urban, 293; of veneration, 261, 281
Cunningham, Alexander, 163
Cunningham, M., 41

Da-lá-byaw-bwe-gyì Village, 314–315
Da-má-reik-hkí-tí, 332–333, 339
Dá-ma-zei-dí, King, 324
dānaṃ, 173
Daśabhūmika Sūtra, 134, 141, 143
Dasabodhisuttappattikatha, 40, 45, 50, 52–53, 59
Dasaratha Jātaka, 24
Davis, Richard, 102
Daw Sàw Mei, 313
Deheijia, Vidya, 65–71, 76–77, 80, 100–101
deities, Hindu, 74–75, 98
dependent origination: attributed to Gotama, 42; doctrine of, 41, 50
Derrida, Jacques, 302–303
Devadatta, 44–45, 54–55, 57
devas, 46–48, 55, 176, 224
devatas, 55
devis, 55
De Visser, M. W., 150
devotees: of Buddha, 83–84; quest for truth of, 82–83
Dhahuli, 132
dhamma, 232, 270–272, 325; ascetic practices in, 297; ascribed to Gotama, 42; contemplation of, 53; corruption of, 302; purification of, 259; questions concerning, 48; source of, 47; teaching of, 24–25, 45, 49, 55, 292; in texts, 293
Dhammacakkappavattana Sutta, 275–276
dhamma-desanā, 325
dhammakāya, 262, 275–276
Dhammapada, 45–46, 49, 62, 165, 278, 286
Dhammapada Commentary, 10, 260, 269–270, 286
Dhammapadaṭṭhakathā, 4, 44–46, 48–49, 51, 53–54, 59, 163
Dhammapāla, 61, 183
dhammaraja, 9, 232
Dhamma-Vinaya, 297
Dhammika, 47
Dhānyakaṭaka, 137
dharma, 124, 158; disappearance of, 134, 150; entrusted to *arhats*, 133–134; given to Rahula, 127; iconized, 99; inscriptions of, 108–109; objectified, 108; preservation of, 121–122, 133–134, 136; spread by *arhats*, 150; survival of, 143
dharmacakramudrā, 71. *See also* Wheel of Law
dharmakāya, 175, 190
dhyanamudrā, 82
dhyānas, 141
diachronic mode, 65
diacritical conventions, x
Dīghanikāya, 25, 35, 183
Dīpaṅkara, 28, 30, 38, 45, 51, 53; encounters with Gotama, 26–27
Dipavaṃsa, 31
Di-pin-ká-ra, 323, 339
disciples: of Ajaan Man, 290–291, 295, 297, 301, 303–304, 308; of Buddha, 25, 43, 47, 138, 149, 164, 292, 297; great, 40, 47, 54
dispensation, of Buddha, 271–273, 276–277, 280, 332
Divyāvadāna, 136, 153, 163, 173, 182
doctrine: Aryan Path, 42; of autonomous personhood, 59; Buddhist, 89, 92, 142; as component, 49; mastery of, 56; paradigmatic, 59; preservation of, 244; teaching of, 73; Theravāda, 19, 32–34, 45
donors: of images, 276–277; to festivals, 178–179; lay, 9; and Maitreya, 206–208; motives of, 206–209; of paintings, 211–212; to *stūpas*, 170–172, 175, 177
Dorje, Sempa, 148
dPag.bsam.ljon.bzang, 145
dreams, 115–116, 122, 125–126; visions in, 290, 300, 302
duḥkha, 121
Dupont, Pierre, 75
Dutt, Nalinaksha, 130–131, 147–148, 152
Dvāravatī, 103

Dynastic Chronicles, 238–239
dynasties, 24, 33, 39

Earth Goddess, 264, 283
East Asia, 5
Eastern Ocean, 115
eclipse, solar, 236–240, 252
Eddy, Mr. and Mrs., 246
Edgerton, Franklin, 154
Ekottarāgama, 121
Elephanta, 102
elephants, 57, 220, 225, 228, 236; white, 53, 195, 199
Eliade, Mircea, 58–59, 259
elites: Buddhist, 143–144; Thai, 257, 303–304, 308
elixir of long life, 141
Elster, Jon, 250
Emerald Buddha, 106–107, 249, 261, 281, 283
empire: biography as, 177–179; Indian, 177–179, 192
enlightenment: accounts of, 35; attainment of, 42, 50–51, 295; of *bodhisattvas*, 152; of Buddha, 24, 118–119, 166; desire for, 51–52; path to, 4, 7–8, 17, 42, 45, 49, 53, 111, 123, 166–169, 174, 272, 275, 292, 315; quest for, 116, 122; results of, 58
Enlightenment (Western), 10, 250
epics, performed, 192
epigraphs, 8, 161–164, 170, 172, 180–181
epistemology, Buddhist, 12–13
ethnography, 10–11, 291; and veneration, 273–277
eulogies, 324
Eusebius, 342
evidence: archaeological, 161–164, 171, 188; art historical, 171–172, 187; epigraphic, 161–164, 181–182, 189; textual, 161–164, 172–174, 180–181, 188

Face Washing ritual, 263–265, 272, 283
Fa-ch'in, 153
Factors of Enlightenment, 317
family, of Buddha, 4
father, of Buddha, 117–119, 196
fatherhood, goal of, 123
festivals, 184, 187; biographical, 179–180; *cakkavattin*, 178–180; Mahāmuni, 272; Śiva's Night, 247; *stūpa*, 170–171, 179–180; temple, 9; *thēt Mahāchāt*, 203–206; worship, 176–177
fields of merit, 20, 46, 133–134, 259, 280; past Buddhas as, 37
filial piety, 37
first meditation, 68, 74
First Sermon, 25, 71, 81–82, 117–118, 196, 275, 278, 317
folklore, 46, 120, 218
Fontein, Jan, 103–104
footprints, of Buddha, 68, 94–97, 285, 330
Forchhammer, Emil, 265, 284–285
Foucault, Michel, 174, 181
Foucher, Albert, 3, 163, 175
four noble truths, 50, 121
frames: biographical, ix, 6, 12, 43, 45–48, 55–56; in *Buddhavaṃsa*, 28; frozen, 76–77; narrative, 3–4
Frauwallner, Erich, 3, 138, 144, 158
French, in Southeast Asia, 242, 252
Freud, Sigmund, 327

gado.pwe, 283
Gaṇḍavyūha, 79, 81
gandhakuṭī, 71. *See also* Perfumed Chamber
Ganesha, 247
Ganges River, 120
Ganz, Arthur, 327
garbhagṛha, 74
Geertz, Clifford, 2
Gehman, H., 46
genealogy, of rulers, 17
genre: biographical, 3, 4, 12; *jātaka*, 21; venerable father, 290
geography, sacred, 269
Gerini, G. E., 196, 205, 209
gestures, of Buddha, 71, 73, 82–83, 263
Ghosita, 47
ghosts, 40, 55, 239
gifts, 173. See also *dānaṃ*
Gilgit, 149
giving, act of, 46
gnosticism, 190
Gopikā, 115
Gorakṣa, 131, 148
Gosling, Betty, 94

About the Contributors

ROBERT BROWN (Ph.D., University of California at Los Angeles) is Associate Professor of South and Southeast Asian Art History at UCLA. He recently published a monograph *The Dvāratī Wheels of the Law and the Indianization of Southeast Asia* (E. J. Brill, 1996) and edited a volume on *Ganesh: Studies of an Asian God.*

GUSTAAF HOUTMAN (Ph.D., University of London) is an anthropologist who specializes in the study of Burmese meditation traditions. He is the news editor of *Anthropology Today* and held the first E. R. Leach–Royal Anthropological Institute Fellowship at the University of Manchester.

THOMAS J. HUDAK (Ph.D., University of Michigan) is Associate Professor for Southeast Asian Languages and Linguistics at Arizona State University. His publication *The Tale of Prince Samuttakote: A Buddhist Epic from Thailand* is a translation of a Thai/Pāli *jātaka* text.

PAUL JOHNSON is a doctoral candidate in History of Religions at the University of Chicago.

FORREST McGILL (Ph.D., University of Michigan), an art historian of South and Southeast Asia, is Director of the Galleries at Mary Washington College, Fredericksburg, Virginia. His recent publications include the essay "Jatakas, Universal Monarchs, and the Year 2000," published in *Atibus Asiae* 53, nos. 3–4.

REGINALD RAY (Ph.D., University of Chicago) is a scholar of Sanskrit and Tibetan Buddhism at the Naropa Institute in Boulder, Colorado, and teaches in the Department of Religion at the University of Colorado. He is the author of *Buddhist Saints in India.*

FRANK REYNOLDS (Ph.D., University of Chicago) is Professor of History of Religions and Buddhist Studies at the University of Chicago. He has published several books and articles. Among them is his *Three Worlds According to King Ruang: A Thai Buddhist Cosmology*, a translation with introduction and notes, coauthored with Mani B. Reynolds.

JULIANE SCHOBER (Ph.D., University of Illinois at Urbana-Champaign) is Assistant Professor of Religious Studies at Arizona State University. She conducted extensive anthropological fieldwork in Mandalay, Burma. Her current work focuses on the role of Buddhism and the state in the Burmese quest for modernity.

JOHN STRONG (Ph.D., University of Chicago) is Professor of Religious Studies at Bates College, Lewiston, Maine. His publications include monographs and articles on Indian Buddhist traditions. He is the author of *The Legend and Cult of Upagupta.*

JAMES L. TAYLOR (Ph.D., MacQuarie University) is Lecturer in Anthropology at Curtin University, Perth, Western Australia. He is the author of *Forest Monks and Nation-State: An Anthropological and Historical Study in Northeastern Thailand.*

JONATHAN WALTERS (Ph.D., University of Chicago) has conducted research in Sri Lanka. He is Assistant Professor in the Division of Humanities and Arts at Whitman College, Walla Walla, Washington.

MARK R. WOODWARD (Ph.D., University of Illinois at Urbana-Champaign) is Associate Professor of Religious Studies at Arizona State University. He publishes on Southeast Asian religions, including Islam, Buddhism, and tribal religions, and has published a recent monograph, *Islam In Java.*